# Insurrection at Bayou Sara

**In A Foreign Country** – *Journeys of a Southerner*
Book 2 of a series

Pat Martin

Publisher's Cataloging-in-Publication Data

Names: Martin, Patrick H., author.
Title: Insurrection at Bayou Sara : in a foreign country – journeys of a southerner / Pat Martin.
Description: Clinton, LA : Comite Press, 2024. | Series : In a foreign country – journeys of a southerner ; 2. | Includes 6 b&w illustrations. | Summary: After the Mexican War, Percy Moorhead becomes a New Orleans attorney, husband and father, and inherits a cotton plantation. After a series of losses, he struggles with his own weakness to prevent chaos for those closest to him. The corrosive effects of African slavery climax in a threatened slave insurrection.
Identifiers: LCCN 2024910763 | ISBN 9781964075037 (hardcover) | ISBN 9781964075044 (pbk.) | ISBN 9781964075051 (ebook)
Subjects: LCSH: Cotton farmers – Fiction. | Veterans – Fiction. | Families – Fiction. | Slavery – United States – Fiction. | Slave insurrections -- Fiction. | Louisiana – History – 1803-1865 – Fiction. | Mexico – History – 19th century – Fiction. | BISAC: FICTION / Historical / General. | FICTION / Action & Adventure. | FICTION / Family Life / General.
Classification: LCC PS3613.A78 I57 2024 | DDC 813 M--dc23
LC record available at https://lccn.loc.gov/2024910763

ISBN (Hardcover): 978-1-964075-03-7
ISBN (Paperback): 978-1-964075-04-4
ISBN (ebook): 978-1-964075-05-1

Published by Comite Press, a Louisiana LLC
Clinton, Louisiana

PatMartinauthor.com

This novel is dedicated to the memory of members of the faculty of the LSU History Department who supported and encouraged my work:

John L. Loos, Anne C. Loveland, John Preston Moore, Burl L. Noggle, and T. Harry Williams.

Time past and time future
What might have been and what has been
Point to one end, which is always present.
   T. S. Eliot – *Burnt Norton*

The past is a foreign country,
they do things differently there.

   L. P. Hartley, *The Go-Between*

# CONTENTS

| Chapter 1. | Alarm Bells in the Night | 1 |
|---|---|---|
| Chapter 2. | Soldier's Return | 7 |
| Chapter 3. | The Family Enlarges | 11 |
| Chapter 4. | Leaving for Law | 17 |
| Chapter 5. | Allied with Judah Benjamin | 24 |
| Chapter 6. | A Lawyer Ascendant | 43 |
| Chapter 7. | Miss Philomena Randolph | 49 |
| Chapter 8 | To Richmond Percy Did Go | 57 |
| Chapter 9. | Sister Lavinia's Readings | 64 |
| Chapter 10. | Recalling Edgar Poe | 74 |
| Chapter 11. | Phil meets Lucy | 80 |
| Chapter 12. | Judah is Charmed by Phil | 88 |
| Chapter 13. | Re-encountering Beauregard | 98 |
| Chapter 14. | Journey Preparations | 107 |
| Chapter 15. | Judah's Special Instructions | 115 |
| Chapter 16. | A *Baltic* Voyage | 123 |
| Chapter 17. | Liverpool | 134 |
| Chapter 18. | Manchester | 138 |
| Chapter 19. | London Town | 146 |
| Chapter 20. | Godstow | 149 |
| Chapter 21. | Oxford | 157 |
| Chapter 22. | The Count and Companions | 163 |
| Chapter 23. | Alderman Duplessis | 170 |
| Chapter 24. | Westie, A Banker Friend | 178 |
| Chapter 25. | Ja-Boo's Roses | 185 |
| Chapter 26. | Yellow Jack's Toll | 191 |
| Chapter 27. | Calvin Comes A Cropper | 202 |
| Chapter 28. | Phil's Heirloom Silver | 209 |
| Chapter 29. | A Mexican Cigar Roller | 213 |
| Chapter 30. | Percy's Skills Mature | 224 |
| Chapter 31. | Informing the Family | 230 |

| | | |
|---|---|---|
| *Chapter 32.* | Return to Mexico City | 236 |
| *Chapter 33.* | An Audience with Juarez | 246 |
| *Chapter 34.* | Percy's Report | 254 |
| *Chapter 35.* | Diana, Manager | 262 |
| *Chapter 36.* | Howard on Reckoning | 268 |
| *Chapter 37.* | Phil's Felicianas | 278 |
| *Chapter 38.* | Diana | 286 |
| *Chapter 39.* | Infidelities and Fidelities | 290 |
| *Chapter 40.* | Summer's Toll | 301 |
| *Chapter 41.* | Taking Charge | 308 |
| *Chapter 42.* | Recalled to Mexico | 313 |
| *Chapter 43.* | Mexican Stand-off | 323 |
| *Chapter 44.* | Comonfort's Cabinet | 333 |
| *Chapter 45.* | A Father's Silence | 343 |
| *Chapter 46.* | Dressed in Yellow | 353 |
| *Chapter 47.* | Philomena's Grief | 368 |
| *Chapter 48.* | Farewell, Father | 345 |
| *Chapter 49.* | Now Philomena | 381 |
| *Chapter 50.* | Moorhead Boyled | 388 |
| *Chapter 51.* | Recrimination | 406 |
| *Chapter 52.* | A Gold Watch | 411 |
| *Chapter 53.* | Meeting Maisie | 419 |
| *Chapter 54.* | Massa Calvin Kills | 432 |
| *Chapter 55.* | Flight to Kwa-zembe | 438 |
| *Chapter 56.* | The Bunch Posse | 446 |
| *Chapter 57.* | Enlisting Odessa | 452 |
| *Chapter 58.* | The Insurrection | 457 |

**In a Foreign Country**
*Journeys of a Southerner*

## About the Series

**In a Foreign Country – *Journeys of a Southerner*** is a series of six historical novels sprawling over the nineteenth century, focusing on a New Orleans lawyer and two generations of families, one free and one enslaved, on a Louisiana cotton plantation. The stain of slavery tainted Southern Whites who did not want to secede but remained loyal to their state and region when war erupted. The series, set in America and England, is a fresh look into the divisions that led to secession's failure. The reader is drawn into the profound conflicts of the era by vivid characters in a tale of adventure, romance, tragedy, and family conflict.

## Books in the Series

1. CANNONS AT THE GATE

   1815-1849: The story of the Moorhead family begins when the father, Howard, flees England to reinvent himself as a successful cotton merchant in Louisiana. It shifts to his son Percy, raised on the family plantation and educated at Princeton, whose ambitions are forged in cannon fire in the American conquest of Mexico.

2. INSURRECTION AT BAYOU SARA

   1850-1859: Percy Moorhead establishes a successful New Orleans law practice but then loses his family and his inheritance to an imposter. He must rise above personal loss to subdue a slave insurrection that threatens the Feliciana parishes.

3. FIRE ON THE MISSISSIPPI

   1861-1862: The Confederacy recruits Lt. Percy Moorhead, now in Virginia. First, he becomes an agent in Liverpool to secure ships for the Navy. Next, he is sent to New Orleans to order its surrender. There he finds that the man who stole his inheritance has been murdered; he must begin anew to restore his fortunes.

4. ESCAPE FROM RICHMOND

   1862-1863: After further missions in England and France, Percy returns to Richmond only to be challenged by false charges. To save himself, he must choose between loyalty and principle.

5. EMPIRE'S FOREIGN AGENT

6. RETURN TO BOLINGBROKE

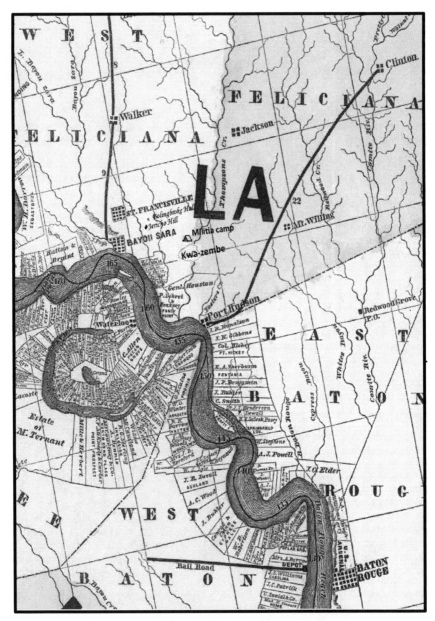

## About the Author

Pat Martin taught at the LSU Law Center until retiring. He holds
B.A., M.A., and Ph. D. degrees in History from Louisiana State
University and a J. D. degree from the Duke University Law School.
Among his publications is *Elizabethan Espionage: Plotters and Spies in
the Struggle Between Catholicism and the Crown.*

*Chapter 1*

# Alarm Bells in the Night

T he plantation bell was made of brass, cast in Philadelphia, by the Point Pleasant Iron and Brass Foundry twenty-three years earlier. The *Caledonian*, a sailing ship, carried it down the Atlantic coast, around Florida into the Gulf of Mexico, and then up the Mississippi to New Orleans. Then the steamboat *Augustus* brought it up the Mississippi to Bayou Sara. There, it was loaded on a wagon to New Troy, where it was mounted on an iron post at the entrance to the plantation on August 10, 1837. Now the massive bell clanged sharply, crisply, urgently, three times, pausing three beats then ringing out three more even more loudly. It could be heard for two miles on a clear winter night such as this. The sound reached Riverbend Plantation.

"What's that?" Annabelle Gipson asked her husband. He was still asleep. It was not yet three in the morning.

"What's what?" he replied groggily. The Gipsons were the third generation to live at Riverbend, the West Feliciana plantation build by his grandfather while the region was still Spanish territory.

"The bell. Don't you hear it?" she said, prodding his side to wake him.

Armstrong Gipson's hearing was not as acute as his wife's. He strained to hear.

Clang. Clang. Clang. Again the bell sounded. Now he heard it.

"Damn," he said, rolling out of bed and pulling his trousers over his legs.

"What does it mean?" his wife demanded, now anxious.

"Slaves. Rebellion. That's the warning."

She was alarmed. "No! Can you be sure?"

"That's McEachern's bell. New Troy. He wouldn't call us out without good reason."

A second bell began to sound, from the adjacent plantation, Woodfair. Three gongs, pause, repeat. Then a third bell, a fourth, a fifth called out in the dark as the alarm sounded and resounded across the parish. Three gongs, that was the signal that all understood. And feared. It rang out revolt. It sounded *Insurrection*!

Armstrong Gipson roused his three sons and put them in the living room. He laid out on the table five long-arms, six pistols and three shotguns, with powder and shot close at hand.

"Lock the doors," he instructed them. "Guard your mother and sister from anything, you hear me?"

Gipson left for town just as the sun rose, glinting on the Mississippi River. Soon, he was at the town hall of St. Francisville. A crowd of men had already gathered, holding guns and talking urgently. One of them — Gipson only knew him as Lucas — explained that Jolly McEachern had just left, on his way to the doctor's office with a wounded man named Bostwick. Lucas said that McEachern had said that Bostwick told him his posse was assaulted by a force of twenty renegade slaves as they tried to capture a runaway slave. The fugitive who the posse were tracking was from Bolingbroke. He killed his own brother and then tried to kill Calvin Bunch. Lucas continued, "Bunch got up the posse, and they went after the runaway. They killed ten maroons before being overwhelmed. Only Bostwick got out. Other three dead."

"Damn," said Gipson.

Another man said, "Bolingbroke? Ain't that Percy Moorhead's plantation?"

"No more," said another, an older man named Cudlow, who had known Percy's father, Howard Moorhead. Or Boyle. "Not since the judge ruled that Irish fellow inherited it. Moorhead's son from Dublin that he abandoned when he come here." After the ruling, Cudlow started saying he always knew something was off about old man Moorhead. Or Boyle.

Just then Sheriff Seymour Lurty stepped out from the town hall. Everyone turned quiet as he stood on a bench to speak.

"Here's what we know," said Lurty, a spare man in his late forties. As spare in speech as in body, he didn't need to raise his voice for men to listen to him. His words carried authority. He was trusted. "Calvin Bunch and a tracker he hired are dead. I told him three four days ago not to go looking for the slave Julius who had run off from the plantation. Ol' Calvin claimed Julius killed his brother Pompey, and Calvin was going to hunt him down. Maybe. Maybe not. Nobody knows how many fugitives and runaways and what not are in that maroon camp deep in the swamp. I wasn't going to send men out there. Y'all know how Calvin can get his dander up. But damned if he didn't go anyway. Now it's a hornet's nest. Wounded man who got away says they killed a number of the niggers, 'cluding Julius's wife, and they're going to rise up and get revenge now that their camp has been located for sure."

A young man, about twenty, who had grown up with stories about the existence of a camp of maroons – fugitive slaves or freedmen who had no papers to show they were free – spoke up: "Wounded man said somethin' about Razmus leading them. You know anything about that?" Razmus was a fearful, if unseen, figure in St. Francisville and Bayou Sara, a runaway slave with ritualistic scars on his cheeks and whip lashings up and down his back. The fierce Razmus was invoked to scare adventurous youth from entering the swamps. Some even claimed he was a cannibal, like others of the African tribe from which he was captured.

Lurty was a measured man, not given to stirring up the people of the parish he was responsible for. "I can't confirm that. I imagine that it's true that two white men have been killed along with a number of the blacks who camp in there. What I can tell you is that I sent a rider to Baton Rouge to notify Governor Wickliffe in person. I didn't send a telegram, because that would spread the story. You all know that Governor Wickliffe's home, Wyoming Plantation, is not far from where the killings occurred. The courier's giving him a message that he should call up a detachment of the Louisiana militia and send them here as quick as they can muster. Now, y'all need to stay calm but keep your families safe til I hear from the governor. Right now, I've got to go to talk with Calvin Bunch's widow and her mother and see what they might know."

As the sheriff and two deputies got on their horses to call on Eliza Bunch and her mother, a paddle-wheeler left her dock in New Orleans to steam north, the same boat that had delivered the bell for New Troy. On it was Percy Moorhead, unaware of the disastrous events unfolding at his home nor of the death of his brother-in-law, Calvin Bunch. Soon he would rush to the edge of the swamp, working with General DeRussy and a company of the state militia to hold back a clash between whites and blacks that could be worse than the River Parish slave rebellion of 1811. Everyone in New Orleans knew it was the largest organized rebellion in the United States. That revolt had begun at Colonel Manuel Andry's plantation in LaPlace, only thirty miles upriver from where Percy had just embarked. Slaves burned five plantations as they marched and murdered their way to the outskirts of New Orleans. It only ended when militia killed or captured more than a hundred of the rebels. An insurrection in West Feliciana could be worse. It could descend into the chaos of Haiti when black rebels massacred 5,000 whites at the order of Jean-

Jacques Dessalines in 1804. What did the slaves have to lose? The Louisiana legislature and the courts had declared that they could never be free, that they could never leave Louisiana. Percy Moorhead is the one man who could prevent the tinder box from igniting and spreading a conflagration that would consume the region.

Ten years have passed since Percy Moorhead returned from the Mexican War. Military service as a private behind him, he enrolled in law at William and Mary College in Virginia. Associating himself as a junior lawyer to Judah P. Benjamin, he shared the brilliant Louisiana attorney's success as Benjamin rose to United States Senator. His marriage to a vivacious young woman, from one of Virginia's most fabled families, the Randolphs, pointed to an illustrious career, filled with honor, respect and achievement, to contentment as a husband and a father. While the cotton plantation he expected to inherit, Bolingbroke Hall, was not among the largest in the state, it was one of the best managed and most profitable. Yet we open this chapter in Percy's life with a most disturbing account of an incipient slave insurrection at Bolingbroke and suggest the multiple catastrophes that have befallen him in the weeks immediately prior to this fearful series of events. He has become an object of pity, even shame.

Who among us has not experienced disaster? We ask, did I bring this upon myself? Is it divine retribution for my own sin? Is God testing me as He tested Abraham and Job? Did not Christ Himself cry out: *Eli, Eli, lama sabachthani*. My God, my God, why hast thou forsaken me?

As he related this period of his life to me, in the comfort of his manor, with good brandy before a comforting fireplace, Percy described this as his time on the cross. On another occasion when I asked him how he could endure such losses, he said, "A furnace and repeated hammering can forge metal and make it stronger. Or it can be shattered if not tempered properly. I was lucky." I protested that it was not luck but character. He demurred in that stoic manner I've often seen him exhibit.

When I asked him to tell me about the slave insurrection, he replied, "Like my father told me, slavery was a Faustian bargain for which a reckoning would come due. He wouldn't have been surprised that Calvin Bunch would be the first to pay the price. The South's reckoning could only follow, of necessity."

But I'll not prolong this prologue to our story in chief. Let us go now and see how a successful attorney and heir to a small fortune was brought low by a conspiracy of events and cascading misfortunes beyond his control. Let us see how he responds to good fortune and to disaster. Let us begin to understand the reckoning for slavery of which his father spoke.

## Chapter 2

# Soldier's Return

The steamer *Portland* arrived in New Orleans from Mexico on a hot mid-June day, 1848. Disembarking at the dock near the Place d'Armes, among many other Louisiana volunteers whose service was complete, was Percy Moorhead. In blue uniform he strode off the plank, canvas duffel in hand, a broad grin across his face. Greeting him proudly, grasping his shoulders and looking him over, his father smiled and insisted on carrying Percy's bag the three blocks to the townhome the family continued to use when not at Bolingbroke.

"Your mother will be happy for me to bring you home in one piece. It's been 18 months. Eliza wants to see her soldier brother as soon as possible."

Not until dinner at a nearby restaurant did his father noticed that something had happened to Percy's left arm. The uniform sleeve had concealed his scar.

Percy winked and tossed it off with nonchalance. "I didn't want to worry any of you. I got in the way of a Mexican gun stock obedient to the laws of physics. A musket ball would have been worse. An officer saved me from the surgeon's scalpel. Perhaps you've heard of the family. Beauregard. Sugar planters at one time."

Howard felt the irregular bones of his son's forearm and pressed down with increasing force. When Percy did not wince, Howard relaxed and leaned back in his chair. He nearly told Percy of his grandfather's time in a company of cavalry but checked himself. Percy would ask one question and then another and then what? Howard would not lie to his son or to Percy's mother, Lucy. Conceal? Yes. Lie, no. A lie was destructive, not because truth was an obligation he owed to others. It was wrong because a lie diminished the integrity of he who made it. Everything of his past and much of his present Howard concealed from his wife, his son, his business associates. But he never lied. He owed duties to wife, son, servants, clients, associates, and friends. But transparency in all that he had done in the past or was doing in the present or would do in the future was no duty. Nothing good would come from telling Percy of his grandfather and grandmother; he did not open that conversation. A time for it would come.

"*Contreras*, if I recall the Beauregard place," said Howard. "Have you made plans? What would you like to do now?"

"I've considered business," Percy began. "When you were my age you had already been at sea for years and had become a ship's purser. Your experiences opened doors for you. I've learned Spanish now and my French is passable. I think I could engage in commerce. Eventually I could run Bolingbroke when it no longer suits you. But the plantation has never been enough in itself for you, and I don't think it would be for me. Times are different from when you settled in New Orleans. Business has become more complex. A man must have a comprehensive understanding of the law. I think I should study the law. What would you say to that?"

Howard leaned forward, enthusiastic. "Splendid idea, son. Splendid. If I were your age, I'd do the same. Now, how would you go about it? Read law with a lawyer in New Orleans? Or study in school somewhere? Judge Bullard stepped down from our Supreme Court a year ago to open a law school at the University of

Louisiana. I'd be glad to introduce you to him."

Just as he was leaving for Mexico Percy had heard of the new school. "Perhaps. Maybe it would be better if I should go back east. If I am to be a success in law and business, I will need many associations. Perhaps Yale or William and Mary. General Scott studied at William and Mary. He said he would see that I am admitted."

Howard dabbed his mouth with a napkin. "The general took an interest? That's good. Many people say General Scott could be our next president if he wants it. You could do worse than follow his example. Of course, your mother would be disappointed to see you so far from home again."

Percy chuckled. "She wasn't keen on my going to Mexico. And you, father? What would you say to William and Mary?" Percy searched his father's face for guidance – one way or the other. As usual, his father's thoughts were inscrutable.

The older Moorhead tore a piece from the baguette next to his plate and used it to absorb gravy left from his meat. He ate it slowly, responding, "Your mother is a strong woman." Smiling, he added, "Head-strong even. Very intelligent and well-read. However, she knows little of the world. You must follow your own judgment, not hers or mine. A man makes of life what he wills. If ambition takes you to New Haven or Williamsburg, so be it. I support your decision."

The next morning early, Moorhead father and son took a packet steamer upriver. Soon enough, they were ascending the wide porch of Bolingbroke Hall, which wrapped around three sides of the home. Percy's bedroom was upstairs, above the front entrance. As a boy, he had been able to see anyone approaching up the twenty-foot wide gravel drive to the house. Two more bedrooms were upstairs and another two below. It was a larger house than needed for a family of four. The man who planned it must have anticipated more. If so, he was disappointed – unless he expected it to be filled with grandchildren.

Howard and Percy Moorhead opened the screen door of the porch and entered the hall of Bolingbroke. They walked to the right, into the parlor, where Lucy and Eliza were seated, Lucy reading a book, Eliza stitching a sampler. The same room in which Percy Moorhead came to life twenty-one years earlier. Eliza remained seated, which surprised Percy; she simply turned and smiled, though blushing, as if concealing something. Lucy rose and embraced her son briefly. He presented his cheek for her indifferent buss, with which he was long familiar. A show of affection was, she knew, what a mother should do who has not seen her son for a year. Or was it two? Would he even notice her hair was showing signs of gray, or care? Why are mothers so seldom appreciated? She sat again. "I'll send Clotilda for tea," she said. It was the proper thing to do.

A boy had departed, gone to soldier in a foreign land. A man had returned. New relations would have to replace the old, though old habits die slowly.

*Chapter 3*

# The Family Enlarges

From letters he received on the army's return to Vera Cruz from Mexico City, Percy had learned of his sister's marriage to Calvin Bunch in April, two months earlier. Now, seated on the sofa opposite Eliza's chair, he slowly became aware that her midriff was covered to conceal how far along she was in pregnancy; he had not expected to find her seven months pregnant. His father had thought it best not to alert him of the circumstances of the marriage and Eliza's condition. He spoke to his sister with warm affection, setting her at ease.

"Eliza, you are positively blooming in the expectancy of motherhood. It agrees with you. When do I meet your lucky husband? I left with only a sister and now I have a brother." His voice carried pleasure and no judgment.

Eliza gripped the arms of her chair and hoisted herself unsteadily to standing. She did not try to disguise her discomfort. "Calvin's in Jackson, helping his father for a few days. He's eager to meet you also."

Eliza Willis was twenty-four, her lean face marked by a narrow port-wine stain down the back part of her left cheek that resembled a map of the Italian peninsula. It had gradually taken shape and darkened when she was about three years old. Her mother made her self-conscious about the birthmark from the time it first appeared. When bathing the small girl, Lucy would scrub the blemish repeatedly, as though it could be washed away. On their infrequent visits to New Orleans, Lucy would take Eliza to see one apothecary and then another and another to see if a cream could be mixed that would cause the dark stain to fade. When nothing would work the desired transformation, Lucy insisted that Eliza's hair be groomed to hide the shame of the imperfection.

"If only you hadn't inherited Mr. Willis's straw-like hair," her mother would complain, putting down the brush. "I can hardly do anything with it. It's . . . ., it's *listless*."

"Yes, mother. I'll do the best I can with it." Eliza naturally thought that others saw her as her mother saw her, a flawed child. But if the birthmark had faded and disappeared, Lucy would have found some other way of reminding her daughter of her deficiencies, as a means to control the girl.

Even now as a grown woman, in Eliza's mind the mark was as obvious as her pregnancy.

Percy encouraged his sister, "Please, you must tell me everything about him and his family."

"Mother tells me his father was a friend of my father." She volunteered little information about Calvin Bunch.

That much was true, as far as it went. Eliza could not speak of the things she knew nothing of; of the things she knew, she was unlikely to be entirely candid.

Calvin's father had been a hunting and drinking companion of Jim Willis. He owned a modest farm north of Jackson, 117 acres, able to support only two slaves, and a general goods store in town. Calvin was a younger son. The senior Bunch gave him no reason to think he would inherit any portion of the property, as small as it was. No matter. Calvin was marrying into a family of two plantations, each ten times larger than his father's farm. Eliza was not visibly pregnant at the wedding. But there had been only a short interval between the engagement and the small ceremony at the Episcopal church in St. Francisville. Few were invited. Fewer still attended. The Bunches of Jackson were not on the social level of the grandees of St. Francisville.

Lucy would have preferred a marriage celebration for Eliza, like the one she had with Jim Willis, attended by more than a hundred. That planning, however, would have necessitated a wedding date that would not have permitted concealment of the circumstances leading to the marriage nor allow for a later fiction that the baby entered the world prematurely. It was left unsaid that Lucy was grateful for a quickly celebrated marriage lest Calvin re-think his prospects and so depart for Texas. The new state was populated in disproportionate number by men who left behind unpaid debts, unfinished sentences and unnamed bastards in a dozen or more states east of the Sabine River. Calvin was neither curious enough to inquire into the arrangements whereby Eliza's family possessed two adjacent plantations nor clever enough to devise a long-term plan to use the division of ownership to his own advantage. It was not so much that he lacked intelligence (limited though it was) as that his mind would not open itself to imagination. Literalism left no room for analogy in his thought. He could read a bill of sale but not a page of prose.

Eliza was drawn to Calvin because she had reached full womanhood and yet she knew few other men to whom she could attach herself. The schooling of tutors resident from time to time at Bolingbroke as chosen by her mother on recommendation from her uncles across the river or recruited by her stepfather in New Orleans had not found fertile ground in Eliza's intellect. She learned to read by rote but never picked up a book unless instructed to do so, and then reluctantly, allowing her eyes to wander over the lines of print with scant cognition. She shared her mother's disdain for New Orleans, frightened by stories of crime and violence and dismayed by muddy streets and raucous sounds day and night. Mr. Moorhead (as she always called her stepfather) took her to several concerts and a play that she found interesting, but the pleasures of music and performance were insufficient to overcome her aversion to the city. The grand dames of New Orleans social circles, in her experience, looked down on the less-refined manners of their country counterparts, irrespective of wealth.

"Your prince will come," her mother assured Eliza from her sixteenth birthday to her twenty-third. "You are heiress to a plantation and possess uncommon good looks. He'll come."

But when Calvin came a' courting (a pistol, but no sword by his side), Eliza's kiss couldn't turn her frog into the prince of fairy tales. It mattered little to Calvin that other young men of St. Francisville and Bayou Sara found Eliza neither lively nor prepossessing. She was two or three rungs higher on the social ladder of the Felicianas than he. Though pleasant company, she had little interest in the conversation of other people, hence they in hers. Without deliberation or intent, Lucy had created in Eliza a dependence from the day Jim Willis's pistol had misfired. Mother and daughter were inseparable. Gentlemen callers at the Moorhead plantation invariably felt the gray, unpleasant presence of the mother hovering somewhere nearby even if not always seen. Eliza Willis was still unmarried and a virgin when Calvin Bunch entered her life.

Calvin was closer in age to Eliza's younger brother than to herself. He and his father were disembarking from a steamboat at Bayou Sara when they encountered Lucy and Eliza at market a year ago. It had been several years since Lucy had seen Woodrow Bunch. She had never met his youngest son (of three). She invited them to call at Bolingbroke on their way back to Jackson if it would please them.

Woody Bunch reluctantly obliged. He had been a frequent visitor at Jericho Hill while he and Jim Willis capered about the

Felicianas like reckless goats. Bolingbroke impressed Bunch. It was much finer and more stoutly built than the Willis plantation.

"This whiskey is real good, Lucy. Mr. Moorhead must be a man of taste," said Woody, sitting on the porch of Bolingbroke Hall sipping whiskey with Jim Willis's widow and daughter. He had not seen Eliza since she was an infant.

"Jim Willis was too, you'll recall," she quickly insisted.

Woody recalled that Jim's taste in liquor depended on who was buying. His weak effort to compliment Lucy on her second marriage was not received as intended. Perhaps it suggested that Eliza's father was a lesser man than her new husband.

"They sure broke the mold with Jim. There was a real man. Sorely missed." Woody saw from Lucy's nod that he had hit a better note.

The events were so long ago. Could he even trust his memory? Yes, he and Jim had been drinking before the challenge and the duel. But was he so drunk that he had been negligent in examining the pistols, that he had not seen that the flint on the pistol selected by Jim Willis was insecure? In those moments between the failure of Jim's pistol to fire and the discharge of his opponent's weapon, did Jim realize why his pistol betrayed him? Did Jim understand it was his second who failed him, more than the pistol? No one but Woody Bunch examined the pistol afterward. Only he knew why it had misfired. And why his friend had died. He had cocked the pistol for Jim before handing it to him. He had seen that the flint was not aligned, that it was probably loose, but it did not register in his mind to delay the duel. The alcohol. The glare of the sun. A quibble about the condition of the pistol might seem cowardice or fear. From the bluff he had cast the weapon, and the Mississippi would never give up the secret that Woodrow Bunch would conceal to his death.

Now Jim's daughter was exchanging shy glances with his own son a hundred plus yards from the room where Jim Willis's wake was held twenty-odd years before. Lucy had never cared much for Woody, but now he was a link to her past. And as much as she had blamed Woody for Jim's lack of responsibility, she had no reason to attribute his death to his friend.

Odessa was skeptical of Calvin Bunch from the first, but she said little to anyone except Big Tom. She was the shrewdest woman on the plantation, a better judge of character and intentions than Lucy or Eliza or any of the other slaves. She was conversant on all activities in the Moorhead family from Clotilda, who kept nothing from Odessa. Even Clotilda, devoted entirely to Miss Lucy and Miss Eliza, had her doubts about Calvin. She saw trouble.

"Sump'n scary 'bout dat Calvin," she confided to Odessa, knowing Odessa never repeated stories. "Like he don't know that fo'ks sees him ugly like he is, like a cur dog what thinks he's the massa's prize bluetick coonhound. Not much better'n white trash an' what don't know it."

From the day Percy was born, Odessa assumed primary responsibility for raising Lucy's son, presenting to Miss Lucy only deference. When Calvin Bunch began calling on Eliza at Bolingbroke, Odessa mostly kept her opinions of the suitor to herself. A few times in conversation with Clotilda, she would ask, "Has the young Massa been courtin' today?" to which Clotilda would respond, "Don't you let Miss Lucy hears you call him dat. You knows what dis means to Miss Lucy to have a man seeing her baby. Eliza still be her baby."

Nothing in the bones cast by Odessa to tell the future disclosed to her what injuries Calvin Bunch would inflict upon her and the grief he would bring to Jericho Hill. But she knew, deep down she knew.

*Chapter 4*

# Leaving for Law

Percy had barely six weeks at home before departing for Williamsburg. He spent some time in the company of Calvin Bunch, to get to know him. He was now his brother, in law if not in blood or regard. He owed it to Eliza, who had always been affectionate and decent to him. The results were not encouraging. No camaraderie ensued, though Percy tried his best to develop a rapport. Eliza's husband was a year or so older than Percy but was defensive from their first meeting – he was clearly inferior to Percy in judgment, education and experience. Percy's three years of college and then campaign life with an army of ten thousand men in combat and field conditions prepared him for encounters with the widest variety of men he might meet in a lifetime. Calvin's acquaintances were largely confined to a thirty-five mile radius centered on Jackson, Louisiana. For a period of five months, Calvin was enrolled at Centenary College, six miles from his home, before returning to work in his father's store. He was incourteous to customers. In an oblique reference to Calvin, Percy's father observed, "The weak man thinks his rudeness is a show of strength."

Congeniality found no place in Calvin Bunch. Casual remarks by Percy were taken as slights by Calvin, who thought Percy was trying to show Calvin's ignorance. Conversations at dinner would become awkward when Lucy intervened to explain what Calvin really meant, taking his side in exchanges with Percy. Howard Moorhead missed most of these as he continued his decades long practice of spending the better part of each month in New Orleans.

Perhaps Percy should have seen the feral ambition that stirred deep within Calvin's crude intelligence. Despite his impatience, Calvin knew that if he waited long enough, he would achieve his plans. Not only would his marriage to an unattractive woman approaching spinsterhood lead to his taking over Jericho Hill, he would wrest Bolingbroke from his oh-so-superior brother-in-law – if he parlayed his advantages. He would show himself to be smarter than the college-educated Percy, once he outlived Howard Moorhead. Percy and Howard were not insurmountable obstacles, only obstructions that would fall away in time.

Lucy absented herself at a church function the day Percy departed for William and Mary. She felt he should have delayed his trip east until after Eliza's baby arrived. He was, she said, putting school ahead of family.

By the time he was ten or eleven, Percy had come to understand he would never have his mother's affection in the way Eliza did. He observed on occasion how their mother allowed Eliza to stay in her bedroom while Lucy read or did needlework by the window looking into the sunlit garden. Once, through a half-open door, he saw their mother take a box from the bottom drawer of her dresser. She opened the top, took out an item, examined it, then put it back. She took out another, looked it over closely and gave it to his twelve-year-old sister. Standing then in front of a mirror, Eliza put on the necklace her mother had handed her. Percy receded from possible discovery of his presence.

A week later, while Lucy and Eliza had gone to St. Francisville to shop, Percy passed the bedroom door. It was open. Clotilda was outside gathering eggs from the chicken yard. No one else was in the house. Percy turned and started to go up to his room for his morning studies. Pausing, temptation got the better of him. He cautiously entered the bedroom. He wanted to see the treasure box from which their mother drew necklaces and who knew what else for the amusement and delight of his older sister.

Setting aside several women's undergarments, in the back part of the right side of the bottom drawer Percy found an oblong box, fourteen inches long, a foot wide and five inches deep. Made of thin wood, it was quite sturdy and finished with a dark stain and a thin coat of shellac. The top was fastened on with two small brass hinges. He lifted it out of the drawer and placed it on the rug next to the bureau. Although he was certain his mother was away for hours, he looked around guiltily to be sure no one was watching him. He shook it gently, fearful something might break. Metallic sounds came from inside, sounds of glass too. With trepidation he opened it, as though some fierce creature kept inside might spring from it, a snake or a small weasel, a guardian of metal and glass objects. Inside he found fifty or more pieces. Silver forks and spoons, five or six necklaces of gold and silver chains, two Catholic rosaries, brooches – one he examined was an ivory brooch depicting Venus in relief. Buttons. A small porcelain yellow bird figurine.

Was this her secret jewelry box, where she kept her special keepsakes away from the servants? Not likely, he thought. She had one jewelry box on top of the bureau. The objects hidden below included many items that were not jewelry. A small, curled briarwood pipe with gold fittings on the top of the bowl and base of the stem. A man's shaving razor with bone handle. Perhaps some of the things had belonged to her first husband, James Willis. Did she keep them from the eyes and jealousy of Howard Moorhead? Or were they items handed down from her father and mother in North Carolina? He had died six months before her brothers had removed Lucy from Bertie County to Louisiana, and her mother a year earlier than he. Some of the items may be her only connection to her father and mother, family heirlooms.

Percy thought the box showed a sentimental side of his mother, a facet of her character that she would share with her daughter but perhaps too intimate for her son – especially if some related to Eliza's father. Now he felt guilty at invading her privacy, an intruder into a world of her memories. He put everything back as he had found it. He shut the lid and returned the box to the drawer and closed it. As he imagined what the box of mementoes meant to his mother, he felt a new affection for her, mingled with regret that she chose not to share those parts of her past with him. He was ashamed of himself for his jealousy at a daughter's special relationship with her mother. What could be more natural than the mother-daughter bond? Near ten years would pass before he would learn the truth about Lucy's box of treasured souvenirs. Still later he would smile at a boy's naïveté.

He went upstairs to his room and returned to the book he was reading, *True Stories from Ancient History* by Agnes Strickland. His tutor was returning tomorrow, up from New Orleans for three weeks of daily lessons and drills, a pedant named Peabody from Boston. What lessons were there for an eleven-year-old to comprehend that his mother was a bit of a thief?

෪෪ — ෯෯

Percy was having coffee and pie with his father at an eating place near the Bayou Sara landing. The steamboat that was taking him to New Orleans for the first leg of his journey to Williamsburg was late. He asked,

"Was Mother cross this morning? I heard her fussing at Clotilda at breakfast. Something about her box. Is that why she's not here to see me off?"

Wryly responding, his father said, "Mother's preoccupied with the approach of being a grandmother. Some of the women are giving Eliza a baby shower later today."

"I thought I heard her accuse Clotilda of taking something. Perhaps from her box of family memories. I saw her looking at it as I passed the bedroom yesterday."

"Family memories?" Howard Moorhead looked up from his plate with some surprise on his face.

"Yes. The one she keeps in her drawer in her dresser. I've seen her go through it from time to time."

"What makes you think it holds family memories?"

"Doesn't it? When we were younger, I saw Mother let Eliza wear a necklace with a small gold cross that she took out of the box. I assumed they were family heirlooms from North Carolina." He didn't tell his father he had once rummaged through the box.

Howard was irritated that his wife had chastised – wrongly – Clotilda for something she had not done and for her spiteful absence from Percy's departure for law school. He sensed Percy's disappointment at his mother's lack of encouragement. She was not keen on Percy leaving again. She thought he should stay and work on the plantations, to be joined eventually by Calvin Bunch. Lucy did little to conceal her displeasure at his plans. At dinner the night before, she had remarked that if he were really interested in the law, he could read law with a firm in New Orleans. Most attorneys admitted to the bar in Louisiana did just that. There was no need to go out of state to college for another year or more, a useless expense. Howard did not want to continue making excuses for her misbehavior.

"Heirlooms? Perhaps," said Howard, pausing before adding, "But not her family's."

"I don't understand."

"Let me express this as delicately as I can, son. Your mother has a problem that has occasioned some embarrassment for our name from time to time. Mother . . . ." he hesitated as he looked for a word. "Mother has a *peculiarity*. Not to put too fine a point on it, she has a penchant for taking things that do not belong to her."

"You mean she is a thief?"

"Thief is too strong a word, perhaps. She thinks of herself as receiving 'souvenirs' – that's her word for it – from people and places she visits. People gift her without their being aware of it. We might be at the home of others for a dinner and she will bring home a fork from the family's set of silver. A gentleman's fine razor might be missed after we have visited during a wedding reception. These find their way into Mother's 'souvenir' box."

"That's terrible." Percy was dumbfounded. What he had thought for years was family sentiment was the savoring of the fruit of petty larceny. This was his mother. They had plenty of money to buy her anything she might want.

"It is an affliction, a compulsion," replied Howard, not without sympathy. "She acts on impulse. The doctors probably have a term for it."

"How long has she done this? Is there anything you can do?"

"Almost as long as I've known her. There's little to do when it occurs near our home. It would be too embarrassing to our family to return items. Among our friends in St. Francisville it is especially awkward. She is suspected of taking things from their homes. But who has nerve to challenge her? When I once raised the question with her, she insisted that Ellie Pritchard had gifted her with a silver spoon to show her friendship. In New Orleans there are shops that turn your mother away if she tries to enter them. With a few others, I've made arrangements with the proprietor that if she is seen to remove an item without paying, to please let me know and I'll be good for the cost."

"I never would have suspected," Percy said, believing it but wishing it weren't so.

"There are worse failings. Cruelty. Extravagance. We all have them. Everyone has a box where we keep our secrets and lies. Your mother can keep hers in a drawer instead of her heart."

"And you, Father, do you carry a box of lies and secrets?"

"A hint of a smile passed over Howard's lips, a touch of mischief in their small pursing, "Only a wee little box lying in the deep, full fathom five."

Percy, with equal slyness, said, "And should I go there, will I find the pearls that were your lies? And where mother's?"

## Chapter 5

# Allied with Judah Benjamin

T he law firm of Benjamin and Micou employed two men in their outer office to admit clients, maintain files and serve as scriveners for court filings. The younger of them, Henri Lepeyre, was about thirty. Percy noted his receding hairline above an angular face as he stood before him. Henri looked up from his desk and said courteously, a French lilt in his baritone voice, "You must be Mr. Moorhead. Mr. Benjamin is running late today. He asked if you would mind waiting for him in his office."

Eight months had passed since he began preparing for this meeting. As Percy researched a topic for Judge Tucker's class, Judah Benjamin had come to his attention. He admired a book in Tucker's library co-authored by Judah Benjamin. If he were to become a lawyer in Louisiana, he would seek to associate himself with the best to be found in New Orleans.

At William and Mary in Williamsburg, Virginia, Percy had expected to find himself in an environment not unlike he had experienced at Princeton. The unexpected was the closure of all departments of the college for the entire school year, owing to a dispute over faculty appointments and resignations, with the sole exception of the law school under Judge Beverley Tucker. Percy found himself in the company of fewer than ten others aspiring to the law. Through his year, Tucker had given Percy close guidance, and he had come to the attention of the acting president of the College, Benjamin Ewell, who was working diligently to repair the damage to the college from a dispute that had strong political overtones.

"Of course," Percy replied to Judah Benjamin's clerk with equal courtesy. "I will wait."

Henri showed him into a large office with wood paneling. Four large bookcases contained the largest collection of books Percy Moorhead had seen outside of the libraries of the two colleges he attended or the Biblioteca Palafoxiana in Puebla, Mexico, in which he had spent much of three months, a respite from the Mexican war. He estimated the number of Benjamin's books at more than three hundred.

In the center of the office was a table about eight feet wide and four deep. Neatly arranged around it were six sturdy oak chairs with arms and cushioned seats, three on each side. Opposite the table was a captain's desk, maybe four feet high, with four drawers on each side that opened to the sides of the desk. A hinged desk top covered a compartment that could hold pens, clips, and paper. A writing set with ink well, pen holder and rolling blotter was on top. Percy surmised, this must be where Judah Benjamin did his writing – standing up, foot propped on a metal rail across the inside bottom of the desk.

The paintings on the wall conveyed a rustic British setting. One depicted a slick-coated black Gordon setter looking on as a pair of willow grouse flew up from their scrape on a heather-thick moor. A larger painting portrayed a bay thoroughbred in mid-step, led by a groom dressed in blue clothing that had been fashionable a century earlier.

Restless after sitting at the table for five minutes, Percy stood and walked over to examine the books. He recognized the titles of many. In English were Blackstone's *Commentaries*, Coke's *Institutes*, *Coke on Littleton*, and Bracton among others. French volumes included Giffrein's edition of Pothier's works, Toullier's *Le Droit Civil, Francais* and three dozen more. In Spanish he found *Novisima Recopilacion de las Leyes de Espana* and the *Siete Partidas*. Here was the Louisiana Civil Code in English and French, edited with annotations by Wheelock Upton and, next to it, the Benjamin and Slidell *Digest of Louisiana Decisions*.

Just as young Moorhead took down and opened the *Digest*, the door to the office opened. Hastily, he replaced the volume and turned to the man who walked in.

Judah P. Benjamin was a bit shorter than Percy expected, a good half foot less than himself. The first thing he noted was the lawyer's broad, boyish smile. About forty, he had not a marked line in his face. Soft black curls fell about his temples and forehead, and his lower face bore a beard that Percy had heard described as Sephardic. He was inclined to be fleshy, even portly. Here, reflected Percy, was a man who hunted no grouse, had no setter at his hearth, and possessed no thoroughbred riding horse. He had more the appearance of the witty bon vivant than the advocate who had appeared several hundred times before the appellate state and federal courts in the last fifteen years. His calm and courtly manner immediately set Percy at ease, as it did others.

"So sorry to keep you waiting, Mr. Moorhead. Please be seated."

The lawyer walked to his writing desk and extracted several papers from a drawer before taking a seat at the table opposite the younger man.

"I received your letter with considerable interest. It was brief and to the point. You were educated at the College of New Jersey. You studied law at William and Mary. But you took a degree at neither institution. You would like to associate with our offices. But you said little else about yourself. Tell me why we should bring you on with us."

The invitation to explain himself carried insistence, though with pleasant delivery.

Percy had planned his words well in advance. "I'm sure many young men apply to you. But none would work harder nor with greater dedication than I. Give me an opportunity. I will prove myself to you." He delivered his lines earnestly, hoping they did not come across as rehearsed or nervous.

Benjamin looked Percy studiously for a moment without speaking, as if carefully framing his response. He put the sheaf of papers down and eased back into his chair.

"New Orleans does not lack for aspiring lawyers. Nor we for applicants. In your case, your name precedes you, young man, and it secured this interview. Seeing the name Moorhead put me on notice to see if you were related to Howard Moorhead, whose name is well-known in business in this city. You are his son, and the Pughs on your mother's side are equally esteemed. Your uncle has been the Speaker of our legislature. I should think you would raise your family connections and the possibility of attracting clients in cotton and sugar to our representation."

The young man insisted that he be considered only for his own record and abilities. "I am seeking employment for myself and do not wish to trade on any connections I may have from my family. As a lawyer I will rise or fall on my own merit."

"I see. Very admirable. Not very practical. A good name is coin of the realm, as good as money in your purse. But tell me, why did you choose William and Mary? Why not Harvard or Yale? Was it because of Beverley Tucker?"

The name and work of Tucker were familiar to Benjamin. Tucker's essays and book reviews in *Southern Quarterly Review* and *Southern Literary Messenger* were read by Benjamin as they appeared. Like many Americans, Benjamin had read Tucker's novels, *George Balcombe,* the serialized *Gertrude,* and the *Partisan Leader,* published under a pseudonym but well known to have issued from his pen. Among Benjamin's law books by Tucker were the *Principles of Pleading* and *Lectures for the Study of the Constitution of the United States.*

Percy had been certain Benjamin would know of Beverley Tucker. "William and Mary is a Southern college. I preferred not to go north again. To be frank, I chose it because of General Winfield Scott. William and Mary is where he studied law. The general was willing to write a letter of recommendation for me."

Dropping General Scott's name into the interview was not casual. Percy anticipated that the politically ambitious Benjamin would respond. While it might appear that Benjamin was conducting the interview, it was Percy who now steered the direction of the questions.

Benjamin's interest indeed picked up. There was obviously

more to this young man than a good name and respectable academic credentials.

"Really? How do you know General Scott?"

"I served under him. In Mexico."

"Your letter didn't mention that."

"Yes sir. I volunteered for Colonel DeRussy's regiment. I was then assigned to General Scott's army in Vera Cruz. We marched to Mexico City."

Benjamin was quiet for a moment, then smiled again. He sensed now that the young man was almost as cunning as himself in reading others. Crafty, perhaps, but could he hold his own when challenged on complex legal matters?

"Professor Tucker is a learned man in law, as was his father," Benjamin said as he began to probe. "But their focus was always on the common law, whether Virginia or Missouri. I would assume, Mr. Moorhead, you relied heavily on St. George Tucker's edition of *Blackstone's Commentaries* that put English common law in the context of Virginia. You do understand, don't you, that Louisiana has a different system? You were holding the Louisiana *Digest* when I came in."

Percy had anticipated that Benjamin's first questions would be about his ability to work in Louisiana's distinctive legal system.

"Yes sir. Of course. I used your *Digest* regularly in Williamsburg in my exercises. A good portion of my year with Professor Tucker was devoted to an essay touching on Louisiana law."

"Oh? What was that?" Benjamin sensed that he was being drawn in by the young man.

"I wrote a study of the reception statutes of Virginia, Texas and Louisiana – comparing the three systems as to how their legal systems were constituted. Professor Tucker was very interested in the topic. When he lacked resources in his own library, he sent me to Richmond and Washington to gather more material."

"And what did you conclude?" Benjamin was surprised. Few lawyers whom he knew were curious about the foundations of a legal system. To Benjamin, a lawyer without such knowledge was like a physician not knowing of the skeleton or the blood system or a ship's captain without a compass and sextant.

Percy continued, "Blackstone had considered the question of law in new lands. If an uninhabited territory is colonized by Britain, then the English law automatically applies in this territory from the moment of colonization. However, if the colonized territory has a pre-existing legal system, that existing law would apply until displaced by new laws of the new sovereign."

"Indian tribes, too?"

"I think Blackstone would have insisted that law must be found in writings, which the tribes lacked. So the Virginia colony had no existing legal system despite the presence of tribes. The common law of England and any statutes of Parliament applied. Unless the Parliament allowed the General Assembly of the colony to adopt local legislation. When Virginia declared its independence, it was now sovereign and was free to make any law applicable that it wished."

"What happened to the old law? How could contracts and property and family law continue?" Benjamin knew the answers to his own questions. But his knowledge had not come in a classroom under the tutelage of a man such as Judge Tucker. As Percy learned from his father and from others to whom he made inquiries, Benjamin had arrived in New Orleans penniless and in desperate need of a job. His studies at Yale were not in law and had not led to a degree but were sufficient for him to offer his services as a tutor to the children of well-to-do parents for whom English was not their first language. He taught them English and they allowed him to further his knowledge of French and Spanish. His diligence brought him to the attention of Mr. Stringer, a public notary, who took young Judah on as a clerk. Stringer had encouraged him to study law when he was not otherwise occupied preparing and copying legal forms. The lawyers who sought notary services from Stringer and Benjamin lent the eager clerk law books on all subjects from their libraries, and he absorbed everything he could get his hands on. Four years of constant study permitted him to stand for admission to the bar, sponsored by two of the attorneys whom he had impressed with his encyclopedic knowledge.

Percy responded, "That's where a reception statute comes in. An early act of the Virginia Assembly received and continued the common law of England prior to the third or fourth year of the reign of King James. I forget which. And all statutes or acts of Parliament made in aid of the common law. The laws of the state's General Assembly then in existence were also continued."

Percy's exposition was almost as complete as he had given a few month's earlier in Judge Tucker's seminar with three other students. The professor had also required each student to deliver his paper as if *ex temporare*, in front of two judges of the Virginia bench – while the student was interrupted with questions.

Benjamin was impressed that Percy was not distracted by interruptions. He might do well in appellate advocacy, facing a panel of judges peppering him with questions that were often unfriendly.

"And Texas?," asked Benjamin, smiling but raising his eyebrows as if skeptical

Without hesitation, Percy answered, "Well, Texas is a little more complicated. It worked by inheritance and by adoption. Following Blackstone, when Texas declared its independence, it retained the Spanish civil law for a time. There had to be some law in place, and land titles depended on it. Let us have no gaps. The law, whatever the jurisdiction, abhors a vacuum, whether it is in title or in inheritance. But the Texas Constitution provided that the Texas legislature had to introduce, by statute, the common law of

England, with such modifications as the Texas circumstances might require. In all criminal cases, the common law was to be the rule of decision. And that's what the Texas Congress did, and it also rejected the Mexican prohibition of slavery. The American settlers in Texas brought their notions of law with them, including slavery."

Benjamin recognized in Percy an extraordinary capacity for observation of the salient and for analysis not unlike his own. He commented, "Very interesting. I have several clients who moved from Louisiana to Texas. They have lands in Louisiana and in Texas. Now tell me what you know of Louisiana law."

What law applies? And why? Benjamin's thoughts returned to these questions many times, and not only because he had studied for admission to practice. He had been born on a little island in the Caribbean, St. Croix, during the brief period the English flag flew over the island, occupied by the British because of Denmark's alliance with France during the Napoleonic Wars. Birth under British sovereignty meant he was a British citizen for life, even when the island returned to Danish sovereignty. He was subject to British law, and he was able to claim the protection of that same law. When his parents moved to South Carolina, he became subject to its law and to the law of the United States. By birth, he was a Jew – a race, religion and nationality. He had been raised to believe he was governed by Mosaic law, whether Jews could claim sovereignty over soil or not. When he moved to Louisiana, he subjected himself to its jurisdiction. Which laws could lay claim to his obedience? Which law could he renounce and be free of? It was more than an academic theory. The New Orleans papers were reporting the debates at a convention of Southern states in Nashville in favor of repudiating national law and for secession from the union.

Percy did not hesitate. "Louisiana's legal heritage is even more complicated than Texas. We have by inheritance both French and

Spanish law. Remnants of both continue. West of the Mississippi River both France and Spain furnished the law over different periods before the United States annexed us in 1803-04. East of the Mississippi, English law applied after the French and Indian War. Then England ceded West Florida to the Spanish during our war of independence. Spanish law continued over the region until 1810 when the United States acquired it after the area where I come from had a brief period as the Republic of West Florida."

"Is that where you grew up? I have the impression that your father lives in New Orleans."

"We live in both places. Bolingbroke, our plantation, is outside St. Francisville. Our townhouse is not more than five blocks from here."

"Please continue." It was not uncommon for plantation owners to have a second residence in New Orleans. Benjamin himself had both a townhouse and a magnificent sugar plantation named Belle Chasse.

Caught up in enthusiasm for his subject, Percy spoke with animation without regard to the fact he was applying for a position. "When we became a state, the law of Louisiana was to apply to the whole of both areas, east and west. Initially, the Louisiana territory simply continued the existing law until new law was enacted locally – to the extent not inconsistent with the constitution and laws of the United States. A digest of Louisiana law was adopted in 1808, essentially a civil code derived from the Code Napoleon. But it continued existing law, some Spanish and some French, that was not inconsistent with the new provisions."

"Oh? Not one or the other? Shouldn't the law have clarity?" Benjamin's question was deliberately provocative.

Smiling as he took Benjamin's bait, Percy said, "That's been up to the courts. And remains controversial as you know, Mr. Benjamin. In the *Cottin* decision in 1817, the Louisiana Supreme Court held that all of the Spanish laws previously in force and not contrary to the Code were still in force. This case is probably one of the reasons why the Louisiana legislature enacted a new Civil Code in 1825 that was supposed to repeal the old Spanish, Roman and French laws. But Louisiana judges and lawyers continue to rely on the old sources. I think that's how your *Digest* treats *Cottin* and the general subject. And that holds true for the annotations in Mr. Upton's edition of the Civil Code. A desire for clarity must be balanced against the leeway a degree of uncertainty gives to judges and lawyers. Hard rules may produce harsh results. Picking from several traditions gives the court flexibility. Why be restrained unduly by rules when you can reshape them drawing on those diverse traditions?"

Percy's display of knowledge of Louisiana law more than impressed Benjamin. But young Moorhead was astute as well as learned. He had the prudence to conceal his knowledge even when its presentation would confirm the depth of his study. He didn't mention the case of *Allen v. Allen* that had excited much controversy in Louisiana and in other slaveholding states – the *white slave case*. The attorney for the slaveholder was Judah Benjamin's partner, William C. Micou. The Louisiana Supreme Court rejected Micou's arguments founded on the Spanish *Partidas*. Micou's pleadings illustrated that Louisiana lawyers continued to rely on ancient Spanish sources despite the enactment of a new Civil Code that attempted to overturn the *Cottin* decision. But it was an embarrassing loss for Micou. As Benjamin himself might say, victories are long celebrated, while defeats are quickly orphaned.

"Well Mr. Moorhead, you have persuaded me that you have the preparation for the practice of the law. But are you the right man for our little firm? How well-rounded are you? Do you read? Are you interested in business? Can you advise clients on decisions that require judgment and discretion?"

Most of the people Percy had asked about Mr. Benjamin had spoken of the breadth of his knowledge of literature and poetry, his quickness in referring to literary examples as precedents for a point he wished to make. Percy said, "When I lack business experience, I will make up for it by preparation. Professor Tucker tells all of his students that his goal is to prepare us to be statesmen and leaders instead of legal drones possessed of more arcane knowledge than others. Both you and Judge Tucker find literature a fitting companion to the pursuit of law. As meager as my learning may be by comparison, I believe that you will find my attachment to belle lettres is unmatched."

Benjamin rightly saw Percy's modesty as to his "meager" learning as an invitation to challenge the extent of his reading. "Oh? What recent books do you like?"

"I just read Mr. Thackeray's *Vanity Fair*. My father's issues of *Fraser's* magazine have his *Luck of Barry Lyndon*, which I find to be the equal of anything by Dickens. I enjoy non-fiction books on travel and geography – Mr. Parkman's *Oregon Trail*, Mr. Dana's *Two Years Before the Mast*, Mr. Mackenzie's *Year in Spain*."

"Mackenzie, you say. What do you know about Mackenzie?" The name was very familiar to Benjamin, as Percy knew. Percy had waited for an opportunity to bring up Alexander Slidell Mackenzie.

"Well, he was brother of our Supreme Court judge Thomas Slidell and of Mr. John Slidell who was an emissary to Mexico around the time I volunteered for service abroad. Of course, I am aware of your relationship with these brothers. But I mention Mr. Mackenzie's book because it helped me learn Spanish when I spent three months in the city of Puebla. In the library next door to the cathedral was *A Year in Spain* together with its translation, *Un año en España*. Reading them side by side helped me pick up the language. When I returned from Mexico, I found out what I could about the man whose writing had commanded so much of my time. What happened to Commander Mackenzie was very unfortunate. In my opinion, Mr. Fenimore Cooper treated him most unfairly."

Clever lad, thought Benjamin, using the brother of my co-author to bring up his knowledge of Spanish. Benjamin was well aware of all that had befallen of Alexander Slidell, who had taken the name Mackenzie so as to claim the inheritance of a maternal uncle. Well-known as an author, Mackenzie was also a naval officer. The *U.S.S. Somers* was under his command in the Atlantic when a plan of mutiny was discovered aboard his vessel. Commander Mackenzie convened a panel of officers. Three of the men who were accused of plotting to turn the *Somers* into a pirate ship were hanged. When the ship returned to the United States, the affair drew national notoriety. The executed ringleader was the son of the Secretary of War. None of the three had been given a real hearing. Commander Mackenzie was put to a court martial. It did not find him guilty of misconduct, nor did it fully exonerate him. James Fenimore Cooper, the best-known writer in America, was a former naval officer who reviewed the transcript of the court martial and published a lengthy report critical of the actions of Commander Mackenzie. Cooper's report carried authority for he had recently published a history of the United States Navy.

Percy had discovered that Benjamin was no stranger to ship mutinies. He had defended an insurance company in claims over the revolt of slaves at sea on the brig *Creole*. The slaveowners' crew had brought on the mutiny, he argued, by their cruelty.

Benjamin told Percy, "Judge Slidell says that Cooper's attack was revenge for an exchange of bad book reviews between Mackenzie and Cooper. Both wrote books about naval engagements, with sharp disagreements between them."

Percy liked the novels of Cooper, but he had no misgivings about criticizing the man himself.

"I think Cooper downplayed the threat to good order posed by incipient mutiny. A leader must act quickly, before something far worse occurs. It's as bad as a slave revolt. Or the St. Patrick's battalion, the San Patricios. They were the Americans who deserted their own side to fight with the Mexicans on the promise from the

Mexicans of land and money. General Scott did the right thing."

"I remember something about Irish deserters," said Benjamin, "but I don't recall what General Scott did."

"We captured about seventy-five of the deserters. One of them was a soldier I had seen in Puebla before he left our army. More than a hundred others were killed in battle. They fought all the more fiercely knowing their fate when captured. Mexican prisoners would be given parole. The San Patricios would not. They would die. The survivors were given a trial, and most were sentenced to death as deserters."

"They had trials?"

"Yes. I was a witness at one of the trials before an army board. General Scott himself reviewed the case of every soldier who was tried. He ordered the sentence be carried out for fifty of the deserters. Some others were commuted to whipping and branding – if they had joined the Mexicans before the war began. He never stopped being a lawyer while he was a general. All of this legal proceeding took place while fighting into Mexico City was going forward. Amazing, I thought. This was a lesson in law. I was there as thirty deserters were hanged at Mixcoac within sight of the assault taking place against the Castle of Chapultepec. Colonel Harney was in charge of the execution, and he wanted the condemned men to see the American deserters take the Castle before they died."

Percy had taken prisoner at the Churubusco convent two of the deserters, then he had identified them at trial as wearing Mexican uniforms. He didn't tell Benjamin that he drove one of the ten wagons, which upon command bolted forward, leaving three men from each dangling from a noose. Percy had felt neither guilt nor regret for being a co-author of their deaths. The deserters had freely chosen their actions. Their execution was the natural consequence of their choice. They had taken up arms against a country whose uniform they had accepted and worn. For all he knew, one of them fired the shot that killed his friend, Jed Barclay. This was no occasion to relate such experiences to Judah Benjamin.

"That must have been a dramatic spectacle. What do you think of Harney?"

"I served with him briefly. He is a man who does what a man must do. But with a relish I would not wish to emulate. I thought of Shakespeare. General Scott's orders for the treatment of the Mexican population were the same as King Henry's on his campaign in France. Even though Bardolph had been Henry's friend for years, he had to be executed for stealing from French churches. General Scott, like King Henry, sought just treatment for the people whom he had invaded and meted out justice to deserters and those who refused his orders. Deserters should have just deserts."

Benjamin cocked his head skeptically. "Are you sure?" he asked. Without waiting for a reply, he walked over to his bookcases. He took down a volume of Shakespeare and flipped through the pages for a minute. From the binding, it appeared to be volume four of the Peabody edition, the same that Professor Tucker had in his library.

"By golly, you're right, Moorhead. I had forgotten the fate of poor old Bardolph. Here's what Henry says. 'We would have all such offenders so cut off. And we give express charge that, in our marches through the country, there be nothing compelled from the villages, nothing taken but paid for, none of the French upbraided or abused in disdainful language; for when lenity and cruelty play for a kingdom, the gentler gamester is the soonest winner.'"

Relieved that his reference had been validated, Percy said, "Baron Jomini said much the same. Or so Lieutenant Beauregard told me. General Scott's order in Mexico was to the same effect as King Henry's in France."

Benjamín closed the book and took a long look at Percy Moorhead. The young man had largely led the interview while maintaining the appearance that Benjamin was in charge. He put his hand on his shoulder and said, "Son, I think I can speak for my partner Micou in coming to some agreement. What arrangement did you contemplate?"

Percy, turning in his seat, answered after a minute of thought. "I'd like to have an office here and to have it known that I'm associated with your law practice. I would be very happy to see you draw up a schedule of fees you would pay me for specific services – drafting contracts, composing briefs and for legal research. Matters which you are too busy to handle I could handle. For any clients I bring to the law firm I will remit one-half of all fees and retainers to you and Mr. Micou."

At that moment the door to Benjamin's office swung open. A man entered. Although he was only in his early forties, he did not appear to be in good health. His eyes were weary, face pale. His tailor must not have possessed the skills of Benjamin's, for his attire was neither stylish nor well-fitting. Percy took note to inquire of the clerks the name of Benjamin's tailor.

Benjamin spoke to his partner. "Ah, William. Permit me to introduce Percy Moorhead. I thought I knew more Shakespeare than any man in New Orleans but young Percy may prove me wrong. We may have to call him Hotspur. With your assent, he will be associating with us to lighten the burdens of our practice."

The reality was that Benjamin was spread too thin. His plantation, a short distance downriver from New Orleans, and his political activities took up much of his time. Micou's health frequently limited the amount of work he could handle. Both lawyers needed competent assistance.

Micou was affable if not energetic. "Moorhead? A good name. An excellent name. Well, young Moorhead, the sooner the better," said Micou as he shook Percy's hand. "If you've survived Judah's withering cross-examination, you must be a capable young man."

Could it have gone so well? Percy wanted to pinch himself to see if this was all a dream from which he would awaken. He said eagerly, "I'm confident I can earn the trust of both of you." And indeed Percy sounded confident but was now daunted by the prospect of living up to the expectations he had created. He was more successful than he had believed possible. But it was only the first step of his longer term plan.

Judah Benjamin had not asked Percy a few questions that would have revealed more about the young man seeking an association with him? Benjamin didn't ask: "Young man, if you are the heir to a thriving plantation and the son of a well-known cotton factor, why do you want to practice law?" Percy had a ready answer, but he would have concealed the truth: Percy's ambition was for a future greater than a cotton plantation, even the largest and best run, could offer. He wanted to be the best at something and to have that "best" be recognized by others. Ownership of land and laborers would bring wealth, but not recognition by his contemporaries. When he joined the Louisiana volunteer company for Mexico, he knew nothing of the military and little of the world. He had not understood he would be looked down upon and answerable to by officers, indeed by every soldier who held rank above private. When he had stumbled in the Aztec Club, he had been embarrassed and humiliated by the sharp rebuke he had received from a captain.

Percy had vowed he would never again be in such a position. He would achieve success in law and use it to become a senator or governor of the state. Judah Benjamin had not asked, "Why do you want to associate with our firm?" Were he candid, Percy would have answered, "If I am to be the best lawyer in Louisiana, then I must associate with the best the state now offers. You, sir, will be my means of gaining prominence, even preeminence in law and then in politics."

❧❧ — ৡৡ

"Let me be sure I understand you, Percy," I said as he related to me how he was employed by Judah Benjamin. "At this point, you saw Benjamin as your instrument to advance your own ambition. It was not the other way around."

Looking over at me with that self-deprecating grin, he said, "You've got it. When I was twenty-three and twenty-four I was the proudest puppy of a litter, as full of confidence and ambition as an over-ripe melon ready to burst. At Princeton and in the army I realized how small my world had been. Once I emerged from my Louisiana cocoon, I thought I was quicker and brighter than everyone around me but they all saw me as a country bumpkin, albeit a kind of diamond in the rough. I always had to show them just how smart I was, even if I was offensive. Becoming a lawyer would increase my standing outside my little patch of Louisiana soil. Going forward in my profession as a lawyer, Benjamin was going to be my railroad car to success. Association with him would open the doors to the corridors of power for me."

"So many metaphors, Percy, for such a young man. I can't tell if you are mocking me or your younger self."

"Tom, words were always my allies. That and my ability to organize them like soldiers in a campaign. To gain entry to law in New Orleans I studied Judah like he was a fort I had to conquer. I read his books and articles. I studied the opinions in the cases in which he appeared. I shadowed him in the streets and followed him into the courthouses to hear him argue. Once I gained an interview, I knew I could win him with my words and the store of information I had gathered. My command of words could carry me anywhere, I was certain. And so, too, were words my weakness."

"How so?"

"I was unprepared for a world that was impervious to words and persuasion. Words will not work with those who are deaf to them, those who refuse to face the consequences even when you warn them."

"Your brother-in-law?"

"Yes, him. And a thousand others like him."

"Still, you were right about Benjamin being key to your success as a lawyer."

"To a point, yes. And for that I have always been grateful. Despite what happened later."

"Yes," I said, "I know." It was too painful a story for him to relate to me again.

*Chapter 6*

# A Lawyer Ascendant

Percy Moorhead, nascent attorney, now wears an affable appearance, an imperturability. His brow is unwrinkled by worry. A shock of dark hair falls across his forehead. Many might mistake him for a dandy. But not those who look closely at his eyes. They are of a deep, dark brown – eyes that glint like flint, eyes that are hard and penetrating, eyes that reveal a rock-like, determined spirit beneath the calm exterior. Few details escape his attention.

Within a matter of months, certainly less than a year, Benjamin and Micou are using Percy Moorhead to develop and prepare their cases and assign him more of their routine business work. The young attorney interviews potential witnesses and prepares their depositions. His research on precedents, statutes and Code articles is impeccable. He soon is entrusted to meet with the bankers and merchants and other business figures of New Orleans who are the firm's clients. He learns as much as he can of their business affairs while preparing their contracts and property transactions. He never proffers advice unsolicited to a client but offers his judgment when requested. It is often followed, and it is always respected.

The senior clerk and office manager in the Benjamin-Micou firm is Frank Koelhoffer, a German immigrant who speaks with a pronounced accent. A heavy-set man of about forty-five, he has worked for Judah Benjamin for ten years. Percy knows that his own success depends on gaining the loyalty and support of Koelhoffer and Henri Lapeyre. In Mexico he had observed the ways in which the enlisted men would subtly undermine the officers above them, men who led by command instead of loyalty. Both men are older than he and more experienced in legal matters. He knows they view him initially with skepticism despite his formal education. In the first months of his work, he invariably seeks the advice of one or the other even when the course to be followed is already clear.

"If this were your case, Frank, how would you . . . .?"

"Henri, you're familiar with Judge Cutshaw's court. What do you think his response would be to the argument that . . . .?"

Clerks are to the legal system what sergeants are to the army – lower ranked than officers but indispensable. Without them nothing would function smoothly or effectively. Having felt mistreated and little appreciated by army officers in Mexico, Percy will not be guilty of the same himself.

The busiest time for Percy Moorhead is summer. Near the end of May, Judah Benjamin will sail to Europe, where he will remain until late August. He has clients in London and Liverpool. They are, however, secondary to his wife and daughter, who reside in Paris. Natalie Benjamin had moved to France a few years earlier and had taken their little daughter Ninette with her. William Micou has a home north of Lake Pontchatrain and regards the climate there as more conducive to his health.

Young Moorhead soon transacts most of the activity of the law office on his own for a quarter of the year. Industrious, competent and astute, he proves equal to the task. His eloquence does not ascend to the heights of Benjamin. But the firm's clients remark on his nobility of expression and his handsome features. He is a confident speaker, full of sparkling metaphor, and elegant comparison. His language abounds in the choice figures of rhetoric that he acquired under Rev. Professor Matthew Hope at Princeton. In his court appearances, there is no hesitation, no want of ideas, nor words in which to clothe them. His affability and air of good humor disarm most other members of the legal community in New Orleans, who welcome him as a worthy protege of Judah Benjamin. The few who are critical and assert he is shallow and facile are prompted more by jealousy than considered assessment.

On most Wednesdays Percy Moorhead has dinner with his father at Lacour's on Royal Street. Howard is as taciturn as he has ever been, never talking about his own business affairs, about which Percy still knows very little. Yet he always is well-informed as to Percy's clients and activities. He offers cryptic but knowing observations about the leading figures of New Orleans commerce. A simple gesture or raised eye is sufficient to alert Percy that this person or that official is to be treated warily or avoided altogether. Howard Moorhead's "good, good" is a seal of approval that validates a course of action on which Percy may have entertained doubt.

When pressed, Percy's father opens up, albeit reluctantly, on developments at home. Six months might pass before Percy could return to Bolingbroke.

"Eliza, Calvin and Nerissa are living in Natchez."

"Now what?" asks Percy. "Another new venture?"

"He's a cotton broker, with two other men."

"That working out any better than his last venture?"

"We'll have to see. He may surprise all of us. Big Tom's health isn't too good."

"Will you hire an overseer? Let's hope Mother doesn't push Calvin on you."

"She means well. For now, Big Tom's boys are taking up the slack. Julius is younger and smaller but he's filling in pretty well for Big Tom."

"I would have expected that," said Percy. "He was always the abler son."

"You and he were almost like brothers," remarked Howard. "I know you would lend him your books."

"It seemed harmless enough. But I assumed you were aware of what I did. It was you who arranged that we were nursed by the same mother. You were aware that Odessa taught me French. We learned to read at the same time, Julius and I. It was a slave who taught Marcus Aurelius as I recall. To all appearances, in Julius the French blood predominates over the African. If Odessa is correct that she was born free and never really a slave, then Julius's status as slave is an accident of birth."

"Is that not true of all the bondsmen in this country?" asked Howard. A waiter hovered nearby, devoting his attentions exclusively to the Moorhead table. Until recently, Moorhead had owned a substantial interest in the restaurant but divested himself as he slowly liquidated many of his holdings. He would still receive attentions as though an owner. Though Percy was ignorant of his father's many ventures, he would receive the same deference given his father.

"I've never heard you question slavery, Father. Is this something new? You own more than many planters in the Felicianas."

"By necessity, not by choice. I take no pleasure owning men, women and children as chattel property. It was, however, a simple proposition – If I were to marry your mother and to own land, it would be necessary to make the land productive. Without bondsmen, there would be no tilling of the soil, no planting of crops, no gathering of cotton. Had I never owned a slave, no slave's life would have been any better. Were I to free every slave we own, not one of them would have a better life than at present."

"I can't disagree. I've always thought slavery against natural law. I never had the courage to speak up to Professor Tucker on the subject. He was adamant that African slavery was part of the natural order. Is there a solution?"

"Would that there were. You and I did not invent slavery. Nor could we abolish it. In India, they have a saying – he who rides the tiger dares not dismount. I have read some of the writings of Judge Tucker on the African. He has tried to make slavery into a Christian undertaking. A morally uplifting enterprise to civilize the savage heathen. I am unconvinced. Nor will he persuade the millions of our fellow citizens in the northern states. They affect purity of heart and intend to radically alter the lives of the millions of us here. They would enjoy the moral pleasure of liberating the black population while suffering none of the consequences. Do they live with the black man? No. Do they employ black labor? Almost never. Do they educate black children? Rarely. I regret ownership of black people, but I do not apologize for it. I do not claim their souls, and I allow for their humanity in ways few abolitionists ever would."

"I am surprised. You've never spoken so freely." Percy has always assumed his father's views were no different from most other plantation owners.

"I don't believe that blacks are inferior to whites any more than the Irish are inferior to the English. They simply have not had the same opportunities."

"Should we provide them?"

"We must take care of our own the best we can while avoiding injury to others. You are my son. What I have built in Bolingbroke and in business for more than twenty years is to be your heritage. I will pass on to you a name and property. Make of them what you will."

"I hope never to disappoint you."

"Nor I, you, son." There is something melancholy in Howard

Moorhead's expression, but it quickly passes. He throws back his head and smiles. "Doesn't Falstaff tell us to drink wine? We shall have more."

As if on cue, the attentive waiter, whom Howard had hired five years earlier for Lacour's, comes to the table and starts to pour from the restaurant's best Bordeaux.

"No, no," said Howard jocularly, putting a finger over his wine glass. "Bring us sherris-sack. Those who drink no sherry are generally fools and cowards."

"I had no idea you were a Shakespeare fan."

"Not like my uncle. He knew Shakespeare like no other. When you visit England, you'll pass through Stratford on your way and then you'll understand."

"Stratford?" Later, Percy would recall and puzzle even more on the phrase that followed. What was on his way? Where? He had no plans to visit England, much less Stratford.

"It's in your blood Percy. Your name is no accident," his father says with a finality that closes the conversation. He has said much more than he had intended. Perhaps the wine, perhaps a sentiment that Percy cannot yet comprehend.

Percy feels that his father is finally opening up to him, moving beyond the stiff, formal communications between them that so long has characterized their relationship. Can Percy bring himself to ask the questions that he'd never had courage to ask? Or would a penetration into his father's past break the closeness that was forming? Does his mother know things of his father that he does not know? Nothing more is said as they leave Lacour's. A moment has passed.

## Chapter 7

# Miss Philomena Randolph

In the course of time, a rising young man will want a wife, a companion to share his good fortune and provide him the comforts of home and family. Many a mother in New Orleans dressed her daughter for strolls in the business district of the city in order to be glimpsed by, and introduced to, the handsome young lawyer Moorhead as he made his rounds of court and client. He would always engage in courteous conversation, smile his winsome smile, and doff his debonair hat as he disengaged politely to continue on his way. Many a father in south Louisiana found reason to take legal business to and seek guidance from the firm of Benjamin and Micou to meet their associate, the son of a successful planter and factor of St. Francisville and New Orleans, to determine his fitness as a prospective son-in-law, one worthy of their clever, convent-tutored daughter and bountiful dowry of land and bondsmen. Scarcely a day went by without an offer to dine with a family at one or another of the city's fine restaurants. Never a weekend passed without an invitation to visit at one of the magnificent new mansions, with Greek and Roman inspired columns and English gardens, erected by sugar and cotton barons, the first-generation aristocracy of a new commercial empire who hoped to extend into a second or third generation through well-planned matrimony to a Louisiana Lochinvar, who, like Sir Walter Scott's character was "So daring in love and so dauntless in war."

The Talcotts of Greenlief had produced mountains of cotton (bales almost measureless to man), three eligible daughters and a son whose absence on an extended European tour was an immense relief to his father. Marcilene was the middle girl, the smaller, more delicate of the three. She set her sights on Percy Moorhead. Her mother concurred enthusiastically and insisted that her husband immediately pay a substantial retainer to the firm of Benjamin and Micou to secure their services. Percy gamely played his part by attending dinner on two successive weekends at Greenlief. Alas, Marcilene's skill at parlor games and clever dinner conversation held no appeal to Percy. The younger daughter was too young and the older daughter too old. The retainer was retained and the eligible daughter remained eligible.

Miss Amelia Prentiss spoke with a vagrant lisp. She cultivated the mannerism during an extended stay at a school for young ladies in Philadelphia. The affectation added, she thought, a touch of mystery to her personality. An aunt and uncle in New Orleans had raised her after her parents perished at sea in a storm as they returned from a sojourn in France. Rumor had it that she was worth $400,000 and that her uncle would contribute an additional sum of $50,000 in ready money to see to her come under the care and authority of a worthy husband. The uncle hosted a charity dinner for an order of nuns and invited Percy to speak on the Mexican War just so Miss Amelia could be seated next to the speaker. The proximity produced only a gracious conversation with the veteran of Cerro Gordo and Churubusco, who was unpersuaded of Amelia's charm nor enchanted by the mystery of her lisp.

The only young woman who had attracted Percy's attention was Julia Rodemacher, the daughter of a German physician and a French woman who was a wine importer. She was intelligent and cultivated, speaking three languages with equal facility. As much as he enjoyed her company, Percy found she was impatient with him when his work precluded some activity she had planned – attendance at a friend's party or a concert performance. Perhaps, he was starting to think, she was right to insist he devote more of his time to her than to his work. Pleasure and leisure were as important as achievement and duty, weren't they, she insisted as she persuaded him from his responsibilities. A future with her could be pleasant; she could be right. Only she never seemed to think she might adjust her schedule from time to time to accommodate his.

Just as Percy was becoming thoroughly discouraged over his feminine prospects, he received a letter from Richmond, Virginia, dated September 16, a simple yet extraordinary piece of correspondence that would alter the course of his life. Its author had made a calculation, and it confirmed she was as shrewd a judge of character as any of her family name, so prominent in Virginia.

Percy was not surprised that his law professor had died. Three months had elapsed since he had received the judge's last letter. The old judge's handwriting had faltered, and he sounded more discouraged than usual. A year earlier, his call for a secession of southern states and the formation of a confederacy was largely ignored by other southern leaders at the Nashville constitutional convention. The Congressional compromise that followed did little to persuade Judge Tucker that the breakup of the union was unnecessary for survival of the southern way of life. Although he welcomed the strengthening of the fugitive slave law, the legislative compromise did nothing to further the expansion of the institution of negro slavery. In his opinion, if the South did not expand it would inevitably recede in national influence. The South would be subject to the North's industrial interests and policies. Better it would be to constitute a small and independent nation than remain part of a larger entity and dependent.

Louisiana was not represented in the Nashville convention. The state legislature, with support from Benjamin, had blocked a delegation from attending.

Holding the letter before him, Percy recalled vividly Judge Tucker's young niece. Freckled and fresh, she took over a room when she entered. She bubbled with enthusiasm, greeting family and friends warmly. She engaged strangers with a familiarity and immediacy that charmed the most reticent among them. Percy had first met her at a reception given by Judge Tucker for a few of his students at his home. The acting president of the college, Benjamin Ewell, was the nominal host. Tucker's law classes were the sum total of the College of William and Mary for most of that year, due the controversy that had riven the rest of the faculty and the College's governors. Ewell was taking it all in stoic stride, noting facetiously to Percy that he was a shepherd who had lost most of his flock, with Judge Tucker tending to the goats who remained.

Through an open window, Percy saw a young woman gallop up to the side of the Tucker home. She fairly leaped from the saddle and patted her horse on his cheek. As she passed by the living room through a hall, Judge Tucker had called her in.

"Philomena, you've already met President Ewell so he needs no introduction. This young man next to him is Percy Moorhead, the sage of Bayou Sara, Louisiana. Percy Moorhead, this is my niece, Philomena Randolph of Richmond."

The young man and young lady nodded to acknowledge the introduction as Judge Tucker continued,

"Mr. Moorhead until a few months ago with our army in Mexico. He's the young fellow whom General Scott recommended to my attention."

"Oh? Really now," said Miss Philomena, slightly exaggerating her Virginia drawl. "Louisiana. You are far from home, soldier. Tell us three reasons how Virginia is different from Louisiana."

Percy thought for a moment and answered, "The rivers of Louisiana are wider, deeper and more turbulent than you find in Virginia, as are our politics. In Louisiana we have only two seasons – 8 months of summer and 4 of winter - while Virginia is reputed to have the full complement of four. And third, in Louisiana young ladies seldom wear paddock boots and arm themselves with a riding crop when they enter a room."

Without hesitation, she responded tartly, "Perhaps in Louisiana women seldom ride horses lest they outperform their men."

Amused by her self-assurance, he said, with only a hint of condescension, "At the risk of characterizing as unchivalrous all my fellow Louisianans of the masculine species, I will take that as a challenge."

"As well you may, Mr. Moorhead." She winked and left the room.

President Ewell chuckled and said, "Moorhead, I think you've met your match. If she beats you riding, you will have difficulty living it down. If you best her, you will appear a churlish fellow. She's a lively young thing."

Percy found himself watching her through the window during the rest of the reception. She was playing outside with three of Judge Tucker's young children in the garden, swinging them and chasing them in circles among the shrubs, her leather quirt serving as a toy in a game of tag. Twice widowed, Professor Tucker had married his third wife when he was in his mid-forties. Now he was sixty-five, and his wife was nursing their seventh child in the next room during the reception.

Over a good bit of the two weeks of her visit, "Phil" Randolph had shown the Louisiana law student the environs of Williamsburg from horseback. She peppered him with questions about the study of law, what it was like to be a soldier in Mexico, and why did cotton and sugar grow in Louisiana but not Virginia and why tobacco would find Virginia soil salubrious but not Louisiana's. She was eager to absorb new knowledge and asked Percy to tell her what books she should read. It was a pity, she said, that women were not allowed to enter college. The college at Oberlin in Ohio did admit them, but it was filled with abolitionists, and her uncle would not hear of her becoming subject to such nonsense. There was nothing more she could learn at Mrs. Mercer's boarding school in Belmont. The ladies' schools in Philadelphia and Boston were not seats of learning. They were stifling institutions for inculcating manners in young women with a view to preparing them for marriage to be ornaments for their husbands. She would have to acquire what education she could on her own, and both of her uncles lent her books any time she asked.

Percy was amused by the young woman but found she was too young to attract him – a frisky, playful, immature filly. The stream of words from her lips was interrupted only when she paused to enjoy a sight or to study a flower or an object in a shop window on a stroll. He was content to listen without comment as she told odd stories about people and places as they rode side by side through Williamsburg's streets and over worn paths around one of oldest towns of the continent. Her families on both maternal and paternal sides extended more than a century in Virginia history. However, her father had passed while she was young. Her mother had chosen not to remarry. They were comfortable but not wealthy, owning only two household servants.

𖠋𖠋 — 𖠋𖠋

Several years had passed since he had seen Philomena but she now leapt from the page of her letter. How different she seemed from the women he had become familiar with since he returned to Louisiana. All were pale by comparison, in fact and figure, dull and unimaginative. All were thoroughly domesticated creatures for whom convention was the measure of value, unreceptive to new experience or thought. None would enter a social event in paddock boots. None would sass him just to provoke a reaction.

Should he now trust his instinct or his reason? If the latter, he saw his future lay with the crinolined socialites whose New Orleans drawing rooms he visited to meet their daughters. Dull, thicker each year, and complacent. And Julia Rodemacher wanted to control him. He shuddered.

With the same impulse and certainty as when he volunteered

for the war in Mexico, he took up pen and wrote:

*My dear Philomena,*

*Your letter arrived this morning. While we must regret the death of our beloved Judge Tucker, we must celebrate the richness of his life and accomplishments and his devotion to family. Surely comets were seen at his passing for it is well said that 'the heavens themselves blaze forth the death of princes.' By coincidence it happens that I have business in Washington that will take me through Richmond in a matter of a few weeks. Should it be convenient for you, I should like to call upon you at that time. And yes, it was a compliment.*

*With sincere sympathy*
*Percy Moorhead, Esq.*

After having Henri Lapeyre dispatch his letter, Percy sat back in his desk chair and calculated the time and route for a trip to Richmond. How long should he remain in Richmond, if he were successful in attaining his purpose? Of course, the reputed business in Washington was an invention of his pen. He conferred with Judah Benjamin about an absence of perhaps six weeks and obtained the lawyer's assurance that his journey would work no hardship on the firm. Benjamin's trust in Percy was such that he made no inquiry why he requested an absence, which was a relief for Percy. There was a certain romanticism about Benjamin, who had the soul of a poet, but it went only so far, and this journey might be seen as merely foolish. Percy saw no reason to write his parents of his plans or intentions. All might prove for naught and his precipitate action the height of folly.

*Chapter 8*

# To Richmond Percy Did Go

By steamboat Percy Moorhead traveled from New Orleans to Mobile. He transferred to another, smaller steamer and rode three hundred plus miles upriver to Montgomery. A railroad carried him to Charleston, South Carolina. After a night in Charleston at the Mills Hotel, he transferred to another steamer that made the 180-mile voyage to Wilmington, North Carolina. From there, it was 162 miles to Weldon on the Wilmington & Weldon Railroad. After a two-hour stopover he caught the Virginia Central line into Richmond for the final 85 mile leg of his journey. He amused himself during travel by engaging other passengers in conversation. A sympathetic listener, he was a pleasant companion to strangers, even when he was weary after days of nearly constant motion and jostling. If another traveler inserted political views into a discussion, he smiled amiably and deflected to another subject without giving offense.

He arrived in Virginia's capital in early afternoon on Friday and took a room at a weekly rate on the second floor of the Exchange Hotel, at the corner of Franklin and 14th Street. It was the same hotel in which he had stayed on his journey back to Louisiana from Williamsburg in 1849, after his studies with Judge Tucker were over. By chance his stay had coincided with a lecture by a writer named Poe on "the poetic principle." Judge Tucker had encouraged Percy to attend the lecture if his schedule allowed. Poe had praised Tucker's novel *George Balcombe* and had maintained a correspondence with Tucker when Poe was editor of the *Southern Literary Messenger*. From Judge Tucker, Percy learned that the orphaned Poe had been raised in Richmond by foster parents, which might explain the haunted and dark nature of the Poe writings Percy had read. Percy preferred the poetry of Wordsworth and Coleridge that his mother had read to him as a boy – among the few fond memories of his mother – who passed on her love of literature. Poe's poetry relied more on its musical quality than its capacity to encourage reflective thought. Benjamin, with whom Percy often discussed poetry, preferred Tennyson and Byron but also had an odd affection for the metaphysical conceits of Donne's poetry.

After hanging his clothing in an oak chifforobe, Percy composed, on a leaf of hotel stationery, a brief letter to Philomena informing her of his arrival in the city. May he call on her tomorrow afternoon at a time of her convenience? The desk clerk at the hotel took Percy's letter and dispatched a messenger to the Randolph residence for a quarter.

Percy removed his boots and lay in bed. For ten days he had thought about what he would say to her. "How are you?" Or "I am just passing through and want to pay my respects for the loss of your uncle." Or, "Because you signed your letter 'Miss,' may I infer that you have not married since I left my studies with your uncle?" No, far too direct. Less direct: "I have a few days to pass before going on to Washington. Perhaps, if your commitments permit, we could once again ride in the countryside as we did three years past?"

If the beginning was so difficult to plan, how could he pursue a courtship that must necessarily be of short duration? He would have to return to New Orleans within a few weeks. What did he actually know about Philomena Randolph? Had his mind transformed a pleasurable brief period of companionship into what he now imagined as a transcendent experience? What if the slim, agile master of horses of seventeen now had the grace of a cow? What if she lisped or limped? Had she been disappointed in love and turned sour at twenty? He could, of course, merely continue on his pretended course to Washington, as though this trip were no more than he had indicated in his brief letter. That might be better. Romance in haste, and later repent, repent.

A tap at his door roused him from his fitful musings of what cauldron of misery he thrust himself into. Another of the hotel lackeys was at his door.

"Mister Moorhead?"

"Yes."

"The manager, he say you needed at the front desk."

"Did he say why?"

"No suh."

"All right. I'll be down in a minute."

Percy looked in the mirror. He needed a shave and a bath before setting out for the Randolph house the next day. There would be time in the morning. He put on his travel jacket and buttoned the lower buttons. He slipped his feet into his worn boots. They would need a shine in the morning.

He descended the staircase and told the clerk at the front desk, "I'm Mr. Moorhead. Did you wish to see me?"

The toothy clerk asked, "Are you expecting a guest? There's someone to see you in the salon." He pointed to his right.

Entering through the open double doors into the hotel salon, Percy did not immediately see who might have summoned him. As he moved into the room, he walked past a large wing chair covered in taffeta, its back to him.

The chair seemed to speak to him. "You haven't come this far to walk right past me, have you?"

Startled at a woman's voice, he turned to his left. Sitting with her right leg crossed over her left, he did not immediately recognize her. Could it be Philomena? Or did she have an older sister?

"Miss Randolph?"

"In Virginia, they teach that it is impolite for a gentleman to keep a lady waiting." The apparent accusation was delivered with a saucy smile.

"It's no different in Louisiana. I came down within 5 minutes of the message to come to the front desk."

"No. You expected me to wait until tomorrow before seeing what the sage of Bayou Sara looks like now."

He examined his dusty, disheveled travel clothes. "I had planned to make myself more presentable. I've been traveling for near six days. And I recall what happened to Essex when he barged in on his queen without giving her time to prepare herself. It cost him his head."

Her reply was, "You see me as I am." She stood and turned around once in front of him. She was wearing a simple wool skirt, leather belt at the waist, a cotton blouse, and a light grey sweater. "I'm no show filly that must be groomed before viewing."

Percy was at a complete loss of words. The woman standing before him far exceeded his expectations. She was at least two inches taller than he remembered, had lost her freckles, and her voice was deeper – confident and no longer tentative. Her breasts were more ample but not large. A tortoise-shell clasp held her brown hair in back. A faint, musky smell of herbs, perhaps calendula oil and olive on her hands and arms, arose from her presence. Percy found her stunning, in simplicity, poise, assurance.

She saw his surprise and responded to his silence by saying, with amusement, "If I'm a disappointment, you are free to leave.

At any time. Or stay. And meet my mother tomorrow."

"No. No disappointment. When I last saw you, you were a girl. Now you are a . . . . a woman," he stammered. "I need a few minutes to adjust to the change."

"I'm glad you noticed. Be quick with something clever, or I'll think I've disappointed. A lawyer who is at a loss for words will soon be at a loss for clients. It's not my fault you waited three years before coming back."

"You're not surprised that I am here?"

"No. I'm only surprised that you took so long. To come to your senses."

"I don't know what to say." Had he expected someone more demure? Had she been, he would have been the disappointed one.

"Of course not. You're a man. You can't understand such things. Don't look for words or anything from reason. You're here even if you don't comprehend feminine mystery. Now let's amble aimlessly around fair Richmond before it's too dark while you try to remember all the clever things you had planned to say to me."

"I should change," Percy protested.

"No, you're fine as you are. If you're not rank after a week in that outfit, you'll survive another hour or two. I'll not ease an escape for you now that you are here." Other men might be threatened by Philomena's forwardness. Percy found it amusing and charming. More than anything, he felt relief – he had made no mistake by traveling this far on a quick judgment.

The couple walked out of the hotel entrance and went left on Franklin. It was but a block to Capitol Square, shaded with stately trees planted during the time of Governor Patrick Henry, adorned with flowers, carpeted with grass. They strolled slowly along the square's gravel walks, stopping to admire the Governor's house, the Washington Monument, and the Capitol itself, designed by Thomas Jefferson with its massive ionic columns. The evening air was cool, a light breeze rising from the James River. Unself-consciously, when not pointing, Phil would put her left arm through Percy's right. She asked about his parents and his sister, recalling every detail he had told her earlier, as though it had been the day before.

Suddenly Percy found himself telling her of the fissures in his family, of the steps that his father had to take to keep peace with his mother, smoothing away the offences of Calvin Bunch that she refused to acknowledge. He confessed frustration that he knew nothing of his Moorhead ancestors and that he felt intimidated by his father such that he would not seek answers. He opened himself to her, something he had done with no other person. She inspired his complete trust. Had he, however, spoken too much of himself? What if this rare creature, now that he had found her, were to reject him?

Retracing their steps on a gravel walk, he sat next to her on a stone bench. He said, "You didn't come back to Williamsburg while I was still a student. I had hoped I would see you again."

"I tried to," she said, laughing, a pleasant laugh of three descending notes, throaty and seductive. "Believe me, I tried." As he listened to her smooth and soothing voice, he heard the night song of a whip-or-will, perched nearby on a low limb. "I pestered Uncle many times. But he wouldn't allow it. He said you were one of his best students in his years of teaching. My presence would distract you from your studies. It reminded him, he said, of his father discouraging him from seeing the sister of his law teacher. His father had been right, his studies must come first. Only later did he marry Polly Coalter, his beloved first wife. Once you finished, he said he would welcome my return to Williamsburg. He encouraged it. He was as fond of you as he was of me. But you never took a degree. At end of term, you were gone."

"I never took my degree from Princeton. William and Mary would not allow me to be awarded a B.L. without a college diploma."

A bright moon was behind Philomena as Percy turned towards her. Where she had been breezy, she was now more earnest and spoke her truth plainly, no matter what the consequence. She was past a point of return. "Then it was up to me to do something. With my uncle's death, I saw an opportunity to give you one more chance to embrace the best thing that might ever happen to you. Or let it pass by, again."

"Could I be so foolish?" He was deeply touched. He wanted to embrace her, but it felt awkward, He was unaccustomed to strong affection. It had never been present in the home in which he was raised.

"If so, you wouldn't be the man I think you are. You need a good woman to nudge you to do the things you are destined to do."

"And tomorrow?"

The chatty young woman returned, her nonchalance intact and undisturbed by the serious exchange that had just occurred between them. "Let's shop in the morning, and at lunch look down on the river from Church Hill. In the afternoon we will ride horses. Mother is expecting us for supper around six."

*Chapter 9*

# Sister Lavinia's Readings

M rs. Randolph – Emily – was a quieter, more demure, version of her daughter. There was a sparkle in her eye, suggestive of an active mind, accompanied by a reserve of manner common to upper-crust Virginians. Her manner of speech reminded Percy of Captain Lee, with whom he had served before the battles at Cerro Gordo and Churusbusco. In fact, her late husband shared a common ancestor with Lee in William Randolph who had fathered no fewer than nine children. She was herself a Bolling before her marriage and was connected with the Tuckers through her own family as well as through the Randolph side. Widowed at a young age, she could have remarried but chose to devote herself to the upbringing of her daughter. The absence of a father or stepfather in the home contributed to Philomena's sense of freedom and her limited deference to male authority. There was no shortage of aunts, uncles and cousins to welcome her into their homes and indulge, even encourage, her spirited ways. Everyone expected that she would eventually marry into a leading family of Virginia, families who comprised their social circle and who dominated the Piedmont and Tidewater regions of the state. But she surprised them all as she turned aside her many Virginia suitors.

Emily Randolph was amused when her daughter fixated on the law student she met at Judge Tucker's. Certain it was a fancy that would pass with no fresh encounters to sustain it, she said nothing to discourage Philomena's enthusiasm for the ex-soldier who had been only a private. When Percy Moorhead of Bayou Sara returned to Louisiana she was sure that Philomena would redirect her attentions to a suitable beau on native soil. A proper West Point man and officer. And she was confident that a young man of good family in Louisiana would find a creole belle eager to attach his name to her heritage. Venus had other plans for Percy Moorhead. Now that Phil's fantasy gallant had reappeared, Emily Randolph was relieved. She could see what Judge Tucker had praised in him and why Phil was attracted to him – polite, deferential, well-spoken, intelligent, serious and educated. Many a Tidewater mother had to settle for less in a son-in-law, even if he were a West Point officer.

Philomena and her mother set the wedding date for twelve days after Percy arrived in Richmond, sufficient time for making a dress, printing announcements, following the formalities of introducing the groom to relatives and friends, and securing the services of the minister. The couple would be married at St. John's Episcopal Church, Grace and 25th street, Church Hill.

When not meeting Virginian aristocracy and gentry, the betrothed couple explored Richmond on foot and the countryside on horseback. Phil seemed well-acquainted with the fabled homes of the area and the stories of the families; she recounted them to Percy. Her enthusiasm was charming and contagious. She loved the complex histories of families and the stories of their connections to homes and lands. All had their ample share of secrets.

One of the plantations Phil wanted Percy to see was Marlbourne, a short distance to the northeast. The plantation was owned by Judge Tucker's friend Edmund Ruffin, who had shared many of the judge's views on the future of the South. Ruffin was not in, but his enslaved foreman, Jem Sykes, showed them around the home and described its modern agricultural innovations.

On the road back to Richmond, about three miles from the city, a rain began to fall. Seeing a tent and wagon with a sign in front, they decided to escape the impending downpour. The sign read:

### SISTER LAVINIA
*Reader of Palms and Tarot*

It was emblazoned with a quarter moon and stars next to depictions of a hand and a card displaying a wheel of fortune. They tied their horses to a wheel of the wagon and entered the tent.

"Come in," said a small dark gypsy woman, turning from what looked like a sideboard behind her. It may have been a sort of altar. She seemed about sixty and wore a long red patterned skirt beneath a blue and green blouse. A red head scarf covered most of her black and grey hair, a beige shawl her shoulders. "Please have a seat," she instructed, quietly.

The couple sat as they were directed, sitting behind a round wooden table covered with a white flaxen cloth. The gypsy lit three candles on the sideboard and two on the table. She sat opposite Phil and Percy. "The heavens have brought you here." The heavy rain could be heard loud upon the canvas roof above them. "Would you like a reading by palm or by Tarot?" To Percy's ear, her accent was almost Germanic.

Phil and Percy looked at each other. Phil said, "One each."

The fortune teller said that it could be done. First she needed to know the birth date for each of them, which she wrote into a small book. She then consulted astrological tables, asking finally, "Now, which of you is first?"

Percy nodded to Phil.

"Palm or Tarot?"

Placing her right hand in front of her on the table, Phil said

"Palm."

With long, crooked fingers the crone took Phil's palm and began examining it closely. "Are you right-handed?"

"Yes," said Phil.

"Then we can tell what you are born with." With her right index finger, Sister Lavinia traced the lines of Phil's hand. After several minutes of examination, she said, "Your heart, head and life lines are of equal length. You are a well-balanced person. Their curves show that you freely express your emotions and feelings. Your heart and head lines are joined together – you have intensity of purpose."

Phil nodded. She saw no reason to disagree.

"Now your left hand. It is where your future can be found." Phil presented her other hand on the table. The fortune teller again examined it closely. She frowned.

"What do you see? Is it not good?" asked Phil.

"You have a travel line that tells me you will make a long journey. But the fate line is uncertain."

Phil became uncharacteristically anxious. "My father died when I was young. Do you see death? Do you see darkness? Can you tell me anything?"

Sister Lavinia took both of Phil's hands in her hands. She bent her head down closer to the table and pressed Phil's palms to her forehead. Her hair had a pungent odor Phil could not recognize, almost like the soil they had been shown at Marlbourne. Her forehead was the texture of parchment. She turned her head toward the top of the tent with closed eyes, and said slowly,

*Death can be a very bright fellow*
*He will come all dressed in yellow.*

Phil was perplexed. "I don't know what that means," she said. It sounded ominous.

The palmist made no response. Seeing that the prophecy troubled Phil, Percy tried to make light of it. To him, the old gal was a bit too theatrical. Was she deliberately frightening Phil?

Percy assured Phil, "It means no more than your wardrobe selection should be limited by avoiding a color that doesn't agree with your complexion in any event. Let's see if yellow turns up in my cards."

The gypsy ignored Percy's casual remark. She turned in her chair and took a deck of Tarot cards from the sideboard behind her. The candles still burned, sputtering occasionally from impurities in the wick or wax. The sound of rain had but little diminished. The woman shuffled the deck of seventy-two cards four or five times and then spread them out in a horseshoe in front of her. Speaking to Percy, she said "Please pass both your hands over them and mix them up." As he did as he was instructed, she continued, "The passing of the hands creates a unity among us – me, you and the cards. Your hands will determine the order of the cards, and they will draw their power of divination from you. Please nod when you are finished." Her accent seemed to thicken. Her words were hard to make out over the sounds of the storm and the rain pelting the canvas just above their heads.

After Percy nodded, he withdrew his hands to the edge of the table. Looking him in the eyes, she assembled the cards without any further mixing. "The first card will identify you. We can then do a three, five or ten card reading. What do you choose?"

"When in doubt, choose the middle way I always say," Percy said affably. It was a harmless and amusing way to avoid a heavy rainstorm. He could not take the reading seriously.

The gypsy placed a card before Percy face down. Her expectant look indicated he was to turn it over. He did.

"That's a Fool or Jester," he said. "Is that who I am?" He chuckled at the thought.

Sister Lavinia shook her head. "No. In the cards, the Fool is a man who is on a journey, who explores the mysteries of life. He is the Fool because he is innocent – all possibility and opportunity. Sometimes he is a trickster, which is why he is always a trump card. He is unnumbered among the cards because he can be the beginning or the end."

"If I must be a Fool, I think that an Innocent is as good as any," Percy said with a skeptical grin at Phil.

The old woman placed another card in the middle of the table and then four more on the sides of it, each face down. She said, "The four to the sides are the Past, the Present, the near Future and the more distant Future. The last card, in the middle, is the card of Potential."

Turning over the Past card, Percy saw it was woman holding a two-edged sword in one hand and scales in the other. "Must be Justice," he said.

"Yes," said the gypsy. "Have you studied law?"

"I confess that I am a lawyer. What if I had turned that one up first instead of the Fool? Wouldn't it have meant the same thing?"

"No. It would have then represented qualities of virtue, considerateness, and harmony in you. The card's meaning depends on position in the spread. And on its orientation when its face is revealed. Just as who you are changes with time and place and with your relations with others."

"Let's see about the Present," Percy said. On this card were a naked man and woman with an angel above them. "Could this be us?"

The old woman smiled. "They are the Lovers. A very positive sign, for the card is up for you. It shows good fortune in love and your relationship."

Percy conceded that the crone was good at her game. He had encountered on steamboats on the Mississippi card sharps whose fingers were so sensitive to shaved edges and small alterations of their cards that they could pull any card they chose from anywhere in the deck. With an affectionate couple before her, she naturally placed the Lovers in an appropriate place in the spread. The riverboat card dealers called it the *set-up*.

Phil said, "We are getting married in six days. And it won't be in a yellow dress. And I'll have no yellow flowers in the bride's bouquet." The prophecy she had been given was making her uneasy.

"Marvelous," said Percy in good humor, attempting to overcome her worry. "Now the near Future." He turned the next card over. Again, the card faced Percy in the upright position. Written at the bottom was Ace of Cups. The card showed a hand holding a cup or chalice overflowing with five streams of water. A dove holding a wafer disc in its mouth descended from above. At the base was a sea, covered with flower blossoms. He said, "Very pretty. Is that an M or a W on the cup?" he said.

"Very favorable," said the woman, nodding approval. "It means happiness, overflowing with love and joy. A person drinking from the cup would see an M."

The rain stopped. Percy and Phil had been in the tent for longer than they realized. The rain and clouds had obscured the time of day. Evening was soon coming on.

"M for Moorhead. Perhaps we should leave while we are ahead," Percy said. He was not superstitious and did not believe any one could tell the future. Percy was convinced the woman was using her sorting skills to flatter her marks and make them more susceptible to her fee; there had been no agreement for her payment. They had stopped on a lark. He began to rise, but the old woman took hold of his wrist. Her boney grip felt as strong as a man's.

"It would be a bad omen to leave the last cards unturned," she said, a severe expression on her face.

"Of course. It will only take a few minutes." Sighing, he settled back into his seat. He turned over the fourth card. Upright, it showed a tall tower pitched atop a craggy mountain. Lightning strikes and flames burst from the building's windows. People were leaping from the tower in desperation, fleeing destruction and turmoil.

"That looks awful," Phil blurted out with a grimace.

The gypsy explained in her slow, deliberate manner, "The Tower signifies darkness and destruction. It could be physical or spiritual or both. The Tower represents ambitions built on false premises. The lightning bolt breaks down existing forms. It represents a sudden, momentary glimpse of truth. A flash of inspiration that breaks down structures of ignorance and false reasoning."

Percy responded, "I was all on board up to here. But if that's the distant Future, how far off is it?"

"None can say."

"Can a person ward off a bad future?" Percy expected a proposal for fee from her, an insurance against disaster, like purchasing an indulgence from a priest to save one's soul. Perhaps, Percy thought, her accent was Polish. He had heard Polish accents among the volunteers of the Mexican campaign.

Without responding to Percy's question, the fortune teller said, "Let us look to the last card. It signifies potential. All five cards must be read together – past, present and future are part of one journey. The final card represents possibility and will shed light on the other four."

In spite of his suspicions, Percy felt some apprehension as he turned the card in the middle of the table so that its face showed. The card was a woman sitting on a throne wearing a starry crown, holding a scepter in one hand.

He observed, "It says The Empress. Who is she?"

"No earthly queen. Most say she is a mother figure, mother earth. Her throne is in the midst of a field of grain, showing her dominion over growing things. Perhaps she can bring you crops of plenty. But her crown is twelve stars. Hers is the sign of Venus. This card tells us she has the potential to protect you, though she cannot completely shield you from fate." Sister Lavinia turned over the six cards and returned them to the deck.

"Are we finished?" Percy asked.

"There is no more I can tell you."

With a sly expression on his lips, Percy asked, "Your prophecy was in verse for my bride. Have you none for me?"

Sister Lavinia clasped his hands tightly. Percy was again surprised by her strength. Again she turned her head up, this time with eyes open. In a hoarse whisper, she said,

*The gods of old have blessed your name*
*What you lose you will twice regain.*

Percy had no inkling to her meaning. But, despite her grim expression, it sounded favorable. He thanked the old woman for shelter from the rain and for an entertaining break for their afternoon ride home. He waited for her to name her fee. Hearing nothing, he asked what they owed. She merely nodded in the direction of a hat sitting on a trunk at the flap of the tent, saying "Whether you believe or not, Percy Moorhead, is of no consequence."

Percy extracted three silver dollar coins from his pocket and showed them to Phil. She moved her lips so as to say "five." Percy deposited all five that he had into the hat.

As they rode into Richmond, Phil asked if he believed the woman. He told her, "People everywhere have their superstitions. The nanny who nursed me convinced the others around her that she has the power of voodoo. You'll meet her soon, and you'll see it's an act she learned in Cuba. You can interpret anything for your own ends. Shakespeare uses it in *Julius Caesar*. His wife Calpurnia has a dream about blood flowing in fountains and she is fearful for her husband. Decius Brutus gives a different interpretation entirely. Dreams are never premonitions, because the future holds infinite possibilities that the human mind cannot contain."

Percy thought it unlikely that Phil had read or seen the play, so she seemed satisfied, without asking whether Calpurnia had rightly interpreted a dream. Percy didn't believe in dreams any more than he did in voodoo, palmistry or Tarot. Dreams and prophecies were only literary devices of an omniscient author who can plot things backward, nothing that could impact his own life. He added, "She could just as easily have said the Tower shows that I will conquer all obstacles in my path. If the Tower had been the first card instead of Justice symbolizing the Past, we would have interpreted the Tower as representing the high walls of the convent at Churubusco where we assaulted the Mexicans."

As they rode the final distance to Richmond, Percy tried to remember if Phil had called him Percy in the presence of the gypsy. Imagination, that's all.

## Chapter 10

# Recalling Edgar Poe

T he next day, Percy visited at Mrs. Randolph's home with Phil's cousin Bev Tucker, who was in town from Washington with his wife Jane and several of their children. He was a son of Judge Tucker's brother, St. George Tucker, who had been a judge and a law professor at the University of Virginia. Percy had met Bev a couple of times when he was at William and Mary and enjoyed his company. He was an outsized character – large, gregarious, often jolly. He was two inches or more taller than Percy and carried substantially more heft. Jane Ellis Tucker was lively, devoted to her children and deferential to her husband.

Bev's politics were as conservative as his uncle's – pro-South and strongly Democrat. Although he was intelligent and articulate, his schooling had not been as disciplined as his father's or uncle's. Bev's family and political connections were to be the source of his successes – more than innate abilities in law, engineering or business. During the Mexican war, at the encouragement of John Y. Mason, Secretary of Navy and a family friend, Bev obtained government contracts making shot and shell for navy guns and for providing coal for Navy ships going to Vera Cruz. Lacking knowledge of armaments and coaling, Bev took on a partner with the necessary skills. After the war, Bev Tucker entered into partnership with a man named Addison, a young lawyer of talent who lacked political and social connections before teaming with Bev. The pair began a practice: advocating claims before Congress and government departments. Projects they advanced, according to Jane Tucker's admiring description to Percy of her husband's work in Washington, included the building of the first sectional dock at Kittery, Maine; obtaining a mail contract for Commodore Vanderbilt's ships for the California mail; the making of Benicia, California as a port of entry; and having Colt's revolvers purchased by the government. She did not describe his work as lobbying, avoiding the whiff of corruption associated with the profession.

Bev Tucker struck Percy as having too much self-regard to loiter in the halls and shadows of government buildings to beg favors even for the most distinguished of clients. And business ventures found in the world of ordinary commerce didn't appear to suit his personality or talents. Percy assessed him as excellent in people skills, a facilitator or coordinator, not a builder or entrepreneur. So Percy was not surprised when Bev described an ambitious plan to start a newspaper in Washington that would advance the political interests of the causes he believed in. Its program sounded much like Judge Tucker's lectures on states' rights under the Constitution, with the national government to champion a strong foreign policy. A garrulous fellow with political connections could find a useful outlet for his talents in a partisan newspaper, and it could serve as a vehicle for his advancement.

"I plan to name my paper *The Sentinel*, Bev told Percy. "If I recall our conversations at my uncle's, you share an interest in literature and good writing. You should think about joining me in Washington if the newspaper proves successful."

Bev offered Percy another bit of whiskey and a cigar. Percy accepted more of the liquor into his glass but declined the cigar and the offer of a newspaper job. He begged off, saying, "Washington sounds like an exciting place. I'm afraid my interest in politics is limited until I master the legal profession. Let me see how Phil likes Louisiana. If my law practice doesn't flourish, perhaps I would consider a move."

ఈ్ఈ — ౬౬

On the day of the wedding, a small group of Judge Tucker's friends from William and Mary arrived for the ceremony, including Benjamin Ewell, now Professor of Mathematics, as did Edmund Ruffin who spent his time talking enthusiastically with Bev about the newspaper project. In place of her deceased father, Bev Tucker walked Philomena down the aisle to give her to Percy. Serving as best man was one of Percy's law school classmates, Talbot Sweeney of Williamsburg.

The wedding reception was held at a handsome home at Sixth and Grace. It was owned by a prominent Richmond attorney, Robert Stanard, and his vivacious wife, Martha Pearce. The effusive hostess greeted the groom and his bride at the door:

"So you're Philomena's honey-tongued beau of the bayous who's bewitched our favorite Randolph. Robert and Professor Ewell assure me you were Judge Tucker's brightest student in many years."

Percy bowed to Martha Stanard and said, "And you are Mrs. Stanard. You are most gracious to organize a reception like this on short notice. Your home is even more lovely in daylight."

The woman was a half-dozen years older than Percy. Tall and stately in figure, she was raised in wealth in Louisville, Kentucky and educated in Latin and French at a fashionable finishing school in Manhattan. The lavish home always impressed visitors with exquisite furnishings from Italy and Paris, some inherited from Robert's father and others acquired by Martha on a trip to the Continent. The frescoed ceilings were worthy of a royal palace. Cocking her head slightly, the perceptive Martha Stanard remarked, "You were here in the evening once?" She did not recall having him as a guest before but would never make the faux pas of failing to remember him.

Smiling wryly, Percy replied, "Yes. A few years ago. There's no reason to have noticed my brief presence. I merely swelled a curious crowd who came and went. It was after Mr. Poe's lecture on poetics at the Exchange Hotel."

Martha Stanard put her hand to her right cheek, exclaiming, "Oh dear me. That poor soul. When they were boys, Eddie Poe was my husband's best friend. This house was his second home. Robert's mother encouraged his poetry, and he would read his verse to her. She always consoled and comforted him when he was unhappy in Mr. Allan's house. He honored her with a lovely poem in which he likened her to Helen of Troy. I fear the Lord taking her so early contributed to the melancholia that haunted him."

This was not the last that Percy was to see of Martha Stanard, and on their next encounter a decade later, she would recall him well.

$$\approx\approx - \ll\ll$$

The day of the lecture three years earlier Percy remembered seeing Poe on the streets of Richmond, a slender and erect figure, dressed in a white suit and Panama hat, dark curling hair thrown back from a broad forehead, a trim mustache beneath a broad nose. He walked leisurely, with an elegant malacca cane topped by a curved brass head. Percy's own father possessed a very similar cane. Richmond had been Poe's home off and on since his actress mother had succumbed to consumption. Her three-year-old son was taken in by a merchant family, Mr. and Mrs. Allan, and separated from his brother and infant sister.

When Poe's performance began at dusk in the Concert Room of the Exchange, before an audience numbering more than eighty, the author had changed into somber black clothing. A few among those seated had known him as a teen or had attended the University of Virginia during his year there. More knew him as the tireless editor of the *Southern Literary Messenger* who, in a short time, increased its circulation ten-fold, while contributing poems, stories, and criticism from his restless, perfervid pen. Among the latter pieces had been his review of *George Balcombe*, a rare item in favoring its author, Judge Beverly Tucker.

Percy observed that Poe had no manuscript. His dark piercing eyes, set in hollows that made him appear more sixty than forty, were fixed just above the heads of his audience, yet each person felt he was speaking intimately to them. He stood unmoving, his measured voice – a rich tenor – holding each of his audience as motionless as himself. If any had expected the macabre narrator of Arthur Gordon Pym or the gloom of a Roderick Usher, they found instead the careful analytic discourse of C. Auguste Dupin, notable for its deliberateness and distinctness of enunciation, an address from a bi-part Soul whose breast enclosed both the creative and the resolvent.

At Princeton Percy had studied the classics of British and Roman literature and had a passing familiarity with recent American poetry – Whittier, Longfellow, Freneau – and English – Tennyson, Wordsworth, Byron, Shelley, Coleridge, Browning. Poe surprised him with his declarations that were counter to those other esteemed poets.

*"A long poem does not exist. The phrase, a long poem, is a flat contradiction in terms."*

Poe had thus dismissed Homer, Vergil, and Milton.

*"The perseverance of composing an epic is one thing and the genius of true poetry is quite another."*

Worst in Poe's opinion was the heresy of the didactic, the most corrupting influence of poetical literature. Poetry's object was not Truth but Beauty.

*"Poetry is the Rhythmical Creation of Beauty. Its sole arbiter is Taste. With the Intellect or with the Conscience it has only collateral relations. Unless incidentally, it has no concern whatever either with*

*Duty or with Truth."*

At first, Percy took Poe's radical pronouncements as perverse, even heretical. Gradually, however, the poet won him over. He realized that Poe was speaking as a poet, not as a critic. He was providing a measure for his own poetry, his ideal of a poem, what he sought to achieve with his unique poetic vision. He was drawn to pathos, to the ethereal, to melancholy, to the sublime, to supernal and sad Beauty. One phrase lingered in Percy's memory: "a certain taint of sadness is inseparably connected with all the higher manifestations of true Beauty."

Only later, much later, did it occur to Percy that Poe's meaning was perhaps yet much more. Was not a man's life his own poem, a creation of his own making? Should not a man begin with an ideal of a life and bring his own measure of value to it?

ॐॐ — ॐॐ

"Mr. Stanard deeply regrets not being here for your wedding and reception," Martha apologized for her absent husband. "He took the train to Washington three days ago to appear in a case."

Percy reassured her. "No apologies are necessary. I fully understand. The lawyer with whom I work is Judah P. Benjamin. The demands of his clients take precedence over all other activities. I trust that Philomena will be as gracious a hostess as you are. Judge Tucker had the greatest respect for Mr. Stanard and for his father, Judge Stanard."

"Now Percy Moorhead, you must take good care of our Philomena. And someday, when she persuades you to bring her home to Richmond, we can all get together."

The next day the newly-weds boarded a train and began the long journey to Louisiana.

*Chapter 11*

# Phil meets Lucy

A Richmond stationer had printed sixty embossed cards for Phil and her mother announcing the wedding of Miss Philomena Eugenia Randolph of Richmond, Virginia and Wallace Percy Moorhead, esq. of St. Francisville and New Orleans, Louisiana. One announcement was dispatched to Percy's mother and father, accompanied by a sweet note in Phil's exquisite hand to her new mother-in-law, Mrs. Lucinda Moorhead. Had the announcement and personal letter arrived at their destination in due course, the difficulties of the initial meeting of the two Mrs. Moorheads might have been avoided. The announcement did not find its way to the postal station at Bayou Sara until three days after Phil and Percy appeared on horseback at Bolingbroke Hall late on a Friday evening – wet, dirty and exhausted.

Percy had hoped to find his father at their New Orleans townhouse when the couple arrived by steamboat from Mobile, but he was at Bolingbroke. The next morning, the newly-weds left early by a stern-wheeled packet boat, the *Grosse Tête*, going up the Mississippi. Stormy weather confined them to the lounge of the boat as it struggled upriver against the current and heavy rains. A few miles above Baton Rouge, the vessel's machinery began a rattle that grew louder and louder until the boiler shuddered and abruptly let out a mighty wheeze as the engine released the steam pressure from the defunctive engine. Most of the passengers ran out onto the rain-swept decks and looked over the railings, fearful that they might need to jump into the swirling waters if there were an imminent boiler explosion. Most travelers knew that boiler explosions were a hazard, a not uncommon occurrence of river trips. The boat slowly turned sideways to the current and began drifting downriver. The captain tried to blow the whistle but the lack of steam prevented the whistle from functioning. With his megaphone, he called out to his passengers not to jump. There was no danger of an explosion. The rain and wind abated. A warming sun peeked from behind clouds.

Percy assured his bride that they would be all right. He was not so confident as he tried to sound. The mass of the boat was no match against large trees, submerged or floating on the current, that could penetrate the hull if they allided. Without control, the steamboat could impact another boat and sink one or both. Perhaps the current would deposit them on one bank or the other or land them on one of the many sandbars that appear and disappear on the river.

After drifting for nearly an hour, with passengers and crew waving helplessly at other boats, the *Grosse Tête* hove into sight of a very large steam snagboat operated by the Army Engineers over on the west side of the river. It was close to the bank, using its crane to remove fallen trees that threatened to obstruct navigation. The captain could not hail the boat from the distance. He ordered two of the crew into a rowboat that they put over the side. In a short time they boarded the army vessel and explained the predicament to the captain of the snagboat. He agreed to help. The snagboat secured its crane and set out after the drifting *Grosse Tête*.

As the snagboat approached the engineless boat, the two crew members rowed over with a line. The captain of the army boat directed them to attach it to the bow of the *Grosse Tête*. Two more lines were used to tie the two boats together, though maintaining a distance of 50 feet between them. Thus joined, two boats floated together for several more hours, the army boat using its engine and paddles to control their speed and direction. The snagboat's whistle warned away other upriver traffic, whose curious crews and passengers gawked at the odd, conjoined craft. Eventually, the snagboat maneuvered the packet boat safely to tie up in Baton Rouge. The docking was difficult, but the captain of the army boat was skillful. As it departed, the snagboat gave a cheerful final salute and made its way back upriver against the current.

At a livery stable, Percy hired two horses and saddles and stored the couple's luggage until they could retrieve it or have it sent on to them in St. Francisville. Percy was apologetic – the stable had no ladies' saddles. Philomena, now wearing trousers and a man's woolen jacket, remained in good humor. "If I didn't want adventure, I'd have stayed in Richmond and married a Methodist minister," she laughed.

Percy looked at the threatening sky and said, "We could stay the night here, if you rather."

"I'm game," she said despite the mishaps so far on their journey. "Let's give it a go."

Percy nodded, glad she was willing. "That's my gal. If the road's not too muddy, we ought to get there before dark. My letter told them we'd probably arrive today. I hope they aren't waiting to greet the steamboat."

Despite the ashen weather and rumble of thunder, they rode north on the post road. A slight drizzle became a storm as they neared Mount Willing, where they took shelter in the vestibule of an empty church. Sitting in a pew, they shared bread and cider from a flask until the rain let up. Then they resumed their dripping journey. It was very dark and well past nine when three dogs barked their arrival at the Moorhead plantation.

Alarmed by the dogs' persistent yelping, four figures, dimly shaped by two lanterns, were waiting in front of the house as Percy and Phil rode to the hitch post.

"Who's there?" called out Howard Moorhead. A pistol hung in his right hand, not menacing but ready if needed.

"Me, Father. We're later than expected. But here nonetheless."

"Son? This is unexpected," said his father with warm surprise. "We've not heard from you in more than six weeks. Your office clerk said you were east on business."

By lantern light, Percy could discern his mother and father, Clotilda and a servant boy, about 12 years old, Isaac – if Percy recollected his name.

"Who is the man with you?" asked his mother, peering into the darkness at the shapes on horseback. "Or boy? Your father said your office has employed a new clerk."

"Neither, Mother. This is Phil, I wrote you about. Mrs. Moorhead."

"You needn't address me formally, son." She was irritated, thinking he mocked her. She hated being awakened for any reason. "I have received no letter regarding a Phil."

"Mother, I meant no disrespect. I was saying simply that Phil, Philomena, *is* Mrs. Moorhead. She is my wife."

"Your wife?" Her voice showed her surprise and disbelief. It was not pleasant.

Percy dismounted his horse and handed the reins to Isaac. He turned to Philomena and helped her down and gave her horse's reins also to the boy. He led his wife over to the lanterns.

"You must not have received our letters. Mother, let me introduce the finest young woman yet produced by Virginia. This is Philomena Randolph, now a proud Moorhead."

Lucy Moorhead took a lantern from Clotilda and stepped over

to Phil, more to examine her new daughter-in-law than to greet her. Skepticism was etched on her face by the flickering light of the lantern's wick. Lucy's hair was spread across her shoulders, unbrushed after being awakened. She wore a thick robe against the night air.

Phil extended her hand and said warmly, "I am so happy to meet you, Mrs. Moorhead. My mother says the Pughs of Bertie County are one of North Carolina's most distinguished families."

Transferring the pewter lantern slowly to her left hand, Lucy limply accepted the proffered hand, without sharing the young woman's enthusiasm. She replied,

"I wish I could return the compliment. Unfortunately, your sudden appearance has precluded us from becoming acquainted with your heritage. I have heard the name of Randolph in Virginia. Have you known my son long? Or was this marriage as hasty as his enlistment in General Scott's marching army?" It was neither friendly nor a question.

Phil ignored her new in-law's uncordial reception. "We first met three years ago through my uncle, Judge Tucker. Our relationship ripened through correspondence." It was stretching truth but, strictly speaking, not inaccurate. She sought to soften awkward facts, not to deceive Percy's mother.

The chill air did not improve Lucy's disposition. An owl hooted then leaped from her perch on a hickory limb. In a few moments she returned to her roost, a small mouse clutched in her curved beak, still twitching.

Phil sensed that Lucy's dissatisfaction was directed more towards her son than herself. Her annoyance with Percy was not infrequent, as Phil would learn. It seemed as if Lucy sought out ways in which to be displeased, a collector of grievances who stored them away in the dark recesses of her mind, to be withdrawn as needed.

"I wish he had mentioned to me that he had a lady friend in Virginia. Perhaps he told his father. Percy has always confided more in Mr. Moorhead than his own mother."

"Well!" Howard Moorhead interceded, taking charge in a cheerful voice. "No reason for us to remain in this wet and chilly weather. You two must be exhausted from your ride. Come inside. Come inside and dry out. Let us get a better look at our new Moorhead. Clotilda, go warm them a plate of food. This is the occasion for opening a brandy I've been saving, warmth and good cheer."

The glance Howard gave Lucy encouraged her to be more hospitable at this unforeseen event, whatever her misgivings and pique. While Howard Moorhead settled his son and Phil in the living room, Lucy went upstairs to find some old clothing of Eliza's. Percy's sister was only a little shorter than Phil. Howard stirred the fire in the parlor, adding wood until it blazed, bright and warm.

"Please take these and change in Percy's room," Lucy said to Phil with better composition, if not grace. "It's the room just above us. Now that we have better light I can appreciate how unlike a boy you are." If this was short of a compliment, it was at least an improvement.

For an hour or so, the two Moorhead couples visited, Percy first recounting the drifting steamer, their rescue by an army snagboat, and their sodden horseback ride from Baton Rouge. The crossing at Thompson's Creek had been difficult from flooding that must have occurred recently. When Percy asked about his sister, Lucy told them that Eliza and Calvin were now in a house near Woodville. Percy expressed surprise. They had been living in Natchez when he had last heard of them. Lucy explained that it was a temporary relocation, in a rented home.

Speaking to Phil, Lucy added, "Eliza is my daughter by my first husband, the late Mr. Willis. Her husband, Mr. Bunch, has been a successful cotton broker in Natchez and has excellent prospects of associating with the bank in Woodville. They have given me my first grandchild, a little angel named Nerissa. It would be nice to have them closer to us. Where will you and Percy settle, now that you have married? Do you think New Orleans a suitable place for a decent family?"

Phil sensed the presence of an ancient family argument about New Orleans. She was determined to do or say nothing to antagonize her new relation nor add to friction within the family.

"We barely spent a night in New Orleans. So I have no basis for an opinion. I will make a loving home for my husband wherever that may be. And as you are the woman who knows him best, I will always seek your guidance how I may be the wife he needs and deserves."

Howard Moorhead nodded gently with the astute response of his son's bride. He observed her poise and self-assurance, despite a long journey and an awkward reception by the Moorhead matriarch. The aged Armagnac he had poured into four snifters was smooth and strong. Howard savored its flavor as he enjoyed the fireside, the return of his son, and the company of the capable young woman who could be counted on to carry forward the Moorhead name. He settled into his leather chair and listened silently to the back and forth of the conversation between his wife and the newcomer. His daughter-in-law showed herself to be a sleek schooner, tacking now starboard, now port, as she sailed into the headwinds of the older woman, whose trust she knew she needed to gain to reach safe harbor. He was relieved that his son had not settled on one of the drab, pretentious belles that seemed so prevalent among the young women of New Orleans.

Howard listened in as Phil continued her campaign to soothe her new mother-in-law, "That's exactly what I told Percy when our train left Richmond. A man is like an untended garden that will go to weeds without a woman's care. I couldn't help but notice even in the dark how lovely your shrubs are in front of your porch. You must devote a lot of time on them, Mrs. Moorhead. What are they called?"

Lucy was surprised that Phil was observant of her gardening even in the dark night. "Oh those? That's dwarf Yaupon. Its leaves aren't prickly like most holly bushes. They're hardy but require regular pruning to keep them from getting too large for their area. They would overwhelm the porch if left alone."

"That's so interesting! You'll have to teach me. I have so much to learn about managing a home and taking care of my husband."

Howard let his mind and memory drift again from the comfortable parlor. He thought of a three-year-old Percy sitting on the porch swing, gently swinging back and forth under the guiding hand of Odessa, while Lucy directed Clotilda on planting the Yaupon, Eliza inside with a tutor. Fond memories, given the limited emotions he and Lucy shared.

His eyes closed, and again, he had a fleeting image of a woman on the dock, a young boy clutching at her left hand. Receding, she slowly raised her right arm and gave a final wave before turning toward Dublin's custom house, while her first born was rowed out to the three-masted ship waiting in the harbor. She had loved him, he had no doubt of that, though she had sent him away on a ship owned by her father – from whom she was estranged. Her husband had determined it was best the elder son be sent to sea, a cabin lad on a great merchant sailing vessel, the *Windrush*. He was too busy, with a rehearsal for an evening performance, to see his son off. The younger, more rambunctious son was the father's favorite, not the ten-year-old who was too young to be so melancholy. It was the last he ever saw of his mother. His melancholy had reason.

## Chapter 12

# Judah Benjamin is Charmed by Phil

The next morning, Howard Moorhead sat with his son on a wrought-iron bench by Bolingbroke's pond. The air was crisp, with a few clouds scudding slowly across the sky. A quartet of geese descended noisily and glided to a landing on the opposite side. The pond was Howard's favorite place on the plantation. He kept it stocked with bass and bream. Big Tom, as overseer, and his family were allowed to fish there on Sundays.

Howard said, "She's a lovely young woman. She'll make an ally of your mother in no time, or I'm a worse judge of character than I have imagined."

"And Eliza?" asked Percy.

"Well, you know your sister. She's perfectly fine when she's one on one. Bring in your mother and then add Calvin to the mix . . . we'll just have to see. Eliza may be jealous that Philomena has made a better marriage than she."

Percy was glad that his father had brought the conversation to Calvin Bunch. He was hesitant to inquire in case the subject was unpleasant to Howard. "What has happened with Calvin? I thought the Natchez arrangement was working out."

Howard frowned and shrugged. "His business associates suspected irregularities in the accounts. After they were cleared up, the others suggested an amicable parting."

"I assume you 'cleared up' the accounts?"

"Perhaps. Calvin assured me it was a temporary state of affairs necessitated by providing well for Eliza and their child. A misunderstanding about his ability to draw on the partnership's accounts. Your mother was indignant at his partners' suspicions of Calvin's good faith." Howard did not mention that he had liquidated several of his assets to cover Calvin's contingencies. He never spoke of his business affairs with his wife or son.

"Woodville's got potential. If Calvin has the good sense to straighten up." Percy spoke with little hope that it would come to pass. It was not a prediction. The conditional expression carried the implication that Calvin did not at present possess "good sense." His father said nothing. He had taken Calvin's measure within a day of meeting him and entertained no illusions about Calvin's likelihood of success nor his stepdaughter's prospects for a harmonious marriage. It was a bad match even if the expectations were low.

Howard Moorhead related other developments on the two plantations. Big Tom's right knee was failing him. Pompey crafted a sturdy crutch for his father to get around. And Pompey took over some of Big Tom's chores in supervising the hands in the field, while Julius was becoming the de facto operating manager in his place, seeing to supplies, equipment, assignments and scheduling of activities and field hands. The two sons of Tom were different but compatible. They complemented one another with little friction.

Odessa had seen well to Julius's preparation for the role of overseer/manager, and naturally favored her own son. She had even performed as a matchmaker for Julius, finding him a suitable wife. The young black woman, Leddie, was something like Odessa in appearance, the light-skinned daughter of a household servant of Dr. Davenport in St. Francisville. The doctor was getting old and turning his medical practice over to a younger physician. He was a widower and had fewer needs than before. He had no wish to sell the young woman away from her mother, who maintained his home. So, he practically gave Leddie to his friend Howard Moorhead when, at Odessa's prompting, Howard inquired of Leddie's availability. Dr. Davenport knew that Leddie would be near enough to her mother. She would have fetched a handsome price in Baton Rouge or Woodville. Like Howard Moorhead, Dr. Davenport was softer in his treatment of slaves than most of the whites of the Felicianas.

Howard purchased Leddie in Lucy's name as a gift for his wife, a decision without significance at the time but of legal consequence later. Clotilda was getting too old to help Lucy very much; arthritis in her hands and knees limited her ability to do many routine household chores. Leddie was articulate and cheerful and glad she could visit her mother regularly.

What did Julius and Leddie think of the match made for them? It was hardly their place to have an opinion. To be born into slavery was to begin a life in a condition not of your own choosing and about which you could do little. All you could control was your own response to each new situation imposed on you. You need not believe slavery a good to conclude you must submit and accommodate your life to living under it. Rage will not lighten your burdens nor better your condition. Rage will not give you dignity, though it may define your identity. The inward self may rebel while submitting outwardly. You make your compromises with the reality imposed on you in order that your life be more tolerable.

Julius and Leddie did not choose one another but they could choose how to live with one another. Under Odessa's guidance, they saw Bolingbroke as the stage upon which they could play the roles they would craft for themselves, to the extent the white masters would allow. Their roles were assigned, but they could play them with intelligence and imagination.

Odessa taught them that the plantation owners could be

influenced in many ways, whether overt or subtle. They could be played against one another once you knew their vanities and fears, once you divined their secrets from one another and from themselves.

So, Julius and Leddie allied themselves. They did not choose to be married but they chose what their marriage would be. They would cooperate. They would protect one another. They would work together to keep white society and law from denying them their essential humanity. Petty takings brought them small comforts. Surely it is no crime to take small items from those who have robbed you of your labor and freedom. Julius took on occasion needles and thread from Miss Lucy's sewing basket so Leddie could sew clothing for herself under Odessa's guidance. Leddie filched fruit from the Moorhead pantry to give to her husband.

ﾎﾟﾎﾟ — ぁぁ

When Percy returned to his law practice after a six-week hiatus, he found a stack of files awaiting him on the sideboard in his office. He stood looking at the folders and papers as he tried to reorient himself. They were daunting. His thoughts of the delightful hours of his new life with a woman whom he was pleased to call his wife should not distract him. He must be both attorney and husband, but he could not be both simultaneously without the one suffering from the other. Work it must be, and he called in Frank Koelhoffer.

"How shall we proceed, Frank?" he called to the chief clerk of the office in the next room.

Koelhoffer came into the room with a sheaf of papers. He told Percy, "Mr. Benjamin left a list of instructions, before he left for his case in Mobile." The German clerk and Percy spent the next eight days methodically drafting pleadings, responding to petitions, writing letters to courts and clients and doing research for briefs.

The noon hour was when Percy returned to being a husband.

Although he was working twelve-hour days, Phil would come to his office each day at noon to join him for lunch at one or another restaurant nearby. Afterwards, she would stroll around the city, enjoying the newness of place, exploring its streets and buildings. She found it garish in comparison to Richmond, combining coarseness and refinement in varying degree, often within the same block.

Phil's new home was a city both ambivalent and unapologetic, unsure of its essential character, yet boisterous. The ostentatious architecture of new buildings resonated with the same harmonics of design as New York City, unsurprising to the observant traveler who recognized the imprint of the Dakin brothers – Charles and James – and their sometime associate James Gallier. The New York bankers and merchants who raised new temples to commerce in their New Orleans and Mobile ventures relied on these New Orleans architects, who had begun their profession in New York before transplanting to new opportunities in the Deep South. Greco-Roman design provided the facade of the massive monuments to business success, or at least, mercantile aspiration, whether on the Hudson or the Mississippi. The columns and friezes of the houses of commerce were echoed in the mansions of the nouveaux riche in the uptown district and in the plantations up and down the Mississippi from the city.

A traveler debarking from a vessel on the crowded docks of New Orleans would find the city's population indistinguishable from the inhabitants she had seen in the ports of Havana or Santo Domingo or Kingstown or any of a dozen or more Caribbean islands. Philomena, however, was unfamiliar with those ports of call. To her, all was new and different and exotic. The people of Richmond were white or black, with few of in-between hues. Throughout New Orleans all shadings of complexion were seen walking, talking and working. And if they looked like islanders of the Caribbean, it was because so many of them had been. Phil's vocabulary had to expand to include all of the new terms of racial variation she encountered in her new home – not only African and black but now colored, mulatto, octoroon, quadroon, hexadecaroon, morisco, chino, griffe, mustee, marabou, sang-mêlé. As she was unusually adept at reading people, she quickly learned to measure the subtle distinctions in mannerisms that marked a free person of color from a person committed to bondage. Few things were more insulting than to mistake a free person for a slave nor more amusing than to treat a slave as though he or she were free. She was surprised to find free persons of color owning successful businesses and slaves of their own, something she had rarely, if ever, encountered in Richmond.

Phil heard languages and accents that were alien to her life in Virginia. Far from being frightened, she found it bracing. She began thinking what she might do to make the city her own. She was well-married. She possessed social graces, education and Virginian refinement. Speaking casually with shopkeepers and milliners, when she identified herself as Mrs. Moorhead, she was immediately offered a line of credit by the owners and shown the utmost courtesy. Her husband and his father were well-known throughout the business district. Boldness had brought her to the marriage she had wanted. Boldness could make her the doyenne of the Crescent City.

Howard Moorhead's wedding gift to his son and daughter-in-law was a deed to the New Orleans townhouse on Royal Street where he had resided for near thirty years. It was characteristic of Howard Moorhead that he went through the formality of a notarized deed in the presence of two witnesses to deliver to his son. It was in character for Percy to file the deed in a cabinet of his law office. To file it of record in the courthouse would have seemed to reflect distrust of his father. Both father and son fully expected Percy to be Howard's sole heir, which would occur by operation of law even if Howard died intestate. Only a perverse fate could procure grief from so simple an omission as the recordation of the townhouse deed.

More than twenty years earlier, after marrying Lucy, Howard had added three rooms to the townhouse by purchasing an adjacent property and knocking out a wall between them. The result was a family room on the ground floor which Phil now transformed into a large parlor suitable for entertaining guests. It opened into the fountained courtyard that was protected on all sides from the streets.

Phil's first initiative was to make Judah Benjamin a frequent guest in the town home for dinner. With his wife Natalie and their daughter, Ninette, permanently residing in France, Benjamin was living the life of a bachelor, though entirely faithful to his absent spouse. His principal companion was Jules St. Martin, Natalie's own dapper young brother. The senior lawyer was impressed with the bright young wife whom Percy had brought back to Louisiana. She immediately charmed him with her fresh wit, and they soon discovered a mutual fondness for poetry. At their second dinner gathering, attended by a dozen guest, Benjamin recited a stanza of *The Lady of Shalott;* Phil took it as a cue to recite the next. Benjamin was surprised. He asked if she enjoyed Tennyson's *Ulysses* as well. She responded immediately, "As senator, Mr. Benjamin, will you mete and dole unequal laws unto a savage race?"

He laughed heartily. "So Percy has shared my little secret with you."

She rejoined in a loud whisper, as though they were fellow conspirators, "He confessed only on the rack, so please forgive him. Now, Judah Benjamin, I come from a long line of political women. There have been Randolphs and Tuckers in the Senate, the House and the Presidential Cabinets since the first days of the republic. And behind every one of them was a strong woman. You could do worse than to have a Randolph woman help your campaign."

"Trust me, Philomena, I'd rather have you for me than backing my opponents."

"What do you think of Mr. Benjamin, now that you have seen him at the dinner table?" Percy asked his wife after their guests had left.

"Truly, I do not believe I have ever met a man so ingenuous of expression and manner. His voice is sweet and beautifully modulated. I'm certain he could charm a squirrel from his hollow and walk away with his winter store of acorns. I mean no disrespect. I understand why he is brilliant a lawyer. You did well coming under his tutelage. And he is an able judge of others, which is why he depends on you and trusts you, my noble husband."

Percy had told his wife that Benjamin's goal was to become a U. S. Senator from Louisiana. Election would be by the Louisiana legislature, of which he was a prominent member, still a Whig but close to Democrats. In no time, the Moorhead townhouse was a frequent venue for the entertainment of Benjamin's supporters. Phil was hostess for events and dinners. The feminine touch lacking in Benjamin's own household was supplied by Philomena Moorhead in political and social gatherings that were essential for his campaign.

Within weeks, Philomena became known as a clever young woman among New Orleans society, a vibrant presence in a social group still striving to find an identity for itself. She was always deferential to the wives of the judges, lawyers and businessmen who attended the soirees *chez* Moorhead. None felt threatened by their hostess who was so obviously devoted to her own husband and to the advancement of Judah Benjamin.

Early 1852 was especially important to Judah Benjamin. The Louisiana legislature was meeting where he could be elected to the United States Senate. At the same time, delegates were being chosen for a constitutional convention that was planned for the summer. Guests in the Moorhead townhouse included the leading politicians and newspaper publishers who supported them. From each, Philomena extracted as much information as she could about their backgrounds and interests, partly from natural curiosity and charm and partly so that she could support her husband's interests. At the end of the evening, she would pepper him with questions.

"Who was the tall man with the receding chin? His name was Kenner."

"That would be Duncan Kenner. He's a sugar planter from Ascension Parish. We expect that he'll be president of the Constitutional Convention."

"Isn't your cousin a sugar planter?"

"Several of the cousins and uncles are. I was at Princeton with two but we have hardly seen one another since."

"Another sugar planter was named Abair, I think he said."

Percy chuckled. "You've got the pronunciation. The spelling would surprise a Virginian. Hebert. Paul Octave Hebert. First in his class at West Point. He was one of the officers I served under at Churubusco in the war in Mexico. He may be a Democrat, but he's likely to be our governor sooner or later. Probably sooner."

"And who was that short fellow from Baton Rouge who was so talkative? The publisher."

"At least you didn't say he was the ugly stout fellow. That's T. B. Thorpe. Thomas Bangs Thorpe, artist, writer, publisher, Whig political candidate. When he first moved to Louisiana from New York, he lived near St. Francisville. Do you remember the portraits of my mother and father in our living room at Bolingbroke?"

"Yes. They were nicely done."

"Those were painted by Thomas Thorpe. I must have been eleven or twelve when he painted them. I think he was trying to follow in the footsteps of John James Audubon, who also painted not far from where I grew up."

"Does he still paint?"

"Maybe. But there's not much money in it. Nor in writing stories and sketches, even if he's been pretty successful. He's tried owning a couple of newspapers in smaller towns, but again, there's not much income when you have few subscribers. His political efforts have gotten him appointments as postmaster where's he lived."

"Do you like him?"

"I do. He's very well read and draws on his learning without ostentation in his humorous sketches of Southern frontier life. I dare say, he's as close as we can get to an American Tristram Shandy."

"Is Shandy the author?"

"Sterne is the author. Shandy is his creation, marvelously funny. Thorpe is funny in the same way Shandy is. Self-aware. Always poking fun at his own expense and not at others."

"Invite him back."

"We'll see. He's living in Baton Rouge."

## Chapter 13

# Re-encountering Beauregard

Percy was returning to his office from morning motions in court a few weeks after returning from his marriage in Richmond. He was a block up from Canal when he saw a man he thought he recognized standing at the construction site of the new custom house.

"Lieutenant Beauregard? Is that you?"

"Captain Beauregard. And you, sir?" the gentleman responded, turning to his inquisitor. Beauregard did not immediately recognize the tall, well-dressed young man who addressed him. "You seem familiar. Mexico, was it?"

"Yes sir. Moorhead. Private Percy Moorhead. Percy Moorhead, esquire, now."

The army engineer walked over to Percy, placing the papers he held under his left arm as he extended his right in a firm handshake. The rank of "captain" was a sensitive matter. He had been brevetted to captain and major from lieutenant late in the Mexican War but did not retain the rank at its close. His principal work for the army now was combatting the Mississippi River. The Army engineers were responsible for maintaining the navigability of the river and fortifying its approaches from the Gulf. The complex hydrology and sedimentation of the river created mudlumps and sandbars that would come and go, up and down the river from New Orleans. Ships would suddenly run aground where only a few months earlier a clear channel had allowed passage. No channel charts were reliable. The river was a continuing challenge to even the most proficient of pilots.

Beauregard's assignments kept him away from his home, on the right bank of the river south of the city, for weeks at a time. If he were put in charge of construction engineering on the customhouse it could lead to a permanent posting to captain and allow him more time for family, a matter of special importance to him. Beauregard was not unfriendly, but he displayed little warmth. There was something shrouded in his eyes, as though an engagement in a social setting was difficult for a man who preferred privacy.

"Esquire? A lawyer, are you? I don't suppose you would look the same out of uniform. You wear the clothes of a gentleman. I remember you now – Cerro Gordo. You looked like a minstrel with your blackened face and arms. And you were at Puebla. Wounded, were you? The maps."

"Your memory is excellent. I'm not sure I've ever thanked you properly for saving my arm. It was you, wasn't it?"

"Perhaps so. What sort of law do you do?" He was not being merely polite. He often had to deal with lawyers, despite his general mistrust of any member of the profession.

"Mostly commercial. Anything the firm's principals assign me."

"And who might they be?"

"Benjamin and Micou."

"Really, now. It is a small world. Benjamin is a name I know. He is often allied with John Slidell, for whom I have a high regard." There was an edge to Beauregard's comment. It was as if he were suggesting he lacked such regard for Benjamin.

"Of course. I see John Slidell from time to time. His brother Thomas compiled the Louisiana *Digest* with Mr. Benjamin. May I take you for a meal? Do you have plans for this evening?"

Beauregard accepted the dinner invitation. From inquiries he made of William Micou later in the day, Percy learned that Beauregard's wife, Laure Villeré, had died in childbirth a couple of years earlier, leaving him with three small children to raise. The sadness and burden of care Percy had seen in Beauregard's eyes were for reasons unrelated to his treatment by the U. S. Army.

The two men met at the Boston Club for a few hands of cards before dining at the St. Charles hotel. Social ritual was essential to success in New Orleans business and politics. Judah Benjamin found Percy to be an eager student who could navigate among the competing groups who sought to further their banking and mercantile interests in the city. That Howard Moorhead was not a founding member of the Boston Club was a curiosity to his son. When Benjamin nominated Percy for admission, it was in part on the strength of the Moorhead name, one familiar to most of the members from business dealings.

Over drinks, the soldier opened up by degrees, though never mentioning his family. Percy was surprised that this was

Beauregard's first visit to the Boston Club. He asked,

"How does it compare to the Aztec Club?"

"Favorably, but not as elegant as a presidential palace." The Aztec Club had been established in Mexico City for the officers who had accompanied General Winfield Scott's campaign from Vear Cruz to the occupation of the capital city of Mexico. Having the entire city under their command, the founding members of the club took as their enclave the palace of Senōr Jose Bocanegra, briefly a president of Mexico. Located in the heart of the city, it was magnificent. "Why? Weren't you there?" asked Beauregard.

Beauregard must have forgotten that Percy was ineligible for membership as he was only a lowly private. Percy recalled vividly his humiliation at being sharply reprimanded by a colonel after Percy knocked over a stool as he delivered a case of wine to the Aztec Club. The degradation still stung Percy, long after he had acquired the title of "esquire," which opened many more doors than an officer's rank from the war in Mexico would have.

"Only on the odd occasion," Percy threw off as a glib reply.

At that moment, Judah Benjamin appeared next to Percy. The younger lawyer introduced Benjamin to Captain G. T. Beauregard. The army officer was slow to stand and seemed reluctant to extend his hand to Benjamin, merely nodding his head rather than speaking as they shook hands. Benjamin commented, "We haven't had the pleasure, but I know of the good work the captain is doing for the river to keep our ships afloat."

With an ironic half-smile on his thin lips, Beauregard responded, "And Mr. Benjamin, your reputation precedes you even to the bayou from which I arose. When you are in Washington, I trust you will be vigilant to the needs of the army here in Louisiana."

"Sir, you can count on it," said Benjamin as he turned his attentions elsewhere.

Beauregard's ability at cards was less than he imagined, and he was unaware that his younger host let him win most hands. It was near dark when they walked to the St. Charles Hotel. The gas lamps of the street were being lit by a city lamplighter making his evening rounds, extending his wick-tipped pole to ignite the coal-gas fixtures. By the time dinner was served at the hotel, Beauregard was describing his frustrations with the Army bureaucracy. He had patented several inventions, but the army was uninterested. Percy was surprised to learn that Beauregard was supporting Franklin Pierce for president.

"I thought your service with General Scott had been very satisfactory," Percy said.

Sipping from his wine glass and then continuing to cut at his steak with his knife without looking Percy in the eye, Beauregard let down the mask that concealed candor in the field of battle. "Not all is as it seems. Like parents with their children, the officers of the service hide their differences from the men they send to face death. If the trumpet is uncertain, who will answer its call? Old Fuss and Feathers was far too cautious a general. Those months in Puebla were largely wasted. We should have marched directly on the Mexican capital. Oh, I know he had his reasons. There's always a reason not to act. But Jomini's teachings would have had us seize the advantage. Napoleon would not have hesitated. Santa Anna had time to rebuild. Scott would be as poor a president as we've had. He heeds the wrong people and fails to give others their due."

From John Slidell Percy would learn that Beauregard chafed that General Scott's reports on the Mexican campaign had given higher marks to Captain Robert Lee for the Engineers' work at Vera Cruz, Cerro Gordo and Churubusco than to Beauregard and several others. Scott played favorites and was too political a general, complained Beauregard.

Percy turned Beauregard from dwelling on his dissatisfactions. "What is your role with the Custom House? I've been watching the progress at the site since I returned from Mexico. It's a huge undertaking."

Beauregard bristled, though not at Percy. "Bah! The architect belongs in jail. Again. This time for incompetence."

"Again?"

"You don't know the story? I thought all New Orleans had heard it. There was a competition to design a new post office and custom house for this city. Man named Alexander Wood was a builder here some time earlier. Before he murdered his foreman. After five years in prison he was ready to return to his profession. He ingratiated himself with politicians in Washington who thought he could help their plans. God save us from the politicians! A Treasury official let him rummage among different plans submitted for the New Orleans project. He stole from his former friends without shame. What did he have to lose? He concocted a grandiose design that appealed to the taste of the Treasury Secretary. The building is fit to be a Mausoleum or Tomb for Egypt's Pharaoh. It will be a sarcophagus, made of granite imported from the state of Massachusetts."

"Massachusetts?"

Beauregard's eyes narrowed. He moved his head closer to Percy's, as if he were imparting secrets to a confidante. "Moorhead, if Washington's going to pay for a building down here, every politician who votes for it will extract some part of the cost for his own constituents. It has always been so. You can be sure that some senator in Massachusetts owes his office to a granite contractor. And in war, when they appropriate money, they will see to it that their friends are the generals and colonels – not the best soldiers. That nearly cost us our victory at Cerro Gordo. President Polk had insisted that Scott take Gideon Pillow as a brigade commander. What qualifications did he have for general? Only his political connection as a lawyer in Tennessee who once shared an office with Polk. No offense to your profession, Moorhead. It's my experience that lawyers would rather argue than fight. Pillow arrived late to battle at Cerro Gordo and took the wrong line of attack in that damned chaparral. He gave conflicting orders and orders that couldn't be carried out. Soldiers died as he delayed to change the order of his troops in formation. He was responsible for our highest casualties that day. Good soldiers die because of political generals. Battles are lost because of political generals."

Beauregard had regressed into his grievances. It was the effect of the wine and the uncertainties of his future assignment with the Army. Percy brought him back to the Custom House. "Is it even worthwhile to build?"

The soldier's face brightened. "Oh yes. Make no mistake. The Custom House is important to the city. We are the great port of inland America. We must have a suitable building near the river befitting our importance as a merchant capital. The problem is that Wood was a better artist than an engineer. He gave them a pretty set of drawings but for a building that cannot be completed according to its design."

"Why not? I know nothing of construction."

"Reflect for a minute where we are." Beauregard paused, waiting for a response.

"This hotel?"

"This hotel sits where? I'll tell you. In the middle of the Mississippi River. At least, where it ran once. And will probably run again. A thousand times this river has changed course. And wherever it has run, it has laid down its sediment. We are sitting on soil which was once the mud lumps and sand bars I'm fighting in the river now to keep our ships going up and down the river. Mr. Wood could build a row house or two and expect it to stand in his lifetime. But when you put ton upon ton of stone on the weak soil of this city it will all sink under the weight. Where you found me today, I was examining how the building is settling too fast and unequally. The outer walls are sinking deeper than the interior ones. As they sink, they are cracking. Within six months, one end will have sunk several feet below the other."

"That's terrible! What can be done?" Beauregard had found an avid listener in Percy Moorhead, a sympathetic ally who might have influence in the city in the future.

"For one thing, the use of groined brick arches bears too heavily on this soft soil. What we must do is to use smaller, iron girder arches. If we install iron plates on the exterior walls, we could bind them to the interior walls. Tying them together would at least equalize the settling. And we could redistribute weight on the higher parts of the building."

Beauregard tried to illustrate his point with silverware from the table but gave up when a fork and spoon could not be induced to stand at attention. The wine was going to his head. Percy nodded as though he understood. Beauregard continued, "It won't change the building from a monstrosity. But I'll guarantee it'll last much longer than the last two the government had here."

"Will they listen to you?"

"Maybe. If they will make me superintendent of the project and increase my rank according to what I merit, I can make it work. But I will insist on being given my elbow room. No interference from people who don't know what they are doing. I am always ready for a fight whenever they will say so. I do what is right and for the best, happen what will."

"I don't doubt that for a minute, sir. I was proud to have served you in Mexico and would be honored to help you in any way I can."

"You may. You have associated yourself with some of the power brokers of the city. If you continue with them, I suspect you will indeed be useful."

Moving a little closer to Beauregard and speaking in a lower voice, Percy said, "Yet, sir, I think I sensed a residue of discomfort or even disapproval on your part when I mentioned Judah

Benjamin earlier today and again when he first appeared at our table. May I be so bold to inquire why? As you suggest, my future is tied to his."

Raising his dark eyebrows, Beauregard said, "Moorhead, you an acute observer. While this was my first meeting with Benjamin, he has been a source of pain for my family. The Beauregard plantation where I was raised, Contreras, was nearly lost to my family because of Benjamin. He was the lawyer representing creditors who sought to seize it while I was in Mexico and unable to help my family meet their obligations. Only the intervention of two of my father's friends prevented foreclosure. He would tell you, I'm sure, that he was only representing his clients. To me, his zeal smacked of the sharp practices for which his race is known."

After he returned to their townhouse, Percy told Phil of his evening with Captain Beauregard. She had not attended dinner with them because her stomach was queasy with her pregnancy. "Beauregard," he related to her, "is an excellent leader. But a poor subordinate. We've not heard the last of him. We shall avoid bringing Benjamin and Beauregard together whenever possible. They are oil and water, fire and ice."

*Chapter 14*

# Journey Preparations

Benjamin's political activities did not cease when he won his seat in the U. S. Senate. A year would pass before he occupied it. In the meantime, he was active in the revision of the state constitution. Philomena continued to serve as his unofficial hostess in gatherings at the Moorhead townhouse and in social functions at the two major hotels. She became a familiar face to the caterers for the events and to the hotel personnel responsible for carrying out her arrangements, made more memorable as her pregnancy became more visible. Although she was precise as to her expectations, she was friendly to all and pleasant to work with. She might say, "I love what you have done, but wouldn't that spray of flowers look just a wee bit better over in the corner? What do you think? Let's give it a try and see." The response was sure to be, "Of course, Mrs. Moorhead." If the wife of a legislator appeared uncomfortable and out-of-place, Philomena would take her by the arm and make her a special friend by letting her speak about her home and family until she entirely forgot where she was and simply enjoyed her hostess.

Percy was now identified as a regular Benjamin stand-in when the Senator-elect was unable to attend to a client or business meeting. At first, the clients who had hoped to see Benjamin were disappointed that he sent a young member of his firm. Percy was not as voluble as the more senior attorney, nor had he yet mastered Benjamin's smooth manner. As it became clear that the stand-in easily grasped the complexities of their problems and could anticipate their needs, they were won over. Benjamin's prodigious talents were best exhibited in the court room – his eloquence, his power to persuade, his analysis of case law and ability to skewer an opponent's presentation. Percy Moorhead excelled in the conference room. His special skill was in structuring transactions, showing businessmen how they could leverage their advantages, how business associates could complement one another in their relative strengths. The courtroom did not beckon him as it did Benjamin, yet he did not avoid it. He thought it a greater achievement to resolve disputes before resorting to litigation. His reputation grew as a deal maker more than as an advocate.

The pressing business of the constitutional convention interfered with Benjamin's annual trip to France to visit his wife and daughter and his customary side trip to England to attend to needs of his clients. In mid-May Judah spoke with Philomena during a well-attended reception at the St. Charles. A new French consul had arrived from Paris and was welcomed by many city and state officials as well as the city's leading bankers, investors, merchants – and their attorneys. All present were intensely interested in the changes being made in the French government and what they meant for the future. Unwilling to leave his presidency, Louis Napoleon Bonaparte had staged a coup, overthrowing his own government, followed by the adoption of a new constitution of his devising only five months earlier. Conversation at the reception was preoccupied with whether the new regime was prelude to a second French Empire.

While Percy was engaged with several of his banking clients, Judah Benjamin took Philomena aside, to a quiet corner. In a low voice that suggested confidentiality, he said, "My dear young lady, I hope you know how we have come to depend on your husband.

He works long hours, and it is likely his load will increase. My annual trip to France must be delayed. Yet we cannot neglect our responsibilities in London and Liverpool. With your consent, and his, I would like for Percy to take my place in England for the merchants and bankers whose interests we represent and those who work with our clients here."

She was surprised that he asked her. "How long would he be gone?" She had picked out a new light blue dress for the occasion a week ago. Her tailor recommended yellow trim, but Phil remained superstitious of the gypsy's warning. Beige accented the dress nicely and would not lend emphasis to her pregnancy. A waiter approached with a tray of red and white wine and champagne, offering her a glass. She hesitated, then selected a champagne coupe.

Benjamin declined a glass but sought Phil's consent that he smoke a cigar. She nodded, "Of course." After drawing on the Havana, he continued, "The voyage is eleven or twelve days each way from New York. His activities abroad would take no more than four weeks. I've not spoken to him yet. In light of your condition, I would not take him away from you if his absence were more than you could accept. I am already in your debt in more ways than can be measured."

"You honor me with your concern, Judah. A woman would be a poor wife indeed if she stood in the way of her husband's advancement."

"Very well then. I will rest more comfortably knowing that my clients' interests will be well attended. It will be in Percy's interests – and yours – that he gain international experience. The steamship has made the world a smaller place. It is to the world what the railroad and riverboat are to the commerce of this country."

తితి — ఆ⊶ఆ

The plans for Percy's trip abroad coalesced within a fortnight.

At a coffee house and bakery a few blocks from his townhouse, Percy told his father that he was leaving for New York and England within the week. It was late May, the weather already stifling. The senior Moorhead was not surprised at his son's news. He reflected, without sharing his thoughts with his son, that Percy's professional life was assuming an arc not unlike his own, drawn to business transactions across national boundaries. Maneuvering among competing laws and interests to complete trades advantageous to the parties he represented – this is what Howard Moorhead had done at the same stage in his own life, only his office had been a cabin in the aft of a merchant vessel sailing port to port in the Mediterranean and Adriatic.

Recalling his own journeys as a young man, when he became a ship's purser his cabin was next to the captain's. The British Navigation Acts required that all commodity trade should take place in British ships, manned by British seamen, trading between British ports and those within the empire. Often his instructions had been of a most general nature and gave him wide latitude – trade a cargo of woolens and manufactured goods for cotton finished fabrics, dyes, spices, silk, flax, wine and dried fruit.

When Napoleon Bonaparte had tried to cut off trade of Britain with Europe by a blockade in 1806, the young merchant was on ships taking exceptional risks on authority of his Majesty's government to keep British trade alive. Not only were goods from the British Isles and from her colonial possessions on board but also secret shipments of gold and silver – British payments to European monarchs to continue fielding armies against the French tyrant. In recompense, the crown allowed his vessel, the *Hybla* (and her sister ships), to import high value Indian fabrics that English protectionist legislation would otherwise prohibit.

For several years Percy's father had successfully accomplished his mission, three and four voyages per year. In time, bankers and merchants looked to the young ship's purser as a man to be trusted with their notes and letters of credits to be negotiated in the ports that his company's ship visited on a regular basis. He advanced their interests and facilitated their export-import business. Only a few of the ship's owners were aware of the special shipments of specie undertaken for the Foreign Ministry.

His ship, the *Hybla*, was a 300-ton, 97 foot, three-masted merchantman out of Bristol, built in Chepstow in 1810 and under Captain Rogers. Had it not been for the events on the French coast in 1815 and the secret cargo of gold taken on for a British consortium he surely would have become a partner in the trading company within another year. He would never share that fateful story with his wife or his son. Only by degrees and by circuitous routes would Percy learn the truth about his father. It required years and many moments of anguish and despair for the son.

Setting aside his musings and feeling pride for his son's professional growth, Howard could not resist sharing with Percy small morsels of his past, crumbs that would later draw Percy on, eager to know more. What prompted these tidbits was his learning he was to become a grandfather.

"That's wonderful," Howard said enthusiastically when Percy finally told him Phil was three months pregnant. "How does Phil feel about you leaving for England under the circumstances?"

"She understands the importance of the work."

Howard asked his son, "But aren't you apprehensive for her safety in New Orleans?"

"Apprehensive? Worried? I don't let those concern me." It was unlike his father to speak of such matters. Percy felt a vague discomfort, an awkwardness at his father's turn of conversation.

"No, I suppose not. You've never been one to express your feelings. Why is that?"

"Why do I so seldom express emotion?" Percy's voice took on an edge, and he put down his cup. "You, of all people, should not ask this question. I am my father's son."

"Indeed, you are. Perhaps I misspoke." Howard turned the conversation in a more positive direction. "And now you're getting deeper into the cotton business – just as I have done for thirty-five years in one capacity or another."

If Howard Moorhead was ready to talk about his past, Percy was eager to encourage him. "You've never told me how an Anglo-Irishman became a New Orleans cotton factor."

"That's a story of many chapters. My understanding of cotton started when I was a ship's purser in the Mediterranean. We were trading English woolens and manufactures for fine Indian cotton goods – muslins, chintzes and calicoes, some so fine they seemed like they were woven wind. Now I knew something about wool from my mother's stories about the sheep on her father's land, sheep raised by his tenants for the woolen industry. But here I was trading wool for cotton. The English public couldn't get enough of the cotton. They thought it was superior to the fabric manufactured in Lancashire."

"My grandmother? Sheep?"

Howard ignored the question. "I suppose I was about the same age as when you went to Mexico that I began to learn of the cotton trade. So, it was some time after my mother had passed. I studied cotton in order to trade it profitably in Mediterranean ports. It was a trading activity that was three thousand years old."

"Cotton has a history?" Percy asked. "I had the impression that it was discovered in the New World. Like potatoes and tobacco."

Howard laughed and said, "Far from it, son. Herodotus wrote of India's wild trees that bore fleece that natives wove into clothing. When Mark Antony sailed to Egypt, he found Cleopatra dressed in cotton clothing dyed in brilliant colors. Marco Polo's travels eastward from Italy brought him in contact with cultures built around cultivation of a wool growing on shrubs and trees, describing what we know as *gossypium arboreum* — the cotton tree. Now, you're right that cotton was in the Americas when Columbus arrived. He thought he had reached India because of the cotton fields he found on the islands of the Caribbean where he made landfall. Even though they were half the world away, the Indians of the New World made fabric and clothing of the same raw material as Indians of Dacca or Surat. From Mexico, Cortes sent his emperor cotton mantles, some all white, others mixed with white and black, or red, green, yellow, and blue; waistcoats, handkerchiefs, counterpanes, tapestries, and carpets of cotton. The colors of the cotton were extremely fine. The native Mexicans had both indigo and cochineal among their dyes, their beauty rivaling the gold Cortes had seized and exported."

Percy smiled, "When I was in Mexico with the army I saw cotton fields on the march to Puebla. I guess that's why I thought it originated in this part of the world."

Howard was more enthusiastic than Percy could remember. It was as though he was welcoming his son into the mercantile world in which he was himself a master. "Well, son, you see that cotton is a world-wide business. What other crop can be made into things that do not rot after ripening? Cotton, and fabric made from it, can be weighed and measured and stored, making it suitable for taxing by a sovereign or transporting over distances by a merchant."

"So, on a ship at sea you decided to become a factor in New Orleans?" Percy wanted to know how his father had come into the world of cotton and found his way across the Atlantic.

"Many parts to the story, as I said, for another day. Other events conspired to bring me connections in Liverpool and London. And I had the support and encouragement of a kind and generous uncle." At the mention of his uncle, Howard's voice trailed off. Percy could sense his father's emotion, as though he was awakening memories of a difficult time.

"He must have been important to you."

"That is an understatement. If my uncle had not been there for me, what would have become of my life? I am still in his debt. I have tried to honor him in the only way I knew how."

Howard smiled and stood. He hugged his son with some emotion, perhaps at the prospect of a grandchild, perhaps at the turn of the conversation of an uncle of whom Percy had been ignorant. Were those tears in his eyes, or merely the sun's rays? Strange that this was his father's first mention of a kind uncle. Percy knew so little of his father. He wished he knew more. Until he regretted learning what he did, from an Irish stranger a few years later.

*Chapter 15*

# Judah's Special Instructions

Early in June, Percy departed New Orleans for New York City, carrying letters of introduction, powers of attorney, and banking transactions for New Orleans banks and financial houses and their New York correspondents. His father saw him off, as he had when Percy had left for Tampico five years earlier and for Williamsburg for law school. Percy asked his father where he might go to visit family connections for the English side of his heritage, especially to see the generous uncle. His father was indirect – inquiring first what cities Percy would go to and how long he planned to stay in each.

Percy told him, "Only to Liverpool and London. Four weeks at most."

"I think your plans would not allow time enough to search out our family roots. It's been some years since I've heard from family and friends, so I cannot in good conscience send you on a search that would likely yield no results."

"But you mentioned something about me seeing Stratford. I had the impression you had spent time there."

Howard shrugged it off. "Did I? There'll be time for that on a later trip."

Howard Moorhead's only recommendation was that Percy

obtain a passport issued by the United States government while in New York. Although identification papers were not required for most travel out of the country, it had been his experience as a young man on a merchant vessel trading between countries that proof of identity and country of origin was often useful. In the event of an outbreak of European hostilities, an American with papers might have freedom of travel that would be denied an Englishman. The ambitions of the new regime established by Louis Napoléon threatened a resumption of the Napoleonic wars across all of Europe. Howard Moorhead had lived through them when he was a young man traveling abroad, his life drastically altered when the Bonapartists had briefly returned after exile. He had crossed France with no papers. It would not hurt for Percy to have such papers as he dealt with merchants and bankers in the cities he visited.

Cryptically, Howard said, "Men of all nations assume new identities, more often than you might imagine." Percy was unaware of his father's irony.

One assignment of his journey Percy did not describe to his father. Judah Benjamin at first had made it seem merely an aside. Yet, on reflection, Percy wondered if it were not the principal reason Judah sent him on this voyage. Had he seen Percy Moorhead's usefulness for his grand enterprise from the moment he first talked with Percy and learned of a background uniquely suited for Benjamin's purposes?

Judah Benjamin's great project was no secret. Only his means and methods were concealed from inquisitive opponents. The vision was as old and imaginative as Christopher Columbus, linking East and West for commerce. President Polk's successful war for American Manifest Destiny increased the urgency of the age-old dream. The goldfields of California beckoned adventurers and visionaries no less than the topless towers of Ilium. Behind them, too, were the merchants who dreamed of a path to the riches of the Orient without the long, treacherous, bitter voyages of Tierra del Fuego and Cape Horn.

Thus far, Benjamin had not shared with Percy the workings and machinations of the grand scheme. The young lawyer was aware of the meetings Benjamin conducted with the backers of the Tehuantepec Railway across southern Mexico and the efforts to gain support for the railway company in the state legislature. Most recently, Benjamin had promoted the long-range plan in a public address to the Southwestern Railroad Convention, which Percy had attended in January. Benjamin described the prime needs of the South in the matter of railways, the most important of which was the route north and south by a railway from New Orleans to Jackson, Mississippi. When extended to Illinois, it would bind the great central and northeastern portions of the country more closely to New Orleans, even as the Mississippi River waterway had earlier. New Orleans would not be the end point, but the indispensable mid-point of a continuous route that extended to the Pacific, to California and its gold rush, and then to the ports of China.

The line of travel would carry straight across the Gulf of Mexico to the narrow neck of land which divides the Pacific from the Atlantic. Nature had bestowed every blessing of soil and climate to this divide between the seas, where she has even lowered the hills as if purposely to point out the way for a railroad.

The audience enjoyed the smooth oratory of Benjamin: "When we cross this Isthmus, this Isthmus of Tehuantepec, what have we before us is the Eastern World. Its commerce has been the bone of many a bloody contest. Its commerce makes empires of the countries to which it flows, and when they are deprived of it they are as empty bags, useless, valueless. That commerce," Benjamin proclaimed to great applause, "belongs to New Orleans."

Now, as Percy's journey to England approached, Benjamin related the complex status of the project. Mexico had initially granted an exclusive franchise to Don Jose de Garay before the

Mexican War. That grant became the object of rivalry and contention, played out in the aftermath of the peace treaty which had failed to settle the future of the project. The Garay rights came into the hands of Peter Hargous, a New York investor with commercial interests in New Orleans, represented by Benjamin. A committee of New Orleans businessmen led by Benjamin secured a charter from the Louisiana legislature to establish the Tehuantepec Railroad Company.

Over lunch at the St. Charles, Benjamin expounded on the project. "Since I became involved three years ago, we've done a great deal of preliminary work. We've dispatched teams of experts to the region in Mexico and completed multiple surveys of the local conditions and the best routes. Our latest report was just published, as a means of advertising our potential for investors and make known our claims."

Percy did not conceal his knowledge of the project nor his interest in participating. "I saw the work when you gave your presentation to the railroad convention."

Judah continued, "Unfortunately, it also encouraged competitors who have exploited the hostility to us among some Mexicans. A man named Albert Sloo, calling himself Colonel Sloo, is seeking favor of the current Mexican government. He has investors and also his own backers in our government. Earlier he was the recipient of subsidies for transporting the United States mail. His mail subsidies will become much more valuable if he has an overland route through Mexico."

"What do you propose, and how may I help?" It was the same question Percy asked each time Benjamin came to him with a client or a proposal. It was Percy's can-do spirit and the intelligent capability that made him so useful.

Benjamin said, "We must anticipate his moves and exploit his weaknesses. Anyone trying to develop a canal or railroad requires capital, enormous capital. We can discourage New Orleans investors by letting it be known that anyone questioning the validity of our grant will face vigorous litigation in our courts in Louisiana. Sloo and his people will have to seek loans. He will have to look to London bankers. Among our acquaintances is Francis Falconnet, a British subject who has represented groups of British creditors in resolving debt controversies in Argentina, Spain and Mexico. Since the end of the war with Mexico he brokered a deal whereby funds owed by the United States to Mexico will be devoted to discounted retirement of Mexican debt to English bondholders. He is uniquely placed for anyone seeking Mexican grants. Colonel Sloo cannot finalize a deal with Mexican interests without securing the support of Falconnet."

Smiling, Percy responded, "So, to the heart of the matter. Where do I fit in this mélange of competing interests and actors?"

"Yes, to the point. I need you to meet with Falconnet's associates in London. He has a continuing, though vaguely defined, association with Baring Bros. & Co. of London. Their agent in New Orleans is our good friend Ed Forstall, whom you have met. When called upon by Sloo's interests, Barings will advance the money to Sloo to confirm his grant with the Mexicans. But with the condition that he assign his grant to them if he fails to meet his payments. When he fails, as would anyone in the same circumstances, the English bankers will take over and then assign the grant to Hargous. The Mexicans will have to deal with our company again."

Percy was aware from the New Orleans newspapers of Mexican political developments. The city was the center of most political intrigue in every country lapped by the waves of the waters of the Gulf of Mexico. Rumors printed in the papers one day became reports of revolutions a week or two later.

"Clever. But won't the Arista government still be hostile to you and Hargous?"

"Dear Percy, you first went to Mexico only five years ago. Can you count how many presidents Mexico has elevated and overthrown since then? It's like the weather in New Orleans. If you don't like it today, tomorrow it will change. We have influential friends in Mexico, and they will return to public favor. If not soon, it will still be timely."

"Until they, too, are overthrown," Percy said.

"Yes," Judah chuckled. "Timing is everything."

"I may need guidance on the transfer of funds." Percy was uncertain what was expected of him.

"You will be my personal representative. You will communicate information and commitments that it would be awkward and imprudent to put into writing. Letters were the undoing of many projects that might have been magnificent had they not been discovered by the wrong people. No funds need change hands right away. It will be enough to make commitments. When necessary, the flow of credit and debit will be through assignment of cotton shipments originating through New Orleans. The purpose behind the transfers will never appear. The fact that our company is now associated with a U. S. Senator increases our credibility and makes challenges less likely to succeed."

Percy commented, "So, my acting as attorney for our cotton merchant clients will blend together with the interests of the isthmus project."

Nodding in agreement, Benjamin said, "Indeed it is. They will be seamless. As to the project, you will convey my endorsement of this plan to confound the efforts of Sloo and his backers to defeat the Tehuantepec Railroad Company of New Orleans. My letter introducing you to them and designating you as my confidential agent on any enterprise with which I am associated will be sufficient. You will help them complete drafts of contracts that they will employ when eventually, as he surely must, Colonel Sloo seeks a loan. They will provide that upon default, any concession or grant by the government of Mexico will *ipso facto* become the property of Francis Falconnet and his investors, subject to his development or reassignment. Are you up for the task?"

Percy didn't hesitate. He was to be the trusted messenger for Benjamin, much as he had been for Colonel DeRussy to General Scott. This mission didn't carry with it the risk of execution by the enemy if captured.

"Sure. I may need to brush up on English finance law. What you suggest sounds little different than what we've done many times for security in shipments of cotton or an advance for the purchase of a plantation or a vessel. It's a right of attachment. Only here, the thing to be recovered from Sloo is not a corporeal but an incorporeal. It is not a thing someone can physically seize but instead a right arising by declaration of the Mexican government. Without regard to English law, may I suggest that you find a way that any concession awarded to Sloo or any other potential grantee be specific that such a right can be reconveyed by the grantee?"

Benjamin reflected a minute and saw that his young associate made a sound recommendation. "Right you are. We have friends in the Mexican capital who will see to that. Falconnet has close relations within the executive and legislative departments in the government."

Percy leaned back in his chair. The dining room of the St. Charles was nearly empty after lunch. "Let me be sure I understand. The Mexicans are invalidating our Tehuantepec railroad grant. Sloo is getting a new railroad grant from the Mexicans. He'll have to get the capital from British bankers to pay the Mexicans. We're getting the bankers to advance him the money so that when he fails to pay them, we get the railroad rights back again. My job is to assure our friends at Baring Brothers that we are good for the capital that they will advance and to see that the deal is structured so we are certain the Sloo railroad grant comes back to us."

"I could not have said it more clearly myself." Benjamin's customary smile was broader than usual. His protégé showed no qualms or hesitancy at becoming a key player in a labyrinthine ploy to defeat a business rival. Someone more squeamish or burdened by too fine a sense of scruple might have declined. There was nothing illegal in the proposal, and Sloo was the interloper, no doubt having secured his advantage by generous transfers to outstretched palms of Mexican authorities. Craft against corruption.

That evening, as they dressed for bed, Percy shared with Philomena his conversation with Judah Benjamin, indicating the confidence the older attorney was placing in Percy. She admitted she did not understand a word about the railroad route in Mexico.

"It's revolutionary," he said with uncharacteristic excitement. "The opening of so short a passage will transform world commerce. Ships won't have to go around Cape Horn or the Cape of Good Hope." Laughing, he added, "And unlike Columbus, we know where we are going."

Caressing her husband's cheek, Phil smiled and said, "Judah and I have that in common. We both know how lucky we are to have found you."

## Chapter 16

# A *Baltic* Voyage

Seven years had passed since Percy last had seen New York City, while still a student at Princeton. He now walked the city's broad streets with a different sense, dressed now in fine clothes, now a successful lawyer representing commercial interests of major consequence for the entire Mississippi Valley. Nothing was more vital for the well-being of his state and the agricultural interests of the delta country, indeed the whole of the South, than the cotton industry. Cotton was the largest business in the world, covering the entire globe in spindly thread.

As a boy, he had watched the small bolls enlarge, ripen and open in mid-summer on the thousand-plus acres of Bolingbroke and Jericho Hill. He had watched the laboring black women and men pluck the cotton locks from the plants and thrust them with a fluid rhythm into large, twelve-foot-long sacks that they dragged behind them. At the end of each row, a wagon waited to collect and empty the sacks after weighing their contents. Thus began cotton's journey – to barn and gin and baler, to wagon again and then to boat, to warehouse and wharf in New Orleans, again on ships to New York City and thence to Liverpool, destined for the mills of Lancashire. It occurred to Percy that he was making the same passage, from birth next to those fields that produced the cotton plants in rich profusion to maturity in New Orleans and now New

York. Perhaps the shirt he bought the day before from a shop on Broadway and wore now had taken the same route, returning to New York from mills in Manchester.

New York was the financing, trading, and insurance capital of the cotton trade. For the better part of four days Percy introduced himself, shook hands and signed documents among lawyers, bankers and merchants. He conveyed bills, notes and instructions of his clients and completed their transactions while laying the foundations for future interactions with these same people. Important business leaders took him to fine restaurants and inquired about conditions in the South. All spoke well of Judah Benjamin and made it known to Percy that they hoped he could serve as an instrument to persuade Senator Benjamin, once he was sworn into office, to further their interests in Congress. He assured them that their interests were the same interests as Benjamin's constituents in Louisiana. Cotton cultivation and finance were as interwoven as the yarn of finished fabric.

Was Percy discouraged in any way by his realization that the welcome and hospitality shown him derived from his status as an intermediary for Benjamin? Not in the least. He suffered under no illusions in that regard. But he was confident that his character and integrity would advance him in the world, as it had his father, as it had Judah Benjamin. In time, he would assume stature in his own right.

On Saturday he boarded the *Baltic*, a new ship of the American Collins line. As he rode up to the Collins Pier at the foot of Canal Street in a carriage from the Astor House Hotel, Percy marveled at the huge steam ship, nearly three hundred feet long and forty-five feet wide, with a wooden-hull and enormous paddle wheels on either side, larger than any vessel he'd ever seen on the Mississippi. A single black and red stack jutted up from near mid-ship, smoke beginning to rise into the cloudless evening sky. The crew were all aboard, some 130 men and women. In small groups, the passengers were beginning to walk up the gangway. The *Baltic* was designed to carry as many as 200 passengers. The dependability of steam travel allowed the scheduling of regular departures. Schedules must be maintained regardless of whether the vessel possessed a full complement of passengers.

Judah Benjamin had insisted that Percy book passage on the boats of the Collins Line. State room accommodations and meals were superior to anything offered by the rival Cunard steam vessels. A crossing by sail would have been far less expensive but also much longer in transit and no where near as comfortable. Time and money were closely related. The *Baltic* could cross the Atlantic in about ten days with little regard to wind and wave. A rapid sailing ship would require three times as long.

Percy's cabin was better than he had imagined. The floor was made of satinwood. On one wall, the room was furnished with a marble wash basin, a dish for soap, and a heavy water pitcher, wide and flat at the bottom so there was no risk of it falling over in rough seas. The mirror near it was cleverly fitted so that it could be adjusted to the height of the traveler. He stowed his clothing in a small closet as the ship pulled away slowly from its berth. The great paddlewheels on both sides of the vessel began propelling her and her passengers out to sea. Sunset's evening light showed through an oval porthole a bit above chest height. Percy looked out and watched the city recede. An hour later, a steward escorted Percy to one of the long tables in the dining saloon, placing him opposite a family of three. Percy reached across the table and introduced himself as Percy Moorhead, attorney of New Orleans. The man whose hand he shook was Sir James Tarkenton. Accompanying him, after two years as British commercial consul in New York, were his wife Clare and their thirteen-year-old daughter, Grace.

Sir James was a vigorous man in middle age, about fifty-four. Educated at Oxford's Balliol College, he had trained for law at Gray's Inn and practiced as a solicitor for a dozen years before becoming a banker, then a diplomat. Percy surmised from their initial conversations that Tarkenton planned to seek a seat in Parliament upon establishing a political base after his stint in public service abroad. His wife could not have been more than forty and was probably closer to thirty-five. Her poise and charm reminded him of Philomena, despite the reserve she exhibited, which was typical of her class in England. Grace was so shy and apparently unassuming that Percy hardly noticed her. In time, he would see that behind the young girl's quiet demeanor was a fierce and critical intelligence that absorbed everything that she saw and heard.

The first dinner of the voyage began with turtle soup. A steward next offered a choice of boiled bass with Hollandaise sauce or veal cutlet à la St. Croix. Plates of vegetables – green corn, peas, asparagus, cabbage – were placed at each table for the diners. After the main courses, a uniformed waiter brought a dessert cart to each table a selection of pastries, fruits and nuts. Percy chose a red currant pie and a small bowl of warm, roasted pecans that reminded him of home. The dinner was as good as anything he had enjoyed in New York City. The Collins line spared no expense to provide luxury.

Over the next ten days of the voyage, Percy had time for reflection and preparation. He wrote, as an *aide-memoire* for his own use, a report on his four days of activities in New York City. He read English newspapers that were less than two weeks old so that he could converse on current affairs with the contacts he would soon make.

Percy became acquainted with a number of his fellow passengers. More than a few were well-to-do Americans taking advantage of improved travel opportunities to spend a summer and fall exploring European countries, their own versions of the Grand Tour that their British cousins had done for more than a century.

Three anti-slavery activists, from a New England abolitionist society, were on their way to London to strengthen their associations with their English counterparts in the British and Foreign Anti-Slavery Society. After six days at sea, having learned that Percy Moorhead represented cotton interests in New Orleans, one of them attempted to engage him in a debate on slavery. Percy merely smiled and deflected her by saying he would not disturb the tranquility of a pleasant sea journey by discussing a topic he found so little open to polite discourse as slavery, whether it related to the institutions of ancient Greece, Rome, the Ottoman Empire, Africa or the United States. As long as it was the law of the land and protected by the Constitution, he was bound to accept it as an established tenet of the law and act accordingly. Unable to engage him in debate, the woman left him without further comment.

Sir James commended Percy on his adroit handling of an awkward encounter.

Percy responded, "Surely, sir, after two years among us, you must have formed some opinions about our society."

The Englishman poured Percy a shot of brandy from a wide-base ship's decanter on the table. He spoke with the shrewdness of a diplomat and the camaraderie often found among men trained in law, no matter the jurisdiction of their practice.

"Diplomacy has taught me the prudence of circumspection. As one of my countrymen was fond of saying, 'An ambassador is an honest gentleman sent to lie abroad for the good of his country.' I am reluctant to pass judgment on the views of others who must live with the consequences of their actions."

Grace whispered to her father. "Papa, I believe Mr. Moorhead equivocates."

Her mother said gently, "You must not embarrass yourself to our new friend." Turning to Percy, she said, "Please forgive our daughter. We have raised her to speak as an adult. Sometimes she forgets the privilege must be accompanied by good manners." In keeping with the luxury accommodations of the *Baltic*, Clare – like most of the passengers – was dressed for dinner as though for an elegant restaurant in London, Paris or New York City. Because of their difference in age, Percy wondered if she were a second wife.

Percy chuckled. "No, really. I'm pleased to see that the young lady can speak. These are her first words I have heard aloud in a week of travel. Let me ask her directly. Equivocate is a mighty big word. Why do you say it describes me?"

The girl did not hesitate to look Percy in the eye. She had enormous eyes and very dark hair that covered her ears and, secured at the neck by a bow, tapered as it descended her back almost to her waist. Like her eyes, Grace's mouth seemed disproportionate to her angular face, distinctive – if not pretty.

"An equivocator is someone who uses words to conceal his true feelings. It's not the same as a liar. My father implied that a diplomat must lie."

Percy replied with a certain indulgence, good-naturedly arguing in return without patronizing her youth. "You are certainly forthright, young lady. As a student of rhetoric, I must disagree. Your father's quote is a favorite of those who love puns in order to equivocate. You see, 'to lie abroad' is to sleep abroad, as a diplomat must. The English diplomat who engaged that word play for amusement surely knew his Shakespeare, for we find the same pun in *Othello*."

The young lady was more persistent than the abolitionist. She refused to be deflected. "If the shoe fits, Mr. Moorhead, you should wear it."

"Very well, Miss Tarkenton, if you insist. What feelings do you think I conceal?"

"When the abolitionist challenged you, you neither defended nor condemned slavery. Yet you appear to be an intelligent and educated man. No man of your age can possibly have no opinion on the subject of human slavery."

"My age? Am I already an ancient? And you wish to know my true feelings. Without equivocation." Now Percy was beginning to feel annoyed. Was this child trying to embarrass him? Or was she genuinely seeking a rationalization of slavery from a man of the South?

"Yes. I do."

Percy replied after a moment. He looked her in the eye, speaking without reservation to her, as though she were an adult. "I detest slavery. I regret deeply that any African was ever sent to the New World in chains. But African slavery is an insoluble problem in my society. I fear that it cannot be resolved without great turmoil. The institution of African slavery was not woven into the fabric of the economy and the culture in the Great Britain as it is in our Southern states, first by tobacco and indigo and now by cotton and sugar. Manufacturing has come to dominate our northern areas while we of the South remain tied to commercial agriculture on a grand scale. Every Southerner knows of the revolts of Nat Turner and Denmark Vesey and Louisiana's River Parish rebellion. A humane and enlightened policy towards the Africans among us might prevent future misery. Perhaps gradual manumission as was done in several Northern states would work. But I'm in a minority favoring this."

The annoying young lady persisted. "Why don't you try to do something to achieve your policy?"

Responding with complete candor, Percy said. "It would be ineffective. To be completely honest, it would harm me and my family. I owe more to my wife, my unborn child and my parents than I do to the Africans in our land. I would lose all my clients and become a pauper. We may admire martyrs but few of us choose to emulate their example. No slave would thank me. Those abolitionists who visited our table would still shun me. It is not to slavery that they direct their anger but to the immorality of the slaveholder. Their objection is to sin rather than the well-being of the African."

Percy could not escape her judgment — that his state of virtue was deficient. "I feel your heart is good. But you do not offer hope, Mr. Percy Moorhead."

Percy poured himself another brandy and accorded her the respect he would show an adult, by giving her a lesson on toleration in her own society – without giving offence to her directly. "And you, young lady, possess the admirable qualities of optimism and enthusiasm which are too often confined to youth. I can only counsel patience and prudence. The Roman Catholics of your country had to persevere for nearly three centuries before the act of only a few years ago that allowed them to be elected to Parliament and most Crown offices. Even now, the man who sent me on this journey would not enjoy such privileges in England. He is a Jew who will now serve in the United States Senate. But in England he would be excluded from your Parliament. Religious leaders in your England preach against our institutions while still practicing discrimination against Jews, Africans and Mohammedians. They ignore Jesus's parable of the mote and the beam."

Percy had found weaknesses in her wall of righteousness. She was intelligent and honest enough to acknowledge it. "Perhaps I am too forthright," she said, lowering her huge eyes. Evidently, she knew the parable.

"No, please," he encouraged her. "My words were not meant to chasten you. Don't lose your hopefulness and your assurance. They are charming. They are qualities that will sustain you in times when others would become discouraged. The Romans had a saying, *nil desperandum.*"

Clare and Grace departed for the forward grand saloon while Percy and Sir James went topside to the smoking room. They sat a few yards aft of the starboard paddle box. Except for low, slow swells, the seas were relatively calm. A nearly full moon illuminated the evening.

"I appreciate your patience with our daughter," the Englishman said. "She is not like other girls her age."

"Has she always been so serious?"

"Yes. It is as though she carries a burden of care. She is forever adopting small animals, especially if they are injured. Even people on occasion. If this voyage were to continue for another week after this, I fear you would become her next project in the absence of smaller creatures aboard the *Baltic.*"

"Me? I trust I do not seem a wounded bird or limping puppy."

"No. She simply fixes upon something and becomes intensely focused on what has attracted her attention. Harmless, generally. Maybe even a good, often. But she has never played like other children. Her enthusiasms are more adult than child-like and seem to occupy her identity. What did the poet say? The world is too much with her."

"Ah, Wordsworth. I hope that my business duties permit me a little leisure to view literary landmarks. I'm inclined to share the poet's sentimentality for a lost time. The other side of me is grateful for the industrial spirit that produces a magnificent machine like the one we are on. The *Baltic* is a city afloat. Triton would be no match for this Leviathan. Never have men so comfortably crossed the seas as we do now."

Sir John shared Percy's enthusiasm for modern transportation. "It is an age of wonders. You must find time to visit us. I think you will find our rail connections most convenient – and better appointed compartments than in your own country. We have a home near Oxford, and we are not far from Stratford. We may be there several weeks, adjusting to our return to England before resuming life in London."

The invitation pleased Percy. His forthrightness with Grace had not offended her father. It could prove useful to have a friend in England. "I will make time. Will you practice law?"

"Perhaps. A reason why I am returning to England is that our government is in flux. Mr. Disraeli has been appointed Chancellor of the Exchequer. He wishes for me to serve in the government he has formed with Lord Derby. The Board of Trade needs to be apprised of all present and future issues concerning commercial relations with the American states. I shall meet with Mr. Disraeli and we shall see if our interests coincide. If not, I will return to my old chambers, at least for a time."

ॐॐ — ॐॐ

Early one morning, nearly nine days into the voyage, Percy was on deck and thought he saw land. A crew member making his way forward said they were off Mizzen Head, a point to the west of Cape Clear, Ireland. The *Baltic* was steering east by south, fresh wind rising, plowing ahead at eleven knots, in thick weather and rain. Several gannets, goose-like, with white body and black wings, were flying near, as though curious about the behemoth that was belching smoke and churning the water with its paddles. Percy Moorhead felt a splendid solitude amidst the waves lapping against the ship, light raindrops pelting his face, impelled by forces far greater than himself yet not in struggle against them, a brief interlude with nature before returning to the commercial assignments before him, with consequences he could neither anticipate nor imagine.

Chapter 17

# Liverpool

With most of her passengers on deck, the *Baltic* arrived at Liverpool. Despite the expansion of the Albert Docks and construction of new warehouses, the *Baltic* was too large to be easily accommodated. The captain had to moor her in the Mersey River, while the passengers waited for the turn of the tide to bring sufficient water for entering one of the three docks used by American steamers. Even then, it was a tight fit for the huge bulk of the vessel. At last, all were unloaded. The firm, solid mason-work of the Liverpool dock where he landed was in sharp contrast to the log-wharves passengers experienced in New York. Percy bade the Tarkenton family goodbye, promising to call upon them in Oxford at his earliest opportunity.

It would take several hours for the ship's luggage and trunks to be unloaded along with the ship's cargo, so Percy explored the city in the area around the docks. A wide terrace had been completed along the river, the Marine Parade. It was much used as a promenade. Several ladies offered him companionship, but he politely declined their services, without inquiring as to their fee.

After gathering his two bags, Percy was taken by a hansom cabman to the Adelphi Hotel, Ranelagh Place. The Adelphi became his base of activity for the next four days while he undertook the round of visits he had arranged by post with the principals of Rathbone Bros. & Co. and Leech, Harrison Partners – the chief trading companies for his clients. He became familiar with their activities and the facilities available for mercantile transactions. He absorbed as much information as he could about all aspects of importing and exporting goods in commerce with England – warehousing, insurance, permits and customs duties. It was work that fascinated him. What he learned would sustain his business dealings long into the future, first as a lawyer, later as government agent, and finally as an entrepreneur. And he discovered that he was really competent in perceiving and understanding hidden webs in commercial transactions.

Percy first paid a call upon the American consul in the city and learned what he could of the consul's principal activities on behalf of American business. The consulate was housed in a shabby and smoke-stained edifice four stories high, at the lower corner of Brunswick Street contiguous to the Goree Arcade, near some of the oldest docks. That he had located the right building was confirmed when he looked up and saw an enormous golden bald eagle marking the entrance. A throng of seedy-looking characters had to be negotiated through to reach the consul himself on the second floor. The supplicants crowded the stairs and the halls, almost as numerous and needy as the urchins and indigents near the docks.

The vice-consul escorted Percy into the next office and introduced him to the consul, Thomas L. Crittenden. Few consulates were more important for American economic interests than the office in Liverpool; few patronage appointments were so prized as this one. Crittenden was only seven or eight years older than Percy. He was not an imposing figure, average height and slight build, with high cheekbones, heavy eyebrows and long dark hair parted on the left. Percy had prepared for the meeting by inquiring into the consul's background, as he did in most of his dealings with officials and judges. Two reasons for his good fortune struck Percy immediately. First was his father, who was a U. S. Senator from Kentucky at the time of the Mexican War and now held the office of Attorney General of the United States. Just as important was the fact that Tom Crittenden had served as an aide to General Zachary Taylor during the war with Mexico; it was President Taylor who named him consul to Liverpool. When consul Crittenden asked Percy where he had received his legal training, the discussion of Beverley Tucker led to Crittenden telling Percy his father had also studied at William and Mary, under Tucker's father, St. George Tucker. Such connections between men were the lubricant that could smooth future encounters when Percy might need assistance in representing a client.

"I don't mean to take up much of your time," Percy apologized, "having appeared here without appointment. I wish only to introduce myself so that I may in the future seek whatever assistance you might render me or one of our clients."

Crittenden shook his head in a gesture that showed that it was no imposition. He smiled, saying, "Mr. Moorhead, you are a welcome break. Most of my time is spent relieving and sending home American seamen, who by accident or misfortune are left destitute. You probably encountered some of them in the passageway and on the stairs. Unfortunately, the duties of the office also carry me to prisons, police-courts, hospitals, lunatic asylums, coroner's inquests, death-beds, and funerals. The consulate brings me in contact with insane people, criminals, ruined speculators, wild adventurers, diplomatists, brother-consuls, and all manner of simpletons and unfortunates, all of whom are our fellow citizens or claim to be."

After swapping stories about their time in Mexico, the two men agreed to have dinner together before Percy parted for London. Both thought it likely that their paths would cross again.

At each of the Liverpool business offices Percy visited over three days, he left a calling card with his name and his business address in New Orleans. Cards were rarely used in New Orleans, but they were regarded as fashionable in New York and in England. In a notebook he kept records of each person he met and relevant information as to costs and scheduling necessities. Anticipating the needs of clients, he visited a dozen or more hotels and inns, together with nearby restaurants, to be able to make recommendations for lodging and meals. These, too, found their way into his notes. They might also be useful should he return to Liverpool.

The large presence of the Irish in Liverpool surprised Percy. One of the bankers he called upon explained that it was due to the depressed state of both farming and labor in Ireland and the ease of transit between Dublin and Liverpool. The voices of the Irishmen in the street sounded somewhat like his own father's, though less refined than his father, who had cultivated English pronunciation and mannerisms in speech. He must insist his father tell him more about his background. "Anglo-Irish" now seemed to Percy far too vague, even less certain in his mind than his fellow citizens in America who were described as "Scots-Irish," as though it were a distinct heritage carrying a rugged ethnic pride. His father had never made clear whether the English side was paternal or maternal. From an off-hand comment once by his father, in a conversation Percy had only overheard, that Moorhead was a good English name, Percy had assumed his grandmother was Irish. His father's speech must have reflected the influence of both parents. He knew his father had been a purser aboard a merchant vessel, but he had never told him from what port he sailed. Perhaps Liverpool? He wondered. Had his father walked these same streets?

Chapter 18

# Manchester

Curiosity about cotton's journey brought Percy at an early hour to the Edge Hill station to board a train to Manchester. Over a hundred textile mills were operating in Lancashire. The damp climate of the region provided the conditions needed for keeping cotton yarns moist and less likely to break. Before nine o'clock he arrived at Manchester's Victoria Station, which dominated the Long Millgate area, and enjoyed a leisurely breakfast at a cafe near the station.

One of the Liverpool agents had suggested to Percy that he contact the firm of McConnel & Co. They were the largest importers of American cotton. From the station, it was a relatively short distance up Swan Street to the Ancoats district of the city. The sun seemed to dim as he approached the area. He felt a low vibration and heard a low hum from the massive amounts of machinery concentrated in the district. The entire area was laced with canals, the principal means of transporting cotton to the warehouses and mills and then the finished fabrics that streamed from thousands of looms housed in brick buildings five to eight stories high. Major canals with many branches connected each building. Percy felt he was entering a labyrinth, but no threads here were spun by a king's daughter.

Black and gray smoke billowed from the stacks of the factories, powered by huge coal-fired steam engines, the smoke rendering the sun a disk without rays. The engines drove the spinning mules that turned fiber into thread and looms that wove the thread into fabric. Steam had long ago supplanted the water wheels that first powered the looms.

At the entrance to McConnel's Redhill Street Mill, Percy introduced himself to a foreman as a cotton grower from Bayou Sara, Louisiana on a business excursion. He said he wanted to follow the progress of the cotton grown in his fields from seed to finished product. The foreman asked Percy to wait for a few minutes. He returned with a young man, maybe a year or two younger than Percy. He said his name was Jockie, and he was a nephew of the McConnels who owned the mill. He would be pleased to escort the visitor on a tour.

They started at the ground level. Here Percy thought he saw something he had not seen since arriving in New York several weeks ago. Black men were engaged in grueling labor, pushing wheelbarrows with heavy loads, looking like half-human beasts, trapped in an inescapable maze under an industrial curse. Drawing nearer, he saw the wheelbarrows were filled with coal and the workers were white men, only black in appearance with coal dust and grime from their job. Inside, there were more grim looking laborers, stoking the furnaces of the boilers in the engine room. In New Orleans, white men seldom engaged in such heavy work.

Jockie showed him warehouses where cotton bales were stored until the bales were broken. The cotton was opened and went through willowing, scutching, carding and slubbing before finally entering the spinning area. Jockie led Percy to a cavernous room, perhaps 150 feet by 100 feet. Thousands of bobbins, atop spindles, were filling with yarn. The machines were in constant movement and Percy found it difficult to hear his guide over the clatter, rattle and clanging that filled the air.

"On these floors we have self-acting mules with 400 spindles each," Jockie explained in a near shout. "Overall in this mill, we operate 276 carding machines, and 77,000 mule spindles. We must keep the spinning rooms hot and damp year-round to prevent the cotton threads from breaking. I would take you along the machines but they throw off oil from lubricating the spindles."

"What are those boys doing?" Teenagers were stepping up on the back of the spinner frames.

"Those are our doffer boys. When a bobbin is full, it must be replaced and a new one begun. That's doffing. You'll see the same function when we get to the looms."

Descending again, Jockie led Percy to the weaving shed. Again, the room was immense, even larger than the last, with row upon row of looms, heavy metal apparatuses in large frames. Percy guessed that there must be a thousand or more of them. Metal shafts ran along the floor and were connected by other shafts and cranks. The looms were powered by leather belts from overhead cross-shafts, on bevel gears from the line shaft that ran the length of the shed. These mechanisms were all tied together to shuttle the looms back and forth. The air was heavy with dust from the cotton, and the floors were oil-soaked. Many of the workers were barefoot. All were lightly clad – women in shifts, men and boys in shirts and rude trousers fastened with cord. Young children, both boys and girls, some not above nine years old, moved rapidly among the machines.

Jockie noticed the expression on Percy's face. He reassured his concerned guest, "The young ones we call scavengers. Debris and droppings from the spindles would foul the machines and bring them to a halt if they weren't removed. The smaller workers can scoot under the looms where an adult can't get. Their fingers can reach into tight places."

Percy pointed to a boy working near him, "And those who stand up in front of the looms and do something with the threads?"

"They're piecers. When a thread of a spindle breaks, they piece the ends together again. If this isn't done quickly, the weaving must stop until re-attaching can be accomplished. If we had stayed in the spinning rooms longer you'd have seen much the same."

The worked looked dangerous to Percy. He asked, "Do you lose many fingers?"

"Well, no more than usual. Children are safer to use, especially the girls. They've got smaller fingers and are more agile. It's no more a hazard than working on a farm. If they were in workhouses, orphanages or back in Ireland, they'd be starving. Here they have steady pay and contribute to the family expenses. If they're under thirteen, we don't work them more than 6 or 7 hours a day, and they get time off for schooling."

"And the older ones?"

The English guide didn't care for the direction of Percy's questions. "No more than 12 hours a day. Breaks to eat. If you look on the walls and on the cross beams above you, you'll see we have gas lighting throughout the mill. We don't need it in the summertime like now. But we can keep working no matter how short the days are."

Percy looked around and said, "I see."

Jockie resisted the disapproval in his guest's voice. "It's a free country. Everyone who labors here does so by choice. They come here from all over England and from Ireland, Scotland and Wales. These factories employ over 300,000 people in and around Manchester. Jobs and wages. We pay a fair wage for a good day's work. The young people grow up and become skilled laborers, as you see. They become the weavers or the tacklers who gait the looms and make repairs and adjustments. May I inquire of you, Mr. Moorhead, how many acres of Louisiana earth do you have in cotton cultivation?"

Percy was surprised by the question.

"About fourteen hundred total, with the two plantations – out of seventeen hundred. The rest is in corn, cattle and timber."

"Very substantial. Imagine, if you will please, that there were no mills of Manchester. Where would your cotton find a market? Spinning machinery in England gave birth to the cotton cultivation in America."

"And without our cotton, would there be a Manchester?"

"Precisely. My point, indeed. We depend on one another. Without your slave labor, we would not have cheap raw cotton. Without our efficient machinery and the labor that keeps it running, you would have no one to transform fine fiber into finished fabric."

Percy had no desire to quarrel with Jockie, who seemed a decent sort of chap, despite the mill's dependence on harsh working conditions and child labor. Did a ten-year-old labor by choice? Did a twelve-year-old orphan girl have other opportunities for employment? He thanked his host and wandered the Ancoats district for another hour or so before catching his train back to Liverpool.

෯෯ — ෧෧

What Percy had seen at Redhill Street Mill was repeated on street after street. Mills, large and small, with machinery making thread and fabric. Why, he wondered, was all this an ocean away? Wouldn't it make more sense to collect the cotton in New Orleans or Mobile or an inland city near where cotton was grown and turn it into cloth there? Instead of ships taking baled cotton to New York for shipment to Liverpool and Manchester and then bringing fabric and clothing back to New York and Boston and New Orleans, why not ships taking finished goods from New Orleans to those same destinations? What a business opportunity there was!

He nearly stumbled in his reverie. He looked around. He was in a block of poorly-built row houses off Bengal Street. He turned to a long-haired old man, in a ragged jacket with a furrowed face. "Where am I?" he asked.

"Gerrards Court," said the man.

"Who lives here?"

"Whoever." The man had an Irish accent and shrugged. He was listless, even resigned.

"Is this where the mill workers live?" Percy persisted.

"Some's. Some's don't have jobs. Used to. Live off my wife and daughter now."

"Which way to Victoria Station?"

The man pointed the direction. As he walked, crossing over a canal bridge, Percy came to grips with the obstacles to his business fantasies.

No machines. The spinning mules and the looms that were here in abundance would all have to be imported into the cotton states. The northern states had imposed heavy tariffs on imports of machinery from England. Comparable equipment was not available in the United States.

No workers. No would-be entrepreneur in the cotton-growing states could draw on a pool of labor to operate the complex precision machines Percy had observed. Employing slave labor in textile mills would require a massive capital outlay. A single field worker would cost in Louisiana the equivalent of ten years of payments to two doffer boys or scavengers, and the slave-owner had to house, feed and clothe his slave. In Manchester, all the workers had to provide for themselves on their meager wages. An injured slave was a capital loss on a plantation. An injured mill-employee in Manchester was instantly replaced and forgotten. There were many poor whites throughout the cotton states, but they were mostly rural people, accustomed to working out-of-doors. They were not peasants who worked the lands of an upper-class gentry. They were not the sort of people who would submit to orders and indignities from mill foremen. Most were small farmers who would sooner starve than send their small children to risk life and limb for excruciating work in a dirty, dangerous factory.

Land was the difference. There were millions of acres of open land in America, free, or nearly so, for food crops and settlement. In England, there were no lands for the poor, for the homeless, for the unemployed.

Land also explained why slavery was the only method for obtaining field workers. Without forced labor, there could be no cultivation of cotton. No one, black or white, could be paid wages to toil so hard in the earth for another if they could work their own parcel of land, however small it might be. Cities with an impoverished population might give rise to wage labor but not a countryside where cheap land is available. Without cotton, there would be no reason to bring Africans to America. Without African slave labor there would be no cotton plantations. Get rid of one and the other ceases as well. Free America's Africans, and they would disperse like leaves on the wind. The fallow cotton fields would be overgrown in a season and would return to forest in a single generation. Lacking slave labor and open land, cotton suitable nations like Egypt and India would not develop plantation economies.

On his train ride back to Liverpool Percy could not shake off his memories of the children he saw and the dismal tenements of Ancoats. Bondage, at least on the Moorhead plantation, was not the moral equivalent of the wretched conditions of labor in Manchester. People might be property on plantations, but in the factories they were temporary extensions of the machinery, to be consumed and tossed aside when no longer useful to keep the machines running. Slavery was not needed in England because the factories could draw on the workhouses and orphanages, on the starving Irish, on the desperate peasants displaced from the English farms where their ancestors had worked since before Roman times. Peasants and children were cheaper by far than chattel slaves.

Chapter 19

# London Town

O n Friday morning, after an uncomfortable night in Liverpool, depressed by the conditions he had observed in Manchester, Percy boarded a railway car on Lime Street in Liverpool and joined the London and North Western Railway to carry him the 200 miles to London. After establishing himself at the Grosvenor Hotel, recommended to him by Benjamin, he passed Sunday sight-seeing in the city. On Monday, he resumed his calls upon clients and financial houses as he had in Liverpool. He felt comfortable in the company of the merchants and bankers. If any regarded him as an unsophisticated or boorish Yankee, they did not convey it in any way of which he was cognizant. He was not the tobacco-spitting, whiskey-swilling philistine they associated with America.

On Wednesday Percy called on the last of his appointments, Mr. Russell Sturgis, a Boston-born investment banker with Baring Bros. & Co., with offices on Bishopsgate. The Barings company felt they had a special relationship with Louisiana; Barings had financed the Louisiana Purchase, the greatest real estate transaction in history.

Benjamin had engaged in transactions with Sturgis before the latter had relocated to London. Russell Sturgis was a rare man of the world, as Benjamin had described him. A lawyer from Harvard, he had abandoned the law in Boston to move to Canton and Macau, where he represented the interests of John Perkins Cushing, a merchant and opium trader. Sturgis founded several trading firms in the Orient before returning to Boston.

"How did you end up in London?" Percy asked the affable Sturgis.

"We missed the boat," he replied with a sly grin. "I was taking my family from Boston to China via London a year ago. The China clipper we were to catch sailed without us. Our vessel was late in making the connection. While awaiting another passage, I was offered a permanent association with this firm, due in part to a family connection. My new wife was apprehensive about our ultimate destination. She proved most persuasive in a decision to remain here."

Percy immediately liked the easy-going banker, despite a hint of vanity in the man's dress and bearing – reflecting expensive tastes. "I'm not sure how much you know about the purpose of my visit. Mr. Benjamin made clear that he preferred that there be no written communications relating to our contemplated arrangements for the Tehuantepec project."

Sturgis leaned forward from behind the desk. "May I offer you tea?" He lightly jingle-jangled a brass tea bell by its ebony handle. A young man appeared to take an order.

Sturgis stirred sugar into his tea and offered a Scottish biscuit to his visitor. "Of course, my dear Percy. We are men of discrimination. We must be as discreet with our communications as we are with the associations we choose to make. The pieces have been falling into place over the past year. Falconnet has made repeated trips between Mexico, the United States and London on behalf of the Committee of Mexican Bondholders. He has been privy to all that has happened with the Hargous grant, which is the source of Senator Benjamin's interest. He has advised us of his dealings with the senator. We are prepared to go forward with advancing him the necessary commitments – up to $700,000."

"The Senator will be most pleased. Tell me what I need to do to bring this to its happy end."

"We need only your signing the surety documents and providing the cotton commitments to back them. Then, with your guidance, we will structure the assignment agreements so that when and if Mr. Sloo defaults on payment to us and Falconnet, we can assign the Mexican railway rights to a party of your designation."

"As it happens, I have prepared the instruments and if they meet your approval, the transaction will be complete." Percy had with him drafts of the commitments and assignment agreements. He, Sturgis and two clerks of Baring Bros. completed their work in mid-afternoon and Percy left their offices with copies penned by Baring Bros.' scriveners.

Sturgis walked Percy to the door. "When you return to London, look me up. With Benjamin taking his seat in the Senate, we will surely have matters of mutual interest. We could use your services."

Percy was elated. He could almost hear Big Tom chuckling and saying, as he did when Percy went off to Princeton and later to Williamsburg, "You be chopping in tall cotton now, Masta Percy."

Chapter 20

# Godstow

H aving completed his rounds a day earlier than anticipated, Percy determined to visit the Tarkenton family in the vicinity of Oxford. In America, he had never met a man with the title of a knight, nor how a man might come by it. Surely, thought Percy, the title "Sir" must represent the chivalrous qualities that Sir James had exhibited when they met aboard the *Baltic*. Like Percy, he was trained in law, and they had interests in common. Should Percy return to England, the Tarkentons were the sort of people he would like to know. By post, which he found was extraordinarily fast and efficient throughout England, he notified them of his intentions.

It was but sixty miles by rail from London to Oxford. A man servant of the Tarkentons met him at the station, collected his bags, and took him by carriage the few miles to the Tarkenton estate, adjacent to the hamlet of Godstow. The servant let him out at the porch of a two-story home made of grey stone. He noticed first the simple symmetry of the dwelling, fire chimneys at either end, windows of identical size above and below on the front. This was the understated, even modest, elegance of the English gentry. Families of the Tarkentons' status had no need for ostentation, unlike most of Percy's wealthy acquaintances in New Orleans, who competed to see who among their class could adorn their palatial plantations with the most columns, even when structurally unnecessary.

Before he took another step, the dark oak door of the house opened. Sir James and Clare stepped out to greet their American guest. Percy felt instantly at ease. Their invitation to visit had not been mere politeness. Inside, they had him remove his traveling jacket and join them in tea, attended by a female servant. He could not help but be struck throughout his stay in England by the number of white servants that he encountered. Later, he learned that the young woman who was cook and maid was the wife of his carriage driver, both in their mid-twenties. They were caretakers of the property when the Tarkentons were away. They lived in an apartment above the stone barn. What Percy knew of feudalism resembled the relationship that still persisted between the English upper-classes and their retainers. More than one servant in the household might be a third or fourth generation resident.

As Percy explained his activities in Liverpool and London, omitting details of his dealings with Baring Bros. & Co. and his disturbing experiences of Manchester's industrial squalor, he became aware of a figure in the garden. The glass of the windows in this, the sitting room of the house opening out to the back, was old, hand-blown glass. It distorted images from outside. Perhaps fifty or sixty yards from the broad flag-stone back porch, a figure was walking from one tree to another and stopping at each tree for a few minutes. After stealing brief glances, so as not to seem distracted from his congenial hosts, Percy discerned that it was young Grace. She appeared to be plucking pieces of paper from low-lying limbs and studying or reading from them. She was much too far away to be heard. Oddly dressed, she wore a boy's cap, a tunic of green, and pant-like leggings.

"Is that your daughter I see out back?" Percy inquired.

Sir James smiled with the indulgence of a father and said "From her perspective it is a regrettable fact. Parents, at her age, are an embarrassment. As you see her, she is playing a role. When in performance she prefers to inhabit the character in every way."

Percy could not come up with a clever response. He might be treading on sensitive ground, though the father's expression was not indicative of any concern. Clare merely nodded in agreement.

"Oh?" he managed awkwardly.

The girl's father said, "Our Grace has embarked on a career as a thespian. How is she to become an actress except by acting? The ground you see as a yard is no yard at all but the stage of Covent Garden. Tomorrow it may be St. James Theatre."

Clare, with similar amusement, added, "I must accept responsibility for her metamorphosis. Soon after our arrival in New York, I enrolled Grace in a proper school for young ladies of good social standing. In addition to literature, she was to learn etiquette and elocution. To provide her with the best examples of proper English, we took her to a performance by our most noted English actress, Fanny Kemble. She had become an American by marriage but remained English to the core. Grace was entirely mesmerized. Fanny's dramatic readings, all alone and dominating the stage for two complete hours, enthralled us with the range and vitality of her impersonations, both male and female. Where did we first see her, James?"

"I believe it was the Stuyvesant Institution, in Broadway," Sir James said to his wife. He continued the story for Percy: "Fortunately my consular duties allowed us to indulge our daughter and to follow Grace's heroine to other venues. We attended performances in Boston, Philadelphia, Lenox. The newspapers were all filled with stories of the bitter divorce her husband put her through. Grace thoroughly sided with Fanny, of course, though the papers were divided as to whom they favored. Her champions portrayed her as a diminutive but strong woman fighting bravely against the largest slaveholder in the state of Georgia. A vicious slave master who would deprive her two young children of their mother as heartlessly as he would sell the children of a female slave from the maternal breast. Her husband Pierce Butler was represented by that most famous American lawyer, Daniel Webster himself – then a U.S. Senator. His co-counsel was George Dallas, your Vice-President and formerly mayor of the city of the marriage domicile, Philadelphia. The press siding with her made sinister even his name change, which they portrayed as opportunistic."

"Pierce Butler wasn't his real name?" inquired Percy, unaware of the famous figure's family history.

It was Clare Tarkenton who responded, picking up the thread of the conversation. "No, it was Mease. His father was a Dr. James Mease, but Pierce Butler dropped his father's name and took the name of his maternal grandfather, so he would receive an inheritance of slave plantations. The grandfather so despised his daughter's husband that he provided that any of his grandsons who changed his last name to Butler would become a joint heir to his fortune."

Percy was taken by the ease with which the couple conversed, complementing one another. Was it despite the difference in their ages, or because of it?

Gesturing outside, Clare said, "Our daughter views the world through the prism of literature. She is made melancholy by the darkness of *Wuthering Heights*. Mr. Pierce Butler, she avers, is the embodiment of Heathcliff's cruelty without his redeeming capacity for love."

Percy knew some of the story of the divorce between Pierce Butler and Fanny Kemble. The name change was new to him. He had assumed that Fanny's husband was son or grandson of the male line of the Pierce Butler who had participated in the Constitutional Convention and had been a Senator. It was his mother who was a Butler. Pierce Butler's partisans made Fanny Kemble out as a masculine figure, devoid of motherly instinct as she abandoned her children to resume her acting career in England. Percy knew nothing of the allusion to *Wuthering Heights* and Heathcliff, whoever he was. The odd name stuck in his memory. He would have to look into this character, whether fact or fiction.

"Perhaps so," was Percy's noncommittal response, pivoting to: "Was Grace able to meet the object of her admiration?"

"Oh, yes," Sir James responded. "Indeed. Fanny Kemble was twice our dinner guest in New York City, once two years ago and again a bit more than a year ago, just before she returned to England. Now that we are on this side of the ocean, Grace hopes to renew her acquaintance with the great actress. Although Grace has every advantage, she believes that women in this country are denied the opportunity to play their proper roles in our society. If Elizabeth and Victoria could be queen, she thinks she at least could become a member of Parliament. It is a harmless affectation on her part now, but should it persist . . . . Well, let's not contemplate that now."

᚛᚛ — ᚜᚜

When Grace appeared again, her attire as Ganymede had been replaced by a blue and white print cotton dress for the dinner prepared by the family's cook. She curtsied to Percy when Clare reminded her that they had met the American on the *Baltic*.

Although she was silent for most of the dinner, Grace finally asked, "Mr. Moorhead, have you a wife and children? You mentioned duties to them when we were on the ship."

Percy was again struck by the size and depth of the child's eyes. "A wife, yes. Our first child will arrive in a matter of a few months."

"Do you have theater in New Orleans?"

"Yes. Several. And opera. And concerts."

"Do you attend? A man who is not moved with concord of sweet sounds cannot be trusted." She spoke with an intensity of feeling that Percy had seen in few adult women, and never in a child.

Clare started to caution Grace against forwardness in speech to a guest, but Percy raised his hand to stay her, despite his irritation at the girl's manner. He replied, "I agree wholeheartedly. Music is a divine gift to man. As I entered your home, I observed a piano in one room. Do you play?"

"Yes."

"Would you play for me?"

Grace looked at her parents for guidance. She was eager to perform, but not without their approval. Sir James looked to Percy but spoke to his daughter. "Our guest must be exhausted from his travels. Perhaps tomorrow would be better."

Percy left no time for the child to respond to her father's effort to discourage her, "Nothing would please me more than an opportunity to hear Grace perform."

Grace needed no further encouragement. She excused herself from the table. The adults followed her into the next room.

For half an hour she played from an anthology she and a tutor had compiled before she had left for America. She performed works of Handel, Mouret and Playel. Her skills were more than adequate but her intonation lacked subtlety. All of the notes were there, yet with none of the emotion of a more accomplished pianist. The performance featured the performer, not the music. Perhaps as she matured . . . .

After Grace finished, she flushed when Percy said with obvious sincerity, "You play exquisitely, Grace. I hope to hear you on stage in London when I return to England in the future."

The odd child excused herself and retired to her room.

Sir James and Percy drank brandy in the drawing room.

Percy slept soundly in the comfort of an upstairs bedroom. Although late July in Louisiana would be suffocating, here in Oxfordshire, England, a pleasant breeze entered through lace curtains. The quiet contrasted with the noises of the English cities and the clatter of the inter-city railroads. He dreamed of Philomena and awoke twice when he realized she was not next by him. Now that his trip was nearly over, he could indulge in the emotion of missing her. She had become so much a part of his life that her absence left him lonely, even in Liverpool, London and now Oxford, where he was preoccupied with many new people and business activities. He prayed she was all right and nothing would happen to their child.

The cook served a hearty breakfast of eggs, a rasher of bacon, beans and toast. "Mistress Tarkenton says you Americans prefer strong coffee at breakfast rather than tea. May I offer you some?" Her face was plain and thin. When she spoke, Percy became aware of the small gap between her two front teeth.

"By all means, please. That is very thoughtful."

Sir James entered through the kitchen. By his attire, he appeared to be returning from an early morning ride.

"I hope you don't mind my leaving you. You were asleep. Grace and I rode to a neighbor's where I left her for the day. I have a few errands in Oxford. Perhaps I could offer you a tour of the city and the university? We will then see you off to your Liverpool train early tomorrow."

"Splendid," said Percy. He was grateful that the self-absorbed daughter was out of the picture for the day. His interest in her playing had been sincere, but he didn't relish entertaining any more of her impertinent questions. She apparently regarded Southern men as boorish slave drivers like the insufferable Mr. Pierce Butler, the cruel American Heathcliff.

## Chapter 21

# Oxford

The carriage left Sir James and Percy at the Oxford Post Office under the Town Hall, near the center of the city. Eben, the driver, was instructed to return in four hours to the same location. Percy's host had more than a dozen letters to dispatch. When Tarkenton inquired whether Percy were a student of history, Percy admitted he was deficient in many areas of knowledge and had only the vaguest of notions of the history of the British Isles, outside of Tucker's *Blackstone* and what he had absorbed from the plays of William Shakespeare.

Sir James took him first to Balliol College, his old school of three decades earlier. They entered its court by a handsome Gothic gate. Facing the entrance was the College chapel, beautifully ornamented with painted glass representing Biblical scenes and stories. On the left stood the Hall, a large and lofty room hung with portraits of Balliol luminaries. Sir James pointed to the Master's House and then to the spot across the street where Ridley, Latimer, and Cranmer suffered death by fire in 1555. The names and context meant nothing to Percy.

"Bloody Mary," said the English host, with evident disapproval.

"Of course," said Percy, as though he understood. "Lovely.

Your Balliol."

"Yes. An ancient seat of learning. A proud history." Sir James's manner assumed more gravity as he spoke. "At one time, Balliol was one of the richest, most illustrious colleges of the University."

"Is its glory past?"

"You must understand. Two centuries ago, when Balliol was at its height, Oxford became the English capital, for a government in internal exile. Our Civil War caused an abrupt drop in student numbers at our college. As a consequence, revenue was reduced to almost nothing. The College was forced to support the King's army, and we had to give to him not only most of our ready cash and all of our domestic silver. Perhaps we are only now recovering."

Percy was struck that his guide spoke of the distant past as though he were a college member during that period. He asked, "Did the College favor the King? Or the Parliament?"

"Both and neither. Obstinate men prevailed on both sides. Obdurate men. Most were unwilling to compromise – insisting always on their prerogatives, whether Parliament or Crown. How many men gave their lives for nothing over a period that spanned seven years – or twenty years if we count the period to the Restoration of the monarchy in 1660? What was accomplished? Very little in relation to our terrible losses."

"Surely there were men of principle and integrity."

"Men choose sides for different reasons. No doubt some had noble aims and principles. Others were venal and vengeful. Ideas, my friend, even principles, are perfectly fine things. Until we try to live them out to their fullest. Then they become monsters that devour us and all that is dear and precious. Worse than Cronus eating his own children. Consider the horrors of the French Revolution for the principles of liberté, égalité, fraternité. For us, the facts remain – a Stewart named Charles was king at the beginning of our Civil War and a Stewart named Charles was the king at the end. A hereditary monarch who wanted control of Parliament was murdered only to be replaced by a hereditary Protector who wanted control of Parliament. Then we returned to our monarchy. And all for what?"

Percy was surprised by the vehemence of his host, who was otherwise the epitome of English reserve. He asked, "Are you bitter?"

Sir James' history lesson was not without purpose. It was a cautionary tale for his new American friend. "Not at all. This blessed isle is still here and we prosper. An awful fever seized us. The illness has inoculated us from like outbreaks and contagion. Were it not for our period of civil strife, we may have experienced something worse than the madness of the French. I tell you all this as warning. What I observed in my two years of residence in your country left me in doubt. Men of compromise in your Senate are being replaced by firebrands on either side of your controversies. There is talk of states' rights and secession."

Percy asked, "What would you have us do?" It would seem the Englishman was more attentive to American political developments than Percy himself was, even though he worked with a U. S. Senator. But it was more than a matter of a lack of interest on Percy's part. He had tried to close his mind to the South's grievances against the North from his first days of studying law with Beverley Tucker. He had admired his law professor but thought Tucker's fixation on Southern independence diminished the clarity of his teaching on common law subjects and on procedure. Accordingly, Percy distanced himself from the controversies of states' rights in law school and continued his avoidance once he represented clients with strong and clashing opinions.

Sir James was diplomatic in his response, just as he had been as consul in New York. "Seek wisdom. But that is weak counsel. Was the advice of Tiresias heeded?"

"I hope your concerns are unfounded. Senator Benjamin, I know, will do all he can to calm the waters. I'm afraid my teacher, Judge Tucker, was among those advocating division."

"I see. Unfortunate. Come, let us cross over and view the two gems of our University. Our Sheldonian Theatre and the Bodleian Library just on the other side of it."

Percy followed Sir James over to Broad Street. They entered the theatre grounds by a gate. The Sheldonian was a massive circular stone building, with a gorgeous, well-lighted interior.

"The Theatre can seat 3,000 people. Magnificent for performances and for all ceremonial occasions. It was built soon after Charles II ascended the throne."

Looking around and up, Percy said, "There's something familiar about the architecture."

"It was designed and built by Sir Christopher Wren, who took his ground-plan from the Theatre of Marcellus, at Rome."

Gesturing to the top of the theatre, Percy said, "Well, that explains it. Look at the cupola. If I were to take you on a tour of my College, William and Mary at Williamsburg, our principal building is said to have been built from plans of Sir Christopher Wren. It is topped by just such a cupola as this one."

A day later, Percy was on a northbound train to Liverpool. It would be a decade before he again would have occasion to call upon Sir James Tarkenton. When he did, it would prove to be a fortunate association.

☙☙ — ❧❧

Percy was back in New Orleans by mid-August. Phil had not let pregnancy slow her down; she had managed well in her husband's absence. He immediately noticed she had rearranged the furniture in the townhouse and had purchased a new sofa and drapes for the room where they entertained guests. He was pleased by her initiative and her taste.

Hugging Phil, Percy said, "You're making this place your own."

"I hope you don't mind. Do you like it?"

"Very much!" he replied. "Mother spent little time here. My father's taste tends to the austere."

"Come see what I've set aside for the baby's room upstairs," she said, taking her husband by the hand.

֍֍ — ֍֍

When his luggage arrived from the steamship later that afternoon, Percy had his wife stay upstairs while he prepared the drawing room for his surprise. From a steamer trunk he pulled a carefully padded small crate. It housed a rosewood music box, a little more than two feet wide and eleven inches high. A wreath of flowers of contrasting wood was inlaid on the top. Inside was an intricate Swiss mechanism that operated by a cylinder whose pins struck the teeth of a comb to produce mandolin-like notes. After winding the mainspring with a key, the cylinder could produce twelve different tunes. Percy placed the music box on the table in front of the new sofa and set the cylinder in motion on "Londonderry Air," while calling Phil to come back down. As she descended the stairs, she saw what Percy had brought her. Her pleasure broke into a broad smile.

"It's beautiful!" she gushed with childish delight. "Where on earth did you find it?"

"A magical little shop of books and musical instruments in Oxford. It plays eleven more tunes, including "Drink to me with Only thine eyes," "Annie Laurie," and my favorite, "Greensleeves.""

"Oxford? I thought you were going just to Liverpool and London."

"Oh, I did. But I had time for side trips to Manchester and Oxford. You must see Oxford. On the *Baltic* going over I met an interesting couple and their daughter. The Tarkentons, Sir James and Clare. The girl I think was Grace. Both from respected old families. He's a lawyer and diplomat and will probably stand or run for Parliament or whatever they say they do for elections over there."

Phil ran her hands over the beautiful music box, admiring the craftsmanship of the wood and ingenuity of the mechanism. "That's wonderful. Exactly the sort of association Judah would want you to make and cultivate. Indeed, *Sir* James. Your shall be Sir Percy, my extraordinary husband. Now put your hand here and feel our little son kick. He began doing that just in time to welcome you home."

*Chapter 22*

# The Count and Companions

A fire of red oak burned in the corner in Percy's office, an odor of seasoned wood in the warm air. The three men at the office table opposite Percy had their backs to the fire and were comfortable in its glow.

"Mr. Moorhead, we have a business model," said the man in the middle. In his early 40s, his name was Alonzo McIntyre. "We have had success with it in Memphis, St. Louis and two other cities. We see no reason why it won't be even more successful in New Orleans."

Benjamin had told Percy what to expect of McIntyre – a good head for business opportunities, a reputation for integrity, yet a man always concealing his wariness of others ready to take advantage of him. Percy observed that the man was well-dressed but not ostentatious – he made a good impression by not seeking to make an impression. He spoke with assurance, not seeming over-eager, as he made his overture for representation. "This," thought Percy, "is the sort of man with whom I wouldn't mind working."

The man on his right next spoke, Damon Simmons, the accountant of the syndicate. He wore pince-nez spectacles; dark hair descended his oval skull to narrow shoulders. His voice had a pronounced nasal quality. Percy smiled at the thought that perhaps it was because the small man's glasses fit too snugly. His large head and leonine mane made Simmons appear larger than he was.

"It is a universal trait of men," Simmons began, "to enjoy games of chance. Where we find civilized people, we find gaming. We offer something more than the desire to better oneself through an encounter with chance or fate. We offer an experience. Instead of the tawdry surroundings of saloons and backrooms, we provide our dinner guests, our clientele, with an elevating experience. We provide an environment congenial to gentlemen and their ladies, where they can spend an evening in the company of like persons of breeding and substance. Our establishments are not saloons but gaming emporia. Each is a supper club, where refined members of the community can congregate for an elegant meal, genteel music and honest games among like-minded individuals. Our croupiers and dealers are required to wear evening dress. We do not accept wagers from those who cannot afford to accept a loss."

Luigi Ottavio, the one they called the Count, took his turn in the presentation, as if on cue. Percy surmised it was a routine pitch they made to investors, lawyers and government authorities in cities up and down the Mississippi and Ohio rivers. The Count's exquisite wardrobe showed the styling and needlecraft of a Parisian tailor. Whether his accent was French, Italian or invented, Percy could not say.

"And ve turn avay professional gamblers who make their livings by nefarious practices, by the dark arts of card marking and enhanced dice. All bets are with the games provided by the house. There are no tables set aside where patrons may be fleeced by *poseurs* pretending to be novices. Ve maintain dossiers on every professional card sharp who plies his trade on the riverboats on the Missouri and Mississippi Rivers and their known accomplices. Ve can identify the itinerant gambler who goes from city to city in search of rubes and suckers. None enters the doors of our emporia. If a guest of ours appears agitated or in danger of becoming volatile, ve gently escort him to another room until he becomes calm. Ve always maintain an atmosphere of decorum and propriety. Anyone visiting one of our salons vould find it the equal of any in Paris or Homborg."

"Gentlemen, your reputation precedes you," Percy said. "Mr. Benjamin has visited several of your establishments in his frequent travels and tells me that they are unique. He regrets he cannot be here. But please tell me what I can do for you."

Percy's fine clothing, professional manner and air of bonhomie reassured the three visitors. He knew just how to make clients feel comfortable that they were associating with one of their own sort.

McIntyre resumed. "Experience has taught us the need for competent legal representation at the earliest date of entry into a new venue. It is better to anticipate than to respond."

The Count interjected, *"nimia cautela non nocet."* Was that a twinkle that Percy detected behind the Count's monocle?

Percy smiled and replied, "I agree. There is no harm in erring on the side of caution. And what are your present needs? Simply to have representation on retainer? For future contingencies?"

"Rather more," McIntyre continued, warming to his subject and showing his preparation for the meeting. "New Orleans has, may we say without giving offence to you, its own reputation that precedes it. Our identity cannot be tainted by corruption. If we enter a new market by bribery or shady payments we will not gain the confidence of the community in our own integrity. A reputation for dishonest dealings is fatal, experience teaches us, to a business whose patrons must believe that dame Fortune possesses an incorruptible character." Pausing as he assessed the young lawyer's reaction, McIntyre said, "Wouldn't you agree, Mr. Moorhead?"

Leaning forward in his chair, Percy replied, "Wholeheartedly, Mr. McIntyre. Distrust is a solvent that will wash over and dissolve even mighty institutions."

"Very good sir. Having agreed on that, I must say we will need licenses and approvals to launch a new club in this city as in any other. Local officials may be more reticent in making demands if they are approached by an officer of the court rather than by outsiders. At a minimum, we need a buffer between us and them. We have a site picked out in the French Quarter but negotiation for its purchase would be better accomplished through an agent instead of one of us. Do you think you are the right man to provide these and other services as we might need?"

"I'm flattered that you have come to me. It would be false modesty if I were to say I am not suitable as your attorney. Have you thought of an appropriate retainer and fee?"

"Yes, it is good to be direct. For similar services in St. Louis our initial engagement was for $12,000 with negotiated fees for specific services thereafter."

Instead of countering, Percy said, "Tell me a little more about your business structure."

This Moorhead fellow was proving more inquisitive than other attorneys in their other locations. McIntyre had not expected such questioning. Had Judah Benjamin assigned a junior attorney to put them off for reasons unknown? He said to the young attorney, "As I mentioned, we are a syndicate. We are the three principals who represent a group of investors. Each investor contributes a portion of the capital in exchange for a share in the profits of each project. Some investors participate in each project but others do not. Thus membership in the syndicate varies by location."

"And for your present project? Have you all of your investors?"

Why should this Moorhead care, wondered McIntyre. "We are at 90% of our targeted funding. Is this relevant? Some of our investors prefer confidentiality."

"What do you anticipate for the remaining 10%?"

"About $35,000."

"Then let me propose this, gentlemen. Let us regard my fee of $12,000 as part of my investment and I will contribute another $22,000 to become a 10% investor in this project. You would in any event have my very best efforts as your lawyer. But I would also have a stake in our success."

Percy had surprised himself as well as his clients. If he were to follow the path of his father and of Judah Benjamin, he must expand his efforts into business ventures as well as the practice of his profession.

"This is unanticipated. May we have a few moments?" McIntyre, it appeared, was the spokesman of the group.

"Certainly." Percy stepped into the antechamber, closing the door behind him. He exited the building on to Carondolet. The rain had almost stopped.

Two blocks away was the bank where his friend Westbrook Haydel had his office. Moorhead's law firm often sent clients to the bank of which Westie was part-owner. The clients needed letters of credit or financing for crops or machinery and equipment. Percy and Westie had talked about the possibility of investing in business together. This gaming house seemed like just the thing for them. If Westie himself wasn't interested, Percy thought he could probably count on him for a loan for his investment.

When Percy returned to his office, he found the door open. The Count and Simmons had put their coats and hats on and were ready to leave. Each shook Percy's hand, broad smiles on their faces, and said they looked forward to working with him as a partner.

"Ve have a boat to board," said the Count. "Und ve leave the hotel, to Havana, then New York."

Percy was elated. McIntyre was left to work out the details over the next few days. Percy and McIntyre sat at the table and sketched out the steps that needed to be taken. They worked out a timetable for securing permits and completion of building renovations. McIntyre took Percy to the disused building they had selected as a desirable venue for their venture. It was on Toulouse, near the Old Levee. Two stories high, it had large open spaces as well as smaller rooms upstairs. It was already well-fitted for gas lighting, a convenience that enhanced the ambiance of an establishment based on nighttime activities – far superior to candles or oil lamps. Percy knew the building was for sale and said he would approach the owner in confidence the next day.

McIntyre said, "It's a little long in the tooth but has a sound enough structure for an older building. These doors aren't inviting, but our contractor says we can knock them out and replace them with double doors that will provide the atmosphere we want."

"Do you have a name for the New Orleans location of your business?" Percy asked.

"*Our* business, Percy Moorhead," said McIntyre in good humor. "You need to think of it in those terms. It gives a man a new perspective. But no, we haven't a name."

"May I suggest one?"

"Most surely."

"Toulouse Gardens. The words have nothing to do with gambling, but they suggest a place where people might visit and socialize."

McIntyre looked at the building and the street sign at the corner. He showed his enthusiasm, "I like it! But please, we prefer the word *gaming*. It suggests entertainment more than risk. The name of a thing is as important as the name of a man, Mr. Moorhead."

"Of course, *gaming*. Let us imagine hanging plants. Flowers. An arrangement of space that reminds the patron of a courtyard. And please, it's Percy."

## Chapter 23

# Alderman Duplessis

The appointment of Percy and Alonzo McIntyre with Alderman Carlos Duplessis was not until 11:00 a.m.. The steamboat north for Count Luigi Ottavio and Damon Simmons was scheduled for boarding at noon. There was time for Percy to join all three of the gaming entrepreneurs for a leisurely breakfast at the St. Charles Hotel. Percy had cultivated the good will of the hotel's morning staff. At his direction, they seated Percy and his guests at a table looking out on the bustling street activities of the river city at its busiest hours. It was a strategic move that Percy often used to his advantage with clients. All who entered or left the hotel passed by Percy's table.

Amusing his new business associates with stories of Louisiana's colorful past, Percy was perfectly positioned to introduce them to the author who was the source of those tales. For after they had enjoyed for a half-hour strong coffee a dapper gentleman with an air of savoir-faire and purpose entered the dining room and directed his steps towards his regular table. In his left hand was a notebook that he carried on his person at all times and a binder with official documents awaiting his signature. A notebook usually had to replaced at month's end as by then it was full of his writing, though his hastily formed words were small and precise. The rims of his glasses were silvery metal; above them was a balding forehead that made his eyes appear even larger. Tufts of hair protruded over his ears. Two black pencils raised their sharpened heads from his jacket pocket. Although twenty years older than Percy, he had a remarkably youthful appearance.

"Charles," said Percy in a friendly greeting as the man drew near.

"Percy," replied the man, nodding in recognition of the bookish young lawyer, whom he had first met at the Moorhead townhouse for a political gathering a year earlier. The two shook hands in the manner of familiars.

Turning to the breakfast table, Percy spoke to his guests. They all stood to meet the man. "Gentlemen, let me introduce Monsieur Charles Gayarre. He is lawyer, a former judge, a raconteur extraordinaire, and presently Louisiana's Secretary of State and foremost man of letters."

Rather than reaching awkwardly across the table to shake hands, the three guests bowed to the well-groomed man before them.

Percy continued, "I say *monsieur* for Charles spent years in France and Spain studying archival documents that have led to his fascinating histories of our state, both in French and English. He promises more to come."

As appreciative of compliments as he was, Gayarre was a creature of habit, eager to begin his writing and execution of formal documents at his own table. It was reserved for him, behind a large planter holding a flowering indoor shrub. It was his office until early afternoon each day. He nodded again and said as he turned to leave, "You are in good hands, *mes amis*," he said to the three men who returned to their seats. McIntyre, Simmons and the Count exchanged glances showing that they were impressed by Percy's association with the state official. It was an impression that Percy had sought, familiar as he was with Gayarre's routine.

Just at that moment two waiters arrived at the table with trays of fresh food that had earned the St. Charles the reputation for serving the best brunch in the city. In turn, each put items on the plates of the four men.

Before Percy had finished two bites of steak and eggs, he saw a couple appear from the interior of the hotel, meaning that they had just come down from the stairs from the rooms above. The man was Percy's brother-in-law, Calvin Bunch. If the woman was a day older than Calvin, then she was certainly a decade older. Perhaps she had looked prettier or younger before the night of drinking and coarse mating the two had experienced.

Preoccupied with one another, the disheveled couple, now seated across the room from Percy and his companions, did not see Percy rise and excuse himself from his table. With mock affability, Percy put his hand on Calvin's shoulder from behind and said, "Why, Calvin Bunch. What a surprise to see you here. Does your Woodville business bring you to our mercantile metropolis?"

If Calvin was surprised or perturbed to see his wife's brother, it did not register on his face. Even if the possibility of encountering Percy had crossed his mind, what was its likelihood in a city of a quarter-million residents. "Business?" he said. Answering the question after a moment, he continued, "Yes, business. Clients. Investors. Bank of Woodville. Your father is not the only man with an eye for opportunity." The words struggled with one another as Calvin tried to find an explanation for being in New Orleans. If he was afraid Percy might report his behavior to his wife or others of her family, he did not show it. Scandal can only be scandal if it is a cause of shame to a person who has behaved scandalously. Calvin had no shame. Indeed, a smirk settled itself upon his face.

Turning to the woman next to him at the table, Calvin said to her, "Noreen, you have the good fortune of meeting a genuine war hero. Private Percy Moorhead. To hear him tell it, he single-handedly defeated a whole company of them Mexicans. Or should

I have said Percy Moorhead, Esquire?"

Sensing Calvin's caustic mood, Noreen giddily joined by responding, "Pleased to meet you Private Percy Esquire." Her mind was muddled by alcohol, a condition that recurred often during any given week.

Still amiable, Percy asked, "And do you live here . . . Noreen, I think I heard Calvin say?"

"I may. If it pleases me. Mr. Bunch and I met on the steamboat down from Memphis. When he boarded at Woodlawn. Not far from his cotton plantation." She was pleased to be with a man of means.

"That would be Wood*ville*. New Orleans may not prove a better venue for you than Memphis. I'm afraid you might find opportunities somewhat limited in here if I'm not mistaken about your calling. Competition will be strong, and the contest usually goes to the young. Don't count on the continuing favor of Calvin here. The cotton plantation is not what the Civil Code would treat as a present interest but instead as a future hope, much as a fisherman aspires that a cast net will return full. And that hope depends entirely on his wife, my sister, who as we speak is at home with their daughter."

Percy's callous words, delivered in sugared tones, were as sharp in their impact as a slap across Calvin's companion's face. Noreen felt exposed that this lawyer had ripped apart the curtain of cultivated cordiality that conceals harsh truth. Calvin seethed.

Leaning more closely to the woman's face and speaking now to Calvin, Percy continued, "But mark you Calvin, though her paint were an inch thick it would not hide what may be seen through the faint half-blush that is exposed along her throat. Pocks that are the outward remains of a visitation of the pox, whether it be called Small or French. Be very careful, Calvin that you not gift Eliza with a souvenir of your ruttings when you return to her."

Calvin grew red in the face and clenched his fists. He started to rise from his chair, but Percy forced him back down. "Son of a bitch," Calvin muttered. "Like your shitass father."

Speaking again to the woman, who was alarmed at the bitterness of the exchange, Percy said evenly, "Ah, do not fear a scene, madam. If Calvin were more a man, or you more a lady, he would already have challenged me to a duel. Alas, you have chosen the company of a coward. He knows well and truly that he must avoid a violent confrontation with me that would be reported to his wife and the rest of our family. Were you now to leave quietly, Calvin can count on my silence to avoid humiliation to my sister. She and I are stuck with him by the legal bonds of marriage but not so with your continued presence."

Hastily the woman left, eager to collect her belongings from the room and to seek a return ticket to Memphis. With downcast eyes, Calvin sputtered impotent oaths at Percy. If he waited for breakfast, it would allow time for Noreen to leave and not add further to his indignity.

Percy returned to the table where his business companions were finishing their breakfast. He sat and ate a final bite as though nothing had just occurred. Awkwardly, McIntyre said "If you have pressing business . . . ."

Smiling, Percy assured the men, "That? It was nothing. An unpleasant acquaintance with whom I have had dealings. A trifle, of which we will hear nothing more."

Count Luigi said in understatement, "Perhaps ve vill find you equally forceful in representing our mutual interests. You demonstrate an uncommon power to intimidate without yourself losing your composure."

Leaving Simmons and the Count to check out of the hotel, Percy and McIntyre exited the St. Charles and walked the few blocks to the new City Hall at Lafayette Square. Alderman Duplessis represented the district in which the Toulouse building was located. No construction or renovation in the district took place without his approval. No license was granted without his concurrence. The recent merger of the municipalities had consolidated New Orleans's government but did little to alter the rules on the ground. The principal rule was that no member of the Common Council would disturb the fiefdom of any other alderman or assistant alderman.

Alderman Duplessis, fiftyish and dark-complexioned, with bushy eyebrows like black centipedes, was courteous. He listened attentively to the out-of-town businessman after Percy introduced McIntyre. Percy fully expected to see little green eyes peep out from the eyebrows at any moment. Behind Duplessis was a pendulum clock, in a dark oak cabinet, on a shelf. Anyone speaking with Duplessis could not help but look back and forth between the man and the clock. A man's eyes would become like the pendulum, back-and-forth, back-and-forth. Duplessis said little, nodding occasionally in apparent acknowledgment of a point, now taking a brief note. When McIntyre finished, Duplessis was silent for a minute and then responded.

"Hmmmm. Well said, sir. Well-said, indeed," commented Duplessis with exaggerated gravity. The centipedes moved up and down on his forehead, now in unison, now opposing one another. Pugnacious, predatory arthropods as Percy recalled from a natural science class at Princeton.

Percy's attention returned to the alderman's disingenuous praise for the gaming proposal. Duplesis told McIntyre, "You may have a project with excellent potential. It could prove very rewarding to you. You have planned well. And it is prudent to hire an attorney to assist you. You must understand, however, this is New Orleans. Not New York or St. Louis. Now that our three municipalities and Lafayette have merged, it is very important that our city's growth not change the city's character. You can appreciate that, I'm sure. Haphazard building and the location of businesses that do not complement existing structures or business activity must be avoided. We have a heritage. People expect to experience that heritage when they come to New Orleans. I'm sure you can understand that, don't you?" The alderman waited for a response.

McIntyre nodded in assent, as he was expected to do. He said, "Let me assure you that our establishment will attract patrons of the best sort. Everything we plan will be first rate."

"Oh, I have no doubt of that. But it is a matter of your project fitting in with the overall character of my district. With existing businesses and those that are in the works and yet to come. Essential. Proper growth, you understand. You can appreciate that."

Again, the silence that sought assent. McIntyre was growing irritated by the coyness of the alderman's manner, a shakedown that demanded complicity from the mark. To show he would not accept the fictive nature of the alderman's expressed concern, he asked, "Is there a plan that we might review to satisfy the Council of the suitability of our project?"

Blandly, the alderman rejoined, "Oh, it's more informal than a written plan. What others in your position often do is to employ a, um, *coordinator* – someone who is familiar with the district's existing businesses. Someone well-versed in local customs."

McIntyre stifled his growing annoyance. He asked, "Perhaps you could suggest a coordinator in your district?" The pendulum behind the alderman continued to swing, back and forth, back and forth.

"Some find Gerald Plauché helpful. I'm sure attorney Moorhead can help you to his office in the Exchange Building." The alderman's bushy-browed eyes returned to the papers on his desk, the gesture dismissing his callers.

With a nod, Percy signaled his client that the meeting was at an end. They both thanked Alderman Duplessis for his time and guidance. On Camp Street, McIntyre was direct in expressing his displeasure with the meeting and Percy's silence. He said "This is not what I expected."

Percy merely smiled and said, "No? You mentioned to me yesterday that you knew of New Orleans's reputation."

"And that's why we want representation. We don't need a translator to tell us that Duplessis's local custom is what the Mexicans call *mordida*."

Percy shrugged off McIntyre's concern, replying, "You needed to hear it for yourself. Alderman Duplessis will be aware of anything that happens in his district. It's better to deal with him sooner than later. Plauché is his man on the street."

McIntyre was not pacified by Percy's calm assurance. "Well, this is not the way we do business. I don't like it. What's next?"

"We make nice. Tomorrow we will have a meeting with Mr. Plauche. He'll let us know what his coordination entails. And yes, in New Orleans *coordination* translates as *mordida*."

"I still don't like it." Percy could sense that McIntyre was beginning to doubt attorney Moorhead's abilities. The client's expression betrayed his thought that he might seek out Judah Benjamin before matters got out of hand with the alderman. He was wary that Duplessis was taking advantage of a younger, less experienced, lawyer.

"Relax," Percy reassured him with a grip on his shoulder. "Enjoy the city. The rain has stopped. Nothing's happened yet. I would show you around, but I need to look in on my wife. We're expecting our first child any day now, and I have someone else I need to see."

Chapter 24

# Westie, A Banker Friend

Percy did not have an appointment with Westie Haydel. He didn't need one. They were close enough that either could drop in on the other to visit if he weren't occupied with a client. Neither would impose on the other's time. Both were making their way in business circles in New Orleans and had recognized they were kindred spirits – young ambitious, rising professionals who were able to combine shrewdness with integrity. After putting his hat and coat on the corner rack, Percy seated himself in a stuffed chair to the right of the banker's desk. He threw one leg over the arm of the chair, comfortable in the informality between close friends.

"You're looking Beau Brumelly today, Westie. New haircut. Whiskers trimmed. Fresh flowers. What's up?"

"Our third anniversary. Flowers are for Polly."

Westbrook Haydel had moved to New Orleans from Mobile right after marrying Miss Dorothy Lockwood, daughter of Herbert and Madeline Lockwood. Herb Lockwood was a New Orleans entrepreneur, importing European goods and buying, selling and investing in real estate in New Orleans and Mobile. When Westbrook came to New Orleans to settle a transaction for a Mobile bank, Herb took him to dinner with his daughter. They hit it off right away. Herb knew he had found a son-in-law. The bright, ambitious young man was quickly placed in a position with many opportunities to share in the wealth of the rapidly growing city of New Orleans. Westie's marriage to Polly cemented a union with her father.

"Congratulations. Let me come to my point right away, Westie. I have an opportunity. I'd be glad to share it with you. If not, I'd like your bank to carry my note."

"All right. What have you got?" Westbrook was round faced, but his light beard extended his cheek line. He was not athletic or vigorous, and in a few more years he would appear soft from sitting at a desk all day. For now, the New Orleans business community saw him as he was, a pleasant professional whose favorable word would open a line of credit that could mean the success of a man's business.

"Let's say you and Polly and Herb and Maddie wanted to go out for the evening on your anniversary. What are your choices? Dinner at a restaurant or a hotel. Maybe there's a theater performance or a concert you've not already attended. New Orleans doesn't offer much more. But what if there were a supper club and gaming emporium where you would encounter only the best of New Orleans society?"

"Gaming emporium? Now there's a mouthful for you," said Westie good naturedly. Aside from his regular cards at the Boston Club, Westbrook Haydel engaged only in the occasional nickel-ante poker game when visiting at a business client's home, strictly as a matter of public relations.

"Casino, if it comes more easily to your lips. I am representing and have the opportunity to invest in a well-run gambling syndicate's project. Or *gaming*, as they prefer. In four cities already and very successful. Imagine it as the Boston Club but open to the public. They entertain with nothing but honest games conducted only through full-time employees. No outside hustlers. No confidence men. A large buffet dinner every evening. Elegant surroundings. Patrons with their wives or special friends, all dressed as though for a concert."

Percy had captured Westie's attention. "Sounds promising. What sort of gambling?"

"Games with showmanship. Excitement. Roulette tables. Baccarat. Faro. Vingt-et-un. In an upstairs room, keno. Poker tables. Music in one room. Instead of going to the theater or a concert, a man and his lady or a friend might spend a pleasant evening in a lovely setting. Sumptuous buffet all evening. A fine, well-stocked bar."

"Percy, you're a great salesman. But I'd never get it past Polly and Herb as an investment for me. I've got enough personal risk as it is. What do you need for your part?"

When Percy named the figure of $22,000 Westbrook Haydel let out a low whistle. He was more than a little surprised at such a sizeable sum. The rewards could be high but so was the risk. Was Percy ready to do this with a wife and a child?

"I won't say no, Percy. I'm confident in your future and your integrity. But I have to get approval from our loan committee. Do you have collateral? Do you own the plantation with your family?"

Percy was sitting upright now and earnest in his effort to persuade Westie to advance the loan. He had never borrowed money. "No. I have the townhouse and some savings. But not the plantation or any of my father's other investments. You know I'm good for it."

"It's not me, Percy. I'm sure the loan committee would be more likely to commit if Howard Moorhead were to co-sign a note with you."

"I'd rather not ask him."

"That's your pride talking. In business, you use any advantage you have, barring illegality. Polly's father co-signs on my investments all the time."

"Judah said the same thing when I applied for a position, that I should rely on my father's good name as I make my own way in the world."

"Hey, look at me for an example. If it weren't for Herb, I'd be little more than a clerk back in Mobile."

"If I must, I must," Percy replied with resignation.

Percy asked Westie about Gerald Plauché. "A knife-fighter in a business suit," said the banker. "Blunt. He's the gate-keeper, the go-between for Alderman Duplessis. Mean as a cur-dog when he's crossed. Nothing gets done without his say-so. Absolutely loyal to the alderman. He's been with him ever since that Supreme Court justice forged McDonogh's signature to a note and got caught. The judge fled to Mexico. Plauche had been his factotum, and the alderman took him in. Beyond that, no one can say why Duplessis has the power he possesses. It's not based on intelligence or charisma. Nobody likes him. Maybe he has secrets on folks, powerful folks."

"Any suggestions on dealing with him?" Westie's office looked under-furnished to Percy. Too bare. Few books, fewer paintings and *objets d'art*. He thought Westie and Polly were contrasting types, the one stolid and a bit too literal, the other frilly, even giddy – but completely reliable to Phil when Phil needed a woman's help.

"Don't try to come between Plauché and the alderman. Whatever he says, it's directly from the alderman. Couple of people have tried to threaten or buy-off Plauche. He went directly to Duplessis. Word went out that it would be a bad choice to do business with them after that."

"Anyone I would know?"

"No. They both left New Orleans for greener pastures."

"Thanks for the heads-up. And tell Polly we appreciate her help."

"She may be at your place now. She was going to check on Phil sometime today."

On his returning to the townhouse Phil told Percy she thought she had felt her first contractions that morning. He asked, "Does that mean the baby is coming soon?"

Phil made light of the question, not wishing to worry her husband. "I'm new to this. If my mother were here . . . ."

"Should we get someone to stay with you full-time?" Percy said before she finished. They had a day-time maid, but she was young and no mid-wife.

Showing uncertainty, Phil said, "The contractions passed quickly. Polly Haydel stopped by on her way to the produce market. She promised me to come again later. She told me early contractions could go on for days. Don't worry she said."

"Did she say it's their anniversary?"

"Yes. She's celebrating with a new wardrobe from Munroe's Clothing."

Percy sent a note to his father at the hotel he usually stayed in when in New Orleans. Percy had told his father to continue to use the townhouse, but Howard preferred not to intrude on Percy and Phil's privacy – or relinquish his own. When Polly returned to sit with Phil, Percy and Howard met for supper at a restaurant close to the townhouse.

Howard Moorhead received the description of the syndicate's plans for Toulouse Gardens with careful attention. He asked Percy a series of questions about the syndicate's other ventures into gambling. If successful in New Orleans, what competition might spring up?

Howard told Percy, "It sounds like the sort of business I would have invested in when I first began in New Orleans. If your friend Westie needs me to co-sign your note, I'll not hesitate. You're right to build up your credit. Your business reputation is as important as the integrity of your name. I could lend you the investment money myself, but it's better you do it on your own."

Percy nodded. He was grateful for the thought but would prefer failure to success of his father's making. Pride is no vice when it insists on a man having his own accomplishments. Co-signing a note was a mere formality. Percy couldn't imagine it to have potential bad consequences, any more than the need to record the deed to the townhouse. If it smoothed the loan, why not go ahead? Even if something terrible should happen to Howard, Percy was his heir.

"That brings me to my real problem," said Percy. "The alderman and city permits and a license for business." Percy described his meeting with Duplessis. His father said he'd had no dealings with the reorganized government.

"So, how did you deal with such problems?" Percy was reluctant to ask for advice that might draw on his father's own business dealings, which were never a topic for household discussion – outside the affairs of the cotton plantation. On Bolingbroke, Howard shared every detail with his son. It was to be his heritage.

Howard replied reluctantly and with vagueness of example. "Trial and error. The problem with corrupt politicians is you can't satisfy them. If they take one bite, they'll always come back for a second or a third. I usually could outwait them or find a business partner who was already thick with the man. You have to find a weak spot or a way around someone who stands in your way. Remember, everyone has secrets and lies."

The advice, while sound, wasn't much to go on. If his father wished to elaborate, he would in his own way. The men drank coffee in silence.

"Phil must be about due."

"Our friend Polly says it'll be in the next few days. Soon."

"Boy or girl?" Howard did not let his concern show. He recalled the difficulties of Percy's birth and how close they came to losing both mother and child. Dr. Davenport had saved both with a timely incision.

"Phil says he kicks like a mule. She thinks he's got to be a boy."

"I'd like a grandson. He'd carry on the Moorhead name. If you don't have one, get a midwife to standby. And be ready to fetch a physician." After another long silence, and apparent rumination, Howard added, "Listen, maybe you should talk to Ja-boo. He still knows more about this city than almost anyone else I know."

"Ja-Boo? I haven't seen him since I went to Mexico. How old is he now?"

Howard responded. "Ja-Boo's over 60. Still strong. Healthy. He's been watching your career as a lawyer. You've walked by him any number of times in three years."

"I've never seen him."

"No one sees Ja-Boo unless he wants them to. He's found safety in anonymity. Always has."

"How do I find him?"

"He'll find you. I'll send him word. Keep your meeting with Plauché. See what he wants. Take it from there. You'll figure it out. Patience prevails."

Chapter 25

# Ja-Boo's Roses

McIntyre and Percy met with Gerald Plauché the next day. Plauché had a regular table at Moreau's restaurant on the south side of Canal street. The alderman's gatekeeper was curt and to the point. He leaned forward, across the white linen table cloth, to share news of an impediment in advancing the project. In a raspy voice, he delivered the somber news, "The alderman wants to help you. But there are difficulties. Some of the businesses in the district don't want to see your establishment intrude on theirs. I've been asking around. Testing the waters. They're likely to form an association to ask the Board of Aldermen to deny any permits. And there are the ministers. Even some of the priests will object to any measure that encourages gambling. The more successful your project, the greater the likelihood of jeopardizing souls."

McIntyre started to speak but Percy intervened.

"Mr. Plauché, it is my experience that dissident voices may be mollified by appropriate persuasion. Do you suppose that you could arrange a few nominal payments as advances on possible economic losses that would lessen the concerns of the businesses of which you speak? Perhaps contributions to the collection baskets of our guardians of civic and moral virtue would advance the interests of salvation. These would, of course, have to be discreet."

"Yes," said Plauché, brightening that Percy was making his task easier than he had anticipated. "Exactly what I was going to suggest."

McIntyre did not approve of his attorney's approach, but he said nothing. Percy continued, soothingly, "Have you formed a judgment about what amount might be necessary? Including of course, your customary commission for serving as an intermediary, or coordinator as I think the alderman termed it."

"A figure of $15,000 should be adequate. Yes, I feel certain that after I receive and distribute that sum, the opposition will cease. And the alderman's concerns will have been satisfied that his constituents do not object to the entry of outsider business interests."

Ruminating for a moment, as though he was reflecting on the reasonableness of the sum, Percy then proceeded as though it was acceptable. "And our ministers?"

Plauché's lips parted in a lupine grin, pleased that Percy was joining in the charade. "Of course, we mustn't ignore concerns for public decency. I will assure them that community standards of morality will in no way be threatened by the proposed establishment."

"Very good. Mr. McIntyre and I will report back to his investors and see if they wish to proceed. Thank you for your time and consideration."

Outside, on the street, McIntyre said, with greater agitation than after the meeting with the alderman, "That's outrageous. The Alderman is demanding $15,000 just for his cooperation on the permits? Too much. Too much. We anticipated that you might have to pay something out of your fee under the table. But nothing so blatant as this."

Percy winked at his client. "It's not over until it's over. How much longer do you plan to stay in New Orleans?"

"I had set aside til the end of this week."

"Good. That gives me a couple of days to work this out. Let's see it through." Percy had nothing in mind. But it gave him time. He did not want to show his client his own uncertainty. Perhaps Ja-Boo could help.

෧෧ — ෧෧

The next morning, Ja-boo was waiting in Percy's law office. He was seated in the chair opposite the lawyer's desk. How he got in was unclear – neither of the office clerks had arrived for work yet. If the mysterious Basque had walked through the wall Percy would not be surprised. He did, however, appear not impervious to the inroads of time. His face was so furrowed that the scar on his cheek was hardly noticeable. The once bulging biceps had lost much of their tone and definition. The pleasure of seeing Percy again was evident in his broad grin, which also revealed a gap of several teeth.

"How you be, Master Percy?"

"Flourishing, Ja-Boo," he responded warmly, embracing his old mentor. "And you?"

"Tolerable, for dis old man."

"My father thinks you might can help me."

"Ya, boss. He say so."

"My problem is a man named Gerald Plauché. He works for Alderman Duplessis. Do you know who he is?"

"Ya, boss. Plauché, he be no problem to you."

"You do know him? Good. But I don't want you to hurt him. No rough stuff. No knives. You taught me how to use a knife. My father tells me you have handled problems like this for him before. He has been unwilling to tell me what methods you use. I don't want to know. Do you think you can resolve my problem?"

"My word. You have no problem with Plauché when you meet

with him. When that be?"

"Tomorrow maybe. Should I set a meeting with him tomorrow? Do you have to plan something? Does that give you time to act?"

"Time 'nuff. Jest, when you meet him, you ware this."

Ja-Boo handed Percy a small sack fashioned out of newspaper. Percy unfolded an edge. Inside was a pink rose, partially bloomed.

"A flower?"

"This flar take care of you. No more problem if you warr this flar when you meet Plauché. Ja-Boo guarantee."

"How?"

"You want to know? Or jest you trust Ja-Boo? All men, they have secrets."

"That's what my father often tells me. And I suppose you have yours. You have my full-faith and credit, Ja-Boo. What shall I pay you for this service?"

"Mr. Moorhead, he take care Ja-Boo."

With a cunning grin, the Basque left. Percy noted that the old pirate's gait was now marred by a slight limp. Was it new? As a young man, Percy had never noticed such things. Now he was becoming aware of change, in the things he had known or thought he knew, and of frailties in the people around him.

えええ — そうそ

The appointment with Alderman Duplessis's man was made for the following day at 2:00 in the afternoon. Before he had left his townhouse, Phil supervised his attire: a white shirt and blue vest tastefully set-off by a silk cravat of darker gray. Percy had a late lunch with McIntyre, who asked if they had made any progress. Percy responded, "We shall see," as he pinned the pink rose to the left lapel of his light-grey waist-coat.

The flower struck McIntyre as odd. "Is that a common fashion here?"

"No. I have employed my own emissary in *l'affaire Plauché*. He assures me this is an enchanted rose that will work wonders on our behalf."

McIntyre's skepticism was ill-concealed. Maybe he should have gone to Benjamin or to Micou after all. Magic flowers? He had heard stories of voo-doo practices in New Orleans but had thought it confined to immigrants of color from the Caribbean. Had the exotic beliefs infected the upper ranks of society in this eclectic city? He had come this far, so he might as well see it through. If it didn't work out, chalk up one more to experience.

Plauché's secretary showed Percy and McIntyre into Plauché's office. The alderman's *major domo* was seated behind his desk. Almost beyond notice, behind a sheaf of papers, was a pink rose, a sister bloom to the one on Percy's lapel. Plauché's eyes went to Percy's rose and involuntarily down to the one on his desk, which he removed with a movement that he tried to make inconspicuous. With similar effort, he removed the grimace from his lips and replaced it with an approximation of a smile. It was a struggle for him. He stood and gestured to his guests to take a seat. He stared at them in silence while he carefully chose his words.

"Well, Mr. Moorhead, you have succeeded where many have failed. The alderman is persuaded that your client's project is of such merit you should proceed, knowing you have his full support."

McIntyre could not help but look at his lawyer in surprise at the unexpected turnabout and the sudden deference in Plauché's manner.

If Percy was similarly surprised, he did not display it. Smoothly, he said to Plauché, "A very wise move. We are most appreciative. May we express our gratitude to you in tangible form?"

Plauché hesitated and then said, with some resignation, or perhaps grudging respect, "When you open your gaming establishment, I hope you will allow me an evening to see if you play cards with the same skill you bring to political affairs."

Outside, McIntyre, in pleased puzzlement, said "I don't think we could have done as well with any other attorney. Would you care to share your secret, now that you are one of our partners?"

Cryptically, because he was himself ignorant, Percy responded, "Where we have acted with integrity and fidelity, we need concern ourselves only with the results we have achieved. If you wish, you may have the enchanted rose which worked the wonders promised by my associate." Percy knew he wasn't responsible for the sudden change of heart of Plauché and the alderman, but he'd be damned if he wouldn't take credit for it. Worse things could happen to a lawyer's practice than to gain a reputation for possessing magical powers.

Percy had no luck in locating Ja-Boo to thank him, nor his own father to discover the secret of success with the alderman and Plauché. By the next day, nothing could have been farther from his mind than the pink rose, for when he returned home, Philomena was beginning her labor. Polly Haydel was with her. A competent doctor lived only three blocks away and came immediately to the townhouse on being summoned. Randolph Howard Moorhead entered the world at 8:35 in the evening with no complications – full-cheeked, rosy as day-break and healthy. Over the next few days, the living room filled with flowers, gifts and food from family, friends and clients. Judah Benjamin sent a silver child's bowl and spoon monographed with the infant's initials.

*Chapter 26*

# Yellow Jack's Toll

**T**wo weeks passed from the birth of Randolph Moorhead before Lucy and Howard Moorhead were able to leave Bayou Sara to see their grandson. Apologizing for being slow and for bringing sad news, Howard explained that Big Tom had died on the same day as the birth of their infant. All the slaves were given two days off to mourn and to bury the man who had been their overseer and buffer from their white owners for many years. His character and fair firmness had earned their respect and loyalty. Although he enforced the white master's law, he ameliorated the conditions of their servitude. Their sufferings were his sufferings. Big Tom would demand nothing of them that he would not himself endure.

"How," asked Percy, "is Odessa taking his death?"

Howard answered, "She relied on him, no question. But was there love between them? Their union was an imposed one. She accepts what she cannot change. Death comes to us all. She has Julius, Leddie and her own grandson, Little Jay they call him, to care for."

Percy listened to his father carefully, inferring that Howard may have been describing his own relation with Big Tom – and his own sense of loss. He asked his father, "What will you do to replace him?"

Howard looked to be sure that Lucy was out of hearing in the next room with Phil and the infant. He spoke in a low voice anyway. "Now that, son, is not without difficulty. Awkward would be another way to say it. Your mother wants to turn it all over to Calvin. Both plantations. I can't stop her giving him Jericho Hill to manage. It's hers. Always has been. I'd rather let Pompey and Julius gradually take on what Big Tom did. I can do that with Bolingbroke. I'll have to play a bigger part than I have in the past."

"Calvin would have to leave his bank job in Woodville, wouldn't he?"

His forehead wrinkling in concern, Howard continued reluctantly, "That was the other news, which I had just found out. He had difficulties in his relations with his *confreres*. They parted company some months ago. In fairness to your mother, she says Eliza only found out a few weeks ago. They were both hesitant to inform me. They've moved into Jericho Hill now, and Calvin says he's ready to run a cotton plantation."

Dismayed at the prospect, Percy shook his head, "He has no idea what it takes."

"No, he doesn't. He's never observed the operations closely. I suppose he thinks cotton renews itself each year like grass growing in a field. The darkies take to their tasks like the starlings who descend each spring and summer to gather fallen grain. I've never seen him enter the gin room. Things are slow this time of year, and there's nothing to disabuse him of his ignorance."

"Hiring a manager would offend him and Mother." Percy's glum outlook matched his father's.

"Of course," said Howard. "Only thing I can do is take on Bolingbroke myself and let him think he's in charge on Jericho. I'll have to see to it that all the hands on Jericho receive the instructions and supplies they need. In appearance at least, he'll believe that the place is running itself. I've wound up all my business activities in New Orleans over the past two years, so I'm spending nearly all my time at Bolingbroke, in any event. Who knows? He may develop an interest in growing crops and reveal an aptitude we haven't seen before."

Percy's little laugh was not one of good humor. "It is a pleasant thought and devoutly to be wished. But not to be counted on. Come into the parlor where the ladies are and hold your little namesake. He will proudly bear the name Moorhead into the next generation."

Howard's darkness disappeared. Percy had never seen his father so happy as when he lifted his grandson into his arms, gingerly, as if the infant were a fragile object. Nor had Percy ever seen his father look upon Lucy Moorhead so tenderly, though her back was to him. Was it a tear in his eye? Perhaps Howard Moorhead was capable of emotion that Percy had never imagined he had within him. The stoic mien slowly came back as Howard's thoughts returned to what awaited him upon landing at Bayou Sara.

No one knew what caused it, so they could only guess what to do to prevent or stop its spread. The *yellow* fever — the name in English was descriptive of the jaundiced skin often experienced by the victims. In New Orleans the disease was usually called Yellow Jack. In Mexico, Percy had known it as the *vomito negro*, its Spanish name from the black retching its victims suffered. He was familiar with the symptoms: fever, headache, vomiting and backache. As the disease progressed, the pulse weakened and slowed, followed by bleeding gums and bloody urine. Unaware that he had been immunized by his exposure while camped outside Vera Cruz, Percy was not himself threatened by the latest of the epidemic outbreaks that descended periodically on New Orleans.

No one would have predicted the severity of the disease when it returned to the city in the early summer of 1853. The first victim was a newly arrived Irish worker, taken to doctors vomiting black bile. Then a second man who had arrived with him on the emigrant ship, the *Augusta* from Bremen, also died. Had the men caught the disease on arrival in New Orleans? Or was the pestilence aboard the ship and spreading outward into the city? If the disease was imported, carried by lower class immigrants, then a quarantine was the best way to protect the people of the city. The same measure would effectively bar the arrival of a class of new inhabitants that the better sort of New Orleanian preferred to do without. Wasn't the city growing too rapidly? Already the small land area, surrounded by river, marsh plain, and swamp, was shared by more than 150,000 people. Yet the business leaders of the city opposed a quarantine. It would severely disrupt commerce that they carried on with the rest of the country and the world. New workers were needed for railroad labor and the wharves. Foreign immigrants, especially the Irish, were much cheaper than slaves. Businessmen discouraged even reporting on the extent of the epidemic, worried that it would impede the influx of trade and drive away their workers and customers. Pretend there was no disease rampant in the city.

Some medical people speculated that the fever originated in the conditions of the city. The epidemic might be checked by improved sanitation. A good start would be to clean up all streets, public places, alleys, yards, lots and everywhere that filth might accumulate. New regulations would improve sewerage and require removal of garbage and every sort of pollution and putrescence of man and nature. All vacant lots should be filled. The city government might require grading of all lots before tenements were erected in order that no standing water could collect and linger beneath dwellings.

Still others blamed the overcrowding of leased apartments by tenants for the spread of the disease. All buildings should be required to have proper ventilation so that foul and loathsome air be not suffered to gather in dwellings and work places. Demands were made for the demolition of all old houses and shanties that were too unhealthy to be occupied by humans. A newspaper urged, "Let there be prohibited the sale or consumption of tainted or putrescent food of every description. Let fresh and pure water be available to every citizen, even the indigent."

But who would pay for the public works required for sewerage and sanitation? Who was willing to bear the costs of new programs of regulation? Why spend money on changes that might do nothing to stop the yellow fever?

So there was no quarantine.

No new sanitation measures.

No public health reforms.

City fathers adopted the least costly preventive measures. They burned smoke pots. They fired cannon to drive away the miasma they thought carried the epidemic. And smoke and cannon blasts were visible, audible signs that the officials were doing something. Preachers preached, priests prayed and burned incense - visible, audible signs that the ministers were doing something. And yellow death held sway in his dominion. A continuous relay of death carts carried his victims to the cemeteries that received two-hundred fifty souls per day, most without coffins. The plague seemed most fearful because it unfairly took its toll among the white population. Making no distinctions among rich and poor, young and old, it discriminated between black and white. Was God punishing New Orleans for slavery?

Many who could, evacuated, in growing numbers. Before the summer was out, a third of the city's residents fled. Banks were depleted of cash as panicked citizens withdrew their savings. Fresh food became difficult to obtain - delivery wagons and boats were reluctant to come into the city. Walking to and from his office, Percy encountered lines of carriages and wagons in traffic jams - all leaving. Yet he dared not move his wife and infant son from their town home. Little Randolph was not a year old and was still nursing.

Phil was willing to move temporarily to St. Francisville if her husband thought it best. They discussed it several times as the epidemic worsened. She remembered the palm reading of the gypsy shortly before her wedding. The gypsy crone had said death would come dressed in yellow. At the time she thought it meant her. Now it seemed it could be a warning for Percy or for their infant. Death might come dressed as the yellow fever – Yellow Jack. Percy again dismissed the old woman's statement as a fable. Yellow could be found every where, an apple, an ear of corn, a banana. They couldn't change everything they ate or wore based on a gypsy's superstition.

Together, they concluded that the stress of moving would be too much for an infant and a nursing mother. Besides, there were stories that many of those fleeing were already infected with the disease, and their flight spread the fever wherever they traveled. Who could say but that Phil and the baby might catch the disease on the northbound steamboat? Except for Phil's occasional walks alone in the early evening, she and the infant spent the entire summer without leaving the townhouse. When no one else was around, she sat with her baby in the courtyard of the townhouse. Occasionally she would dip her fingers into the tiered fountain and pat her face and her child's cheeks and forehead with cool water. At night, she stood at a window and looked down at the fires of the burning tar-barrels, billowing black smoke at every street corner.

The coffin-makers and undertakers could not keep up with the numbers of deaths. By the end of summer 20,000 people were victims of the fever and more than 4000 had died from the epidemic. Priests performed rites at mass burials. Unnamed dead lay in unmarked graves. Few families had not been touched by the death of a loved one or a neighbor.

Phil made no complaints to her husband at being confined to

the townhouse most of the day. She loved her infant and took pleasure in nursing him. Although they had a maid (an enslaved woman who was rented out by her elderly mistress) who came three days a week to clean the townhouse and wash clothes, Percy insisted that she hire full-time help. Phil interviewed several women of color to help her with keeping up the household. Buying a slave for a few months would make little sense. Short-term labor for a free woman of color was much less costly. Unlike a bondswoman, a free servant had to clothe, feed and house herself. Phil hired a plump, caramel colored girl named Beckah, about 18 years old. The girl was intelligent and polite; she did as she was told and required little supervision.

After Percy came home from work, Phil might walk along the river bank if the evening were cool and a wind blowing up from the Gulf. She missed the gaiety of entertaining Benjamin's political allies and the visits of Percy's clients and associates. Dinners and parties had no place in a time of plague. After two or three guests collapsed at New Orleans social gatherings in late May, all soirees had ceased. Still, Phil had no second thoughts about marrying Percy or moving to Louisiana to be his wife and the mother of his child. No good could come from thinking on the unthinkable. A Randolph accepted adverse fortune without fuss, without regret. What the conscious mind will not entertain, however, the will may harbor without acknowledgement.

ôôô — ôôô

By mid-July Percy noticed his wife was drinking wine more frequently in the evening. At his office, he could not observe that she numbed herself in the same manner at times during the day. With Beckah helping with the baby, she did not have to keep up her guard; she could take a little time to herself. She was still capable of laughter and wit, even if they were less frequent. In a time of plague, who could not be sad?

When the first fall weather arrived, the epidemic abated. The cemeteries had gained in population, but in a city experiencing such growth as New Orleans, the losses soon receded and were accepted as a part of a natural order. The urgency of civic reform dissipated almost as rapidly as it had arrived with the outbreak. The tar barrels grew cold, the cannons silent. Mourning fades. Yellow Jack had ceased his reign, relinquishing his dominion. For now. Life resumes.

Percy's law practice had suffered little. In a time of plague, priests and lawyers are in demand – the former for confessions, the latter for wills. The constant reminders of earthly mortality put many men and women in mind of the need for cleansing the soul for the final judgment of Christ and for a will for the final judgment of the judge. Every Louisiana lawyer tells his clients, "le mort saisit le vif." Legal title vests immediately in the heirs upon the death of the person through whom they claim title, and the final judgment of the court confirms the action of the testator. Percy was writing eight to ten wills per day. Briefs had to be filed for cases that had been put on schedules months before the outbreak. And, surprisingly, work on Toulouse Gardens was nearing completion. Laborers could not flee the city like their well-heeled counterparts in the professions and the leisure class. Those who succumbed to the plague were quickly replaced by new workers.

Each day, Percy inspected the progress of his first business venture. True to his word, the alderman did nothing to impede construction and renovation of the property. Alonzo McIntyre, the Count and Damon Simmons conferred with Percy in late August, and together they set the opening of their supper club for the last Friday in September. They introduced him to Linton Scruggs. He was assistant manager at the group's St. Louis gambling operation and would head the operation here. Scruggs was familiar with New Orleans, having lived here earlier as a shipping agent. He had an urbane manner, slick hair and was on the portly side for a man in his early thirties. A trim beard made him appear older and lent gravity to his carriage. Percy was satisfied that Scruggs would work well with a New Orleans clientele and politicians.

On the appointed day, shortly after noon, Toulouse Gardens opened its elegant double doors. Nature cooperated fully. The sun was bright, yet the temperature did not exceed eighty degrees. A string ensemble played music that pleased passers-by, inviting them in. Those who entered were treated to free spirits dispensed by two genial bartenders in green and white silk vests. The games of chance had not yet begun but visitors were encouraged to walk throughout the rooms, upstairs as well as down.

When evening arrived, accompanied by a cooling breeze, the afternoon personnel were replaced by an evening crew who dealt cards, operated the gaming wheels and supervised the dice tables. All were dressed formally. Individual invitations had been delivered to several hundred of New Orleans's leading citizens and to proprietors of plantations within a 50-mile radius of the city. Percy met five of the other investors in the enterprise who had come from as far as Memphis to attend the opening. They congratulated the young lawyer for how smoothly he had achieved the tasks they had expected of him. Senator Benjamin was unable to attend but sent a telegram to wish the enterprise great success. Little Randolph had come down with colic, and Philomena thought him too little to be left in the care of Beckah while ill.

Captain Beauregard made a point of seeking out Percy and thanking him for his invitation. "After all," the engineer said, "we are near neighbors. My Custom House appointment has come through channels. We will be working a few blocks from each other for some time to come perhaps."

Percy detected a degree of respect from Beauregard he had not shown earlier. That regard was amplified when Beauregard began to introduce his companion, Thomas Slidell, who had become Chief Justice of the Louisiana Supreme Court six months earlier. Slidell interrupted to say he was well familiar with Percy Moorhead, who had recently won a significant victory before the court. Percy had argued the defense of an insurance company on a maritime policy for the carriage of goods. He convinced the court that the insured vessel was sent to sea from Galveston with a load of cotton in an unseaworthy condition. Thus, the loss of the ship and cargo was due to the negligence of the shipper and not from a risk during the voyage. Percy deflected the praise with modesty, while enjoying the expression on Beauregard's face – Slidell was impressed that Beauregard knew Percy, not that Percy knew the army officer. Slidell, Benjamin's co-author of the acclaimed Louisiana Digest, was well-aware that Percy was Benjamin's protégé. Percy was no longer the private soldier in Mexico, the enlistee who could only enter the Aztec Club as a laborer.

Percy warmly greeted Westie and Polly Haydel when they arrived. He showed them around the gaming rooms. He saw to it that they had a full meal from the generous buffet and the best wine the house had to offer. A magician whom Scruggs had hired for the event was entertaining other of the patrons with demonstrations of sleight of hand and feats of juggling. The string ensemble had returned after a two-hour break in late afternoon and provided a festive air. The rooms were so well furnished with gas lamps mounted on the walls and hanging from the ceiling, turned to their maximum output, that the guests were astonished with the light they provided. They were brighter than the lighting in the best hotels in the city. No expense had been spared in setting up the operation.

It was near two in the morning that closing was signaled by the dimming of the lights. Scruggs, the manager, turned down the central gas valve of the pipe coming into the building. A tally of the evening's takes would have to wait until later on Saturday. Every report from the dealers, the croupiers and others indicated it should be very good.

When he returned home and entered their bedroom, Percy found Phil nursing their son. The infant was feeling better. In a little more than a month, he would celebrate his first birthday. Phil could tell that Percy was happy with the outcome of the evening and told him how proud she was of her successful husband.

"You dear," he said, kissing her lightly on her forehead, "you always think of others before yourself." He collapsed into deep sleep without taking off his clothing. Philomena gently removed his shoes, put his legs upon the bed, and covered him with a light blanket. Only when she removed his evening dress jacket did she notice his vest, a gift from Alonzo McIntyre for the grand opening of Toulouse Gardens. Trimmed with gold thread, it was made of yellow satin. Phil's slender shoulders gave a shudder; she picked up her infant and drew him close to her breast. "Nothing can get you, child. Nothing."

Chapter 27

# Calvin Comes A Cropper

Despite the passing of Big Tom a year earlier, the cotton crop on the two plantations came a good harvest. Had Calvin Bunch taken a more active role, no doubt the crop would have suffered. A nasty confrontation between Percy and Calvin had caused Calvin to retreat from supervision. It occurred on a day while Howard Moorhead was in New Orleans and the three women of the Moorhead family were in St. Francisville for a Saturday shopping outing.

Percy was in the library of Bolingbroke Hall reading the latest issue of the *Southern Literary Messenger* when he heard Calvin's rude voice shouting in anger. Walking over to the window, he looked out and saw Pompey hunched over, holding his arms to his chest while Calvin Bunch thrashed him repeatedly across the back with his leather quirt.

"You no-good black sombitch," Calvin yelled. "Don't you sass me, boy."

Julius was several arms-length away, pleading with Calvin.

"Mr. Calvin, Pompey didn't mean no sass at all. He just be sayin' the ground be too wet for plowin' today."

"You sassin' me too, boy?"

Just as Calvin was turning to hit Julius, Percy was at his back and grabbed his right wrist. The quirt fell from Calvin's hand as he winced in pain at Percy's strong grasp.

Angrily, Percy told Calvin, "There'll be no beating of slaves on either of these plantations."

"They just niggras, Percy. Just niggras." Calvin was taken back by Percy's unexpected intervention and vehemence.

"They are our workers. We depend on them. We no more beat them than we do our mules or cows. Pompey and Julius are two of our best men. They know what they are doing."

All three men understood that Percy was saying that Calvin didn't know what he was doing. The ground was, in fact, too wet for effective plowing. It was a day for using hoes to till the soil.

"Do I make myself clear?" Percy demanded with force in his words.

Picking up his quirt, Calvin responded, "Oh, I think we understand each other well enough, brother Percy. You've made your point."

Percy turned and walked away. His interference stung Calvin more sharply than the blows he had managed to land on Pompey's tough and broad back. The scruffy Bunch had been humiliated in front of the slaves. Snickers would attend him among the other slaves until he established his own dominance. A price would have to be paid, sooner or later by one or both of the black half-brothers.

Under his breath, a furious Calvin seethed to Pompey, "Your turn will come. There'll be a time when you won't have Percy Moorhead to protect your black ass."

When Calvin was out of hearing, Pompey asked Julius, "Why you s'pose God made no'counts like Cav'n Bunch?"

"White folks say it's the curse of Ham upon us. More like there's just some men who think they can be big only by making others small. If slavery were the natural order for all people of African descent, there'd be no free men and women of color. You and me, we got the same daddy. But my mother says she was born free in San Domingo. The Cubans put her down as a slave by mistake. That means I'm supposed to be free, too. Son of a free woman is free too."

"I dunno," replied Pompey with a half-grin. "You best 'splain that to Cav'n Bunch and Miz Lucy."

A chastised Calvin Bunch avoided any further possibility of correction at the hands of a Moorhead. A beaten dog slinks away from danger. Howard Moorhead had deftly managed the plantations' operations so that no further confrontation with Calvin Bunch occurred. Calvin never knew if Percy had told Howard about the incident. He dared not risk a repetition. Calvin already resented Howard for bailing him out on two occasions, but he was too weak to express it except passively. Calvin did, however, insist that Jericho Hill's cotton be kept segregated from Bolingbroke's so that he could manage a sale on his own. He would show that he was a businessman in his own right and that his experiences in banking and finance in Natchez and Woodville had prepared him to be a shrewd trader. Among his business contacts was a friend in New Orleans who was privy to inside information on the New York and Liverpool markets. The friend encouraged Calvin to store his bales until the conditions were optimum for the best price of the year, offering his own warehouse for storage at a reduced rate.

Thus it was that all of Bolingbroke's cotton was sold by late December 1853, but not, it was soon learned, Jericho Hill's. The baled crop of Bolingbroke was half-way across the Atlantic when fire bells rang out in the early hours of a cold February morning. Their frenzied clanging called the New Orleans volunteer firefighters to a raging fire on the Mississippi River. The conflagration of the ships and warehouses was too great to be contained. It quickly engulfed a half-dozen large ships tied to the levee or anchored nearby.

Cotton on New Orleans levee
Source: Library of Congress

Thus, too, it was that all of Jericho Hill's cotton was consumed by the massive flames, though it could not be determined if Calvin's cotton was still in his friend's warehouse or loaded aboard the *Natchez* or another of the lost ships or the *Charles Belcher*, where the fire was reported to have begun. In any event, it did not matter whether the cotton, and risk of its loss, was at the warehouse or aboard a vessel. Determination of place of loss was only important if it allocated risk between buyer and seller or between one insurer and another. Calvin's risk was all Calvin's – and his family's.

Percy Moorhead was among the on-lookers who walked to the river to survey the damage early that morning. His was a professional interest. Clients would be making claims – planters against the warehouses; sellers and buyers of cotton and other goods as to which was the owner at the moment of loss; planters, warehouses, and owners of consumed commodities and merchandise against insurers. Percy was unaware that Calvin had retained ownership of the crop of Jericho Hill, awaiting the precise moment of the best price which his insider friend had yet to announce. Nor did he know that Calvin had decided it was a waste of money to purchase insurance against the loss of the baled cotton while it was in storage, before having the risk pass to a purchaser.

Percy did not anticipate that Calvin, as foolhardy as he was, would be so foolish as to leave an entire year's production at the risk of uninsured loss. But in a matter of days the magnitude of the loss became clear.

Calvin's family searched for him until someone told Howard Moorhead that he was at a hotel in Baton Rouge. Fortunately for him, his female companion had already departed when Eliza located him and told him of the fire. When Calvin and Eliza finally arrived in New Orleans two days after the river inferno, they met with Percy and Howard at the Moorhead townhouse. Calvin insisted the cotton crop was fully insured. His friend with the inside information would have seen to it.

"Good," said Percy, as though he actually believed Calvin's words. "Let's go see him right now. Let's find out who the insurers are and we'll begin the claims process immediately."

"I'll just stay here with Eliza," said Calvin. He would not look Percy in the eye. "No reason to stress her." Howard looked on skeptically. It was good that Lucy was not here to watch the inevitable unfold – and take Calvin's side.

Within an hour Percy had returned. He confirmed what he and his father suspected even before Calvin's arrival. The friend was vehement that Calvin had been informed of the risks of storage and that he declined to purchase insurance from a broker to whom he had referred Calvin. The warehouse's own coverage extended only to the structure itself, not to its contents. All loss was at the cotton owner's sole risk.

"Well, he's lying," Calvin said heatedly. His round face had avoided a razor – and soap – for more than a week. His eyes betrayed the furtiveness of an opossum surprised while rummaging in the garbage. "I want you to sue him, Percy. He said he was insured or getting insurance and I took it to mean he was insuring my bales."

"Did you pay him the premium for the coverage?"

"He was supposed to get it when we sold the cotton."

"That's not the commercial custom here. Do you have a written agreement with him?"

"I think so. I don't carry it about with me. We just got here from Baton Rouge. What is this? Some sort of interrogation?"

Howard spoke up. "I have the storage contract here. Lucy and Eliza found it and gave it to me when they first heard of the fire." He handed the document to his son.

Percy read over the contract. More for his father, sister and wife than for Calvin, he said, "This is what we call a bailment for hire. It makes clear that all risk of loss while in storage is with the bailor, not the bailee. As owner of the cotton you are the bailor."

Cornered, Calvin fought back with the vehemence of a weasel. "Bailor? Bailee? I don't care what it says. I know what he told me. I want you to sue him. That's what you lawyers do, sue people."

"I'm afraid I can't do that, Calvin."

"Why the hell not? If not for me, then for your sister and mother. It's their cotton as much as it is mine."

"For one, a written contract takes precedence over an oral one."

"Screw precedence. Just tell the judge the verbal contract controls. You can do that. We're family. We're supposed to help each other."

Percy continued patiently, "For another, to make a claim I must have good faith basis for its merit."

Calvin did not quite get Percy's meaning, but Eliza did. She spoke, accusingly, "You're saying you don't believe Calvin. You're taking the other man's side."

"It's not a matter of taking sides, Sissy. It's what a lawyer can establish in court. And Calvin just doesn't have a case that can be won."

Calvin was angry, "Where does that leave us then if we can't turn to the courts for justice?"

"In a word, nowhere. Fire. Crop failure. Flooded fields. These are acts of God. Lacking insurance, your complaint of injustice is with Him and not the courts. You'll have to find a way to get by and put together enough to get a crop next year."

"Look, this is a loss for your mother and your sister, not just me." Calvin spoke in the direction of Percy, but the words were intended for Howard. It was unstated but understood by all: he was placing the onus upon Howard Moorhead to see them through another year's planting and harvesting. He acknowledged no responsibility for the loss. In his view, it was a reasonable risk to go without insurance. How could he be blamed for taking a justifiable risk? Percy himself said it was fate or God's fault, not Calvin's. And besides he had spent the money in other ways, for which he had no clear recollection. He was angry that Howard and Percy gave him no support at a time when he most needed it. Lucy, he knew, would be more understanding, if not for his sake, for Eliza's.

A quarter of a century had passed and Howard Moorhead found himself where he was before. Full circle, the wheel of fate rotates back to where it began. Again, Howard Moorhead would bail out Jericho Hill from financial woes, inflicted now by the recklessness of the husband of Jim Willis's daughter rather than Jim Willis. Mother and daughter would again be rescued by Howard. Yet their dependence bred resentment, not gratitude from Lucy and Eliza. It exposed their gross misjudgment in choosing husbands of irresolute character. Howard accepted their indifference to his generosity as a burden he bore – duty to those who depended upon him. He was no stranger to the harshness of fate nor the failures of family long before he met and married widow Willis.

Chapter 28

# Phil's Heirloom Silver

A week after the warehouse fiasco, Phil discovered that she was missing items that she was certain had properly been put away in the downstairs cabinet of their townhouse.

"What are you looking for, my dear?" Percy inquired at the perplexed expression on his wife's face.

"Our silver napkin rings. The ones with a R monogram for Randolph that mother gave us for a wedding present. We had six. Now there are only four. They've been in our family for three generations. I'm afraid that a servant may have taken them."

"When did you notice they were missing?"

"About a week ago, I think."

"Right after my parents were here?"

"Why yes. I had two girls give the place a thorough cleaning. I imagine it was one of them who took them. Should we report them to their owner? Or to the authorities?"

Percy was slow to respond, uncertain as to how candid he should be. "I suspect the items will turn up."

"Why? Do you think they will bring them back?"

"No. I doubt that the young women would risk stealing them."

"Then what?"

"I think we'll find them at Bolingbroke. Mother has a special place where she keeps her souvenirs."

"Souvenirs?" Phil was reluctant to accept Percy's implication. Why would Percy say such a thing about his mother?

"Mother has a bad habit, a peculiarity as my father called it. Sometimes she takes things that do not belong to her."

"Why? She has her own set of silver and napkin rings. She can afford to buy anything she wants." Phil and her mother had never coveted a thing belonging to another. Petty theft was a vice of the lower sorts of people.

It was painful to Percy that he had to acknowledge to his wife the truth about his mother's habit. He didn't understand it himself, but he attempted an explanation, though not offering an excuse. "I think something in her wants to believe she is getting something for nothing. They are never a thing a person needs. It's as though they are little trophies, representative of small victories. I think my father said she treats them as souvenirs, as though given her by people she has visited or a shop where she has made purchases."

"I'm sorry for you, Percy. It must have been difficult growing up with her." She walked over to where her husband was standing. She put her hands on his shoulders. "Now I can share your burden. Any other thoughts?"

Percy put one hand over hers, saying, "She's never been willing to give up the mantle of widowhood. She enjoyed being Jim Willis's widow more than being Howard Moorhead's wife. A widow evokes sympathy. 'That poor woman,' people say. 'So brave, so strong.' Who has compassion or admiration for a wealthy wife? Apparently, she thinks people should give her gifts to compensate for her loss."

"Why did she marry your father?"

"She probably realized that the sympathetic widow was a façade that no one really believed; if they had believed initially, the sympathy had ceased. It was a story she told herself. She had been foolish to marry Jim Willis and most people, including her brothers, thought she got what she should have foreseen. Had she not married my father, she would have lost everything, including the sad tale she had told about herself."

"Then why did your father marry her?"

"There's much about her he admired. He still does. She has intelligence. She was young and strong and healthy. He had a passing business acquaintance with her brothers, so he knew she came from good stock. She loved books and was well-read. Her father had provided her with excellent tutors in North Carolina. My father was a cotton factor, and she had a cotton plantation. He was old enough that he wasn't lured by the superficial beauty of a New Orleans belle. He wanted a young wife. They seemed a natural match."

"He wanted her so he could have you and provide me with my own husband," she said with a broad grin. "And he wanted a Moorhead dynasty in Louisiana."

"Like the Randolphs of Virginia? I've often thought that to be the case. He's talked so much about carrying on the family name and heritage. He once told me that his plantation was twice the size of Grandfather Moorhead's in England."

"Your grandfather? Or his?" Phil thought it odd that Percy seemed to know so little of his own family history. She was raised with constant reminders of forebears of the Virginia dynasty carrying the Randolph name.

"I really can't say. He just said Grandfather Moorhead. It's curious that he's told me so little about the history of the Moorheads."

"Have you asked?"

"Very tentatively. Each time he has deferred the subject, always saying 'In good time, son. In good time.'"

*Chapter 29*

# A Mexican Cigar Roller

Judah Benjamin, now Senator Benjamin, had recently returned to New Orleans from his first session of Congress in Washington. Over lunch at LaBelle's, he and Percy were revising the relationship that they had maintained for close to five years. With Micou's health deteriorating, Benjamin was forming a new partnership with two other men and informing Percy – after the fact. The conversation was awkward and required delicacy, with which Judah was amply supplied.

Benjamin had not conferred with Percy before associating himself with Bradford and Finney, two men whom Percy barely knew. Anticipating Percy's look of surprise and resentment, Benjamin sought to mollify the younger attorney. He would propose work on his Tehuantepec project as an alternative for Percy's consideration. It had enormous potential for the commercial development of the South and the United States and could bring many clients to Percy.

Percy was not a good fit with Benjamin's new firm. Edward Bradford was from Connecticut – with a patrician education at Yale and Harvard. President Fillmore had tried to put Bradford and then Benjamin's partner William Micou on the Supreme Court but failed to get either confirmed. Bradford brought with him a younger attorney, John Finney. Both men regarded Percy's background and Louisiana origins as inferior to theirs. Neither wished to be associated with Percy Moorhead, and they bluntly told Judah he would have to make a choice.

Benjamin, Percy felt, took his loyalty for granted. He did not like being slighted. Perhaps Benjamin thought him still too young to be fully in his confidence. Behind that cheery grin, Benjamin was both calculating and subtle, as subtle as any man Percy would ever meet.

The reason Benjamin gave to Percy for not inviting him into the new firm was that the clients that the partners would bring unfortunately posed conflicts with Percy Moorhead's own business interests. And Percy's commitments to his family in St. Francisville would limit his ability to respond to an expanded practice. It was then that Benjamin suggested that they could continue an informal arrangement in which Percy would serve as an independent party in assisting certain Benjamin projects and clients. Percy said that would be agreeable to him, and he asked if Benjamin had any in mind.

It was then that Benjamin announced, "Tehuantepec."

"Tehuantepec?" replied Percy. Benjamin knew this would appeal to Percy. "Have there been new developments? Has Falconnet acquired the Sloo concession?"

"Come, come," Benjamin instructed Percy as they rose from the table. "You'll see for yourself," he said with a wink and a grin. Judah Benjamin was always amiable. He was pleased with himself that he may have navigated the revision of a relationship with Percy in the interest of his new firm. From LaBelle's they walked three blocks to the Custom House and soon entered the offices of the *Louisiana Courier*, the city's leading morning newspaper. Standing at a desk and talking with an editor was a short, dark man, about fifty.

"Percy," said Benjamin, "I'm sure you already know this man.

Emile La Sere, this is Percy Moorhead."

Shaking the man's hand, Percy said, "Yes, we've met. I know your brother, Eugene." Though small in stature, La Sere had a firm grip and a strong presence, an air of confidence. The sort of man unafraid of duels. He had survived eighteen of them before he was thirty.

Emile and Eugene La Sere were born of French parents in San Domingo during the period of revolt by the former slaves of the island. Like so many other refugees of the Caribbean islands, the family made their new home in New Orleans.

Percy was struck by the resemblance that Emile La Sere bore to Odessa in physique and facial features – large round eyes, small nose, distinctive cheek bones. It was no coincidence, no accident of nature. As Percy suspected, they shared a common ancestor, a wealthy French planter on San Domingo. Odessa's French father was first cousin to the father of the La Sere brothers, one family emigrating to Louisiana, the other to Cuba, to escape the political turmoil of their ancestral island. Despite their closely related parentage, in Louisiana Odessa was a slave, while her La Sere relatives were prominent political figures.

The La Sere father set Emile on a path for business and Eugene for law. He taught them from an early age that success in any field arose from intelligence, hard work and determination, but only if joined with close bonds established with like-minded people, bonds that needed to be nurtured and reinforced with regularity. Percy knew Eugene as clerk of the Louisiana Supreme Court, where he was associated with the Chief Justice, Thomas Slidell. Emile's principal political connection was the other Slidell, John Slidell, Benjamin's fellow Louisiana Senator. Each La Sere brother was linked to a Slidell brother.

Emile La Sere had succeeded to John Slidell's seat as a Louisiana representative in Congress at the beginning of the Mexican War and sat for six years. Emile and John Slidell were now co-owners of the *Courier,* and Emile served as its publisher. Like Bev Tucker's *Sentinel* in Washington, the paper was set up as a mouthpiece for the state's Democratic Party. The national party was expanding its southern base and identity.

"Judah has said good things about your abilities and discretion," said La Sere, looking Percy up and down. "And my brother says you have been an effective advocate in his court."

Accepting the compliment with modest grace, Percy responded, "They are more than generous."

"Shall we continue?" said La Sere. It was not a question but an indication that they were to depart. Evidently Benjamin and La Sere had set up a meeting that would include Percy. It was news to Percy who wondered how this related to Tehuantepec. The connection he was about to make would be the second most fateful of his life, exceeded in importance only by his association with Judah. The three men turned a corner and walked up Bourbon Street until they arrived at a location just north of St. Peters street. At a shop under the sign of "Fernando Borrego, Cigar Maker," they stopped. As they entered, a bell jutting from the door ding-dinged their arrival. A stout, swarthy, fiftyish Cuban greeted them.

"Ola, Fernando," said Benjamin. "Is our friend here?"

Borrego the Cigar Maker shook the men's hands and said, "*El presidente*? *Si*. In back."

Passing through a parted thick curtain, Benjamin, La Sere and Percy entered a larger room that smelled strongly of cured tobacco. Large casks of imported tobacco lined the walls. Four men and a woman sat at tables rolling thick brown, aromatic tobacco leaves into cigars, wrapping each with a distinctive band, and putting them into small wooden boxes to maintain their freshness. Three of the men and the woman appeared to be of mixed race, probably from one or more of the Caribbean islands. The fourth man, a bit smaller than the others, was of a type Percy had seen in Mexico – a full-blooded Indian. Almost fifty, his skin was dark and hair well-oiled. A broad nose, wide mouth and high forehead gave character to his face. He was the only tobacco roller to look up at the visitors. They were here to see him and were expected. He stood and came from behind his cigar bench, his expression at first indecipherable but breaking into a broad smile as he greeted La Sere. Throwing his arms around him, he said "Amigo Emile!"

With similar affection, La Sere inquired, "*Como esta mi amigo Benito?*"

Cigar rollers
Source – *Practical Magazine*, I. 265 (1873)

The two men were about the same height and shared other features. The Frenchman and the Mexican were both exiled in polyglot Louisiana, both exhibited to Percy the similarities of the Mediterranean and the Meso-American races – dark complexion, raven-black eyes, spare frame. The two men chatted in Spanish about family for a few minutes while Benjamin and Percy stood to the side.

Benjamin quietly explained to Percy, "Emile La Sere has had a long association with the New Orleans trading firm of McLanahan & Bogart, which did business with merchant houses in Mexico. When not dueling or engaging in Democratic politics, Emile made trips to Mexico on the firm's behalf. He is nothing if not astute, and has cultivated many business and political figures. You are meeting one of the most influential in this unpropitious setting."

Now "Benito" turned to La Sere's companions. Emile's role was as a friendly contact, and Benjamin was the focus of the meeting, not Percy, but Benjamin was pulling Percy into an ongoing project.

"Señor Benjamin," the Mexican greeted the Senator. "You have been very busy in your national capital. I read that you have a treaty."

"We do, indeed, Benito. It has not been easy."

Percy understood the men were discussing the Gadsden Treaty, negotiated by James Gadsden, the American ambassador to Mexico. The United States paid Mexico a sum of money to add a strip of land of northern Mexico to the American side, suitable eventually for a railroad. As with most other public policy matters west of the Mississippi, the treaty raised fears in the north about the expansion of slavery, and fear in the south over the constriction of its peculiar institution. Several provisions of the treaty concerned the Tehuantepec rail line on which Benjamin had expended much effort for several years. But what had it to do with this cigar maker?

"Señor Juarez, allow me to introduce my associate, Mr. Percy Moorhead. Percy, this is Señor Benito Juarez, the future president of Mexico. Do not let his appearances fool you. He was a lawyer and judge in his home state of Oaxaca. In fact, he became governor of Oaxaca during your year-long engagement in his country. He is a guest in our country owing to his opposition to President Santa Anna."

Juarez smiled in amusement at the change in expression of

Benjamin's associate. Percy recovered quickly and extended his hand with a warm grasp.

The Mexican said, "Did you take me for a peasant? Do not be embarrassed. I am what I am. A peasant. A peasant lawyer and a peasant governor. Now I am a peasant cigar maker. In this life, a man may play many parts, no? It is true that I oppose our president, and I work for his overthrow. The treaty he has just signed with your government is illegal. The plan of government we are making will undo the treaty when we overthrow Santa Anna. Senator Benjamin knows very well that is our intention."

Benjamin, as always, remained affable as he spoke. His words to Percy now were for Juarez's ears. "It's true. Señor Juarez is a true patriot. If I were a Mexican senator I would oppose Santa Anna's treaty. But even if the treaty is unmade, as Señor Juarez will seek, the Tehuantepec rail project will still be a very good thing for his country and for ours. There are no Mexican businessmen with the capital and resources to build a 150-mile railroad across the country. Whoever is president, whatever political party is in control in Mexico, the Mexican people will have to look abroad to have someone build the railroad. Would a Mexican patriot look to the British? Would he look to the French? Señor Juarez is more skeptical about both those monarchies than he is about the Americans. If our *amigo* Benito were president, he would look to us for protection from the British and the French."

Juarez nodded slowly and spoke to Percy. "You see why Mr. Benjamin is a successful politician. He just negotiated the sale of La Mesilla through his government and is already negotiating with me for a new treaty to replace this one before the ink is dry. But tell me Mr. Moorhead, what is your interest?"

Percy would not again underestimate the small, dark man found in these inauspicious surroundings. The Mexican native spoke with candor, conviction, and certainty that reflected a strong force of character and of will.

Replying to Juarez's question, Percy said, "A priest in Puebla taught me much about your country and your people. I have seen the remnants of the great civilization that existed before the Spanish arrived. There could be another civilization if the corruption of the likes of Santa Anna could be replaced by honest government, one that doesn't suppress its native population. Mexico has abundant land and resources. After spending a year in your country, I would like to be a part of its future development."

"Mr. Moorhead, it would be more persuasive if I did not see around me in your state an enslaved population serving white masters."

It was not the first time, nor would it be the last, that a foreigner would challenge Percy on slavery. He replied,

"Our democracy embraces a contradiction that is difficult to defend. When slavery is ended, as it surely will, it must occur in a manner that does not consume both master and servant. The transition will require men who are sympathetic to servant and to master."

"The same was said in my country. Yet the Spaniard still rules the native held in peonage. I would like to know more about American law. May we look to you for assistance? Other men of my country are here, too. We need guidance if we are to frame a new government. Do you speak Spanish?"

"Well enough. And I'd be gratified to share what I know of the law." Percy's response was not insincere. The differences in legal systems and their historical foundations were of great interest to him. In his daily practice, he had to weave together threads of English common law, Louisiana statutes, and the French and Spanish civil codes that among the sources of Louisiana law. And there was something compelling about the force of Juarez's personality, especially in his confident exchanges with a sitting United States Senator.

As they left the cigar store, Benjamin said, "Men like Juarez are the future of Mexico. Does work on the Tehuantepec project appeal to you?"

Percy's eagerness was apparent. "Very much."

"Good," Benjamin said. "Good. If you haven't already surmised, Emile here will be a very important man in our railroad project. There's no one in Mexico he doesn't know, no matter what their politics. He and John Slidell are among our investors and both share our confidence that this isthmian railroad will be a key link in world commerce. But we face challenges and rivals."

As the three walked, nodding to all and sundry on the way back to Canal Street, Percy grew more certain that Benjamin had never intended to bring him into the new law firm. He had other plans for Percy Moorhead. What they were was inscrutable, but Percy felt less disrespected by Benjamin. Perhaps the U. S. Senator had a broader role for Percy to play, one on an international stage. If he were manipulating Percy, so be it. He had never expressed dissatisfaction with Percy's work; Percy doubted that he had been misused by Benjamin.

Over several months, Percy had more meetings with Juarez. The Mexican introduced him to others in exile, including Melchor Ocampo, who had practiced law, then studied in Paris for a time before returning to Mexico, rising to be governor of the state of Michoacán. In New Orleans Ocampo was eking out a living as a potter. Both men were strongly anti-clerical, if not atheists, and shared an enthusiasm for land reform. When they learned that Percy had studied law in Virginia, they insisted he explain how Louisiana's civil law differed from the law of Virginia.

Three times Percy called on Juarez at the rooming house on Marais Street, near the Pontchatrain Rail line, where he stayed for eight dollars a month. If his wife and children were with him, Percy never saw them. When Juarez asked about the courts in Louisiana Percy offered to take him to a  hearing in the Louisiana Supreme Court. Percy arranged the visit in advance through Emile La Sere and his brother, Eugene, the court's administrator. Dressed in his only suit, Juarez showed up early for the hearing. Percy escorted him into the court room where they heard arguments in three cases. The last of these involved the measure of damages for gross negligence in a case against the New Orleans and Carrollton Railroad Company. A music teacher had been badly injured and was awarded damages far in excess of her income lost from her lessons. After the justices filed out, Percy and Eugene La Sere took Juarez to meet Thomas Slidell, who had become Chief Justice of the court a year earlier. Slidell called three of the other judges together to meet the Mexican lawyer and former governor of the state of Oaxaca. A bottle of bourbon appeared from a judge's cabinet and Juarez was given a toast. Juarez's appreciative glance to Percy suggested that it was one of the few times the displaced Mexican had felt welcome in New Orleans. The next day he resumed the life of an exile cigar maker, but he would long remember the attention, and respect, showed him by the earnest Louisiana lawyer. The meeting would have lasting consequences for both.

෯෯ — ෯෯

"Let me put this in perspective," I said to Percy as I stopped taking notes on our conversation. "Your ambition was to be an eminent attorney and political figure, so you hitched yourself to Judah Benjamin. But then he derailed your plan by shuffling you off from his new partnership, leaving you to fend for yourself with a vague promise to send unwanted clients on to you."

"Yes. I was hurt. I was angry. I was resentful. It was the exclusion from the Aztec Club all over again. It was especially galling because Finney had studied law at William and Mary a year before me. He was from an old Virginia family that was at odds with the Randolphs. I never told Phil about him."

"But you continued to associate with Judah."

"Yes. He held out to me a new possibility, the Tehuantepec Railroad. It redirected my ambition. Instead of achieving success in law in New Orleans and in Louisiana politics, I could seek it on a world stage. I believed in its potential to increase vastly world commerce by becoming the path between the oceans. I had seen that when I met with Russell Sturgis on my first trip to London."

"Well, the Tehuantepec railroad never worked out, but you've more than made your mark on world commerce. Your coal depots have provided the fuel for ocean trade."

"Tom, nothing succeeds unless it first experiences failure."

"The same day Judah Benjamin ended his practice with you, he introduced you to Benito Juarez. Was that part of his plan?"

"Probably. He must have seen Juarez as a future ally on the Tehuantepec project. But what I saw that day was a man in exile. He was a stranger in a foreign country in a menial job. But he endured and worked for a better future. Not to be overly dramatic, I felt that I, too, had just been exiled. If this Mexican peasant could survive and rise again, so could I."

"And you did. But so much more loss to suffer."

"As you know so well, my friend."

Chapter 30

# Percy's Skills Mature

Both Jericho Hill and Bolingbroke Hall produced good crops for several seasons after the dock fire disaster. Yet the harvests cost a good bit of Howard Moorhead's remaining capital. His health began to show his years. What resources he had and where he had them still was known to no one except himself. His diminished vigor and spirit were more apparent, especially to his son Percy, who was concerned that his father had taken on too many responsibilities.

Chastened by the fire losses, Calvin Bunch nevertheless still acted the role of country squire but refrained from actual involvement in the operation and maintenance of the plantation. At regular intervals of a few weeks, he would announce that cotton affairs required that he take an extended business trip to Woodville or Natchez or New Orleans. Affairs there were, but they had little to do with cotton. So long as he was away, there was little damage he could do to the people and property of the joined plantations. Lucy had tacitly accepted such misbehavior in Eliza's father, so she was hardly surprised that Eliza's husband displayed the same traits.

Percy's law practice in New Orleans was flourishing, and he visited St. Francisville only irregularly. The gradual decline of his father had lately become more apparent to him. He and Philomena enjoyed an active social life in New Orleans. Now closer to three years than two, little Rand, as he was generally called rather than the more formal Randolph, was an active, precocious child. Endlessly inquisitive, he peppered his mother with questions as they strolled in a nearby park so that he learned the name of each new thing he saw. His vocabulary grew rapidly.

The routine of this small, happy community of three was to change at the first reports of yellow fever threatening another epidemic.

In late May 1855, Percy decided his little family must be removed from danger. It was too much to expect a woman who loved the outdoors as did Philomena to remain indoors for an extended period, nor for an active child to be rendered immobile by fear of death from Yellow Jack. Percy and Phil discussed the relocation at length. It was a decision not to be taken lightly. They agreed that it was only temporary, that by early fall Phil and Rand would return to the townhouse in New Orleans. If she were apprehensive at being lodged at the home of her in-laws, Phil did not betray her feelings. She was a dutiful wife and feared the recurring outbreaks that New Orleans suffered. Better to endure discomfort than disease and death. "When you think it best, we will leave," she assured her husband.

They packed Phil's clothing that was most suitable for country life. Her gowns for evening wear remained closeted for her return. All that little Rand might need fit into a corner of one steamer trunk. He was growing so quickly, he needed new clothes at six-month intervals, and they would surely return by then.

When the steamboat tied up at Bayou Sara's landing, Howard Moorhead and Pompey were waiting with a wagon and with two horses for Percy and Phil. Pompey loaded the trunk and baggage. Howard lifted Rand and seated him on the coach seat between him and Pompey for the six-mile ride to Bolingbroke.

ᢒᡒᢒ — ᡐᢙᡏ

Opposing counsel leaned forward on the table across from Percy and his client and held his thumb and right index finger an inch apart to demonstrate his seriousness. His manner was meant to be menacing, but Percy retained his bland expression. He had learned from observing Judah Benjamin that nothing disconcerted an opponent more than ignoring provocation.

"Look, here's how we see it, Moorhead. Your client promised my client, Felix Girod, he'd finish up all construction no later than February 15. It's the end of April and we're still not near to completion. We're about this close to suing for fraud as well as breach of contract."

Percy replied soothingly, "I'm certain you mean to give no offense, Mr. Brundage, by your last remark. We assure you that we proceed in a spirit of goodwill. Before this day is out, a resolution will be reached to the contentment of your client and mine. By the way Mr. Girod, how is your wife? My Philomena said Mrs. Girod missed the last altar society meeting because she was feeling poorly. We do hope she's all right."

Such exchanges had come to characterize Percy Moorhead's practice after his first few years lawyering. As he grew confident in representing clients, he became more relaxed. His smile appeared readily, his voice grew more resonant. When tempers rose in tense confrontations, whether commercial or domestic, Percy carefully adopted a conciliatory approach. Following Judah's example, he greeted aggressiveness with easy affability, quickly disarming his opponent. He would direct his attention to the other lawyer's client to establish a personal connection. Opposing counsel saw through Percy's gambit, but their clients did not. Most often, Percy Moorhead showed them more respect than did their own lawyer. Regardless of whether he met client, counsel, judge, or friend, Percy never failed to recall details of his last meeting with each nor to inquire about their family. After his early experiences in practice, he realized he need not bear the burden of conversation. He could instead rely on facial gestures, nods, winks and shrugs that could be taken as either comprehension or agreement. He learned that silence and gestures of empathy (feigned or genuine) were preferable to expressing his disagreements or opinions. Counter-arguments, he found, never persuaded another with whom he differed, and the satisfaction of speaking out passed quickly with no proportionate gain to him or to his client.

The most effective way of dealing with an obstinate opponent who would not yield to pleasant invitations to harmony was the cutting remark dressed as compliment, especially when delivered in the setting of a court room:

"My dear Mr. Kelly, your intelligence and learning are exceeded only by your rhetorical skills. You deploy arguments that mere reason could never sustain. They are, more often than not, magnificently inscrutable."

On another occasion he was recorded as declaiming to the assembled justices of the Louisiana Supreme Court:

"My learned opposing counsel's logic is impeccably impenetrable. Our leading jurists have been unable to grasp his subtlety when they have repeatedly ruled to a contrary conclusion. No fewer than four decisions of this court have opined in the manner favored by my client. But Mr. Belsom's view is the more imaginative proposition and indeed a radical departure from those settled principles. If your honors wish to be seen as bold architects of a new legal regime for our state, then by all means rule as my esteemed opponent urges you. If your goals are more modest, less adventuresome, then follow the boring but well-trod path of fidelity to the judicial norms set forth by this honorable Court for two generations."

What response could a lawyer Kelly or Belsom make to Percy's rhetorical flourishes? They suffered a sting for which they could not answer. If he did not always prevail, Percy unfailingly made the day in court a more pleasant experience.

For all the success he enjoyed as a lawyer and for all the contentment he experienced as husband and father, Percy Morehead suffered periodic episodes of despondency. The origins of these fits of depression were unknown to him. Fight them as he may, in their grip he felt like a man drowning. In the company of others, it was as if the maleficent spirits went into hiding, preferring to remain unseen by others, only to reemerge as he sat on the sofa after Phil and Rand were asleep. He struggled against the malicious demons by opening a copy of Robert Burton's *Anatomy of Melancholy* that he kept on a neglected shelf.

> Methinks I hear, methinks I see
> Ghosts, goblins, fiends; my phantasy
> Presents a thousand ugly shapes,
> Headless bears, black men, and apes,
> Doleful outcries, and fearful sights,
> My sad and dismal soul affrights.
> All my griefs to this are jolly,
> None so damn'd as melancholy.

Burton's self-deprecating lines could bring a smile, but still Percy had a sense of foreboding. What had Sister Lavinia told him?

> *The gods of old have blessed your name*
> *What you lose you will twice regain.*

What was he afraid of? If she were right, there was some significant loss ahead of him. Was it premonition keeping him awake at night?

Nonsense! No one can tell the future, no one. She was just a scheming gypsy, and he was foolish to pay her any heed. His bouts of melancholy had preceded encountering her with Phil.

Concealing his fears and apprehensions behind a confident face and manner, Percy grew in stature in the eyes of fellow lawyers, judges and politicians of all persuasions. Avoiding party identifications, Percy was neither Whig nor Democrat nor Know-Nothing but nodded sagely and sympathetically when listening to partisan acquaintances. Invitations by leaders of the political parties for Percy to seek a seat in the Louisiana legislature were politely declined.

Percy's reputation among New Orleans lawyers and businessmen assured that he never lacked for clients. His preference was to accept designation as appellant counsel in complex cases. Percy's appellate briefs were unaffected by the dark moods that descended upon him with little warning; judges and opponents noted their clarity and rhetorical skill and could not have imagined the bilious humors from which they emerged. Appellate cases were easier to schedule than trial work. But his routine, often pleasant, was interrupted by Benjamin's consuming Mexican project, his highway between the seas.

*Chapter 31*

# Informing the Family

Developments in Mexico in late summer 1855 altered Percy's plans to have his wife and son rejoin him in New Orleans. The plan for a new government that Benito Juarez and his compatriots had drawn up in New Orleans was adopted when the government of President Santa Anna was ousted in March. Juarez had immediately returned to Mexico. An interim president and a new government were installed. Juarez was to have a leading role, potentially the next president. The political changes now under way would determine the fate of the Tehuantepec Railroad. Senator Benjamin, Emile La Sere and other principals of the railroad project asked Percy Moorhead to leave as soon as possible for Mexico City to assess the new political climate and to press the case for recognition of the validity of the grant the company held through the assignments made to Falconnet.

A hasty trip to Bolingbroke followed a day after Percy met with Judah Benjamin and Emile La Sere. Phil and Percy had a joyful reunion. Four months had passed since they had last embraced one another.

"It will be good to sleep with you and not your shirt," she whispered into his ear.

"My shirt? Why?"

"It smells of you."

"My lord, I hope you would have washed it. Surely I sweat."

Phil wrapped her arms around her husband. "No washing. I miss your odor. A wife knows the odor of her husband and her children. I would know you in a room full of people entirely in the dark."

"I better leave you several. I don't know how long I'll be away. I'll explain at dinner."

Little Rand remembered his father but was shy. He walked slowly from Howard to Percy and looked his father in the eye when Percy picked him up and kissed his cheek.

Percy asked his son, "Have Mama Lucy and PawPaw taken good care of you?"

"Yes, Papa." Rand returned his father's kiss and clung to his hand when Percy set him down.

After a dinner of pork, potatoes and snapbeans, Percy told them of his intention to go to Mexico to further the railroad project of the Tehuantepec Company.

"Is it safe?" asked his mother, her tone suggesting disapproval.

"In the places I'll be going to, I'll be as safe as in most American cities."

"Aren't there a lot of Indians?" said Eliza. She was, as always, seated next to her mother, moon-like in orbit around her, moon-like with her dull, round, pasty-flesh face. Percy cared for his sister, retaining affection from the years when she was lively, inquisitive, more receptive to the world around her, when she took delight in the kittens and cock-a-tiels that Howard would bring up to her from New Orleans. Fear of not marrying had diminished her. Marrying Calvin Bunch had diminished her further.

"Not like the tribes in our West. One of the men I hope to work with is a Mexican Indian. His name is Benito Juarez. I met him in New Orleans while he was in exile. He's educated in law and was governor of one of their states."

Eliza was not convinced. "Calvin says all Indians are ignorant savages. That's how God made them."

"Perhaps he is closer to the Deity than I am. Those savages once had a great civilization. Their pyramids rivaled those of the Egyptians. I climbed them when I was in the army in Mexico City. Great feats of engineering." Softening at his sister's shrinking reaction, he said more gently, " I'm sorry I'll miss seeing Calvin before I leave. Please give him my warm regards."

"He's on business. Natchez, I think."

Howard turned the conversation away from the son-in-law. "Are you the company's lawyer?"

"Not on any matters in Louisiana yet. Not since Judah Benjamin formed his new law firm. But I'll go as a registered agent of the company. No one expects me to transact any business. There have been two different concessions granted by Mexico and we made a treaty two years ago that affects our rights. When I went to England, we set it up so that a Mr. Falconnet would succeed to the rights across Mexico and could assign those rights. But there are different opinions among the Mexicans about whether any grant should be recognized by a new government. They may want to renegotiate with the Tehuantepec Company or with our government. My assignment is to learn as much as I can about the people who will be the new Mexican government and what they think about the railroad project. After I meet with the British bankers in Mexico who have been our contacts in the past, I'll try to meet with Señor Juarez and Señor Ocampo. And Judah Benjamin assures me that I can expect the full cooperation of our ambassador to Mexico and his staff."

"Do you have a stake in the company?" asked Howard, raising his eyebrows.

"They've given me a sum of money to work with in the next

few months. I don't have any shares in the Tehuantepec Company, but I do have a counter letter with the company that provides that I will be assigned a two percent interest in the net profits of the railroad for ten years from the date of the first commercial transit of goods or passengers on the railroad."

This information reassured Howard. "Good. A strong incentive. That could more than justify the time and effort you need to put into the project."

"I'm sorry it will take me away from Phil and Rand for an indefinite period."

"Nothing would make us happier than your letting them stay here with us. Phil and Rand have become so much a part of our lives, I don't know how we could do without them."

Percy turned to his wife. "Phil, how do you feel about staying at Bolingbroke?"

Philomena put her fork beside her plate. She spoke carefully. "I like New Orleans. I like St. Francisville. I love Bolingbroke. I love my husband and my husband's family. Since I can't be with you in any of those places, I am equally happy to remain here. If Rand can't be with his father, I would hate to take him away from his grandmother and his PawPaw. He and Mr. Moorhead have grown very close. PawPaw takes him everywhere on the plantation with him. Pompey has made him a rocking horse he loves to ride. And Julius hung him a swing in the old oak at the back of the house. He wouldn't have those or PawPaw if I took him back to New Orleans now."

Everything Phil said was true. But it was incomplete. In truth, she longed for the first year of her marriage to have continued. She had flourished as a new entrant into New Orleans society and its political community. Her wit and social skills had been at their shining best. The visitors to their town home and at the political gatherings where she played hostess had admired the bright young wife and her dashing lawyer-soldier husband who had in short time occupied a place of prominence in this cosmopolitan, exotic city. She was fresh, vibrant and pleasingly irreverent. However, she was a mother and devoted to her husband and New Orleans society would have to wait. She would make the best of the situation. The months spent shut-in because of the yellow fever epidemic were disturbing to her. With that, and the rearing of an infant, she had not yet recovered her former ebullience. Soon, she would try to recapture it in her new surroundings.

Percy turned to his father. His expression told him everything. The company of his grandson in the past four months had revived him in body and spirit. Together he and the boy walked in the woods and fields, naming the animals – big and small – the birds, the trees, the flowers. "That is a squirrel. Can you say squirrel?" "Squrrrr." "This is a horse. Can you say horse?" "Horrrz." "This is a cow. What does the cow say?" "Mooooo." "What color is the hen?" "Ret."

Everything was new to the child, and everything was re-newed for the grandfather. Calvin Bunch receded from Howard's cares while his attention was occupied by the child, who was all innocence, all potential. The supervision of two plantations was easier when he could make a visit to the gin shed into an adventure for a three-year-old, when the gathering of eggs became a game of hide-and-seek. And the companionship of his daughter-in-law greatly eased Howard's burdens. He could talk to her. She listened to him with greater attentiveness than Eliza ever had and with more sympathy than Lucy would. Phil would volunteer for a trip to town if he needed something or take up a hoe to show a young field-hand how she was to plant a seed at the proper depth with a protective mound shaped over it.

Percy said, satisfied, "Well, there's our answer. Randolph Moorhead is the new master of Bolingbroke Hall for the time-being. New Orleans' loss will be St. Francisville's gain."

Chapter 32

# Return to Mexico City

Three days later Percy was on a ship out of New Orleans steaming south for Vera Cruz. The vessel was a pleasant contrast to his voyage of less than a decade earlier on troop transport boats, though lacking the luxury of his trans-Atlantic crossing on the *Baltic*. Tropical breezes offset the end-of-summer heat of the Gulf of Mexico. He spent the few days of travel reading newspapers he had collected in New Orleans on political changes in Mexico over the previous six months. A correspondent on his way to Mexico City for the *Daily Picayune*, named Drury, filled him in on some of the political personalities who were active in the latest overthrow of Santa Anna. And he brushed up on his Spanish by chatting with two Mexicans returning home.

Percy and Drury spent one night in a hostel in Vera Cruz and quickly departed early the next morning by mule-drawn coach, after a breakfast of goat meat and tortilla. They feared the *vomito*. The road past Cerro Gordo had been improved, but little, since Percy's nights in the dark seeking a flanking path northeast of the bend. There were few signs that it had been the scene of a decisive battle of a significant war between the two countries. Percy wondered if the body of the Mexican youth he had hidden in the chaparral had received a proper burial. He doubted he could find the spot even if he tried.

In Puebla Percy parted company with the American journalist. He was pleased to find Father Pablo was still associated with the cathedral and seminary. He treated the priest to a meal at a modest restaurant and was candid with him about the purpose of his trip. He asked for the priest's views on the current ouster of President Santa Anna.

"Be careful what you pray for," the Franciscan said ruefully. "You may get it."

"What do you mean?"

"The reformers. They are more honest. But they blame the conditions of Mexico on the church. They see wealth in the church and poverty among the people. They mistake the former to be the cause of the latter. If the church is stripped of its authority, the people will be wealthy and the church poor, they believe. I do not doubt the sincerity of some. But others? I think they would take the lands and buildings of the church and give them to their own supporters. This is what they did in England, yes?"

"Yes. King Henry Tudor."

"These reformers, the ones who would tear down the church, they are the ones educated by the church. Juarez and Ocampo. People say that both are native peasants without parents. They were educated at seminaries by clericals like me. Would they have learned to read and write without the church? They say we make the people superstitious and keep them in a child-like condition. But what will the Mexican people become when we have been run out?"

Percy had sympathy but no answers that could reassure the priest. He only shrugged.

Fr. Pablo now asked, "But tell me, what has become of your friend, Jed?"

Percy hesitated. "There was no way you could know. How shall I say this, except to say – he was killed outside Mexico City.

At the convent of Churubusco. In combat."

"Oh? I'm sorry to hear that. He was very troubled when he came to me."

"Yes," agreed Percy. "He apparently thought of taking his own life before joining the army."

The priest nodded vigorously. "As I surmised. That would have cost him his soul. Becoming a soldier was not the right answer for him either. He came to see himself as fighting a war for a slave-holding president who was expanding slavery into Texas and westward. He was afraid he was killing Mexicans to keep Africans in chains."

"What did you tell him?"

"What I would tell any man. It is no sin to kill another in a just war. It is murder and a mortal sin to kill a man in an unjust war."

"Even if the other man is trying to kill you?"

"Even so. It is better to die in a state of grace than commit the mortal sin of murder. The soul will not perish. It is no different from what we teach the peasant girls – they cannot consent to carnal knowledge even if a rapist threatens to kill them. Canon law teaches they must resist to their last breath."

Percy said nothing, though he found the priest's thinking foolish. God could not be so scrupulous an accountant that self-preservation was debited as sin. He would not tell the cleric that his teaching surely produced Jed's death. Nor would he open a debate on the features of a just war. Each man owes loyalties and duties to family, friends, neighbors and country that may conflict with a priest's analysis of a just war. Fr. Pablo, should he be apprised of Jed's unloaded gun, would surely say Jed had died an honorable death, assuring him of salvific grace. Percy thought it a useless death. *Requiēscat in pace,* Jed Barkly.

Emerging from the restaurant off the plaza, they encountered a religious procession. Amid the clanging of bells and a strange dirge of whistles and drums and horns, the procession issued from a church near the Casa de las Diligencias. A dozen or fifteen priests and monks preceded a long train of waxen saints and angels set on low wagons, rigged in costly finery and bedecked with gold and jewels. A crowd of spectators knelt reverently in the dust along the route until the objects of veneration had passed. Percy made the sign of the cross each time the priest did.

At Fr. Pablo's urging, Percy hired a guide sent to him by the priest, and a horse to take him to the capital. They set forth in mid-morning the next day. On their second day, they came to a bend in the road. Just a few yards from the road was a tree on whose bare branches hung three swarthy Mexicans, their corpses already putrid, fly-infested. Their hands were tied behind their backs, in their stocking feet, their boots having been stolen. What good are boots to a dead man? Each had pinned to his chest a paper on which was scrawled – *bandido*.

"Are there many bandits here?" Percy asked the guide, a stout, unkempt man of about forty.

"*Si*. Not so many as last week. No bandits will come while you travel with me."

The guide did not explain how he was able to protect him with such assurance. Perhaps it was professional courtesy. Glancing at the boots of his Virgil, Percy noted they were freshly oiled, out of keeping with the rest of his worn clothing. Were they newly acquired?

Percy and his guide spent the last night of the journey at an inn in Ayotla, a few hundred yards from where he had camped with General Twiggs's army in the summer of 1847. The final twenty-five miles to the plaza of the capital were covered by early afternoon the next day. As they rode on a pleasant morning he recalled the well-cultivated rich sandy soil, the road bordered by cactus, fields of ripe corn, and, along the lake, over a causeway, numerous ducks and starlings. Distant hills on all sides of the widespread valley were as picturesque and beautiful as he remembered. Entering the city, the guide accepted his payment and turned his horse back to the east, leading Percy's hired mount back to the stables in Puebla.

The desk clerk of the Hotel Iturbide spoke English well. He efficiently located a reservation in the name of Moorhead, Percy. Percy was fortunate to have arranged his accommodation in advance. The hotel was a hive of polyglot activity – Spanish, English, French and German predominating. Formerly the palace of Agustín de Iturbide, the first emperor of Mexico, the building had been reincarnated as a hotel to rank with the best in Paris or London. The hotel's name showed the shifting views of the fickle Mexican population: Iturbide was loved, hated, loved again, now venerated like the wax and wooden icons in any of Mexico's recurring pageants. Percy paid $30 a month for two months in advance and was escorted to a room twenty feet square, with a window opening down to the ground, and a wide balcony overlooking a bowling-alley, well shaded by trees. Two hours later, he eagerly ate in the hotel restaurant, the first satisfying meal he had had since setting out.

Sipping coffee, he reflected on what he should do in the coming weeks. His goal was clear enough – to advance the Tehuantepec Railroad project. Necessarily, this had to be done at the capital city, many hundreds of miles from the planned route. Engineering skills were required to survey the best route, to remove layers of growth, to break ground, to lay crossties and rails. But it took political and legal skills to make a concept into a reality. At Princeton Percy had learned of the *demiurge,* a figure of ancient philosophy and myth responsible for the fashioning and maintenance of the physical universe, who turned the force of the *potential* into the *actual.* The demiurge preceded the engineer, as the architect did the builder.

When last in Mexico, Percy was part of an army of conquest, working with the tools of cannon, musket, pistol and sword to win an objective. Now, he returned as a supplicant, seeking support for a project from some of the same politicians who were forced to relinquish to their northern neighbor title to vast areas formerly subject to their sovereignty. What instruments could he employ to win new concessions from them?

Percy rehearsed his legal arguments on a pad:

*Contract*: The new government, inchoate as it might be at present, was bound by the grants conferred by prior rulers to Garay, Hargous, Sloo, and Falconnet – whose claims were held by the Tehuantepec Railroad Company, existing by charter of the Louisiana legislature. Solemn obligations. Binding under the laws of men and nations, no matter if tainted at the inception.

*Utility*: the Tehuantepec Railroad would open the trade of Mexico to the world, bringing jobs and prosperity to the country as never before experienced.

*Self-interest. Mordida. Quid pro quo.* A Mexican official might seek more immediate personal persuasion in the form of coin of the realm. He would simply have to deflect, to feign a lack of understanding of Mexican law, language and custom. Percy had no money to pay bribes, even if he were willing to resort to the unsavory, albeit nearly universal, practice.

But who would be his audience? All of the leaders of the latest revolt against Santa Anna were assembled in Cuernavaca, fifty-five miles to the south. Many of the members of the Mexican Senate and Chamber of Deputies had gathered in Mexico City awaiting developments. The only certainty in the mass of confusion was that Santa Anna had to go. Upon his abdication, regional differences among the remaining officials had to be ironed out and conflicting interests harmonized. Juan Álvarez was a compromise candidate who was named chief of the revolution and was the assumed choice for interim president until a consensus could be reached. Until a new government was fully formed, until there was a functioning Congress, no one would know who would exercise the power to recognize the claims of the Tehuantepec Railroad Company. It was pointless to go to Cuernavaca when those in Cuernavaca were sure to relocate to Mexico City in the immediate future. In the interim, he would present himself to the American ambassador and see what support and guidance he might expect from his own government. After getting a sense of the major players coming to power, he would try to establish a relationship with Benito Juarez or Melchor Ocampo, based on his prior associations in New Orleans.

Over a couple of weeks, Percy met with American envoys and attachés and found them unable – or unwilling – to answer his questions. He was puzzled by their indifference to a project that was surely important to the commercial interests of their country. After repeated inquiries, one of the American clerks finally explained what Percy should have already inferred. The ambassador, James Gadsden, had a personal and political stake that was opposed to the Tehuantepec project.

A railroad president himself, Gadsden had negotiated with Santa Anna the acquisition of territory from Mexico at its northern border to facilitate a railroad to California westward from Texas. He was part of a political plan to divide California into two states, with the southern portion to be admitted to the Union as a slave state. Gadsden would do what he could to impede the development of an Isthmus of Tehuantepec crossing that would compete with his favored overland route and the expansion of slavery to California. Percy understood the futility of seeking support from the United States Department of State so long as Gadsden remained ambassador.

Percy settled in to a routine. Much of each day he established himself into a large chair in the hotel lobby, crafted of mahogany and bull leather and stuffed with horsehair. He would read all the newspapers on local and national developments and jot notes in a small notebook. He listened to passers-by and watched who was talking to whom. The same would-be politicians would talk on one day with a petitioner and on the next to his opponent. He regarded the exchanges with some amusement and not a little disdain. Hangers-on are always found in the doors and lobbies of government, waiting to grab the attention of some official who can influence a decision in their favor. And then it came to Percy Moorhead that he was one of the hangers-on himself. A moment of self-awareness settled on him, like a garment that appeared ill-fitted when he viewed himself in a mirror. He was less an attorney for a noble project of international importance and more a seeker of political favor from politicians whom he regarded as tawdry if not contemptible. But duty required that he continue on his course. He had signed on to this role for Judah Benjamin; he must follow it through. He struck up conversations and made acquaintances among the many people, Mexican and foreign, who were seeking favor with the new government.

If he were to play the character, he must look the part. Percy grew himself a mustache in the style of locals and found the tailor who made the clothing of the well-dressed hacienda owners and politicians. Espinoza the Bootmaker measured his feet and cobbled a pair of boots that fit better than anything Percy had ever found in New Orleans. For Philomena he purchased several pieces of fine silver jewelry that would be easy to carry home – and to conceal during his journey. For his son, a small silver horse. When not walking around the Plaza Mayor, he enjoyed strolling in the park at the west end of the city, the Alameda.

கூ கூ — ఆ ఆ

On his second Sunday in the city, Percy made his way up the Paseo to the Plaza de Toros, the bullring. He found a large stadium with an immense crowd, perhaps as many as 3,000 in attendance. Amid bursts of music and shouts of the people, the first bull came bounding in from a gate on the north side. Bewildered by the light and noise, the bull stopped, pawed the ground, and then with a furious bellow rushed at the nearest horse. The rider held him off with his spear. Turning, the bull attacked another horse, this time more successfully. Both horse and rider rolled headlong to the ground. The rider picked himself up and, with an exaggerated stroll and waving with his right arm, showed the crowd he was uninjured. His dying horse was dispatched by a blow to the head with a wooden mallet and replaced by a fresh mount.

Percy was both fascinated and depressed by the spectacle as the slaughter resumed. Several more horses were ripped open, to the cheers and shouts of the crowd. Now three men on foot threw short lances covered with fireworks into the bull's flesh, till he was raging with pain, the fire-crackers adding to the din. Then, over the yelling of the bull, a bugle sounded. The matador stepped forward, bowed to the crowd, then engaged the wounded animal with several passes of his crimson cape. As the angry, injured bull snorted and pawed the ground, the bullfighter plunged his sword over the horns and into the animal. The first bull of the day collapsed and was finished.

The same sequence of events was begun again, with the outcome never in doubt. Why, Percy wondered, were the Mexicans so attracted to the carnage? The only uncertainty seemed to be the ratio of horse deaths to each bull that entered the circle of animal mortality.

Between events, the crowd was treated to displays of horsemanship and lasso tricks, but these received little attention from the bloodlust mass. Percy could work up no sympathy for the bulls, but it pained him to watch a gored horse lying on his side, raising his head in wild-eyed agony and finally subsiding, usually with a clubbing to its brain, then dragged ignominiously away by a pair of horses pulling ropes tied to the hind legs of the dead animal. Percy and most of his fellow sons of the South were familiar with cock fights and dog fights but nothing he had experienced could compare for ritual violence with the savagery of Mexican bull fights. Only war was worse, and too much of that was yet to come.

## Chapter 33

# An Audience with Juarez

You are in a foreign country. You are an observer, gathering information that may be useful to you as you represent the interests that have sent you on this mission. You do not think you are being observed at the same time. Then someone calls out your name, and it jars you. Briefly, you are dislocated.

"Ola, Moorhead. Is that you? I thought you were a Mexican."

Turning in his seat in the Iturbide Hotel courtyard, Percy saw a lean figure wearing brown canvas trousers and a cotton long-sleeve shirt walking toward him, his back to the setting sun. He recognized the craggy face of Drury, the New Orleans newspaper man with whom he had parted company in Puebla a few weeks earlier.

Standing, Percy extended his hand. "Mr. Drury. Well, I'm not sure if I am flattered or offended. I hoped to be inconspicuous but did not expect to be mistaken for a native."

"Only an angry editor would call me *Mr.* Drury. Kit it is. Kit Drury at your service."

"Kit it is. I know you're here for the *Picayune*. But tell me how you happened to end up in New Orleans."

"I'll treat you to the short version and skip the wife and girlfriends parts. Originally, I'm from Vermont. After a couple of years of college, I knocked about New York and Pennsylvania in odd jobs before discovering I have a knack for stringing words together that I could convert into coin more readily than as a saloon keeper. A newspaper in New York City hired me to investigate City Hall and police arrests. Restless legs and two threats on my life took me south, landing me eventually in New Orleans, with assignments to Cuba, Mexico and Central America. My arrangement with the *Daily Picayune* allows me to correspond to a London newspaper as well."

"Beer or dinner? Your choice," said Percy. "I'll buy and we'll compare notes. We may have different purposes but common means to those ends."

"Guard your wallet, Percy. My spare frame belies a large appetite."

Over dinner, the two men compared their notes and agreed that the political scene was highly fluid. Drury had just come from Cuernavaca and reported that the two men Percy had known in New Orleans were certain to be powers in any new government – Ocampo and Juarez.

For the next week or so, Percy and Kit Drury met nightly in the bar of the Hotel Iturbide to swap stories. Drury was a leathery man of forty plus years, with a droll sense of the comic and absurd, which allowed him to view Louisiana politics and Latin American revolutions with amusement. He would report on both with wry wit. He smoked the dark cigaritos favored by both sexes of Mexicans and maintained unconvincingly that they soothed the persistent cough he had picked up through frequent encounters with tropical diseases. Kit downed two drinks for each imbibed by Percy but never showed effects until his eyelids drooped and he shuffled and stumbled his way back to his ground floor room, sometimes aided by Percy's shoulder. Percy enjoyed his company.

Based on Drury's information, which came from better sources than Percy's own, it appeared that a new government was nearly formed. With little more that he could learn or accomplish in Mexico City, Percy decided it was time to contact Juarez or Ocampo or both. Kit Drury gave him the names of three contacts Percy might find useful.

On a horse he hired, Percy made the journey to Cuernavaca in two days. It was early October. The city had an excellent climate and was alive with flowering bougainvillea. After inquiring around, Percy learned where Juarez was staying and had a note delivered to him requesting an appointment. Within an hour Juarez replied and set an appointment for five in the afternoon.

The Mexican received his American visitor pleasantly, but he was not given to small talk, nor to smiles, nor to any other displays of emotion. His habitual expression was etched in stone, little different from those of his ancestors carved in the pyramids of Mexico.

"Have you come all this way to see me? For your kindness, I owe you a respectful reception," Juarez said from behind a desk, neither rising nor extending a hand.

Although his Spanish was adequate for conversation, Percy and Juarez had spoken in English in New Orleans; he thought it more respectful to speak in English to Juarez now. "Señor Juarez, as glad as I am to see you, I am here because of the Tehuantepec Railroad. It is not to further Mexican democracy or reform of the church. I do not care about land redistribution. I pity the *peones* and am glad I am not one of them. They are not my concern. It is to Mexico I appeal. For many years, the government of Mexico has committed itself to the railroad project. The principals in the Tehuantepec Railroad Company have relied on those commitments and have invested their money and time based on Mexico's solemn promises in an unbroken chain stretching back fifteen years. Anyone who succeeds to the leadership of Mexico should give full faith and credit to Mexico's binding promises."

Juarez's face still showed no expression. "A pretty argument,

Mr. Percy. If it were a treaty between sovereigns you might persuade me. But the commitments you represent as being made by Mexico were obtained by corrupt means. Is it not true in your state that an order of a judge secured by bribery is void? How can a contract be otherwise? If I am to be Minister of Justice, that is what I will tell our President."

Percy was undeterred. He had anticipated Juarez's response. He now urged that the present holders of the concession rights must be distinguished and separated from the original grantees. And he would try to persuade Juarez of the utility to Mexico of an American-built railroad.

"Senator Benjamin and his associates were not parties to the original negotiations. They are good faith purchasers of what they believed to be valid obligations. How were they to know whether the grants were obtained through irregularities? Regardless of that, I will tell you and any of your reformers or your opposition that the Tehuantepec Railroad will be good for Mexico. You have capital, but no one has enough capital for a project of this size. Near the Hotel Iturbide where I am staying, there is a fine mining college. But you do not have engineers who have laid hundreds of miles of track across rivers and mountains. You have no foundries to manufacture the rails. The steamboat and the railroad have made the American south wealthy. They have made England wealthy. They will do the same for Mexico. But you can kill the railroad with paperwork and corruption and taxes and customs duties."

Juarez leaned forward ever so slightly. "Señor Percy, I think you are like your Senator Benjamin. You and he have studied political history and you both understand duty. You do not pretend to be what you are not. You are honest. You make no secret of what you want and why you want it. Your only flattery is not offering me any bribes. You know that would be useless." Juarez continued, without rancor, "Have you not found paperwork and corruption in New Orleans? Are my people so different from yours? I have heard stories from my friend Emile La Sere. He told me that the judges I met with you at your supreme court are good men. But he also told me of the one who was not, who left in dishonor." Little in New Orleans had escaped Juarez's attention.

Showing his earnest agreement, Percy responded, "Men of good will must work together. We must work with what we find and try to better it." On his fifty-mile ride from Mexico City Percy had tried to frame the arguments he would make to Juarez, drawing on his lessons in rhetoric at Princeton. Ethos, Pathos, Logos. Use the particular. Appeal to the highest motives. Evoke your auditor's emotions. "Does not destiny call you to something higher, Señor Juarez? If you think Mexico will be better off with mule packs carrying two hundred pounds of corn or cotton at two miles an hour from village to village than with a steam engine carrying 100,000 pounds of goods of all sorts across the entire country at forty miles an hour, then you should oppose the railroad. But if you want to leave a better Mexico for you having played your part, you should support the railroad."

"If more of your countrymen were like you, . . . ." The diminutive Mexican left the sentence unfinished. "I am not *el presidente*. There are many others in Mexico who will have a say. But I must ask you this. Have you been to Coatzacoalcos, to Minatitlán, and Ixtepec and Tehuantepec?"

Puzzled, Percy admitted, "No. I haven't."

"In New Orleans I heard the Isthmus described as if it were a land of milk and honey, all flat and filled with native labor, smiling and cheerful. I have been governor of the state of Oaxaca. It is nothing like what Senator Benjamin's investors believe it to be. A railroad and ferries will require more money and time that any of you have described in promoting the plan. If you value your life, do not go there to see for yourself. If ladrones do not rob and kill you, mosquitos, scorpions and pinolilloes will."

Percy had heard of the pinolilloes – tiny red insects so small as to be scarcely visible to the naked eye. They bury themselves into a man's flesh and work their way in, till they die. They keep their victims in a fever for the space of three days.

Undeterred, Percy continued, "We always say Rome wasn't built in a day. I haven't been there, but I think the Romans had to drain their swamps to make a great civilization. Was it not true of Mexico City also?"

"You are an advocate always, Señor Percy." Juarez was now smiling at Percy's perseverance. "I am not your enemy. But do not look for me to sell your project to my people. La Reforma must come first. We must end the *fueros* of the Catholic Church and the army. Until then, no progress is possible for my people. Without reform first, your project will entrench the conservatives who oppose all change."

Percy nearly spoke but suppressed the urge to ask Juarez who were his people. The Mexican saw his hesitation.

"Your Senator Benjamin, do you know why I like him, why we understand one another?"

Percy replied, "I would be presumptuous to respond."

"He is a Jew. I am Zapotec. We are both from conquered tribes. He must live and work with Christians who despise him as an alien among them. As I must. My native language is taken from me. I was made to worship a god from foreign lands that the Spaniards brought with them when they took our lands. The descendants of the *conquistadores* are only a small percentage of the Mexicans, but they own most of the land and control the church and the voting and the political offices. Benjamin understands this. He does not pretend otherwise. You are like him in this, this lack of pretense. But you do not have his personal ambition or his guile. A jew in America cannot be a leader of jews. He can only serve his masters and himself. An Indian in my country can serve his people and justice. Have you had to ask yourself who you serve?"

Juarez's question was not meant to reprove Percy. It was an honest query, and invited Percy to reflect on it, not to answer it. The discussion was over with it. Juarez had other work that pressed upon him. The two men shook hands, and Percy exited into the evening.

Kit Drury had warned Percy that housing in Cuernavaca was hard to find. Percy recalled seeing a private home that had posted on its porch a notice of vacancy, taking advantage of the temporary political circumstances that had put a premium on available space. He ate a light supper provided by his host and retired for the night.

Percy's trip of two days had yielded a conversation of a half-hour. But what an important half-hour in Percy's long life. Although Percy Moorhead and Benito Juarez, because of cultural and political differences, could never be friends, they had solidified a connection of mutual respect that transcended those differences.

The next morning, Percy contacted the sources suggested by Drury; they confirmed that President Alvarez would name Benito Juarez as Minister of Justice and Melchor Ocampo would become Foreign Minister. Both were to be named to positions likely to affect the future of the Tehuantepec Railroad project.

Leaving Cuernavaca, Percy took the same route to return to his hotel in the capital. He resumed his routine in the lobby's easy chair. He began to compose a report for the Tehuantepec Railroad Company on what he had learned and what they could expect from the new government, but not while Gadsden was the ambassador.

In mid-November President Alvarez rode into Mexico City and step-by-step installed his new government. Percy was homesick and encountered continuing futility in trying to accomplish anything worthwhile. The new president would not grant him an audience. Juarez and Ocampo were both preoccupied with organizing their ministries and had no time to take up a project that would take years to yield results. The American commercial consul expressed his interest and sympathy for Percy's project but could only encourage him to persist – without substantial involvement of the American government.

Percy packed his bags and settled his bill at the Hotel Iturbide. He left on a very good horse he purchased and would sell in Vera Cruz. He hired no guide, concerned that his boots made by Espinoza the Bootmaker might find themselves on other feet when Fr. Pablo was not choosing the guide.

A few miles outside the city, Percy was stopped by a pair of Mexican soldiers. The larger of the two demanded that Percy exchange horses with him in the name of the new Mexican Republic. He asserted that the military had the power of appropriation, and the condition of his horse did not permit him to fulfill his duties. Percy had had enough of Mexican lawlessness. He pulled out a large revolver concealed by his riding coat. He replied that his duties to his superiors did not permit him to relinquish his horse without an order from a court of competent jurisdiction. He would have to resist their entreaties under the authority of Samuel Colt. The soldiers shrugged and rode lazily on. They were amused that they had met a norteamericano who would not be intimidated.

*Chapter 34*

# Percy's Report

After waiting for a vessel in Vera Cruz for several days, Percy was finally on board and on his way back to New Orleans. The waters of the Gulf were rough but did not threaten the voyage. He resumed his report in his cabin, while rain pelted the porthole.

To: The Tehuantepec Railroad Company

From: Wallace Percy Moorhead, esq.

Re: Conditions of the New Government of Mexico

It is not customary in Mexico to decide Presidential elections by the ballot-box. Aspiring candidates resort to revolutions and conspiracies as the means of fulfilling their designs. Accordingly, a standing army has been an inevitable feature of Mexican rule. The Mexican military is composed of two branches: one, the *Estado Mayor*, corresponding to our regular army, the officers being well educated, and the men well drilled and uniformed. The other branch resembles our militia. When President Alvarez came to the capital, he brought with him many of the latter, which are called the Army of the South, who now guard the Palace and overrun the city. These tribal militia are known as *Pintos*, or painted ones, as some still wear war paint of the jungle. Although the troops are in the service of the government, and receive regular pay, when the government has money and rations, recruiting is generally carried on by resorting to strong measures. Loyalties shift rapidly, and different strong men hold sway over their own militia in their regions. As a new government settles in, it is unlikely that we can count on stability over an extended period. If, as expected, Ignacio Comonfort becomes president, our contacts Juarez and Ocampo will leave the government and likely return to their own states. Comonfort is irresolute and unable to continue on a stable path. The prospect of continued uncertainty about the tenure of Mexico's leaders will affect the ability of the Tehuantepec Railroad to attract new investors and to raise capital through loans.

The law courts of the country have little status. The military and the clergy have from the days of Spanish rule been exempt from the ordinary courts. Their privileges are called *fueros* and will not be given up without further civil war. There is little correspondence between written law and what is dispensed in the courts, which remains largely customary law.

The revenues of the country, if properly levied and collected, and not subject to the peculations of officials, would be much more than sufficient to carry on the expenses of government. The numerous interior custom houses annually collect large amounts of duties, and a good income is also derived from the mines. Owing to the exorbitant duties, smuggling is extensively engaged in, particularly on the Pacific coast and the Texas frontier, and many large capitalists who can now count the dollars by millions, have amassed their fortunes by this illegal practice. During the rule of Santa Anna, a certain merchant was on terms of intimacy with the recurring *Presidente*, and frequently obtained exclusive privileges for the introduction of goods without paying duties. The enormous profits would be divided with the greedy *presidente* in return for his kindness in granting the privileges. Thus, they were mutually concerned in swindling the country. So, too, with other merchants. Commitments made by Santa Anna are, as a result, looked on with disfavor by many Mexicans, including those who have recently overthrown him. Our claim for the Tehuantepec route of course is derived of a grant by Santa Anna.

In several ports, the business of introducing contraband goods is carried on very extensively, by an English commercial house, and British ships of war have frequently been known to afford protection to the smugglers, in the very faces of the authorities of those ports. The mercantile house which engages so largely in these transactions, on the gulf of California, is immensely wealthy, and completely rules the district which is the scene of their operations. Some Mexicans fear that a foreign controlled railroad across the Isthmus of Tehuantepec will only increase opportunities for contraband. Paradoxically, our railroad project threatens the lucrative contraband elsewhere in Mexico.

Bribery is very openly practiced, and justice is always obtained by the parties who have the most money. Important cases are carried on by the plaintiff and defendant holding a controversy, in which the arguments are written on sealed paper, the cost of which is a great source of profit to the government, and placed in the hands of the judge who is to decide the case. When the parties have disputed and answered each other on paper, to their own satisfaction and to the detriment of their *bolsas* (pockets), the documents are examined and the merits of the case decided from them. This is a mere outline, of course, and numerous technicalities exist which serve to annoy and impoverish the disputants, and greatly add to the welfare of the lawyers, who draw up the documents and render themselves otherwise useful. The rule of law to which we are accustomed is completely lacking in this country, so our appeals to the obligation of contract represented by the Garay and Sloo and Falconet concessions fall on unlistening ears. We cannot look to the Mexican courts for support.

*Peonage* is a system of bondage in which the bondsman is compelled to work for a master in payment for debt. All the large plantations, called here *haciendas,* are owned by very wealthy men. Nearly all pride themselves on the purity of their Spanish heritage. So, too, is it with the military officers, who are often drawn from the ruling Spanish-blood families. Individual planters frequently possess tracts of land forty or fifty miles square. These immense farms are principally devoted to cattle-raising or the production of corn, the labor being performed by hundreds of Indian *peones*. According to the old Mexican laws, or usage, for the Indians appear to be the only ones who are thus used, a creditor can obtain payment by compelling his debtor to labor. Should the labor of a lifetime fail to accomplish the liquidation of the debt, the children of the *peon* become responsible for it. This is known to be the practice, whether allowed by law or not. This system would never be tolerated by any race of men but the ignorant, careless, down-trodden Indians of Mexico, who, did they but know it, are by far the most numerous, and might be the most powerful, class of the inhabitants of the country. There is no class of free labor, such as the English enjoy from the Irish nation, to draw upon for construction of a railroad. Labor will surely have to be imported.

The owners of the haciendas and the military invariably support the church, and the leadership of the church reciprocates their support. Nevertheless, some of the parish priests take up the cause of the *peones* of the villages. Such priests become radicals, even revolutionaries.

Reformers like Juarez and Ocampo of Indian blood would redistribute lands of the church and the haciendas and would eradicate the church from the lives of the Mexican poor – who are mostly Indian. But what will replace these in the lives of the *peones* if the reforms take place? The ancient Indian gods will not return. The *peones* would live by subsistence farming and remain in poverty. The masses will be subject to manipulation by numerous political factions mounted by regional strong men, *caudillos*. It would be little different from the chaos that would ensue if all the bondsmen of our southern states were instantly manumitted.

All concerns with the Mexican government are transacted with the greatest inefficiency. The most trivial affairs are surrounded by ceremonies and difficulties, apparently, for no other purpose than to give annoyance and vexation. The uncertainty of all things depending upon Mexican promises, and, in fact, a great deal of their character is expressed in these two phrases, which are constantly used, and are the words always learned first by foreigners: *Quien sabe*? God knows. *Mañana*, Tomorrow.

I must reluctantly conclude that the Tehuantepec Railroad project is at a standstill for the foreseeable future. The struggles among the haciendas, the church, the army and the Indian masses, with their radical leaders, prevent anyone in the government from accepting responsibility for promoting a private project in the way we do in our country.

Only when the project becomes a government-to-government undertaking with substantial benefits to whatever ruling groups emerge will the project be able to move forward. And a government-to-government project, secured by a treaty, will not be possible so long as the present American ambassador to Mexico represents the interests of our government. When he is replaced, it is imperative that his successor is an envoy sympathetic to the Tehuantepec route between the oceans.

In conclusion, I would recommend a fresh start with the new Mexican government. The backers of the project could reorganize the endeavor and seek a new grant from the Mexicans, overlaid upon the existing rights and claims – old wine in a new bottle. This approach would absolve the new government in Mexico City of validating earlier wrongs imposed by the now reviled Santa Anna. It will be more effective to appeal to Mexican pride than to insist upon their adherence to obligations they consider as ill-gotten. The express backing of the United States government, joined with a postal contract for the US mail to cross the Isthmus of Tehuantepec to connect with California, would go far in negotiating a new arrangement with the Mexicans.

Respectfully submitted,
W. Percy Moorhead, esq.

On a chill December morning, Percy disembarked from his steamer. He collected his mail from his clerk at the law office and left his report to be copied for Benjamin and two others.

The townhouse was dusty from his absence. A fire quickly dispelled cold from the living room but could not displace the loneliness Percy suddenly felt in familiar surroundings that were devoid of his wife and son. He separated his correspondence into three stacks and put those with the highest priority in a satchel to carry with him to Bolingbroke.

He left word the next morning with his clerk that he would be back in two weeks. Then he boarded a steamboat, which a day and a half later deposited him at the Bayou Sara landing. It was a joyous reunion. Phil called him "Señor Percy" and Rand tugged at his mustache as he laughed in his father's arms. The melancholy he experienced in Mexico in his final weeks was temporarily held at bay.

After lunch Percy said to his wife, "We should discuss the future." He had been at Bolingbroke for a week. Phil and little Rand seemed to have settled into life on the plantation quite comfortably. Percy was reluctant to move them back to New Orleans after they had been away the better part of a year. Who could say but that the yellow fever would not return again in the late spring? She had made friends with the lieutenant-governor's wife and family and with the wives of several merchants in St. Francisville. She attended services at the Anglican church with Lucy and Eliza on Sunday and met parishioners there.

Lucy, in recent months, had become increasingly occupied with the church in St. Francisville. She was active in the building committee for a new church. Through her brothers she had come to know Bishop Leonidas Polk. The bishop owned Leighton, a sugar plantation not far from her brothers' sugar plantations near Thibodeaux. Bishop Polk was now based at Trinity Episcopal in New Orleans but traveled throughout the state. Through Polk's ministries, Lucy had accepted Jesus as her personal savior. He new-found religiosity gave her a new reason to chide her son, for his continued indifference to organized religion.

Lucy would say to Percy as she and Eliza left for Sunday services, "It's that little Jew who keeps you from embracing Jesus, isn't it? They killed Him, you know."

Patiently, Percy would respond, "Judah is about as Jewish as I am. And as I recall, Jesus Himself was a Jew."

Howard ignored Lucy in matters of religion. He was glad she had an outlet for her energy and did not try to involve him. He contributed generously to the new building fund. When Lucy organized a parish dinner for the bishop on one of his visits to St. Francisville, Howard sat next to the pious man, so unlike the general officer he would become.

Philomena answered her husband. "I would be equally happy staying here in St. Francisville or returning to New Orleans. I want to be with you wherever you choose to live."

"I think I should spend more time here at Bolingbroke. It is more than my father can take care of at his stage of life."

"What about your practice?"

"I'm a good lawyer, but I don't have the gift and drive that Judah Benjamin has. There's quiet here in the country. And time to read books. We can ride together like we did in Williamsburg."

Phil listened attentively. She would not push her husband in one direction or another. He needed to work it out himself. She knew that the time in Mexico had caused him to reflect on the arc of his life. She had pondered the possibilities in her mind and now asked Percy, "Have you thought about becoming a judge in this parish? You would make a fine judge. You have the temperament.

And the mustache gives you a certain distinguished appearance. Now if we could turn your hair to grey . . . ."

They both laughed. They decided to give it a year or two of thought. He would spend two weeks in New Orleans each month and reside at Bolingbroke the rest of the time. It was not unlike the schedule his father had followed while Percy was growing up.

The next day, he boarded the packet steamer to New Orleans. Philomena now resumed her plan to make St. Francisville-Bayou Sara her own dominion, just as she had taken on New Orleans in a successful campaign to establish herself. It was too early yet to surprise him with it. She was as certain that he would be pleased as she had been certain that he would return to Richmond and marry her.

*Chapter 35*

# Diana, Manager

More than five months had passed since Percy had last set foot in Toulouse Gardens. In mid-afternoon, while he awaited his clerk transcribing letters and documents for his signature, he decided to visit Linton Scruggs to see how the business was doing. The manager was not in his office. Instead there was a woman, a pretty woman in her late twenties perhaps, in Scruggs' chair in his office. She wore no earrings or make-up. Her light auburn hair was tied in a chignon bun that ended at the base of her neck. She had cat-like oval eyes that were instantly alert.

"I was looking for Mr. Scruggs," he said.

"He's upriver, in Natchez, for a week. What can I do for you, Mr. Moorhead? Or Percy, if I may be more familiar." Her voice was both pleasant and confident.

"You know me?" Percy searched his memory. Surely if they had met, he would have noted the small mole on her left cheek.

She smiled, "We haven't met. But Linton said you'd probably be by after you returned from Mexico City. You haven't been by to collect your share of the year's profits. And I knew of you from my late father."

"Your father?"

"Forgive me for not introducing myself. I'm Diana Watkins.

My father was Florian Dodson." Diana stood and walked from behind the desk to shake Percy's hand. "Call me Di." She leaned back against the edge of the desk, crossing her arms over her ample breasts.

Percy knew the name Florian and the man. He was one of the investors in Toulouse Gardens, from Philadelphia. He had visited the supper club soon after it opened – an elegant man with sharp nose, wavy gray hair, and rounded vowels to his avuncular speech. Had his hair once been of reddish-brown hue like his daughter's? Or was red hair a trait passing from the mother?

"I'm sorry. I did not know he had passed."

"It was sudden. In April."

"I see. Eight months." He had no other response.

The woman filled the space left by his obvious discomfort.

"My father left me his interest in Toulouse Gardens. I wanted to see it for myself. Linton and I talked with your managing partner, Alonzo McIntyre. They agreed that I could become an employee, a co-manager with Linton. Under the by-laws, there was no need to get approval from the other investors. I hope you have no reason to object to the arrangement."

"No reason. I believe you said your name is Watkins. Did your husband accompany you?" A gold wedding band on her left hand was the only jewelry she wore.

The smile faded from her face. "That is one of the reasons I was glad to be employed here. You see, my husband died a little over a year ago. His estate is in litigation over his family debts. With my father and mother both passed, I had nowhere else to turn. My inheritance from my father is free from my late husband's legal problems."

"That's terrible. Are you so alone? What happened to Mr. Watkins?" Percy's protective instincts were moved by a woman in distress, Diana appeared vulnerable.

Briefly, Diana was silent. She looked away, towards the window. She turned slightly to the side and placed her hand on the desk, as if for support.

Percy apologized, "Please, I don't mean to intrude."

Her eyes returned to his. "No, no. Please forgive my emotion. It takes me a moment to come around. You may have heard of the accident. All of the newspapers carried stories of the tragedy. He was returning from a trip to England on the *Arctic*. They were not far from Newfoundland when they were struck by a French steamship. He was one of three hundred who perished."

"A horrible accident! The *Arctic* was a sister ship to the one I took over the same route two years before. I read about it. The crew of the *Arctic* took the lifeboats for themselves and let the women and children all drown."

"Yes, they abandoned him. He would never have put himself before others. Such a dear man, a minister at a church near Philadelphia, the assistant pastor. Everyone in the congregation loved him. So kind, so gentle, so educated. He attended Yale in the theology department and was ordained soon after completing his study."

"You have had a great loss. I cannot imagine what it is like to lose someone you love so much."

Diana dabbed her eyes with a delicate white handkerchief, trimmed by blue floral net lace. "It is difficult to be alone. A new start. When my father died soon after my Jonathan, the pastor recommended I move away for a time. Two funerals in less than a year was more than anyone should have to bear, he said. Now that I have been here for two months, I see that I have an aptitude for keeping accounts. It helps me to keep things in good order. There is comfort in numbers. And I have my cat, Cheddar. Do you like cats, Mr. Moorhead? Percy." She favored him with another smile, making an effort to return to matters less sad.

"I've never given them much attention." Cats, for the Moorheads, were simply farm animals – useful in the barn and storage sheds but a nuisance in the house. He recalled that Eliza occasionally had kittens as a small girl, but she had never kept them to adulthood – they were too inviting as prey for foxes and wildcats. The caged birds her stepfather brought from New Orleans were more to her liking, though she often forgot to feed them. When a bird would die from neglect, Howard would replace it with a near identical bird of the same species, and the family all indulged in the fiction that it was the same bird. It was called by the same name, Sophia. Even if the species had to be changed when no similar bird was available, the name always remained the same, to maintain the fiction that it was always the same bird, or at least that the soul of Sophia had migrated – a Pythagorean continuity.

"No, I suppose not. Most men think it unmanly to have cats. And you were a soldier. But tell me, is there anything I can do to keep you informed about your ownership in this business?" She returned to her chair behind the desk, no remnant of a tear for her late husband lingered on her cheek. "My father was very interested in the everyday operations and the changes when they were made. We have two new dealers since I arrived. Lady Lindy came from our Memphis club. And Joseph from Hannibal. And a lottery wheel was replaced last week."

After they visited a bit more, Diana took from her desk a draft on the Mechanics and Planters Bank for his share of the casino profits. Percy excused himself and had an early dinner at the buffet table. He returned to his law office and worked til near midnight.

Three days later, Percy returned to Toulouse Gardens for the dinner buffet. It was more convenient than a restaurant and the food was generally to his liking. Diana Watkins descended the nearby staircase. Her face brightened when she saw him at a table. Now she wore cosmetics – tasteful, not garish – highlighting her full lips and dark, oval eyes. Her auburn hair seemed darker now and was pulled to one side, spilling over her left shoulder.

"So, you've come back. I was afraid the selection didn't please you when you were last here. Or perhaps that a woman was managing the business."

"If a woman can sit on the throne of England, I see no reason to object to a woman in management of a business such as ours. As to the food, it is very good. I prefer my wife's cooking, but she is at our home north of here. With our son." Percy was not unaware of the import of his words; Diana was thus informed that he was married but that his family were not with him in New Orleans.

"Not everyone feels safe in New Orleans. What can I put on the menu to draw you back?"

"It's very good. No complaints."

"Surely you must have favorites. Give me a challenge."

"A challenge? All right. Crêpe. Or something I had in Mexico – *sopaipillo*. But tell me," he continued, what are those earrings you are wearing? They recall something I've seen, but I can't remember what they are called."

"Ankh. An Egyptian cross. My husband gave them to me, and this silver necklace. He studied the Egyptians at Yale. The ankh was their symbol of life."

"Interesting," commented Percy approvingly.

The next night, when he arrived at a little after seven, Percy found on the buffet table, just after the beef, boudin, rice, gravy, and vegetables, a tray of crêpes, kept on top of a candle-lit warmer. Diana walked from the back of the room and prepared him two crêpes, into which she folded sliced fruit and topped with whipped cream. She sat at a table with Percy and asked him about his work for the day. Routine, he replied. Conveyances and contracts.

Linton Scruggs, she said, had told her Percy might answer legal questions concerning Toulouse Gardens. He would be glad to help. What sort of problems? Nothing yet, she said. It occurs to me that we might have disputes about terminating a dealer, or a person who supplies us with food or liquor.

"Of course," he replied. "I'll be glad to help."

Over the next few weeks, Percy told himself he was spending his evenings at Toulouse Gardens for the food and to get away from the cares of law practice. In fact, he was enjoying the company of the co-manager. She was charming, outgoing without being pushy, always sympathetic. Someone to talk to at the end of the day. Nothing more. And she needed help. Who would fail to help a sympathetic widow?

## Chapter 36

# Howard Speaks of Reckoning

Howard Moorhead would speak with Percy about the economics of the paired plantations from time to time. Even when cotton prices were down, he would say that he was comfortable that Bolingbroke was profitable. Percy would note the singular nature of his father's comment.

"And Jericho Hill?" Percy asked in late January 1856. He was home on one of his regular visits from New Orleans. The two were again sitting on the wrought-iron bench overlooking the pond. It was early evening. A group of three grey-green mallards, a drake and two hens, slid their way to a wings-outstretched, feet-down soft landing in the cattails and rushes off to their right. Percy knew his father preferred to avoid discussing Calvin Bunch's mismanagement.

Reservation in his voice, Howard replied, "We leave it to Calvin to keep the accounts on Jericho."

"I have the impression you're bearing all the costs of both plantations out of Bolingbroke's revenues."

"Probably." Howard said. His manner indicated that he most certainly was paying the bills. "Your mother is covering for him on some of his debts. She has money of her own, of course."

Howard had had to sell more of his business interests to

maintain the soundness of the plantations. He acknowledged as much. "I have put some additional money into the land to keep it fertile. On some of the acreage we are trying crop rotation and alternative plantings. I want to be certain that when I am gone, you will inherit a viable enterprise. A year ago, I receded from my work as a factor. My clients I turned over to another factor I've known, Henry Hope Stanley. He's a good man, the managing partner of the Mississippi Cotton Press."

"I recognize the name and the building he and his partners own. They are sometimes clients of Judah Benjamin."

"I left them in good hands. Now, you may choose not to take over the plantation. I want that to be at least an option for you. And for your wife and child. They enjoy life here, unless I mistake Philomena. She will make a good life for you and your heir wherever you are. Nothing can complete a man and his family like having a piece of the earth for their own. It's not incompatible with having a life in New Orleans, too. A man needs *land* he can call his own. With a townhouse, you are never more than a visitor. No matter how magnificent it may be or with all the things you fill it. You must have buildings and animals and gardens and soil of your own. Don't you feel like this is your own?"

Percy noticed his father's eyes sometimes squinted in bright sun. Was it a sign of declining health? "I do, Father. Not perhaps the same way you have made it yours. Or ours, I should say." Percy was always conscious that he had not built Bolingbroke but was born to it. It would always be his father's achievement, not his. He yearned to build something of his own, something that reflected his ability to create, to build. Winning a law suit or concluding a successful negotiation was satisfying but briefly so. He wanted something that would last and could be seen as his own achievement. Owing to his exclusion from Judah Benjamin's revised law partnership, Percy's legal and political ambitions were stalled. The new law firm sent him some cases, but he was not adept in attracting his own clients. The Tehuantepec Railroad project was going forward, and he had great hopes for his involvement when his services might be needed. Percy was not sure he could be satisfied with owning a cotton plantation and managing the demands.

"Good, good. I like that. *Ours*. It has always been ours. Now tell me about the law practice. And your investments."

Percy explained that under the arrangements for Toulouse Gardens, his interest was largely passive. His share of the profits was distributed at the end of each year. Nominally he was attorney for the casino, but there was little need for his services. Under the charter, management was by a committee.

"There was an incident you probably should know about. At the casino," he told his father.

"Hmmm. Oh?" grunted Howard, perking up, sensing unpleasant news was to follow.

"I'm sure Calvin wouldn't have told you about. Or Mother or Eliza. A couple of months ago, Calvin turned up one night at Toulouse Gardens. When he tried to sign a note to obtain chips, the faro dealer turned him away. Calvin tried to give him a hard time. He sent him to our manager, a man named Scruggs. The manager told him he'd been instructed not to give him credit. 'Who says?' Calvin demanded. 'My brother-in-law?' Scruggs told him he'd have to take that up with me."

"Did he?"

"He avoids me when we're both here. I'm sure he'll hold that grudge a long time, even if I explain I didn't make the credit policy. Our manager could have handled it without implicating me. When I returned from Mexico, I found that the committee had hired a co-manager. A woman named Diana. She's a widow who inherited her interest from her father."

"From New Orleans?"

"No. Philadelphia."

"Able to cope with New Orleans?"

"I've gotten to know her. I'm confident she will keep the business on course. Scruggs comes back and forth for a new business a group is starting in Mobile. He's still active with our project and another in Natchez."

"A woman with a substantial role in running a gambling business is unusual," Howard's skepticism was evident.

"She's a remarkable woman. I've told her not to hesitate to look to me for help. After all, I've got an investment to protect. It's not enough to live on, but I expect that I will find other investments as my practice grows. Eventually my involvement in the Tehuantepec Railroad project will pay off. When we get a new president this fall, we may get a new ambassador to Mexico and a new Secretary of State who will support the Isthmus route. Judah Benjamin says he'll be sure that I get an ownership interest when he forms a new company for the project."

"Good. In the meantime, you should consider adding more acreage to Bolingbroke. If I were younger, I'd add land and experiment with some different crops. Diversify. Grow things that do not depend so heavily on forced labor. But I'm not getting younger. A man doesn't like to confront his own mortality. It's certain to occur even if the timing is uncertain. Bolingbroke is yours in all but title. I'd sign it over to you now, but that would require unraveling its ties to your mother's property. I would encourage you to invest in other railroad projects. Insurance syndicates."

Percy replied, "Yes. I shall. But cotton is still king. And I know how much this place means to you."

"It does, son, it does. But . . . " Howard's voice trailed off, as though uncertain of what he should say. He was quiet for a moment, then said with a grave expression, "Your knowledge of Shakespeare is solid, I know. But your Marlowe. How is it?

"At best, fair. Offhand, I only recall *Tamburlaine*." Percy was surprised at the question. He knew his father was widely read but seldom talked about his books.

"They say he died over a reckoning at a pub in Deptford. You might want to read *Doctor Faustus*."

"On your recommendation, I certainly will. What brings it to mind just now?"

"It must have been written shortly before his death, when he died over a settling of accounts. *Faustus* is about a reckoning. The doctor Faustus of the play signs a contract in his own blood. For a term of years, he will get knowledge and the service of a devil. When his time is up there must be a reckoning. He loses his soul to Lucifer."

"I see. In the end it's a bad bargain. When there is a reckoning as you put it. You see it as a parable?"

"Cotton. There will be a reckoning." Percy's father's eyes were grave, sad.

"I don't think I understand."

"The South is Doctor Faustus. Lucifer has given the South wealth in the form of cotton and an enslaved multitude to cultivate it, and the South has given its soul, which the devil will one day claim. A reckoning will come."

"Father, I am stunned. It's been so much of your life here."

"I can't deny that. I am a willing participant in a cruel system, but every act I have done in it has lessened its severity. Had I never raised a boll of cotton, had I never bought a slave, had I not accepted the benefits of slave labor, would the life of a single African have been better? It is a paradox, isn't it? I won't lie to you. There will be a reckoning, and others will bear the burdens of the moral debts we have incurred."

In silence the two men, father and son, stood and slowly walked together back to the house. Percy wondered what prompted his father's reflections on Bolingbroke and slavery. Had Percy himself set it off by nudging his father to take up Calvin Bunch's mismanagement of Jericho? Howard's contemplation of his legacy to Percy would entail disentangling Bolingbroke from Jericho. It left him feeling unsettled. The system of slavery cast a pall on everything touched and fouled by the institution.

ৰ্ফ ৰ্ফ — ৰ্ফৰ্ফ

A day after talking with his father, Percy sought out Julius. He found him in the barn. Mid-morning in mid-February, the air was crisp outside but comfortable enough inside. The bondsman was at a bench, seated on a stool, repairing a saddle that needed re-stitching where the coarse thread had worn through. Other leatherwork was nearby, being prepared for plowing and for harnessing mules to wagons in the busy weeks ahead. An odor of oil rose from a bucket on the bench. Julius believed in applying it liberally to all leather used in the farm work.

"You be doing good?" Percy said to Julius, affecting the speech that whites often adopted in conversations with their servants when they wished to seem friendly to an underling, much as an adult will speak to a child in a child's vocabulary.

"Tolerable well, Mr. Percy." It had been "Mr. Percy" ever since Percy had returned from the war in Mexico. Percy never asked that he be called by honorific. The two had grown up together as friends, having nourished from the same breast and received guidance in youth from Big Tom. The transition simply happened and was inexorable in the sharply divided society – racial boundaries that were invisible yet rigid and insurmountable and reflected in language.

"And Little Jay and Leddie? I saw them outside yesterday. They looked fine."

"We all good," Julius replied affably. He liked leatherwork. It required patience and improvisation. Plow harnesses, reins and shoulder straps had to be inspected and maintained for eight plows on the two plantations. Similar riggings were used year-round on the wagons, carts and carriages owned by the Moorheads. Seven saddles of varying sizes required upkeep, along with girths, martingales, halters, headstalls and reins. If not cared for, the leather would rot and break, injuring a rider or a worker.

"Julius, you're here all the time and I can't be. I have to continue my law practice in New Orleans. So, I want you to tell me what you think. Just how well are things on the place?"

"We mostly deal with Mr. Howard. That's good. He's a good man. But he's not around as much as he need be. He spend most his time with Mass' Randolph. They're real happy together."

"Is Rand a distraction for him?" Rand had his own small saddle for the pony Howard had given him for his last birthday. PawPaw would place him on Gingerbread and lead him around the grounds. Rand held the reins in his little five-year-old hands.

"That's not what I'm saying. Mr. Howard, he is getting old. He doesn't know who all the slaves be on the two places. Some think they are supposed to look to Mr. Calvin and others to Mr. Howard."

"Is Calvin trying to run things now?"

"Oh, no suh. We don't see him much. When he does come round, he tries pretend'n he's in charge. Make a show. Tell someone off. He knows the hands laugh at him ahind his back. But he's not gonna do anything that's make Mr. Howard take him down a notch. Or you. Especially you."

"If I'm hearing you right, there's a problem with organization. The hands need more direction than they're getting."

"Afore Big Tom died, everyone knew who was in charge. He kept him a firm hand. Mr. Howard has me and Pompey doin' much of what Big Tom done, but we're not in charge like Big Tom."

Percy hoped Julius was seeing where he was trying to take him without being too direct. "We need an overseer, is that right?"

"I'm not sayin' Mr. Howard's running things badly." Julius

had stopped his stitching to make eye contact with Percy. Julius would be frank without being critical of Percy's father. Looking down again, he began rubbing neat's-foot oil into the saddle with a rag, working it with his long fingers to penetrate the leather.

"I know that. You're just saying he's not up to tending to all the details of looking after ninety-some workers. Someone needs to be in charge – more in charge. Is that something you could do, Julius? Or Pompey? Is that something you would want to do, be the overseer?"

Julius paused before saying thoughtfully, "Pompey, he is a good man. A big man, a strong man. He can do anything someone tell him to do. Fix anything what broken. He's not so good at knowin' what to do. Doin' and knowin' be two different things. And Pompey, he don't have a mean bone in his body. He's too nice to everyone to tell 'em what they got to do. Ain't no kindness to be kind sometimes."

Percy nodded in agreement. "I understand, Julius. Pompey is not a problem solver and he can't provide direction to others. Sometimes a leader has to be harsh to be effective."

Percy leaned against one of the massive vertical beams holding up the roof and pulled out his pocket knife. He took an apple from his coat and cut a slice. He handed the first to Julius then cut another for himself.

Julius chewed on the apple, nodded affirmatively and returned to his leather work.

"That leaves you, Julius," Percy finally said.

"No suh, I didn't say that. I'm not big like my daddy or Pompey. I don't carry much weight with the other slaves. They are afraid of Odessa because they think she got voodoo on them and some of that rubs off on me just cause she's my mamma. I don't think I could be very good overseeing."

Now Percy disagreed. "Don't sell yourself short. I know you're intelligent, and I think you could handle people. But who else is there? I don't want y'all to come under Calvin, and I don't want to have to hire a white man who's trained in harshness and cruelty. Enough of them already."

With a wry expression on his face, Julius retorted, "Ain't nobody elsed here. Except you, Mistah Percy." Julius was turning the table on Percy, making him face the obvious problem.

Julius had caught Percy in a contradiction. He was himself unwilling to assume responsibility for managing Bolingbroke but was trying to push Julius into the position. He acknowledged his predicament, hoping Julius could be persuaded yet. "I'm a lawyer, Julius. I like to argue and persuade. But I've got no stomach to be a boss man. I could no more whip a man as punishment than I could beat a child. I know it has to be done, but not by me." He offered another slice of apple to Julius, which he declined.

"Where's that leave us, boss?"

"You do have a sly sense of humor, Julius. Look, you think it over and see if you have it in you to become the overseer."

His voice carrying exaggerated irony, Julius replied, "Yes suh. I just be the slave. I do's what massa' tell me to."

"Now you're playing me, Julius. You know how it is with me. I don't like slavery."

"No suh. I don't expect that you do. That doesn't make me like it any more'n you. It doesn't make me any less a slave."

"Even if we could free you – mind you, the law makes that difficult and expensive – what would you be able to do? Go north? Go back to Africa?"

"There's no going back to somewhere I've never been. Odessa says I'm as much French as African. Or San Dominican. Or Cuban."

"That's true. And you've got no people in the north. Black folks aren't really welcome there. I know. I've lived there."

"You saying I got no place but here? Reckon I'd rather have

some say in it. Freedom's choosing."""

"Choice is an illusion. Neither of us chose the world we were born into. It's nothing you did that made you a slave. Nature is a lottery. And it's nothing I did to be a master. A wheel of fortune. It's something I thought about when I was in the army and something of what I learned from Judge Tucker. When I was a soldier I was a private. I had to do what my officers told me to do. There's hierarchy. Has to be. Where there is no hierarchy there's only anarchy. If the privates and corporals didn't obey, we'd have all been killed."

"Difference be, you chose be'n a soldier. And you stopped be'n a soldier. I can't stop being a slave less I be ready to die tryin'."

Percy couldn't deny what Julius's truth. He shrugged in resignation, continuing, "You're right. We didn't choose the order of things, but we're all constrained by the order. We all have duties. Judge Tucker thought it was a natural order, master and servant. I don't think he was right. But the law is the law. For now. And neither you nor I can change that by ourselves."

Julius put aside the oiling rag. He looked Percy in the eye. "I ain't disagreeing with you. What you need to think about is this. If you don't take charge, ain't you leaving all the rest of us under Calvin Bunch when your daddy passes on? That would be a hierarchy and order you choose, if you don't choose. There is choice in this world, whether you say so or not. Where be your duty, Mistah Percy?" The words were not bitter, but they were meant to sting.

Percy flinched at the thought. Julius had hit a nerve. He left without responding, but it continued to bother him. What were his duties?

Chapter 37

# Phil's Felicianas

That evening, Percy told Phil, "I'm torn." They were sitting on the bed in the upstairs room where they slept. They were getting ready to turn in.

"What's wrong, dear?" soothed Phil. "You didn't seem yourself at dinner."

"I'm not sure who myself is."

"Silly, you're my Lochinvar who carried me off from far Virginia."

"Would that it were so simple. We earlier put off a decision about our future – my future. I've been dividing my time between here and my practice. It's not working."

"Why not?" She took his hand. "What can I do? Move to New Orleans with you again?"

"It's not that. I love the law. I like the company of lawyers and my clients. I like having my office and two clerks. My trips to England and Mexico have been very fulfilling."

"Then it is simple. We go back to the townhouse. No? You're shaking your head."

"No. It's not just a matter of what I want. Bolingbroke needs me. Jericho needs me. A talk with Julius today made that clear to me. Talking with my father made it clear to me. He's slipping. Growing old. Growing weary. Calvin will destroy my sister and mother's place and all the people living there. And Bolingbroke won't survive long under a manager if it is separated from Jericho. What will happen to all the people who have depended on the Moorheads for thirty years? If I don't assume control, it all falls apart."

Phil responded sympathetically. "I'm afraid that's true. But you don't have to give up what you love for others. Do you feel so strongly about the slaves?"

"The truth is I don't want to be a slaveholder. My father created this plantation for me. It's a great heritage, but it comes at a price. I love the land, maybe even more than he does. I love the river, the seasons, the rhythm of life – land and people and animals all joined to one another. But not slavery. Yet we can't have the one without the other. Without slavery, there would be no cotton crop, no plantation. If we sell the plantation and the slaves, I'll condemn them all to a much different life than they have here."

"I know how hard this must be for you," she said.

"But what would you do? What would you want? It's your life, too, and Rand's."

"We will make our home and life with you, wherever you choose. It is no marriage where the wife doesn't support her husband."

"If we stay here, what will you do? Don't you get lonely?"

"No. I don't. Maybe this is the time to show you my book." She stood and smiled.

"The book I've seen you writing in when I come home?"

"Yes. Let me get it." Phil walked over to a chest of drawers and drew out a large notebook. She handed it to her husband.

Percy opened the book. The first three pages were hand-drawn maps. Here was the town of Bayou Sara. The Mississippi River was at the top of the sheet, with the town's namesake bayou at the right, draining into the Mississippi. Below were six streets parallel to the river and six intersecting them. Small boxes depicted the principal stores and houses and the Methodist church. Most boxes had a line out to an identification, in Phil's small, neat lettering, of the business or home – Whiteman Bros., Hatch & Irvine, Mumford's Bank, China Grove Hotel, Barton's Books & Stationery and many more. The second page was similar but with St. Francisville's layout, with the parish courthouse at the center. She had written at the top "two miles long two yards wide." Again, each business, church and house was shown and labelled. The third map was a brave effort at showing roads in the parish that connected the major plantations with the town. There were small boxes identifying 14 or 15 plantations and a half dozen more with question marks in pencil next to them. Each plantation was numbered. Among them he could read were Wyoming, Lamplei, Meadowdale, Woodfair, New Troy, Riverbend, Elm Grove, Auburne, Bonnie Doon, Cumberland, Dorset Villa, Seven Oaks, Candlewyd – and others. Leafing through the pages, Percy saw that each page was numbered, and each plantation of the third map had its own page filled with notes that Phil had made.

"Good heavens, Phil. Did you do all this?" He had no idea she had devoted so much effort into exploring the area. She knew more now about the Felicianas than he did after spending most of his life there.

"Yes. Me and Leddie. Do you like it?"

Percy was impressed and pleased with her initiative. "It's amazing! When did you start? Why?"

"A couple of months after we first arrived with Rand. I wanted to know my way around the two towns, so I made the maps. With the third, the book took on a life of its own."

Phil was pleased to have surprised him, but she was not entirely candid. When she first met him as a law student, she had asked him why he sometimes said he was from Bayou Sara but at other times St. Francisville. She had thought he might be referring to the bayou and the town as interchangeable. His answer had been a shrug. As she began exploring the two, she came to see that they were two distinct towns, one above the other on the bluff overlooking the Mississippi River.

Equidistant from his house at Bolingbroke, either community could be described as the town nearest his home. So close, yet so different. Did they reflect two parts of his identity? Or perhaps his father's? Bayou Sara was a rough riverfront town, populated by hustlers and itinerants, some laying over on a voyage upriver, some just laying low, evading the law. The more respectable, successful merchants, who once had stores on Front Street of Bayou Sara, had removed their families to the town above, St. Francisville, where they enjoyed a genteel life away from the common sort. Safe in their neat cottages on Royal and St. Ferdinand Streets, they were spared the shootings and knifings in the saloons and on the streets of Bayou Sara. Four churches were within walking distance of the St. Francisville courthouse. Bayou Sara had but one church, peopled irregularly by a congregation of Methodists. Sunday services at that church were less attended than Saturday soirees at Madame Lascaux's boarding house, tolerated as an unacknowledged whorehouse run by a free woman of color. None of this seediness of Bayou Sara could be found on the maps of her book.

"The plantations?" he asked.

"I thought I should get to know the neighbors. When you went to Mexico, I assumed we'd probably be here for a good while. I had already been attending Episcopal services in St. Francisville with Eliza and your mother. When the minister asked for volunteers to gather old clothing for the poor, I saw an opportunity to learn more about the community. I began visiting a different plantation every other day for weeks, meeting the lady of the house. I was afraid of getting lost on my own, so I got Leddie to ride with me. Your father lent us the buggy and his horse, Happy Jack. Leddie's been such a help. She grew up in the home of Dr. Davenport and knows all of the plantation families through the doctor and through her mother, who often assisted the doctor. She would go with her mother when the doctor would send her out with medicines for his patients when he couldn't call. Leddie's given me so many stories. That's where I got many of the notes on each plantation. Every plantation has its own story. The slaves on every one know the stories and the secrets of their masters, and they share them from plantation to plantation."

Percy had no idea that his wife had been so active. It was not that she had concealed anything from him. His time at Bolingbroke always took precedence over her visits to plantations.

"What other surprises do you have for me?" he asked.

"Only if you approve. I've gotten to know some of the other mothers through my visits as well as some at our church. I've talked with some of them and with the minister about starting a Saturday program. We'd meet every two weeks at the church hall so the children can learn drawing, crafts, games and songs. Two of us would be in charge and the other mothers can have the day for shopping and visiting."

"That's wonderful! I've been thinking you were pining away in the countryside wishing someone would carry you back to old Virginny. I should have known. You always make the most of a new situation."

☙☙ — ❧❧

"I see you talkin' to Master Percy today," Pompey said to Julius as they ate supper together. Leddie and Jessie Mae were sewing in the next room while Joshua and Little Jay played on the floor at their feet. "What be on his mind?"

"He says it's not easy owning slaves," Julius said wryly.

"Ha," laughed Pompey, bringing a chunk of cornbread to his

mouth. "Tell him try being a slave fo' a while. Then he know how easy ownin' slaves is."

"He doesn't mean anything bad to us. He thinks one of us oughta be overseer."

"You mean, like Big Tom was?"

"Yeah, I s'pose."

"Can't nobody take Big Tom's place. Don't see how no man can know just what to do like Big Tom was. What was dat story he used to tell, what you liked so much?"

"Bout the little bird?"

"Yeah. The froze bird."

"I can't tell it like Big Tom could."

"C'mon. You say it better than me."

"Aw right." Julius took on Big Tom's voice and mannerisms. "You see, there was this little bird what was freezin' and he up and fell out of the top of the barn. And he be laying there just a shiverin' and knowin' he 'bout to die and he be praying to God to go to bird heaven. And jest 'bout then when he done give up all hope this big ol' horse saunters over an' dumps a load of horse dump all over that po' lil bird. Oh lord, thought that lil bird, you gonna add indignity to my final moment on this yere earth. But then somethin' happened. That horse dump was all warm and pleasant an' after a few more minutes that lil bird started to warm up. Now here is where Big Tom would stand up from the chair he be sitting on and he be that lil bird standing up in all that horse dump and start shakin' hisself off. And he get a big smile on his face and stretch out his arms like they was that bird's wings and then he hold his head up and he start singing jest like that lil bird. Then he look at us and say, that lil bird jest at happy as he could be. That bird thanked the good lord and he took to singing as loud as he could. 'Bout that time Ol' Calico the barn cat heard that sing'n and come over to see what it was all about and saw that lil bird jest a sing'n and sing'n and Ol' Calico snatched that lil bird out of the horse dump an' et him up, jest like that. And that be a lesson to you boys, Big Tom would say. Not everybody who dump on you is your enemy, not everybody who takes you out of the dump is your friend and if you is alive and warm even though you be covered in the dump jest keep your mouth shut."

Pompey laughed, more in sadness than at the story, and shook his head, "Ain't nothin' the same since he gone."

"Yeah, that's true. Mr. Howard kinda leaves things to you and me but he's forgetful of late."

"I notice that too. His heart jest ain't in it."

"Percy, he's worried what gonna' happen when his daddy die."

"Reckon he might set us free?" Pompey sounded hopeful.

"Who? Percy? Or his daddy?"

"Eith'r one. Miz Lucy, she not."

"Nah. I don't think they's can. Odessa says some of us belongs just to Miss Lucy and others of us maybe not. Percy asked me what I'd do if I was free."

"What'd you say?"

"I didn't."

"What would you do?"

"Guess first thing would be to go see New Orleans. Heard all about it and I've seen it in books. They say it is one of the biggest cities in the country, maybe in the whole world. They say there are thousands of free black folk who live in New Orleans. Reckon me and Leddie could make a life in New Orleans. Leddie, she could work for some rich white woman in New Orleans as well as she could right here. Me, I can read and write as good as any. Could get me a nice easy job working in a store. Get Leddie and little Jay store-bought clothes. Odessa says she worked at a store in Havana for a

Jew."

"What kinda store you be workin' in?"

"It don't matter. They say there are stores that sell nothing but shoes and coats and hats. There are shops that sell nothing but bread and cakes and such like. Or coffee. Imagine that. A store that sells nothing but coffee and tea. But Pompey, what would you do if'n you was free tomorrow?"

"Reckon I could carpenter. Or blacksmith. There be a free man-of-color who be a carpenter in Bayou Sara. He say he makes good money as long as he stay sober and don't gamble too much. Jessie Mae, she keep me from drinkin' anyhow. An' I don't gamble none." Pompey leaned forward at the table and sopped a chunk of cornbread in the black-eyed pea gravy on his plate. He took a bite and said, "Best thing 'bout bein' free would be to get far away from Cal'n Bunch. That man mean to get me if he can. I see it in his eye every time I sees him. Something about me he jest don't like."

"I think that's one of them things weighin' on Percy Moorhead. He don't think much of Calvin."

"Ain't no good can come from Calv'n."

Chapter 38

# Diana

Asurprised and solicitous Percy asked "Di, what's happened to you?"

Diana Watkins had been talking to several of the customers of Toulouse Gardens at the bar when Percy walked in. Her face was bruised on one side, and her left arm was in a sling fashioned from a red silk scarf. She led Percy into a quieter room, where they wouldn't be overheard.

Nearly whispering, she confided, "I thought I was safe in New Orleans. I guess I was wrong. A man robbed me. He struck me in the face and pulled my purse from my arm."

"Is it broken?" Percy gently put his right hand on her left shoulder and held her hand with his other.

"The doctor said it was only a sprain."

"When? Where?"

"After closing. After midnight. I was walking to my apartment." She had been smiling as he walked in. Now, she sounded sad, shaken, putting on a brave front after a harsh experience.

"Was it a white man? No blacks should have been out after curfew. The police patrols would have picked up a black man out after hours."

She shook her head. "It was so sudden. I didn't see him very well at all."

"It must have been very disturbing. Are you frightened?"

More emphatically, she said, "Your wife was right about New Orleans. It's not a good place for a woman. Someone found my bag in the morning near a wharf. My money was gone but nothing else. I don't carry much with me. Don't worry, I'll be okay."

Diana left Percy, resuming her chats with customers and overseeing the card dealers and others running the games. At the end of the evening she collected the money at each table and gaming station and put it in the office safe. Percy lingered, chatting with clients and occasionally playing *vingt-et-un* for small stakes.

"You're still here," Diana observed pleasantly.

"Yes. I'm concerned about your well-being."

"I'm sure I'll be fine." She hesitated, then looked at him. "Would you walk me home? I'd feel better."

Diana turned off the gas lights at the main valve and locked the doors to the building. Percy followed her into the night. Street lamps flickered as they walked up Royal Street for six blocks. She said, "I hope you don't think me silly and afraid. But I feel safe with you."

"If you would like, I could give you a derringer pistol for a pocket or your purse."

Di took Percy's arm in hers and shook her head as they walked, "Oh, no, I'm more afraid of guns than of robbers. I would more likely shoot myself or a friend than a thief."

When they arrived at her door, she said, Well, here we are. You are Sir Galahad to see me safely home." She extended her gloved right hand for a handshake then gave him a brief kiss on the cheek – no more than affection and gratitude.

As Percy left, he thought he saw a man nearly hidden in the shadows. Was it someone looking to attack Di again? He continued to walk, more cautiously now. When he looked over his shoulder, he saw someone walking slowly in the opposite direction on the other side of the street. There was something familiar about the walk. Almost like Ja-Boo.

The next night Percy walked Di home again. This time he came inside and sipped whiskey before leaving. She no longer needed a sling for her arm. Her bruise was fading from her face.

Two nights following, Di asked Percy, "Will you not kiss me? I need to be kissed," when he stood to leave. She placed herself between him and the door. He did as she bid, tentatively. Then deeply.

"No, I shouldn't," he said, pulling back from her. He felt shame that he was attracted to her.

Di took his coat lapels in her hands and gently pulled him back to her. Looking him in the eye, she whispered, "You're married, I know. But I'm no threat to your marriage. You love your wife. You have no reason to love me, and I don't ask for you to love me. Or pity me. I had a husband and loved him and lost him. I'm lonely. I'll never ask more than friendship from you, so help me on the memory of my husband."

As she spoke, she unbuttoned the buttons of his trousers and closed her right hand around his erection. "You want this as much as I do," she whispered. She was right. Minutes later they were naked and in her bed, his shame overpowered by passion.

Percy returned to Di's apartment, and bed, on a regular basis for the next couple of weeks. As promised, she did not introduce romance into the relationship. No endearments, no little efforts to please him when he was in her apartment. Yet, he found himself thinking of her while in his law office working on document preparations and briefs. He wondered that he felt no more guilt than he had initially. She did make him feel good about himself.

She was a retreat from his worries and cares. She kept him from thinking about Bolingbroke and what he should do to prevent both plantations from falling under the control of his brother-in-law. His melancholy was at bay, at least for now.

Percy thought about what Phil had said, that he didn't have to give up what he loved for others. Yes, he did have his own life to live. The commitments he thought he had to Odessa and Julius and Pompey and Leddie and all the others on the plantation were not of his own making. Those relations were created by his mother and father, not by Percy Moorhead. Why should he be bound by them any more than being bound by their debts? Yes, he must take care of his own – Philomena and Randolph. Practicing law in New Orleans would accomplish that. His mother and sister were, of course, his own flesh and blood. But their problems with Calvin Bunch and Jericho Hill were of their own making. Like his father, he had tried to reduce the consequences of their embrace of Calvin, a man of low character and modest ability. There was a limit to what he must do to protect them from their repeated bad judgments, and the limit had already been exceeded by himself and by his father. Perhaps he would, in due course, tell Phil that New Orleans was the better choice for their future than Bolingbroke. His ties to the law were proving stronger than those to the land. Or was he rationalizing? For now, he was living in the moment. For now, the future was of no concern.

## Chapter 39

# Infidelities and Fidelities

When Percy made his next regular trip to Bolingbroke, he found Phil, his mother, and Rand sitting before an open fire in the living room hearth. It was late afternoon. He put his leather case next to the door that was now his study, where he carried on his law work from home. Phil stood as he approached her. They hugged, and he kissed her lightly on the cheek, a sign of affection more than emotion. If she sensed a difference in his manner, he was unaware of it.

"Where's father?" Percy asked. "Usually, he's on the porch or by the pond at this time of day."

Both Philomena and his mother were vague about his absence. "You know your father," Lucy replied indifferently. More than likely, they did not know where he had gone. Phil only shrugged. Percy handed Rand a tin whistle with four holes for his fingers. Lucy started at the sudden shrill sound as Rand blew but then resumed knitting.

A day later, Howard returned. Percy made inquiry but his father only responded, "Business. An investment in the future. Of sorts. Part of your patrimony." He seemed more distant than usual. "Pass the butterbeans please," he said to Percy. Was there disapproval in his voice?

Later that evening, Percy listened as his father read little Rand a children's story about an ox and a rooster. He would get up from where he sat and go through ox-like walking motions, and the boy would laugh. Howard would make rooster crowing sounds and the boy would laugh. Percy was struck by two things. Howard was much closer to Rand than Percy himself was. The two enjoyed each other's company and a mutual trust. And Percy had no memories of ever being close to Howard in the way Howard was close to his grandson. Had his father read to him, made animal noises, laughed at absurdities? He felt himself an outsider to a little society. Had he put himself outside by his relation with Diana (he could not regard it as an affair, or so he told himself)?

Philomena offered her husband a small dish of salted pecans that Clotilda had roasted earlier. "Don't be a Gloomy Gus," she said, putting her hand on his shoulder. "You look sad."

"Do I? Just reflective. I'm happy to see Dad and Rand get along so well. It might be bad for both to take Rand back to New Orleans." He poured a glass of bourbon and nibbled on pecans.

"I wouldn't disagree. We miss you, of course. I hope you haven't been too busy with your work. It's been a month since you were here last."

"That long? Yes, I suppose so. Seems like the work comes in cycles – too much and too little. How are your plans for the Saturday program coming along?" He remembered he should show interest in her activities.

Phil was eager to share her thoughts. "We started two weeks ago. Twelve children showed up and took part. Nine to three. They loved every minute. Two other mothers helped me. We expect even more children this Saturday. We've gotten very good reports from all the families."

"Marvelous. And your plantation visits?"

"Yes, indeed. The stories continue. Two more last week.

Always interesting." She said no more.

☞☞ — ☜☜

Phil was not ready to give details to Percy about the visits. White people seemed to know less about their neighbors than their black servants did. Surely this was willful – an unacknowledged realm of truth that could not be confronted, an alternate reality that would displace their carefully cultivated vision of their society.

For several months, Leddie had told Philomena which plantations included slaves that were the mixed-race offspring of the owners. Until last Wednesday the mulattoes that Leddie had described were all the result of a white man and a slave woman. On Wednesday, however, Phil and Leddie had called at Woodfair, presided over by Mrs. Opal Higginson, a diminutive, irascible woman of about sixty. She was the imperious owner of the plantation, having inherited it from her parents. Her husband was a weak man who had married her for her property and for convenience. Though nominally a member of the Grace Episcopal congregation, she was an infrequent congregant. She resented being called upon by Phil without an invitation and did not invite Phil inside. Leddie had remained seated in the buggy, holding the reins.

"That was unpleasant," Phil said to Leddie as they rode away from Woodfair.

"Yes'm. I don't s'pose you heard about Miss Opal. Most whites don't know."

"No, I haven't. Tell me."

"Miss Opal be the mother of a slave. Shadrach. His daddy be called Amos. They say Amos be the overseer at Woodfair when she inherit it when her daddy died."

Phil was wide-eyed and eager to hear the story. "My heavens! What did she do with the baby?"

"She give that baby over to a slave on another plantation to raise as her own child. She pretend she never gave birth. Wouldn't give him no name at all. My momma know it be true cause she was with Dr. Davenport when that baby come into the world."

"And where is Shadrach now?"

"He still be at Bonnie Doon."

"Does he know who his mother and father are?"

"Yes'm. But he never know what happen to Amos. Miss Opal sold Amos when she married Mr. Higginson 'bout year later. Amos be sent far away. Nobody never hear from Amos again. Nothin' worse off than a boy with white mother and black daddy. Nobody claim that poor child. When it be white daddy black mother, it be okay. Shadrach be looked at like he a freak. Both black and white. Nobody want nothin' to do with Shadrach."

The buggy jostled as they crossed the rickety bridge over Alexander Creek. A group of buzzards at the creek bank were tearing at the decaying flesh of a dead opossum. The skies were iron gray, threatening rain.

Phil commented to Leddie, "I guess you're right. White folks don't want to believe such a thing could happen. Men can be weak. But a white woman is expected to protect the white race."

"Yes'm," said Leddie in full agreement.

The next day, Phil and Leddie had called at Meadowdale, owned by the Bradshaws. The current owners were the third generation attached to the same plantation, which had been founded when the area was under Spanish rule. The patriarch, Charles Bradshaw – Don Carlos as he was called – had occupied for a time the office of *alcalde*, a judge-administrator within his own jurisdiction. Despite his success as a planter and having a loving wife and three children, he became despondent – with no apparent cause. One evening, after a quiet dinner, he walked out of the home with a lantern, without telling anyone where he was going. The next morning his hat and boots, together with two loaded pistols, were found next to a bayou near the home. On a closer look, the sons who were searching for him found his body just below the surface, a ghastly expression of anguish on his face. He had apparently walked into the water after weighting himself with bricks in the pockets of his pants and coat. No one suspected foul play. The creek became known as Bradshaw Bayou. Twenty-five years later the eldest son of Don Carlos, the one who first found him, went upstairs to his office after a quiet dinner with his family and blew his brains out with a shotgun. Now, his eldest son was approaching the same point in his life, and the Bradshaw curse lingered over the plantation. Would Cole Bradshaw succumb to the same fate?

Cole and his wife Alice Bradshaw were as hospitable to Phil and Leddie as anyone she had met in St. Francisville. They were eager to learn about her upbringing in Virginia and spoke admiringly of Howard Moorhead and how lucky Phil was to marry such a fine young man as Percy. Alice hoped they would see more of Phil and Percy. They filled two croker sacks of clothing to contribute to the church drive.

Yet, there was something disquieting about Cole Bradshaw. He was austere, with a lean build and sad, dark eyes. Phil heard he had studied medicine in New York but had never practiced as a physician. In the middle of a conversation with Alice and Phil, he stood abruptly and walked to the window, staring out. Phil could discern no activity in the yard or beyond that could have drawn him away. His expression was vacant, lost and inscrutable.

Because Percy seemed troubled about his own future, Phil decided not to discuss the history of the Bradshaws. No reason to invite into Bolingbroke Hall any of the ghosts who haunted the Felicianas.

Philomena handed the reins to Leddie and stepped down from the buggy. Leddie drove the buggy to the barn, where Julius was replacing a broken batten from the side of the barn. He greeted his wife and led the horse and buggy into the barn. As he unharnessed the horse from the shafts of the chaise, he asked where she and the mistress had been.

"Calling on more of the neighbors."

"Do I know them?" asked Julius.

"That Miss Opal. The one who had a baby out of Amos."

"I reckon that is why she hates black folks so much."

"And we visited those Bradshaws. Over across the creek."

"Miss Phil know about the Bradshaw curse?"

"She do now."

"I don't know how folks that have so much can take their own lives. Most like they goin' end up in hell. Miss Phil still spendin' mos her time with you?"

"I suppose she be lonely. She trying hard to make a place for herself in the town. The women think she be putting on airs with her Virginia way of talking. They trying to be refined while she be what they trying to be. And they know she better than them."

"You not gittin' tired of her?"

"She's lots better'n Miss Lucy or Miss Eliza. Miss Lucy, she's just sour and gettin' old. Eliza, she born old. She don't know what to think less'n her momma or Calvin tell her what she think. Way she look outta the side of her eyes look like some kinda spook."

"Who does she think you are?" Julius asked cryptically.

Leddie understood his question perfectly well. "You mean, who she think my daddy be?"

"You know that is what I mean.

"I think she think he be Doc Davenport."

"And who you think he be?"

"Mama won't ever say. She won't stop me from knowin' it was a white man."

"No chance it being Mr. Howard Moorhead?"

"No chance at all. I'd know from how mama would act and she don't act like he mean nothing at all. I still be guessin' coulda been old man Bradshaw."

"That be why he kill hisself?"

"No. That just be the Bradshaw curse."

"You not worried it get you?"

"No. If'n he is my daddy, it be the curse of the menfolks. Besides, you ever hear of a woman killin' herself?"

"Maybe a man killin' himself is the only way to get away from some women." Julius's eyes wrinkled with amusement.

Leddie gave out a rich laugh. "You watch out now what you be saying Julius. Com'n over here and I give you a good enough reason to stick around."

"Right here? What if Pompey come back to the barn."

"Won't be the first time he walk in on us. We can climb the ladder to the hay loft if you want."

ॐॐ — ॐॐ

At dinner Phil had seemed to avoid talking about something. Percy felt a shiver of guilt. Did his wife suspect something? Was he displaying signs that he was unfaithful? He had difficulty dissembling. He had no desire to pull away from his wife and son. He knew he couldn't maintain a double life. A shot of whiskey might divert his attention from stirrings of self-reproach. What man has not strayed? Fidelity is an over-rated virtue. Do wives really expect it of a husband? Are they not content so long as they are well-provided for and have only modest demands made of them? Eliza, for example. Surely she knew that Calvin ran around with other women, almost from the earliest days of their marriage. Yet it did not diminish her love and need for him. She was merely grateful that he did not flaunt his infidelities. She would never confront him. And yet. Percy knew that even if Phil had no inkling of his involvement with another woman, his relationship with his wife was already subtly impaired. His self-reproach now was evidence of that. There was a part of him now closed off to her, a corner of his heart on guard, blocked off from her love for him. His loss, more than hers.

Phil sensed the uneasiness in her husband. She put down the book she was reading by the light of the lamp between them. Bending over as she left, she lightly kissed his forehead. "Goodnight, dear. Come to bed when you can. I love you. It's good you are home."

Percy squeezed her hand. Phil left, off to sleep. He stared into the fire in the hearth for another hour as he drank more whiskey. Must he not choose?

ҩ҉ҩ — ҩ҉ҩ

A week later Percy was back in his office in New Orleans. For three days he devoted himself entirely to his work before returning to Toulouse Gardens. On Thursday evening he showed up for the buffet dinner. Diana Watkins was nowhere in sight as he put food on his plate. After eating a small amount, he pushed his plate away, motioning the kitchen help to come get it. He walked back to the office where he expected to find her. The door was ajar. He slowly pushed it open. Behind the desk was Linton Scruggs.

"Good evening, Mr. Moorhead," said Scruggs, looking up from a group of papers. His sleeves were rolled up. A half-eaten plate of food was at the side of the desk.

"Good evening, Scruggs. I thought you were spending most of your time in Mobile."

Scruggs pushed back from his desk, disengaging from the work before him to respond to one of the business owners. He slid his fingers through his hair as if to make himself more presentable. "I was. And I'd rather be there. But this establishment needs me more. How have you been? I haven't seen you in some time."

Without naming Diana, Percy said, "I thought your co-manager was handling matters here adequately."

"That was then. This is now," he said wearily.

"She was here just two weeks ago."

"That's the then. She up and quit a week or so ago. Of a sudden. I got a telegram from the executive committee to return to New Orleans post-haste. That's the now."

"Where'd she go? Did she take another job?"

"Well," he drawled, "your guess is as good as mine. Real mysterious-like. Left the books in pretty good order. No one made any complaints. Just up and left. Vanished. Gone. Left a resignation letter on the desk. So it's not like she was abducted."

"That's strange. I'm surprised. I thought she added something to the ambiance of the place. No offence to you, of course. A feminine touch." Percy was wary. He hoped she had said nothing to Scruggs about their relationship.

Scruggs shook his head. "You never know."

"Perhaps she was mugged again. Some weeks ago she was assaulted on her way home for the night."

"First I heard of it. She's a pretty tough cookie, you know."

Percy did not tell Scruggs he knew a vulnerable side of Di Watkins. Scruggs may have been one of the men at Toulouse Gardens who had tried to take advantage of a widow in a new city.

Inquiries the next day at the apartments where Diana had lived yielded no further information. She had left no forwarding address and her neighbors knew nothing.

At his townhouse, he tried to recall every word of their last conversation, the details of their last intimacy. What had he said or done to drive her away? Or was she being noble? Having lost her husband and her father, had she decided she should not cause another woman to lose her husband and a child to lose his father? She had been married to a minister. Did she share a minister's conscience? If she had felt guilt in her affair with Percy, she had never displayed it to him. Or perhaps she had, and he was too insensitive to have seen it. Perhaps she left on impulse and would come back when she began to miss him. How would she find work?

Percy considered asking Alonzo McIntyre and others of the executive committee if they knew where she was. But that would be too obvious. It might make them demand of her why she had left the New Orleans establishment. If she exposed their relationship, it could have detrimental effects on his law practice, not to mention the damage it would bring to his marriage. He would have to suffer her absence in silence, remaining ignorant as to the reason she abandoned him. He had been torn between his duty to his wife and child and his attraction to Di, but he was not prepared to give her up. She had needed him, perhaps as much as his family did, and he had taken pleasure in her company. She was one more reason for his reluctance to give up New Orleans for Bolingbroke.

When Percy was working in his New Orleans office the next day, he was surprised when his father appeared at his door.

"Dad, what brings you to New Orleans?" It was the first time Howard Moorhead had visited his son's law office.

"This is a business call, Percy. I need legal guidance."

"Please be seated. I'll do my best."

"As I know you will. This will affect you, and there's no one else I can trust with my intentions."

Percy had never seen his father so grave. He replied, "Of course."

Howard resumed, "In one of our luncheons you may remember I told you of my concerns about slavery.

"Yes. You spoke of a reckoning."

"Precisely. More to the point, I suggested you would do well not to count on a future dependent on a cotton plantation."

"I do recall."

What Percy recalled was his father recommending that he diversify with other investments. Now he realized that the future of Bolingbroke was under consideration.

"Then what I would like from you is to tell me how I might go about giving freedom to all the slaves that I own. You, Phil, and Rand, would still enjoy a generous inheritance. But your wealth should not depend on the forced labor of others."

Percy was taken back, but quickly realized this was the logical progression from his father's musing on the reckoning coming due on the Faustian bargain of slavery. "I can't disagree," he said. "Is this something you want to do now, or as part of planning for a will. May I ask, do you have a will now?"

"No, no will. But I will need one, sooner or later. Let me know my options. You will still inherit the land. If our workers wish to remain, that will be up to them and to you."

"All right, Father. I think I know the law at present. But there have been developments I must review."

"I should have done this long ago. When Big Tom passed, I lost as dear a friend as a man can have. Now I understand, no man should be the property of another."

Howard stood, put on his hat, and left as quietly as he had appeared. Percy assumed he would have a few weeks to follow up on his father's request. He would regret that he been unable to act on it more quickly.

## Chapter 40

# Summer's Toll

A t first, they attributed it to the summer heat. August was always a hot month, mid-nineties every day. And always the humidity, always. Cool breezes never came from the Mississippi River, not more than six miles to the west of Bolingbroke. Howard Moorhead had not engaged in any strenuous labor. But the summer sun takes a toll on an old man, even when he's wearing a straw hat and has a blue bandana around his neck to soak up sweat and mop his forehead. PawPaw was walking with little Rand up from the pond. He had crafted a toy sailboat for the boy from pine wood, with two little masts and two small silk sails. They launched the boat from the end of the pond's pier. A string at the bow supplied motion in the absence of winds.

Julius was the first to see Howard stumble and drop the toy boat. The old man bent over and held his hands on his knees, waiting for the dizziness to pass.

"You okay, Mistah Moorhead?" Julius bent over to look the white master in the eye. He put his hand on Howard's shoulder, to steady him.

"Just give me a minute, Julius. I'll be okay." Howard continued to bend over, his breathing difficult, his speech an effort.

Rand stood a few feet away, a worried look on his face.

"PawPaw?" He looked to Julius. "Is PawPaw awright?"

"Don't you worry, boy." Julius looked around for help. He put his fingers to his lips and issued a piercing whistle. Pompey emerged from the barn, then ran to his brother, dropping an iron bar used as a lever for the baler.

Howard Moorhead drew himself upright again, shakily. His face was pale and covered with sweat. He removed the neckerchief and wiped his face and brow. "I'm okay. Just felt faint for a minute. Haven't been sleeping well." He tried to pass it off with humor. "Guess little Rand here is getting so big, it's hard for an old-timer to keep up with him."

Howard began walking towards the house, limping and bent. Pompey and Julius were on either side and tried to guide his arms. He gently declined their assistance as he struggled to straighten his posture. He made about a dozen steps before his legs buckled under him. The two black men rushed to his side and raised him, supporting him by holding an arm over each of their shoulders, carrying him into the house. His legs dragged limply beneath, leaving a trail in the dust all the way to the front porch. Lucy came running in as they laid him upon the couch.

"What happened to Mr. Moorhead?" she demanded of Julius. Fear was in her voice and on her face.

"Passed out, m'am. Must be heat." The slave tried to sound reassuring but was unconvincing. Lucy recognized the seriousness of Howard's condition.

"Take his boots off. Open his shirt." Lucy was normally passive but she now took charge of her husband in a way that Julius hadn't seen before. Julius and Pompey quickly did as they were told. She called Clotilda to bring water. She instructed Julius to go to town for Dr. Davenport or Dr. Shay. "And get Odessa to come here quick."

Howard's body stirred weakly. His eyelids opened but then his eyes rolled in their sockets, uncomprehending, and he slumped again. Odessa came in. She took the wash basin and pitcher from Clotilda and set them on the floor next to the couch. She mopped his forehead with a damp cloth. He was still on the couch when Dr. Davenport arrived less than an hour later. The old physician seldom made calls after turning his office and practice over to Dr. Shay, but he rushed to his old friend's home when Julius appeared at his door.

"Let's get him to bed," the doctor instructed Pompey and Julius. "Get dry clothing on him," he said to Lucy and Odessa. Philomena entered the room with Rand holding her hand. Her look to Odessa and the nod of her head made clear that she would take charge in caring for her father-in-law.

The doctor listened to the patient's heart, took his pulse, felt his brow, observed his breathing, squeezed his arm and leg muscles for tone. Bending over Howard's face he opened each eyelid and saw mostly the unresponsive whites of his eyes. He pinched Howard's right little toe and got a reflex from his leg.

"Probably heat stroke and seizure," he said to Lucy softly.

"How bad?" she asked.

Reluctantly the doctor answered, "Possibly brain damage. His body has shut itself down. He's unconscious. How long he stays like this I can't say. Maybe a few hours. But it could be days or weeks. His heart seems strong enough and he is not entirely unresponsive. His temperature has come down to normal. See if you can sit him up and give him some water and a little food if he doesn't come around in a few hours. He'll need nourishment. I'll come back in the morning. Or I'll send Dr. Shay. I'd like for him to see Mr. Moorhead, too. I wish I could tell you more."

"It's serious?" Lucy asked.

"Yes. We'll just have to wait and see."

ॐॐ — ॐॐ

Percy arrived at Bolingbroke two days after his father's collapse. He had received Phil's telegram that his father was seriously ill. Immediately he closed his office, anticipating an absence of several weeks, then boarded the next upriver steamboat.

Julius had met Percy at the Bayou Sara landing with the buggy. The two men did not talk as the buggy rolled past the hands still busy in the fields, as if nothing were amiss in the big house on the other side of the ridge. It was mid-afternoon now. Lucy and Eliza were on the front porch when he arrived. After greeting him, they led him into the living room. The family had installed Howard into a chair in the living room. Lucy and Eliza went into the adjacent parlor, leaving Percy with his father and his wife.

Philomena explained Howard's condition. She was nearly in tears and had slept little since Howard had collapsed. If anyone was in charge of the house – and the patient – it was Phil. Despite her fatigue, she tried to sound positive for her husband.

"Dr. Shay says your father is not in a coma. That's good, he says. His heart and breathing are good. He has some level of consciousness. He opens his eyes when we feed him. When the doctor holds a candle in front of his face, his eyes will follow the flame as he moves it from side to side. I think he sees Rand when he walks into the room. It may be my imagination, but I think I saw him smile when Rand said something to his PawPaw."

Phil sounded more hopeful than Percy could bring himself to be. Although he had seen men wounded in battle, he had never seen a man in the condition of his father, sitting upright but eyes nearly closed, skin clammy, face expressionless.

Percy asked, "He seems to be asleep right now. Is that a good sign?"

"Yes. The doctor says if he has a sleep cycle, it shows brain activity."

"So what is it? A stroke? Can he recover?"

"Only time will tell, he says. It could have come on from the heat and over-exertion. Sometimes something just happens in the brain. Just like we can't explain why an old person becomes addled."

Percy asked Phil, "What does he say we should do?"

"Feed him. Bathe him. Move him from one position to another several times a day so he doesn't get sores and abscesses. Make something like diapers for when he soils himself."

"Will he come out of this?"

"The doctor says he could. He's seen it happen. Once. In New York. We need to care for him as if he will."

Leddie walked in with a pitcher of lemonade and glasses. She put them on a small round table between Percy and his father.

"Glad you back, Mister Percy. We needin' you."

"Thank you, Leddie." He poured several glasses near to full. "Can he drink?"

"Let me help," Phil said. "It can be tricky." She stood next to Howard and held a glass in one hand and a napkin in the other, under his chin. She placed the glass rim on his lips and tilted it slightly. His eyes remained unopen, but he pursed his lips on the glass and some of the drink entered his mouth; he could be seen to swallow.

"Well, that's something at least," Percy said. He sat silently as Phil slowly gave Howard more to drink. He felt helpless to see his father helpless. Never had he seen Howard Moorhead unable to care for himself and everyone around him. Finally, a positive thought struck him.

"In New Orleans I've seen some chairs on wheels. They're called Bath chairs in England. I'll have one sent here as quickly as possible. At least he'll be able to go outdoors." Percy looked around, trying to see what else needed to be done for his father. "Maybe we could read to him?" he said to Phil.

"Of course. But there are other considerations," she said in a low voice.

"What?"

"Let's go outside."

Percy was puzzled. He followed his wife into the back yard.

"We can hope for a quick and full recovery," she said. She sat on the wrought iron bench in front of a rose bed. He stood looking down at her.

"Yes?"

"But if not . . . . . ." She paused. "I know we've talked about this. But I don't think you've resolved it in your own mind. I wouldn't speak . . . . but this is urgent. Everything will fall apart if all this falls to Calvin to manage. Are you prepared to let that happen?"

Percy frowned. His wife was right. "That would be terrible. I've told you, I plan to spend more time here. But I hadn't expected it to be so soon. I still have my practice to consider. I suppose we could hire a man to oversee."

Phil's weariness sounded in her voice. Lucy and Eliza were not of much help. It was not so much an absence of caring as it was uncertainty about what to do in a household crisis. They had depended on Howard Moorhead for so long – all of them had – they could not imagine his depending on them. Phil spelled it out for her husband.

"This is the busy time for the cotton crop. Time to pick, gin and bale. Do you think we can find an experienced man for the job? Someone who will understand how these two plantations work together?"

"What's the alternative? For me to take it over, right now?" It was not annoyance in his voice but frustration.

Philomena said nothing. She looked at her husband. He understood her without words. He could tell she disapproved of his reluctance to respond as a dutiful husband and son.

"If I must, I must," he finally murmured in resignation.

"Isn't it what your father would have done?" Phil knew her husband's thoughts. She knew duty and filial piety, once examined, could not fail to guide him. Had he not chosen her for his wife, to coax forth the better man within him?

Percy chided himself. "He's the man that I am not."

"There's no better man than you, Percy Moorhead. You have no idea how proud he is of you. In the two years Rand and I have been living here, he's made that clear. He's said he couldn't imagine any one more worthy to bear the Moorhead name. A special future awaits you, he's told me, more than once."

Whether she intended it or not, Philomena's words of praise could not have hurt him more. He felt shame at his affair with Di Watkins and that he had not already assumed a larger role in managing the plantation, easing the burdens on his father. He was a weaker man than Howard Moorhead, little better than Calvin Bunch in his self-estimation.

"Enough said. I'll tell my mother and sister tonight that Father would expect me to take up the reins for the time-being. I hope I don't get resistance from them or Calvin."

Chapter 41

# Taking Charge

In his New Orleans office, Percy explained to Louis, his law clerk, that circumstances at home required that he spend an extended period away. A lawyer who shared offices and a library with him agreed to handle Percy's court appearances if he were unable to attend on the dates as they were set. He had the *Daily Picayune* publish a weekly notice that he would be available to write briefs and arguments for other attorneys. Percy's ambition to become a leader of the New Orleans bar was fading.

Percy was fortunate in having a good law library available to him in St. Francisville. Governor Robert Wickliffe allowed Percy to use his office and library near the courthouse for a small rental. He had relinquished his practice when he became governor more than a year earlier. Wickliffe had moved to Louisiana after marrying the daughter of a Louisiana congressman from St. Francisville. Their home was Wyoming Plantation, located only a few miles from Bolingbroke.

The day-to-day operations at Bolingbroke proved more challenging than Percy expected. He gained new appreciation for the abilities of his father and of Big Tom. After a few days in his new role as manager, he concluded that he needed a complete inventory of all assets of both plantations and a full review of all of the accounts. He grew concerned as it soon appeared that at least seven male slaves and two females were missing. The ledgers for expenses for Bolingbroke were mostly in order, but they were balanced only through infusions of cash by Howard from sources unidentified in the books. Concern grew to suspicion as Percy discovered that the accounts for Jericho Hill were in complete disarray, from the laxness or incompetence of Calvin Bunch.

Approaching the plantations' suppliers in Bayou Sara and St. Francisville, Percy learned that substantial debts were owed for charges made to both plantations, mostly incurred by Calvin Bunch. A banker in St. Francisville extended a loan to Percy against sales of cotton, so he was able to bring all accounts current with merchants in both Bayou Sara and St. Francisville, with firm instructions that only he was to make purchases in the future. If the plantations were to survive, he must deal harshly with Calvin, regardless of recriminations from his mother and sister.

Two days later, Percy was climbing on a buckboard wagon on his way with a young slave to pick up supplies at the landing at Bayou Sara when Calvin came riding up on a bay gelding. As was his habit, he held a riding crop in his right hand and used it for gestures. He pointed the crop at Percy and accused him, "Hey! You cut off my credit in town." Calvin's face was redder than usual, sweat dripping from his full jowls.

"Yes. If I hadn't, the creditors would be at our door."

"You can't do that," said Calvin, puffed up and indignant.

"Let's both get down and walk a bit." Percy was calm, but not conciliatory. He told the slave boy to take Mr. Calvin's horse to the barn then watch the wagon while the two men talked. They were near the garden adjacent to Bolingbroke and walked to a bench.

"Now Calvin, I meant no disrespect," Percy said with patent insincerity.

"The hell you didn't. This isn't the first time I've had this happen. You cut me off in your damned casino."

"Really? House rules for anyone with weak credit. No exceptions."

"So, what now? Why did you humiliate me in town with the merchants?"

"It would be more accurate to say you had done that yourself over a few years. You charged, and Howard always had to make good on your debts. The books are bad. I had to take a loan to bring the accounts all current with our creditors. I can't let anyone run up debt on either plantation unless it can be paid out of current receipts. Howard's been keeping the places going by selling off his investments in New Orleans. On their own, we'd be bankrupt with what you've been spending."

"I could have taken care of the debts in the near future if I'd known of a problem." Calvin saw he was making no progress with Percy. No, his brother-in-law was simply toying with him, drawing it out to increase his pain of embarrassment.

"And there are discrepancies." Percy's inflection was ominous, an elongation in the pronunciation of dis-crep-an-cies.

"Meaning?" Calvin responded cautiously.

"To put it directly, meaning the nine slaves that are unaccounted for."

Calvin was so accustomed to evading and lying to his wife and mother-in-law that he tried the same with Percy.

"I'd say ask your father but he's not able to tell us, now is he?" Calvin should have learned better at the time of the dock fire, where all of Jericho's crop had burned, when Percy had exposed Calvin's lying about having insurance on the baled cotton.

Percy was not merciful. He drew Calvin further out.

"You know nothing about them? Their absence leaves us short-handed at a very busy time."

"I'd have to go over the lists," Calvin replied, haltingly, looking for a credible response. He found none. "With two plantations, I can't be expected to know every nigra in the field."

"No, I suppose not. Well, I'm on my way to town with the load of cotton, and I plan to stop at Sheriff Lurty's office to report nine runaway slaves. I have a list, with the descriptions of each one who is missing. We'll post a notice in a couple of locations for bounty hunters. Care to come with me?"

Calvin suddenly adopted a less abrasive tone. "Today's not a good day. Why don't we make it tomorrow?" He stood, as though he needed to be somewhere else.

"I always say, there's no time like the present. I'll just go on without you. You don't seem to have anything to add."

"Let's go to the house and maybe go over the list. Talk with your mother and sister."

"Oh? Do you think *they* can add anything?"

"Maybe," Calvin said nervously, sitting back down.

Percy had had enough. It was time to end the charade.

"Actually, they can't. But the sheriff could. I've already visited him, Calvin. With the list. Three of the missing men and both females you sold months ago. The four other men you have hired out to other plantations. You needed the money. You're no more than a thief, Calvin. You're stealing from your own family."

"Damn it, Percy." The excuses rushed out. "That money is as good as put back into the plantations. If I hadn't used it to pay off some debts, the creditors would have come against Eliza's interest in Jericho. You know that. And we're better off without them nigras that got sold. Hell, they were troublemakers. Would've caused more problems than they were worth. I put that on Howard Moorhead. Harsh methods are necessary. He's always been too soft, too easy on the nigra. They don't respect you if you spoil them. They're not any different from children. They'll talk back and be insolent unless you whack 'em ever so often. My daddy took a belt to me if I sassed him. Same thing with the nigra. Only with the nigra you got to use a whip. You try and run this place the same way Howard has and you'll see I'm right. The nigra is happiest when he knows his place. Don't blame me. Blame the nigras. I'm not the problem. It's Howard's fault for being so soft. Everbody knows that."

Although he had been caught, Calvin worked himself up into self-righteousness. He again stood and walked off indignantly toward Jericho Hill, face rosy-hued, rooster-strutting. Of course, he felt no guilt over selling off assets of the plantations and concealing it from Howard. He quickly overcame his embarrassment at being called out by his wife's brother.

Percy had expected no remorse from his confrontation. It did, however, serve a useful purpose in forestalling further controversy with Calvin, at least for a short time, over the handling of the two plantations. Calvin knew now that Percy was firmly in charge and would not overlook Calvin's small larcenies and misappropriations as Howard had done for the past eight years.

Chapter 42

# Recalled to Mexico

W hen he picked up Judah Benjamin's telegram at the St. Francisville post office, Percy's initial reaction was to respond immediately that another trip to Mexico was impossible because of his father's stroke three months earlier. His visit two years earlier had seemed a waste of time, with no visible results. Before replying, however, he would talk to Philomena. Percy and Julius finished gathering supplies in Bayou Sara and returned to Bolingbroke. He showed Philomena the telegram the operator had transcribed to paper from the clicks of code.

> Leaving for Mexico in two weeks. Urgent you accompany. Please meet NO Fri. Will explain. JPB.

"I think you must go," Phil told her husband.

He looked at her gravely. "I can't leave you to care for everything. Not with Father like he is. And the plantations. Soon, it will be time to gin and bale."

She took his hands in hers, as though they were clasped in prayer. "I know your sense of responsibility and duty. At least go meet with Judah. You need to go to New Orleans for a few days anyway. You have been so burdened, you need a break."

"If going to Mexico is out of the question, there's not much point in getting together with him. You know how persuasive he is."

"Yes. And he's never done you wrong, has he? Surely, it's just a short trip. He's a U. S. Senator. It wouldn't be for four months like your last time. Look, we'll be fine. He's in good condition, no worse after three months. Dr. Shay and Dr. Davenport both say that. Odessa, Leddie and I have no trouble caring for him. And your mother. She's helping more now. We've settled into a regular routine. Calvin's not giving us any trouble. Pompey and Julius know everything that needs to be done to harvest and bale the cotton crop. Little Jay and Rand are constant companions. They amuse each other for hours. He's the smartest black child I've seen."

"Are you sure you'll be all right?" He was reassured by her confidence. And he admitted, to himself, that he'd be glad to get away for a while. Ruining the plantations was an entirely different sort of responsibility from the practice of law. Upwards of a hundred men, women and children looked to Percy every day for guidance and orders. That most were chattel labor was a great discomfort to him. Julius, Pompey, and Odessa were the buffers between him and the captive workers.

She responded, "Of course. Go to New Orleans tomorrow and meet Judah on Friday. Give him my love. Pack a bag as though you will be in Mexico for a few weeks. Send us a letter or telegram from New Orleans when you find out. If we can't manage, we'll let you know. You've already invested a lot of time on this project. Judah depends on you."

Reluctantly, Percy accepted his wife's guidance. She was right about his investment of time and effort in the project. Three days later he met with Judah Benjamin at Emile La Sere's row house, 229 Royal in New Orleans.

☙☙ — ❧❧

Benjamin said, "Thank you for coming, Percy. I heard about your father's condition. I can only imagine how difficult it is for you as you two are very close." Benjamin would have been surprised to learn how little Percy knew of his father.

Benjamin and his own father were never close. The persons of most significance to Benjamin were his sisters, Rebecca and Hatty, and Jules St. Martin, his wife's younger brother. Benjamin's wife and daughter were in Paris again after briefly trying to make a home in Washington as a Senator's wife. She, and their daughter, had found the nation's capital crude and inhospitable.

"Thank you. Phil assures me she can nurse him in my absence."

Turning to another man who was present, Benjamin said, "Percy this is Louis Heyliger. He will be working with us." Percy shook hands with the new man. He was in his mid-thirties, with brown hair and brown eyes and no distinctive features. He was business-like and quiet. "I'll let Emile explain," added Benjamin with no further words of introduction.

Emile La Sere spoke next, with his Caribbean creole accent. "The letter you wrote to the company about your impressions of Mexico and our status with them was very helpful. We re-organized our approach as a result. A fresh start is needed, like you said."

"That's good," was all Percy would say. He had never gotten a response from anyone about his work in Mexico and meeting with Benito Juarez.

Sensing that Percy was more interested now, La Sere continued. "Yes. Following your observations, we became the Tehuantepec Company of Louisiana in April, and the board named me president. Our new structure is effective today. The board has instructed us to go to Mexico City immediately. We've been working with President Buchanan for the last month. He is enthusiastic about our project. Louis Heyliger will serve as our Secretary and Treasurer. We have new capital and a number of new shareholders."

Percy was unaware of the changes in the company or what had happened with the conflicting claims. He asked, "Aren't there still complications with the Sloo grant? I recall there's been a lawsuit here in the past year."

Benjamin responded, "Sloo is uncooperative. He's challenging the rights he gave up to Falconnet. The purpose of the trip to Mexico is to put the relationship with the Mexican government on a new footing. Ten days ago, Secretary of State Cass endorsed a long letter for delivery to the American envoy, John Forsyth. Do you know him?"

"No. When I was there, the ambassador was James Gadsden. And he was our biggest problem."

"Forsyth could be, too. But the letter of Secretary Cass is explicit in support of our project."

La Sere handed a copy of a letter of 12 or 15 pages, opened to page seven. The little Creole pointed to the pertinent lines in the instructions to be delivered to ambassador John Forsyth:

Mr. Falconnet, the Tehuantepec Company, and the owners of the Garay grant have united their interests, and now seek to obtain from the Mexican government such modifications in the Sloo grant as will secure the construction of the road. If these modifications can be obtained, it is confidently believed that sufficient capital, energy, and enterprise will be enlisted to accomplish the object. The Hon. J. P. Benjamin, senator in Congress, from Louisiana, and Emile La Sere, esq., of New Orleans, president of the Tehuantepec Company, will proceed to Mexico for this purpose, and the latter will bear you these instructions. You are hereby instructed, upon the request of Messrs. Benjamin and La Sere, to make known to the Mexican government the object of their mission, and to give them such aid in its accomplishment as you may deem advisable and effectual.

La Sere took the letter back and placed it on an armoire. "President Buchanan himself wrote most of these instructions, in line with our guidance. The letter makes clear that we represent the policy of the Buchanan administration. Even though we are a private company, the rest of the instructions to the ambassador spell out the terms of a treaty he is expected to negotiate with the Mexican government."

Percy was impressed. "I see. A very interesting development. Why now?"

Judah Benjamin saw that Percy was being drawn in and now added his voice. "Why? We need to get this done early to forestall Sloo's efforts. We've made progress on the coach road for part of the isthmus route. We have a steamship on the Coatzacoalcos River, the *Lenora*. But the Sloo operatives have impeded our efforts. They've been making contracts in the name of our company. We have work crews in Tehuantepec, and a government survey of the area is soon to take place."

Still reluctant to become involved, Percy turned to Benjamin and asked, "And me? What do you need me for? I haven't kept up with the political changes down there. I understand they have a new president and a new constitution. It's General Comonfort, isn't it? I saw him but never met him when I was there. And I have no idea who ambassador Forsyth is."

Benjamin came over to sit by Percy. Placing his hand on Percy's left arm, he said, "You have a keen sense of conditions in Mexico. We don't know what we may encounter after we arrive in the capital. We may need to seek help from Benito Juarez, whom you know as well as we. We expect that you will have a continuing role in the Tehuantepec Company. If it had not been for your need to be home with your father, we would have made you a member of the board for the company."

"I'm very flattered. But I'm hesitant to leave my family for an extended period."

"Of course. Six weeks at most. Probably less."

"Starting two weeks from now?"

Benjamin stood and said with an abruptness that meant quick action was needed, "We've moved up our departure by a week. Can you leave the day after tomorrow? It is an imposition, I know, but we need you."

Nothing in Benjamin's manner was demanding, and he fully sympathized with Percy's concerns. But Phil was right: he could not turn him down. It was not a matter of conflicting loyalties or priorities but of balancing duties to father and to mentor. He had no commitments to Emile La Sere or the Tehuantepec Company, but he could not say no to Judah Benjamin after more than six years of close association. Benjamin was too much like a second father to Percy.

Still uncertain, Percy inquired, "Is Peter Hargous still backing the project?"

"Indeed, he is. And some of Louisiana's most prominent businessmen," said Benjamin.

Heyliger spoke. "No doubt you have worked with some, and their names are familiar. Paul Hebert, our former governor, has joined our board. We have investments by the presidents of two New Orleans banks, James Denegre and Alfred Penn. You probably know William Starke, cotton broker, and Duncan Kenner, sugar planter. I could name others, but you get the idea. All good men."

Heyliger was subtle enough. He didn't need to spell it out – these were leading figures of commerce in New Orleans and could prove important clients to Percy Moorhead should he wish to continue or expand his law practice in New Orleans. It was something to reflect on, even if he weren't committed to Judah Benjamin by long-standing obligation. He knew he must. He had not given up his ambition to become a prominent New Orleans lawyer. He might yet join Judah's law firm.

☙☙ — ❧❧

The sun's heat at noon on the first Sunday in August was too much for the passengers of the steamship to wait on the wharf before boarding. Cargo was still being loaded aboard the *Texas*. She was a large sidewheeler – eleven hundred tons, two hundred sixteen feet long with a beam of thirty-five feet, owned by Harris & Morgan's Southern Steamship Company. Percy found his group seated at a table outside the restaurant nearest Jackson Square: Judah Benjamin, Emile La Sere and a man whom Percy barely knew, Mandeville Marigny.

After Percy sat, Benjamin nodded in the direction of a nearby table and said in a low voice, "He's here." He must have meant the elegantly dressed, distinguished gentleman seated alone, not thirty feet away. He was handsome and in his mid-fifties. The man saw Percy look at him and bowed his head slightly while lifting a glass of beer in acknowledgement. A sly smile briefly played upon his lips. Percy felt he had been caught spying and flushed with embarrassment. His companions avoided the other man's amused staring at them. The man did not lack in self-assurance and enjoyed their discomfort.

After boarding an hour later and putting their bags in their cabin, Percy and Benjamin sat on the upper deck. Percy asked who the man was.

"Our predecessor in the Senate. Pierre Soulé. Some think him a brilliant orator. I say he's simply *orotund*, a man in love with the sound of his own voice – sound and fury without significance. Yes, *or-o-tund*," Benjamin repeated with a grin, lingering on each syllable.

Percy kept to himself his thought that Benjamin could just as easily have been describing himself. He instead asked, "Why's he here?"

"No doubt to make mischief for us. Soulé and John Slidell are implacable foes for control of the Democratic party of Louisiana. They've been fighting each other for years. Slidell became Senator when President Pierce appointed Soulé minister to Spain. Now that Soulé has returned, he won't rest until he takes either my seat in the Senate or Slidell's. He's hell-bent on making Stephen Douglas of Illinois our next president. I can only guess that Sloo has hired Soulé to undermine our mission to get a new concession from Mexico. Soulé and Sloo have many friends in Washington and in the State Department. These friends must have told Soulé what we are up to. That's why we're leaving early, so Sloo won't have time to organize against us. Looks like we aren't fast enough. He's been busy, too."

"Why would Soulé go to all this trouble?"

"Spite partly. It's known that John Slidell has a significant ownership stake in the Tehuantepec Company. And Slidell has unique connections for trade in the Pacific, especially Japan."

"Why is that?" asked Percy.

"His brother-in-law. That would be Commodore Matthew C. Perry. He's married to Slidell's sister, Jane."

"Ah," said Percy. "That Perry. The naval officer who opened Japan to commerce. Was it in two visits a couple of years ago?"

"There's no Westerner better known in Japan than Perry. Slidell's personal connection will make our Pacific connection especially valuable in expanding commerce between East and West. Now, anything that harms Slidell advances Soulé. Sloo's got friends and investors in New Orleans just as we do. Soulé may be holding his influence with them. A politician has to hold on to his base of support. Maybe they gave Soulé a stake in Sloo's outfit. And Soulé's got other interests in Central America. He's one of the faction that wants us to wrest Cuba away from Spain. We'll just have to see when we get to Mexico City."

As the ship began its journey southward, Bolingbroke receded from Percy's thoughts. He remembered his voyage from New Orleans to Tampico a decade earlier, when he was a twenty-year-old volunteer in the Mexican War. He felt he was again involved in an immense international undertaking, this time in a larger capacity. He was glad to be a part of an important project. The Tehuantepec Railroad had enormous potential.

సీసీ — ఆఆ

Upon landing at Vera Cruz, the Louisiana travelers were greeted by the American consul resident in the port city. He was a native of Kentucky, a very tall, muscular man about five years older than Percy. Judah introduced him as John Thomas Pickett.

As their luggage was being transferred, Judah told Percy more about Pickett. "Pickett's facility at Spanish comes from living abroad with his father who was a diplomat. He dropped out of West Point at the age of eighteen to become a consul in the West Indies. He's done some work for the Tehuantepec Company in the past year."

Percy observed that Pickett seemed to greet the Benjamin party and Pierre Soulé with equal favor. Perhaps, Percy thought, Pickett was unaware of the divisions and competing claimants. Indeed, Pickett had arranged for Soulé and the Benjamin party to ride to Mexico City in the same Troy coach, capacious enough for eight passengers, pulled by a team of six large mules. From their familiarity, Percy concluded that Pickett and Soulé were well acquainted. He observed Soulé give Pickett an envelope, which the consul passed to a Mexican with a leather pouch. The man on horse was a courier of some sort, and the condition of his horse suggested that he was well-paid. Percy later learned that through Pickett and the courier, Soulé was able to notify ambassador Forsyth of his expected arrival in Mexico in advance of his appearance in Mexico City. The swift mount allowed the courier to arrive in Mexico City eighteen hours before the men traveling by mule-drawn coach.

Two hours after sundown the coach rolled out of Vera Cruz, preceded by two Mexican soldiers, armed with rifles and pistols. Mexican drivers had no hesitancy about driving the highway to the interior even on the darkest nights, relying on the light from two lanterns and a torch. Throughout the journey, the silence of the Louisiana travelers was broken only by the constant lashing and cracking of the whip by the driver when the road became difficult. In many places the road was made of cobblestones but much damaged by heavily laden wagons, military tactics and torrents of rain. The coach bounced over the rough rocks, plunged over steep pitches, swayed and reeled in deep gullies at the rate of nearly six miles per hour, the mules pushed by the determined driver, cursing loudly at them in guttural Spanish. Periodically the riders and mules rested for an hour or two. The Mexican interior was long overdue for a railroad network. Percy's initial enthusiasm for the American built stagecoach was diminished by spending two days in increasing discomfort on the road. As their route carried them past Cerro Gordo, Percy felt a pang of conscience as he remembered taking the life of the young Mexican to prevent discovery of the reconnaissance for his army assignment.

*Chapter 43*

# Mexican Stand-off

At the coach depot near the Hotel Iturbide, the secretary of the American legation met the stagecoach and welcomed the road-weary arrivals. Percy was relieved to out of the hot, crowded confines. Taking Soulé aside, the secretary told him that the ambassador had arranged private quarters for him near the presidential palace and that that evening, Soulé was to dine with the ambassador, John Forsyth. The Benjamin group was not invited, not a promising start. Percy attributed the apparent slight to the fact that Benjamin and La Sere had not yet delivered the Secretary of State's letter of instruction showing the official imprimatur given to their mission.

When Percy appeared at the reception counter of the hotel, the clerk informed him his room would be ready in two hours. Fatigued by the journey, he set his bag aside and found his way to the leather chair he had occupied so long on his last stay. He was awakened from dozing by a familiar voice.

"Hola, Percy Moorhead. You have been restored to your seat of honor." It was Kit Drury, ironic smile upon his lips.

Percy said, "Why am I not surprised to see you? Have we just had a revolution or is another about to take place?" He was glad to see the familiar face of an old friend.

"Perhaps both my friend," grinned Drury. "Are you on railroad business again?"

"Yes. But not solo. A party of four this time."

"Not with Soulé, are you? A friend told me they saw him."

"No. He's our opposition. I'm sure you're familiar with our group – Senator Benjamin, Emile La Sere and Sheriff Marigny. Their rooms were ready. Mine's not yet."

"Coffee or whiskey?" offered the reporter, always looking for a story on Americans in Mexico. "I'm buying if you're going to fill me in on what's what."

The weather was pleasant in the courtyard. Percy took coffee while Drury ordered whiskey. For the next hour, Percy told the reporter what he knew about the reorganization and progress of the Tehuantepec Company. "Full development can't occur until the competing claims for the Mexican concession are resolved. And that, my friend, is why we are here."

"So, Soulé is for Sloo, and they're your rivals?"

"Exactly. Can't be any other reason why he's here. He's not one of our party."

Speaking more confidentially, the reporter inquired, "How well do you know Pierre Soulé?"

"Just by name. I've tried to stay away from Louisiana politics, except for working with Benjamin."

"Arrogant sombitch if you want the truth. You know about him and Walker, don't you?" Drury's disdain was obvious.

"The filibuster? Can't say that I do."

The Mexican clerk walked up and announced that Mr. Moorhead's room was ready.

Drury rose to leave, saying, "Talk with me in the next day or two and I'll tell you some Soulé and Walker stories."

At a late breakfast the next morning, Benjamin and his small party discussed what they should expect. They had been unable to confer in the stagecoach because of Soulé's presence. "Benjamin said, "Soulé's warm welcome by Forsyth is not encouraging. But it's Comonfort and his Interior minister we need to persuade, not Forsyth." Percy decided not to mention his friend Drury might be able to help."

When they reached the American embassy in the capital, they were greeted by the secretary, Walker Fearn, an ambitious and capable Alabama lawyer, younger than Percy. He took them in to see the ambassador. Benjamin made the introductions of La Sere, Marigny and Percy Moorhead to John Forsyth and presented him with the long letter of instructions from Cass, the American Secretary of State.

The poorly concealed expressions of concern on Forsyth's face observed by Percy betrayed the ambassador's allegiances as he came to the paragraphs giving Benjamin and La Sere the status of special envoys, whom the ambassador was expected to assist. Forsyth's dinner with Soulé the night before had prepared him on the likely topics of the Tehuantepec concession but not the extent of their support in Washington. Subtly, Soulé had set the stage for the detailed instructions to be taken by Forsyth as an affront to his own role as ambassador. It was an effective ploy.

Recovering from his initial reaction to the missive, Forsyth smoothly offered Benjamin and La Sere all the assistance his office could provide. He would immediately contact President Comonfort and the Minister of *Fomento*, Señor Manuel Siliceo, which office, he explained, was the Department of the Interior, Colonization, Industry, and Commerce of the Mexican Republic.

Forsyth said, "The meeting and the appropriate officials may take a little time to set up. The Comonfort administration is facing opposition from his left and his right, and elections are about to be held. My offices and my staff are always available to you. Please enjoy the city in the meantime."

Benjamin asked pointedly, "Is Pierre Soulé seeking a presidential audience also?"

The ambassador cleared his throat and adjusted his posture in his chair, showing his discomfort at the boldness of the Senator's question. "As a former Senator and ambassador extraordinary, Mr. Soulé is extended courtesies just as we would to any other prominent American citizen."

"I will take that as 'Yes.' And I will assume he is here as representative of Mr. A. G. Sloo." Percy admired the smooth manner in which Benjamin skewered Forsyth's partiality.

With some stiffness and formality, Forsyth said, "Perhaps it best you take up the nature of his interests with Mr. Soulé himself. I will keep you informed as to our progress in arranging a conference with the Mexican leaders."

Over dinner at the hotel that evening, Marigny asked, "Did I discern that the ambassador was peevish about the instructions you brought from Washington?"

Percy still didn't have a sense of why Marigny was along on this trip. Perhaps it was because he was Sheriff of Orleans Parish and that might impress the Mexicans. He was probably one of the investors in the Tehuantepec Company, but Percy wasn't sure. Marigny's father had been one of the richest men of New Orleans but had gambled most of his fortune away and sold most of the property his son would have otherwise inherited.

Benjamin responded, "We must make allowances for the ambassador's exalted sense of himself. He comes by it naturally, if undeservedly. His father was Governor of Georgia, U. S. Senator, and Secretary of State for both Andrew Jackson and Martin Van Buren. No doubt he feels he is more qualified than Lewis Cass to be Buchanan's Secretary of State. His credentials as a newspaper editor in Mobile do not make likely his further advancement."

Emile La Sere turned the meeting to planning for the eventual conference. He said to Benjamin, "You've established that Soulé is here to represent the Sloo claimants and will be meeting with Comonfort to oppose our plan for a new concession grant. What is our approach?"

"We are under certain constraints," said Benjamin, lighting another thin, light brown cheroot. "Our appeal to the Mexican president must not be one of legalisms. As Percy explained two years ago, going to the Mexican courts to resolve the many conflicting claims going back to the Garay grant in 1842 is a dead end. Soulé will probably appeal to the sanctity of the Sloo grant and argue that it is enshrined in the Gadsden Treaty. Our argument will be that Comonfort should simply declare that all the existing parties with claims have failed to fulfill their obligations to have portions of the route completed as promised. Thus, the concessions have terminated of their own accord. The president has authority to grant a new one along the lines of the old. We have the difficulty of ambassador Forsyth sitting with us during the meeting with the President and the Minister of *Fomento*. We must be careful what we say against Soulé. Sloo was very clever in sending Soulé. It puts us in a tricky situation. We should not make broad declarations about American policy towards Mexico. Forsyth thinks that is his job and that we are usurping his authority. If Forsyth is an ally of Soulé, then he could report back to Secretary Cass and President Buchanan that we are undermining policies Forsyth has been trying to achieve for the administration."

Percy spoke up. "That was my experience two years ago. Ambassador Gadsden had his own program and wouldn't lift a finger to assist our project."

Benjamin nodded, tapping his cigar into a saucer on the table. He took another draw and said, "So, let's put ourselves in the place of Comonfort. What's on his mind? From all I gather, he is a good man, a genuine patriot. But he's a compromiser, not that different from our own president. He believes he can satisfy the conflicting strains among the Mexican political interests by meeting all of them half-way. That only means he's pulled in different directions and will never satisfy all of them. The 'puros' are the anti-clerical, anti-military party and think he has abandoned their ideals. The church and the landowners, with the support of many military, believe he has already gone too far and that he must be overthrown if they are to survive. We need to convince him that an American presence with a Isthmian Railroad will help stabilize his government. And a new treaty that affirms that relationship will forestall the possibility of British or French intervention in Mexico on the pretense that Mexico hasn't paid its debts to their business interests."

Benjamin looked around the dinner table. The other three men all nodded in agreement. "Cheers," he said, lifting his glass of French wine. "Cheers," responded his chorus. Their grave expressions showed they knew the way would not be easy.

ॐॐ — ॐॐ

Kit Drury suggested to Percy that they talk somewhere other than the bar of the Hotel Iturbide. He was unsure whether Benjamin would approve of a *tête-à-tête* of Percy with a reporter. The two men walked to the Alameda, a lovely park enclosed by a low stone wall and filled with grand old forest trees. Fountains played among the cool, shaded walks as they found their way to a billiard saloon, operated by a German, adjacent to the park. Percy ordered a glass of Mexican beer while Drury enjoyed a whiskey with his usual *cigarito*.

Percy was as candid with Drury about this visit to Mexico City as he had been about the last, two years earlier, explaining the status of the Tehuantepec Company and its hope to gain a new concession. He was telling him no more than was common knowledge in several New Orleans newspapers. Gaining useful information was an exchange, and Percy gave as much as he had. Drury reciprocated, for his own purposes. The reporter had no reason to favor the Tehuantepec Company, but he was eager to see

Soulé fail, whatever his claimed goal.

Drury said to Percy, "I mentioned Walker and Soulé and you seemed to draw a blank."

"That's right. I assumed you meant William Walker, the filibuster who's tried to take over Nicaragua. Does he have a connection to Soulé?"

"A connection? They are joined together like those Siamese twins in the traveling show. Co-conspirators. I spent a good bit of the last year going in and out of Nicaragua covering Walker's takeover of that country's government. He was the self-proclaimed president for much of a year. Walker thinks it's the manifest destiny of the white race, particularly Americans, to expand their dominion to all lands washed by the Gulf of Mexico and the Caribbean Sea. Southward the course of empire. He wants to re-introduce African slavery to the entire region as he did in Nicaragua and begin the slave trade again with Africa, the rest of the world be damned."

Drury paused while he lighted another black *cigarito*. He exhaled smoke and admired the glow of the setting sun on the edge of the mountains, far from the valley surrounding the city. They were not far from where Percy had lived in camp for seven months in 1848. Their walk had taken them past the site of the Aztec club, where Percy had stumbled and suffered embarrassment from an officer.

"You know what they say – poor Mexico, so far from God, so close to the United States. Well, who is Walker's biggest American supporter? Pierre Soulé. In New Orleans, Soulé raised funds to purchase munitions and supplies. He recruited soldiers for Walker's invading army. I was in Nicaragua just a year ago at this time when Soulé arrived there to help the Walker government. He worked with them to issue bonds to finance their programs. He wrote the proclamation published by Walker in September that allowed the return of slavery. Around that time, Soulé paid $50,000 for a cacao plantation near Granada that had been confiscated from a Nicaraguan government official."

"Did you get to ask him about it?"

"No, I never interviewed him, but people around him said he intended to settle on the huge estate. That deal fell through when Walker was driven out. But you can be sure that Walker and his friend Soulé still have their hearts set on conquering central America, Cuba and eventually much of Mexico. They view the peoples of these areas as inferior races ripe for plunder. A railroad in that part of Mexico under Soulé's control would help them achieve their dreams."

"I gather you think that's a bad idea," Percy said with a grin and a wink.

"I dislike the arrogance of my fellow Americans. I think slavery's a terrible thing. But I also dislike the arrogance of the abolitionists. Men like Walker and Soulé are rapacious adventurers who destroy the lives of others in the name of civilization. The abolitionists would destroy the lives of others in the name of virtue and righteousness."

"That sure sounds hopeful!" He added with good humor, "And who do you not dislike?"

Sipping his whiskey, Drury continued, "Those who see the folly of human progress and are amused by man's insignificant presumptions. People such as yourself who understand that all these politicians who surround us are so many roosters crowing on their own little dung heaps, thinking their cackles cause the sun to rise."

"Yep," Percy nodded in agreement, and took another drink of beer. "Are you not concerned that President Buchanan may seek the same ends as Soulé?"

Drury shrugged, "Maybe. He was Polk's Secretary of State during the Mexican War. But he's a bumbling fool, not a wild-eyed adventurer. He backs away from controversy."

"And Benjamin? Perhaps he wants Mexico. Why would you trust him more than Soulé? Or me, for that matter." Percy was more serious now.

The reporter scoffed. "No. Not Benjamin. The Southern empire builders don't trust Benjamin because he's a Jew. Besides, he's not interested in establishing colonies. Not in his character. And you, Percy Moorhead, are incapable of dissembling. I saw that two years ago, night after night while we talked. You were born with a soul with no spark of meanness and that can never know greed. That's why Benjamin looks to you. It's what he would like to think about himself."

Rejecting Drury's description of his character, Percy replied, "Don't mistake me for one of King Arthur's knights. I'm a lawyer who takes his duties to clients very seriously, whatever my own inclinations might be. What you've told me is very helpful. Sloo and Soulé may have a larger agenda than the commercial success of a path connecting the two oceans. I know for fact that Benjamin is interested in trade, not territory."

"Maybe I can be more helpful. Check with me in a few days. The courier who takes my dispatches to the mail packets in Vera Cruz twice a week tells me Soulé wants him to take his letters also."

For the next couple of days Percy strolled the streets of Mexico City by himself and read the Mexican newspapers to get a sense of the political situation. With his group at their nightly dinner, he exchanged views and rumors, without mentioning Drury. One evening they enjoyed an outdoor concert given by a small orchestra in the Alameda.

True to his word, on Wednesday Kit Drury passed on to Percy two letters written by Pierre Soulé to a man named Jennings, one of Sloo's investors in Louisiana. Soulé had entrusted them to the courier to take to Vera Cruz.

"And the courier just passed them on to you?" said Percy.

Winking, Drury said, "I wish I could attribute it to my charm. No, he's a courier I use on a regular basis. He felt he was treated rudely by Soulé and had no hesitancy in allowing me to delay the letters' departure for a day or two so that I could examine them." It was not the first time Drury and the courier had entered such a transaction, with suitable reward. What resourceful reporter has not made use of underhanded means for gathering news and intelligence?

Percy promised Kit Drury that he would not tell others in his delegation and that he would return them shortly after reading them. They proved most interesting, even if Percy was uncertain how he could put them to use. Soon the opportunity presented itself, though not by Percy's design.

*Chapter 44*

# Comonfort's Cabinet

As he mounted the steps of the magnificent archbishop's palace in Tacubaya, Percy recalled his first entry into the buildings ten years earlier when, as a private, he had taken reports to General Winfield Scott. Like the American general and several Mexican presidents before himself, President Ignacio Comonfort preferred to hold office in the palace in Tacubaya, a short coach ride from the center of Mexico City. Instead of coming as conquerors, Percy was now with a small party of American supplicants seeking favors, not territory.

As the audience with President Comonfort began in the early afternoon, ambassador Forsyth made the introductions of the four Louisianans representing the Tehuantepec Company. The president seemed weary to Percy. *The cares of office sit heavily on a man who takes his responsibilities seriously.* Comonfort was in his mid-forties, from the city of Puebla, where Percy had spent a pleasant three months recovering from his wound as Cerro Gordo and learning Spanish. *El presidente* had a receding hairline, a modest beard, and bore the extra weight of comfortable middle-age. Of moderate height, he had no trace of Indian blood about him.

Next to Comonfort was Manuel Siliceo, the Minister of *Fomento* whose department would be responsible for oversight of the completion and operation of the Tehuantepec railroad while under the American company's control. His very dark skin and broad facial features revealed a substantial African heritage. African blood was rarer in Mexico than in the American south and the Caribbean. Siliceo had encountered relatively little race prejudice as he rose in the Mexican military and the government but was acutely aware of the attitudes of most Americans.

Percy watched silently the back-and-forth of Benjamin and La Sere as they took turns making their case to Comonfort for the voiding of the existing grants of rights-of-way. As planned, they emphasized the economic benefits flowing to Mexican commerce from a trans-Mexican railroad and why an American company was preferable to a British or French company. They did not mention the name of Pierre Soulé, though he was an unseen presence in the room; he had been there two days before, as Benjamin had learned from a contact in the legation staff. President Comonfort had studied law. He listened respectfully and interjected only a few questions as Benjamin spoke.

When it was his turn, Mandeville Marigny spoke briefly on the amity and natural affinities between the city of New Orleans and Mexico City. He then turned to the expanded steamship service that could be offered by the Southern Steamship Company to Vera Cruz and Tehuantepec, should the proposed new concession be granted. Percy suddenly understood the presence of Marigny on this mission. He was representing the interests of the steamship company owned by Charles Morgan of New York but run from New Orleans by his son-in-law Israel Harris. It was the largest shipping company in the Gulf of Mexico and another of Judah Benjamin's clients. Of course, it should have been obvious long ago to Percy: the Tehuantepec Company was nothing without ships connecting it to ports throughout the Gulf.

Now President Comonfort turned to Percy and said: "Señor Purs-see," pronouncing Percy's name with two sibilants. "You sit in silence. Have you nothing to say? Come, I would hear your thoughts."

Surprised at the sudden attention, Percy managed, "Mr. President, I am the junior member of the delegation. Mine is a non-speaking role in this performance."

Comonfort seemed amused by the response. "But you know my country. You have been here several times. have you not?"

"*Si*, that I have Mr. President. I was with General Scott for a year and spent a pleasing interlude in your hometown of Puebla. Again I was here for a time two years ago. As an observer for the railroad project."

"My friend Benito Juarez says you are a good man, an honest lawyer who speaks his mind."

"Señor Juarez is too kind. We had stimulating conversations on the nature of government when he was a resident in New Orleans."

Comonfort was insistent. He would hear from the friend of Benito Juarez. "Then you should add your voice to what I have heard from Senator Benjamin and President La Sere and Sheriff Marigny."

Percy remained reluctant. "My thoughts might not be gracious to the ears of my compatriots. They speak for our government and for the Tehuantepec Company. I can only speak for myself."

"Then we shall ask them to leave us for a short interval. From your lips to my ears alone. Minister Siliceo does not understand English, so he will remain. Benito said I must hear from you. He said I must insist. Please, indulge me, or Benito if not me."

Percy looked at the other men uncomfortably. Judah Benjamin's face was frozen in his enigmatic smile and betrayed nothing of his thoughts. Emile La Sere fidgeted nervously, concerned that his relationship with Juarez was of longer standing than Percy's, yet Juarez had urged Comonfort to sound the opinions of Percy Moorhead. Marigny was indifferent; he had said his piece.

Forsyth's demeanor showed that he was taken completely by surprise. Like others in the capital, Forsyth was uncertain of the present relationship between Juarez and Comonfort. Apparently the two men remained personally close even if politically estranged. The American ambassador had paid little attention to Percy and was unaware that Percy even knew Juarez. Now Forsyth's position was subverted by an upstart from the rude town of Bayou Sara. Without protesting, he reluctantly departed with the other men. It would not do to offend the Mexican president.

Now Percy was alone with the two Mexican officials, sitting opposite them, Comonfort testing him and the Minister of *Fomento* looking at him with an inscrutable expression that seemed hostile, even menacing under his hooded eyes. Percy and the president continued to speak in English, Percy understanding that Comonfort preferred that Minister Siliceo not participate fully in the exchange.

Comonfort said, "A man is on a road. Suddenly he finds himself at a fork with two different paths. If they will both arrive at the same destination, why should he prefer the one path and not the other?"

Juarez had recommended Percy as forthright, so forthright Percy would be. "Your Excellency makes a good point. If Mr. Sloo's company and the Tehuantepec Company both have the capital and the expertise to build a railroad across the isthmus, why should you prefer one over the other? If that were the sole consideration, you might as well flip a coin or turn a card to determine the winner. Both will build the railroad."

Comonfort was pleased that Percy immediately grasped his use of parable. "But that is not the only consideration you seem to say, Mr. Purs-see. What else would you consider if you were seated where I am sitting? Do not be reluctant. We have a saying: *Arrieros somos y en el camino andamos.* Do you understand?"

"Yes. We are all mule drivers in the fields. We are all human beings making our way through life as best we can. If I were a Mexican and I loved my people, as I know Benito Juarez does, I would look upon Mr. Pierre Soulé and Mr. Sloo as a grave threat to my country."

Percy had Comonfort's full engagement. The president said, "He is your countryman and is very well spoken. Why should I not trust this man?"

Earnest now, Percy spoke as a lawyer advising his own client. "Do not be misled by his French birth nor his elegant Castilian Spanish. He is ardent advocate of American expansionism and the reintroduction of slavery and the slave trade everywhere from the isthmus of Panama to the Texas coast."

Comonfort affected a stern expression, saying, "That is a strong allegation."

"I do not make it lightly. Surely Mr. President, you know of William Walker's invasion of Baja California and Sonora to separate them from Mexico. And you know he took over Nicaragua just a year ago and made war with Honduras and Costa Rica."

"Of course. What has this to do with Pierre Soulé?" Comonfort had been told by Forsyth only that Soulé was a prominent American statesman. He now wore a frown, but it was not directed at Percy.

Percy pressed on. "Soulé is the strongest supporter of Walker in the United States. He was in Nicaragua as an unofficial minister in the Walker government. He drafted the proclamation for slavery. Walker plans to return to central America with more men, and he hopes to have the support of the U. S. government. Walker and Soulé have designs on Mexico. Control of a railway through Mexico, distant from Mexico City but close to your southern border, would give them the means to carry out their long term plans."

Comonfort was suspicious that Percy might be throwing a false light on Soulé and his interest. He demanded, "Wouldn't the same concerns be there for the company you represent?"

"No, Mr. President. Senator Benjamin and Senator Slidell, who also is an investor, are interested only in commerce. Both are political rivals of Soulé. Both look on William Walker as a dangerous man who can only harm American interests. Neither of them believes the slave trade should be reopened."

"If what you say is true . . . . . Well, I can look into whether Soulé was in Nicaragua as you say. That alone would be enough to reject the Sloo grant. Still, I must address the other claims. What can you tell me about Soulé's argument that Sloo's grant is still valid because Falconnet has only a mortgage or pledge and until the mortgage or pledge is foreclosed in a proper legal proceeding, he has no interest in the concession he could assign? Have you thought about this?"

"Yes, Mr. President. It is an ingenious argument. But this is a type of contract, a special contract between two parties concerning the grant by a sovereign government. As with any contract, we look to the intent of the parties. I can speak to the intent of the contract because I drafted the terms of the contract when I was in London. Judah Benjamin sent me to London to protect the interests of his company when the English bankers financed the Sloo project. Senator Benjamin thought Sloo was stealing his project from him and Mr. Hargous, but that Sloo could never get the work done. So he wanted us to be in a position to get the rights back. The contract I drafted was no mortgage or pledge. It was an assignment subject to a condition, namely that the money be paid. When the condition occurred by the failure of Sloo to pay, the assignment to Falconnet was immediately effective without further action by the parties. Such an automatic feature is consistent with both English and Mexican law."

"I see," Comonfort said slowly and thoughtfully. "I still must deal with Minister Siliceo. He was very impressed by Señor Soulé, the smoothness of his presentation."

Percy hesitated. He had Soulé's letter in his breast pocket. How would it be received? He put aside misgivings. "Mr. Soulé is facile and insincere. Perhaps Minister Siliceo would like to know Mr. Soulé's true opinion of him."

Percy drew a letter from his coat pocket and handed it to the Mexican president, who could read English well-enough, with the page folded to show the paragraph he wished to show Comonfort. It said:

*The support of the Minister of Fomento, it is understood, can be had for one hundred thousand dollars. His name is Manuel Siliceo, and is a full and dark mulatto, just such a being as would run great risk to be put at auction in New Orleans. In New Orleans we sell them, here they sell themselves.*

Comonfort then read the entire letter slowly, from beginning to end. It had to be genuine, because it had information from a meeting only two days earlier at which only Comonfort, Siliceo and Soulé were present. The handwriting and signature were identical to a summary of arguments on behalf of the Sloo grant that Soulé had presented to Comonfort at that meeting.

Comonfort handed the letter to his Minister of Fomento. "Manuel, *Señor Soulé dice en Nueva Orleans serías su esclavo.*"

Siliceo looked at the letter without comprehension but muttered, "*hijo de puta.*"

Percy told Comonfort that he had not gotten the translation of Soulé's letter quite right, that it was not as harsh as he made it.

Comonfort smiled, almost indulgently. "Señor Purs-see, you are as naïve as you are honest. If I am to reject Mr. Soulé, I must have Minister Siliceo fully in opposition to Soulé as well. Here, take the letter and keep it. Otherwise, the minister will get Soulé to explain it and ask for the money. He can be bought for much less. Or he may cut Soulé's throat. Siliceo is capable of either. Thank you in any event. You have given me much to think over. I must ask questions about Walker and Soulé. You may join your countrymen."

ᕱᕱ — ᕽᕽ

At dinner that evening, the group were eager to hear what Percy said about his meeting with President Comonfort. Percy deflected them for as long as he could, but they were insistent. Finally, he told them, "El Presidente wanted to know what I thought about American railroads. He had never seen one. I said they were wonderful. He said Mexico has only two small sets of tracks, the one opened a month ago at Vera Cruz to a village nearby and the three-mile line here at Tacubayu. I told him about my father taking me to see the arrival of a steam locomotive brought by barge up the Mississippi River when I was ten. It was called the *Woodville*. Magnificent."

"You can't be telling the truth," said Marigny.

"No, I can't. But that's the story I'm sticking with until the next snowfall in New Orleans or in Hell, whichever occurs first." The others laughed with Percy at his fable.

ᕱᕱ — ᕽᕽ

The first of the Mexican government's two decrees was issued on Thursday, September 3. A messenger brought it to Judah Benjamin at the Hotel Iturbide. He and the other three were having morning coffee and read the proclamation. In Spanish, and signed by "Citizen Siliceo," it said:

> His excellency the president of the republic has transmitted to me the following decree:
>
> Ignacio Comonfort, president of the Mexican republic, to the inhabitants thereof: Know ye, that, using the powers granted to me by the plan of Ayutla, remodelled at Acapulco, I have thought proper to issue the following decree:
>
> Sole article. The privilege granted on the 5th of February, 1853, to Mr. A. G. Sloo and associates, and to the company entitled

- 340 -

Mixed, for the opening of interoceanic communication through the Isthmus of Tehuantepec, is declared null and void, the grantees having violated the obligations imposed by the decree of the above date.

Issued in the Palace of Tacubaya, September 3, 1857.

Marigny only understood a little of the Spanish. "Does this mean we've won?"

Benjamin replied, with cautious optimism, "Not yet. It's halfway there. Comonfort could still deny ours. Too early to celebrate."

On Monday, September 7, Ambassador Forsyth summoned the Benjamin party to the American embassy. Ushered into his office, he told the group, "Sit down, gentlemen." As they sat, Forsyth said, "It looks like you got everything you wanted. President Comonfort just issued his proclamation. I'll translate the first article for you: "A privilege is conceded to the company formed in New Orleans on the 30th of July of the present year, called the Louisiana Tehuantepec Company, for the opening of an inter-oceanic communication across the Isthmus of that name, according to the conditions expressed in the present decree."

"Magnificent," said Benjamin. "Do you have copies for us? Anything unexpected?"

"Two things perhaps. You had asked for an exclusive grant for seventy-five years. He gave you sixty. The only other thing that might surprise you is article 17. A condition of the grant is that your company assumes the payment to Francisco P. Falconnet of the six hundred thousand dollars, with interest and damages legally due, lent to the Sloo enterprise, to enable it to comply with the 14th article of the contract of the 5th February, 1853, liberating the Mexican government from all future responsibility, and without diminishing its share of net profits fixed in article 16. Sounds like a small price to me, and eminently reasonable. It relieves the Mexicans from litigation."

Percy assumed that Forsyth was upset that the Mexicans had

not backed Pierre Soulé as he had sought, but he had the prudence not to let it show. This was a U. S. Senator he was dealing with, one who had the backing of the President and the Secretary of State.

The four Louisianans contained their elation until they were well on the way back to the hotel from the legation. Riding in the coach, La Sere was first to speak. "Incredible. We have nearly everything we asked for and far more than we expected."

Benjamin said, "Indeed, and just how that happened, I can't say. The president wasn't leaning our way in our meeting. It must have been something in private with Moorhead here. Percy, you are either the shrewdest negotiator in the Americas or the holiest fool in Christendom."

Percy deflected the compliment. "Neither, I'm sure. I'm pretty sure our success is to be found in something Pierre Soulé said or did that gave offence to the Mexicans. Now, if you gentlemen don't mind, if I ride fast there's a steamboat leaving Vera Cruz for New Orleans in a few days. You have plans for the next couple of weeks in making arrangements for surveying and road building. Those needn't include me. I have been away from my family longer than I had intended."

Three hours later Percy Moorhead was on his way home.

## Chapter 45

# A Father's Silence

ating a leisurely breakfast at the St. Charles, Percy read morning editions of the *Picayune* and the *Daily Crescent*. The return to New Orleans from Mexico City took a week. Percy had slept late on this, the morning after arriving. The packet steamer that would take him to Bayou Sara would not depart until 2:00. He was surprised that both papers carried accounts of the new grant of the Mexican government to the Tehuantepec Company. The Southern Steamship Company steamship that carried him must have carried also Drury's dispatches, perhaps others, too.

The *Picayune* reported that the sudden arrival of Benjamin, La Sere and Soulé gave rise to all sorts of rumors, including one that they bore offers to purchase Sonora for $20,000,000. Percy chuckled that the paper said that this rumor was not looked on with disfavor, the Mexicans pleased with the idea of having so much spare change in an hour of necessity. It finished by noting, "As to our distinguished citizens themselves, they were the cynosure of all eyes in the public streets and at the theatre." Percy was sure that "cynosure" was Drury's own ironic touch and not an addition by a New Orleans editor of his dispatch.

More accurately, the other paper reported that the negotiations had been successful, granting all or nearly all asked by Benjamin and La Sere: "the Sloo and Garay grants are both entirely ignored, and the affair is placed on a perfectly new and independent basis." Another portion of the paper printed the new charter of the Tehuantepec and a list of the company's thirteen shareholders. Percy regretted his name was not among the company owners but felt confident that Benjamin would see that he was issued an appropriate number of shares. The company's reorganization had taken place before he agreed to join the group on the mission to Mexico. It was on the expectation of shares that he had not charged a fee for his work in going to Mexico City.

In the six weeks he was gone, New Orleans had paid little note of Percy's absence. The papers told him what he had missed and what he would yet miss this very evening. At the Théâtre d'Orléans on Saturday a sold-out audience enjoyed Donizetti's *Lucrezia Borgia*, which was to be followed this evening at the same theater by Donizetti's grand three-act opera, *Maria di Rohan*. The cast would include as *Armand* Signora Felicita Vestvali and as *Maria* Signora Luigia Caranti. Cast as *Ricardo* was Signor Mario Tiberini and as *Enrique*, Signor Corradi Setti. The traveling company was owned and managed by Signora Vestvali who often followed her opera turn by a performance in a male Shakespearean role, generally Romeo in the tomb scene from *Romeo and Juliet* or Hamlet in the graveyard scene. Percy was one of the insiders in New Orleans who were aware that Signora Vestvali was actually born in Germany as Anna Marie Staegemann. A new name and a fabricated background went a long way in establishing an enhanced persona for Fräulein Staegemann to display her talents in a new country. At Crisp's Gaiety theater, *Rob Roy* was still being performed, as when he had left. The bill of fare at the St. Charles Theater were Rumsey and Newcomb's Minstrels, a troupe consisting of eighteen Ethiopian Melodists and Extravaganzists, performing songs, ballads, dances, burlesques, and plantation scenes. The shows, Percy reflected, would go on whether he attended or not.

Walking towards the river, he observed that shoppers continued to shop on Canal, Royal and Chartres, heedless of his return from Mexico, just as they surely had shopped daily while he was away. Now he approached the lines of wagons and handcarts that were next to the wharves, waiting to load or unload goods on the thirty-five or forty steamships and sailing vessels anchored and docked along the levee. Visible along the levee also were numerous stacks of five-hundred-pound bales of cotton awaiting transshipment from river steamers to the sailing ships that would carry them to New York and Liverpool. Ships relying on sail were slower, but far more cotton could be carried by a ship that needed no large boilers nor bunkers of coal to fuel them across the Atlantic. Which, if any, of the hundreds of bales were from the Moorhead plantations? Life had gone on without him while he was away. And what would he find on return to St. Francisville and Bolingbroke? Was his father still alive?

And then he realized -- his thoughts of the opera and the entertainments and the shoppers and the ships and the cotton were not about their indifference to his absence but to his father's absence. Life in New Orleans and its multifold pleasures went on without Howard Moorhead to enjoy them. His father had loved the opera. Three decades of Howard's life had revolved around cotton and its commerce, and he had witnessed the growth of New Orleans into one of the world's most important ports in part because of the cotton trades he had transacted and the market innovations he had made. Percy did not love New Orleans as his father had. Or the opera. And today was his father's birthday. Or tomorrow. He wasn't sure. The same year that Howard Moorhead had taken little Percy to see the arrival of the locomotive *Woodville* at Bayou Sara, he had fitted Percy in a suit tailored to a ten year old to accompany him to the Théâtre d'Orléans for a performance of Giacomo Meyerbeer's *Robert le diable*. Percy's sadness was sadness for his father and for the transience of all things human. And yet . . . . . . is there not comfort in seeing that sadness too shall pass?

ﾟﾟ — ﾟﾟ

Philomena had been right. Howard Moorhead's condition was unchanged – no better, no worse. Phil was happy to have a husband again and Rand to have a father. Percy dispensed the small souvenirs: the three adult women were each given silver jewelry crafted in Mexico City; to Nerissa, he gave a cloth Mexican parrot to hang from her bed post; for Rand, Percy unwrapped a carved wooden bull with horns made of bone. For his father, Percy had brought a small bottle of cologne that Phil could apply to his face after she shaved him. He placed it next to the bowl on the wash stand in Howard's bedroom.

The plantations were in as good a shape as when he had left at the end of July. Now September was soon to end. Cotton had been picked and much of it ginned and baled. The two wells still pumped. The ginning equipment had not broken. Mules and horses still grazed and performed chores. The milch cows still gave milk, chickens laid their eggs as before, and two sows had recently given birth to litters of seven and nine piglets. Corn was harvested and put away in two storage sheds. Julius and Pompey had seen to all that needed to be done. And Percy was relieved, but he needed to be sure things continued to run smoothly. He updated all accounts and made a schedule of maintenance and tasks that had to be done to continue the successful operations on the two plantations. Without planning and organization, all would slowly fail. More than ever, Percy was certain his role was indispensable.

The winter passed mildly, the cotton yield better than expected, and prices were relatively stable. Percy had weathered the challenges of running the plantations. After the initial confrontation, Calvin had left him alone – albeit remaining antagonistic. Steamship service had improved to the point Percy could spend three or four days a month in New Orleans without losing too much time in transit. He was able to keep some semblance of a law practice going. He hoped he could continue it with spring planting approaching.

Percy seldom saw old friends in the city and had no time to call at Toulouse Gardens, not since Scruggs had told him of Di's departure. If, by chance, she had returned, he didn't want to know or to see her. He had not seen or heard from Judah Benjamin after returning from Mexico City. The senator was again in Washington. He read in the New Orleans paper that the Tehuantepec Company had made its first successful transit with mail and passengers from California. He was able to schedule his time so that he made a few court appearances, but he was disappointed in that he never felt as well-prepared as he should be.

The only memorable event was a chance encounter on Tchoupitoulas Street with Kit Drury. After pleasantries, Drury said he had recently returned from Mexico City. Percy again thanked him for his guidance on Soulé and apologized for not having paid much attention to the news of late. Drury was surprised that Percy had not heard that Mexico's new president was Benito Juarez, who had ascended to the office from his post as Chief Justice.

"How long will that last?" Percy asked. Few lasted very long in the Mexican presidency, so another vacancy was certain to arise. Even now, a struggle was growing between Juarez and a coalition of the religious and military elements of the country. Drury had interviewed Juarez several times, and Juarez always asked about his friend Percy Moorhead.

"How very kind of him," Percy replied, "but I'm sure he was merely being polite to a New Orleans reporter."

"I don't think so," said Drury. "He said you are honest and learned. You treated him with respect and never insulted his intelligence. He was sorry to have missed you when you were there last August." Shortly before returning to New Orleans, Drury reported, a croupier at a public gambling saloon named Zuloaga had become a general and then named head of state in Mexico City, while Juarez was in retreat in Guadalajara.

"And Comonfort?" asked Percy.

"As usual, going in opposite directions – for Zuloaga and then against him in a matter of weeks."

"I suppose your paper will have you reporting on another Mexican civil war in the near future. Pity the Mexicans can't govern themselves."

His forehead furrowed, Drury warily responded, "Since I've been back here, I'm beginning to wonder whether Americans can."

"Talk of secession is overblown," said Percy confidently. "My law teacher, Judge Tucker, was calling for it a decade ago. Reasonable people will see that the economies of North and South are bound to one another. The slave states don't have the resources to go it alone. We're more civilized than the Mexicans and can resolve our differences without fighting one another."

The newspaper man was skeptical. "I'd prefer that you prove right. But I can't be too hopeful. In Congress, members in both houses now arm themselves in the capitol because of Preston Brooks beating Senator Sumner within an inch of his life. With no more than a token fine as a consequence. I haven't seen anything as bad as that in Mexico."

Affably, Percy replied, "That's a good reason to avoid reading the news. My hands are full with the things I can influence."

かかか — みかか

"Is PawPaw going to get better?" asked Rand one evening. The five-year-old missed his grandfather. They had been constant companions for nearly three years, seldom separated by more than a few hours.

"We can hope so," his father said, without conviction. Rand had never experienced a death in the family, nor even a serious illness. Percy didn't know how to prepare his son for the inevitable. Do you draw examples from what a child knows of animals? Do you talk of heaven and eternal happiness on leaving this world? Do you ward off your own sorrow by telling your child a story you don't yourself believe?

Rand said, "I see you talking to PawPaw. Does he talk to you?" The child sounded doubtful. Percy owed it to him to be upbeat. There were truths he could honestly impart.

"Sometimes people can talk without words."

"Can he hear you?"

"I like to think so. And when I talk to him, I can hear words he once spoke to me, even long ago. Sometimes I imagine what he would say to me if he could speak. It's almost the same."

"Mother talks to him."

"Oh? What does she say?"

"When she pushes him in the garden, she asks him if he's warm enough. Then she'll adjust his blanket. She will pick a flower and let him smell it. Things like that."

It pleased Percy that Philomena preferred that she take care of Howard rather than one of the servants. She thought it a shame that a man could find himself in such a condition and not enjoy loving care. If Lucy were a more affectionate woman, she would have devoted more time to her husband. It just wasn't in Lucy, and she wouldn't pretend to be a person she was not.

After eight months, Howard's condition had changed little. Sometimes, after a late lunch and coffee, Percy would spell Phil by walking his father's wheelchair around areas of Bolingbroke familiar to his father. They almost had a routine. He would put a fresh shirt on Howard and lift him into the chair. The old man must have lost thirty pounds, yet he was not completely frail. Phil supervised a young servant moving Howard's arms and legs twice daily to maintain muscle tone. Percy would then groom his father, combing his hair, trimming his mustache and beard and eyebrows when needed, tucking his arms beneath a woolen blanket, even on a warm day.

Moving slowly over the shell and gravel paths, Percy would speak to his father. His father's silence had broken his own. Percy was now able to ask his father questions that had remained unvoiced of many years.

"I know so little about you, Father. Who were your father and mother? You never tell me of my grandparents. Why did you leave them for America? Why did you leave New Orleans to grow cotton? You did not need the money. What drives a man to do the things he does? You said my name was no accident. What did you mean? Have I not proved myself a success? Am I not worthy of your trust, no matter what I might learn?"

Occasionally Percy would stop pushing the invalid chair and then sit on the bench by the pond, turning his father to look towards him. On one occasion Percy spoke at length on something that had been troubling him, something he could tell to no one else.

"You may wonder why I haven't brought up the subject on which you sought my guidance a short time before your *condition*." Condition was an awkward way of describing Howard's present physical state. *Condition* was a convenient circumlocution. "Before your condition, you asked about freeing some or all of the workers of Bolingbroke. I haven't forgotten. Even if your condition did not limit your ability to free them, the law now forbids you to act — whether by an act of manumission or in your will.

"Our Supreme Court paved the way for the legislature to enact a new law. The court said that emancipation is not just a private matter but concerns the state. They wrote that emancipation tends to substitute a free colored population for the system of compulsory labor which involves to such a vast extent the fortunes of Louisiana citizens, and the production of her agricultural staples. Acting on this fear of masters freeing their slaves caused our legislature this session to prohibit the freeing of any slaves at all."

Percy knew that there was already a legal wall around the state forbidding masters to take their slaves to any Free State. Now all avenues to freedom for a person held in bondage were closed, even for the most generous masters. The advocates of slavery knew that the successes of free people of color were daily proof against their assertions of the inferiority of the African. Threatened by this, they were determined to prevent a growth in the free black population.

Percy saw that the blanket over his father's legs had slipped to the side. He adjusted it and resumed speaking: "This deprives all slaves in this state from hoping to ever gain freedom for themselves or for their children. Slave status is permanent and irrevocable. When your condition improves, we can return to the question. Even if we had made a will for you last year freeing every person on Bolingbroke, the court has just ruled that the will cannot be carried out as it is subject to the new legislation absolutely prohibiting manumission."

If Howard were at all conscious, he would have heard how discouraged Percy sounded. His son thought the legislation was unconscionable. Percy looked for signs of cognition. The man's eyes were open, but looking past Percy. Perhaps, thought Percy, his father was thinking of the reckoning that was to come.

Focused on his father, Percy was unaware that a passing field hand had overheard him talking aloud to his father, telling him that no slave could be freed in Louisiana. The story quickly spread, confirming rumors about the new law that had made its way from plantation to plantation. *Never free*, they told one another.

જ્જ્જ — ≪ં≪ં

Sometimes at night, after others had gone to bed, Percy would lift his father from his bed, carry him into the living room and sit him in his favorite leather chair, close to the fireplace. He would pour a small amount of Howard's favorite calvados into a brandy snifter and pass it under his father's nose. If some of the mind's functions were incomplete, might not other senses be enhanced? He would place the liquor on the table nearest him. He would pour a like amount for himself. "Here's my problem," he would say as he puzzled over a legal issue for a brief or a decision concerning the operation of the plantations. "Tell me what I should do." And by the time the fire's embers extinguished themselves, Percy would have his answer.

On one occasion, an excess of whiskey turned Percy uncommonly sentimental, almost maudlin. He had told his father little of his experiences in the Mexican war. Now he said to him, "Would you mind if I call you 'old scout'? When I was first in Mexico, serving under Colonel Harney, he made me a scout. I think it was the best thing in the world that a young man could do. It was adventure. It was purpose. I was the lookout for danger and tried to protect others from any threats that might show themselves. I was looked to by others to guide them in places that were treacherous. Isn't that what you have done for me, for Mother, for Eliza? For all the men and women and children who belong to these plantations? And how many others? You've been our scout. Our guardian. Our sentry always on duty. And now you have your rest. Now the responsibilities fall to me. Will I measure up? Stay with me, old scout. I need you still. You've always been here."

*Chapter 46*

# Dressed in Yellow

Could heaven have made the weather any lovelier this gorgeous spring day? The weather was pleasantly warm. A light breeze played among the trees, Spanish moss swaying gently. Azaleas were in glorious bloom. Dogwood greeted Easter with white radiance. Percy told Phil and Rand he would make a short trip into St. Francisville for the mail and supplies.

An hour later, as noon approached, Phil decided to take Rand and Howard for a picnic. She prepared a basket with sandwiches, fruit and jam cookies that Clotilda had baked that morning. Lucy worked in her greenhouse, preparing camellias for planting. Phil hung the picnic basket from the back of Howard Moorhead's wheelchair and rolled him slowly towards the pond, while little Rand skipped along a few steps ahead, grasping at four-winged dragonflies that darted immediately from him.

In the shade of Howard's favorite oak tree, Phil spread a striped cotton blanket a little before noon. She began unpacking the basket to lay out their little lunch. Rand walked slowly towards the pond, looking closely at the ground, hoping to find a toad or turtle along the way. He loved to find turtles and place them in the pond to swim away. Bright green baby turtles would dart underwater and disappear. The pond did not worry Phil. The boy had been taught to swim at three and now, approaching six, could easily take care of himself in the shallow water. Besides, she was no more than a short distance from him, no more than thirty paces. When she saw him stumble, she was not concerned. He seemed merely to trip and started to get up, a smile on his innocent face as he turned to wave at his mother. But then he cried out. Now his arms were thrashing wildly at his head and sides. He screamed, "Help me! Help! Help!"

Phil was startled. She leaped to her feet. Then she saw what had happened. Her son had stepped into an in-ground nest of yellow jackets. They were swarming all over him, hundreds of them bursting from the earth, stinging him over and over and over. Phil ran as fast as she could. By the time she got to him, he was lying on the ground, barely moving, the yellow wasps still attacking him. She lifted his small body and did the only thing she could think of to protect him. She jumped into the pond with him to escape the stinging, swarming, fierce, venomous insects. Some attacked her but she hardly felt their stings. After a minute, the yellow jackets were all gone. She looked at her boy, moaning, nearly unconscious, his curly hair wet. Already she could see welts rising on his tender skin – his face, his arms, his legs below his shorts.

Phil waded from the pond and ran with her boy to the house, crying out for help as she ran. She had to leave Howard where he was, hoping that the angry insects would not make him a target of their wrath. As he had been for eight months, he was silent, motionless. The yellow jackets were as unaware of his existence as he of theirs. Nearly simultaneously, Lucy, Clotilda and Odessa converged on Phil as she frantically carried Rand up the front steps to the downstairs bed.

"What happened?" said Lucy urgently.

"Wasps. They've stung him all over. Please get Percy. Get the doctor. Percy will know what to do. Oh God, what now?"

Phil carefully removed the shirt Rand was wearing by cutting it with scissors up its front and arms. She now saw that the insects' stingers had penetrated the light shirt. He was in shock, his eyes open but slowly moving, unfocused. His breathing was difficult. He struggled to speak. "Papa, Papa," his lips were forming to say. But sounds did not emerge. The toxins in the insect venom were causing swelling, constricting his throat. Respiratory congestion was setting in.

All of the male slaves were in the fields working, and most of the women, too. Lucy told Odessa she'd have to saddle a horse and ride as quick as she could. She instructed Clotilda to get the ointment she kept for small wounds and rashes that was in a kitchen cabinet, third shelf – a compound of cocoa butter, beeswax and shea butter. She began to spread the salve gingerly on the child's arms and chest. The boy was unresponsive to her touch. Phil stood at the foot of the bed, bent over, sobbing convulsively. She watched her child's life slowly ebbing away, his breath diminishing to feeble gasps. Lucy saw the futility of her ointment and stepped back from the bed.

By the time Percy and the doctor arrived forty minutes later, all life had left the boy's small body. Lucy was embracing her daughter-in-law. They had never been close, but now Lucy held Phil tenderly, sobbing with her in mutual loss. Clotilda wailed. Odessa murmured prayers quietly, whether in French or English was not clear.

Percy stood over the small, immobile form on the bed. Only three hours earlier, Rand had bubbled with life and joy. This innocent's death – random, purposeless. This father's grief – uncomprehending, despairing. Was the universe only chaos? Was fate malevolent? Percy had never felt so helpless.

శౌౕౕ — ౕౕౕ

That night, Percy did what he could to console his wife. Her voice carrying her despair, she said, "Don't you see, Percy? We were warned. We should have known."

He could only say, "I don't understand."

Tears were again in her eyes. "You must remember. The old gypsy in her tent outside Richmond. She told us. *Death will come dressed in yellow.* It was true, all true. Moving to Bolingbroke had been to flee yellow fever. Yellow Jack. But yellow death was waiting for us here, hiding until it could draw us out."

"You mustn't think that, Phil. God doesn't work that way."

"Doesn't He?"

&#8198;&#8198;&#8198; — &#8198;&#8198;&#8198;

Pompey was the best carpenter on the plantations, the best in the Felicianas. He crafted a small coffin, four feet long, of pecan, and stained it a deeper brown. Where his tears streaked the stain, he reapplied stain more carefully. From leather and brass fittings he fashioned four handles, for pall-bearers to lift their small burden and carry Randolph Moorhead on the short, final journey that he must take. Too soon, too soon, not yet six.

No hearse, no horses, were necessary. When Howard Moorhead designed Bolingbroke, the plan included a family plot two hundred feet behind the home. It had a wrought iron fence, like the railings on the second floor of their townhouse in New Orleans, and an iron lattice arbor with lettering that spelled Moorhead, now entwined with climbing purple wisteria. Howard had told Percy that he expected to be the first to be interred there. He couldn't have known it would be his grandson.

The family marched in slow procession from the house to the vacant cemetery that was large enough for thirty Moorheads. Percy and Philomena walked behind the four bearers of the small coffin, then Lucy and Eliza and Nerissa, with Calvin pushing Howard Moorhead's Bath chair. Several Pugh cousins had arrived in time from across the river. A dozen members of the St. Francisville Anglican congregation were in the background. Among them were four of the mothers who helped Phil with her Saturday morning children's program.

The minister spoke words at the grave site, but they were meaningless to Phil and Percy. Yes, God's love is a mystery and God has gathered His young to His breast, the Innocent shall sleep in Peace, and so forth and so on. None brought comfort to a grieving mother or a shattered father who could not understand the cruelty of nature. Why would a loving God send a plague of wasps upon His Innocent Children. "Dust to dust," continued the minister. With an aching heart, eyes filled with tears, Percy gently put a shovel into the loose dirt at the side of the grave and spread the soil slowly at the head of the dark coffin beneath him, as if not to disturb his son. Then another, and another and another until finally one of his cousins relieved him. Reluctantly, the distraught father relinquished the shovel. And his son.

Chapter 47

# Philomena's Grief

Percy had no choice but to remain at Bolingbroke to run the plantations. He had little help from Phil or Lucy and none at all from his worthless brother-in-law. A few days after Rand's funeral, Calvin Bunch again absented himself from unpleasant tasks and responsibility. This was the time of greatest activity in cotton cultivation, weather sensitive and labor-intensive. Pompey and Julius were capable of supervising the field-hands and operating the machines, but it fell to Percy to take care of all the business affairs, from cash advances for staples, to the ordering, purchase and delivery of hardware and implements and other supplies. If a plow or scraper broke or a piece of broken equipment could not be replaced immediately, crucial time was lost in cultivation or production. No slave, no matter how competent, would be able to commit the funds necessary for new equipment or deal with a merchant in St. Francisville or Bayou Sara for its delivery.

After five weeks of mourning, Philomena had appeared to regain a measure of equilibrium, though often deeply sad. She busied herself about the house. She offered to help Lucy with her garden. She tried to engage in the education of her niece, reading with her in children's books of history and geography. At first, Eliza welcomed the attention to Nerissa. It freed up time for Eliza to devote to her own activities, shopping in St. Francisville or participating in the church choir. She was in the choir that sang when Bishop Polk set the cornerstone for the new church, while Lucy stood at his side as a major donor on the finance committee.

Phil could be entirely child-like when walking with Nerissa or learning a new card game. Nerissa enjoyed the attention of her aunt. Then Eliza began to imagine that Phil was attempting to take her child from her, to replace her lost son with another mother's daughter. Words were exchanged. Phil retreated.

Continuing the Saturday program became unbearable to Phil. Nor could Phil resume her visits to plantations collecting stories of their owners' past and present for her book on the Felicianas when her loss would be the only topic.

Hoping to find an outlet for his wife, Percy bought his wife a new horse, a young and spirited mare. Phil had always taken pleasure in riding but had ridden little since the birth of her son. She accepted the horse with gratitude. "Does she have a name?" Phil inquired.

"She shall have the name you choose for her," Percy said.

"Her name will reveal itself," she said, pleased with Percy's gift..

The next morning, Phil proudly announced at breakfast, "Her name is Niobe. It came to me in a dream."

"Niobe, it is," Percy said, smiling, concealing his immediate apprehension at her choice. The name must have lodged in her memory from something she had read. He couldn't tell her that Niobe in mythology was the mother of sons killed by Apollo with poisoned arrows. She still regarded the fortune-teller's prophecy as a gypsy's curse that she should have heeded. If he said anything about the name, she'd take it as an omen and have the horse sent away.

Phil, however, was hesitant to take the new horse out of sight of Bolingbroke Hall. Grooming the horse and saddling her would occupy Phil for near an hour before she would mount. When she finally stepped into the stirrups, she took the mare only for short rides, sketching circles and figure eights in the yard nearest the house. She would not ride in the direction of the pond; she had avoided it since the day of Rand's death.

After two weeks of little more than exercising Niobe in the yard, Phil put on a riding skirt, a crisp pink shirt with puff sleeves and a jaunty hat and rode off on the trail in the direction of St. Francisville. Percy looked on as she went over the ridge west of the house. It was an encouraging sign that she had ventured out.

An hour later, Percy looked out the window from his upstairs office. He saw the new horse grazing, rider-less on the lawn. He rushed out and discovered the reins were broken and hanging loose to the ground. He began running in the direction he had last seen Phil riding. As he crossed the crest of the ridge, he saw her stumbling in his direction. Her hat was gone, her blouse torn and her skirt muddy. When he ran closer, he saw that she was crying, that her face was scratched.

"My God! What happened? Did she throw you?" Percy took her in his arms, and she sobbed on his chest.

She clutched at him and cried, "I'm so incompetent. I can do nothing right."

"What did you do?" Percy took a handkerchief from his pocket and dabbed lightly on her face to absorb the small streaks of fresh blood.

"Nothing, nothing," she shook her head sadly. "I was enjoying the ride. I was trying to think of anything but Rand and how I let him down. I hadn't tied the reins together. I dropped one rein. The mare stepped on it and stumbled. To hold on, I pulled the other rein. My little horse panicked and began running wildly. It wasn't her fault. It was mine. She's a wonderful horse. But I could hold on only to the one rein and could do nothing to control her. She ran into a thicket of brush and thrashed about. She threw me and ran off."

"Now, now," soothed Percy.

She buried her head in his chest. "I'm so sorry, Percy. You were trying to do something nice for me and now I've ruined everything. I couldn't control the horse. I couldn't even protect our son. And he's dead now. Oh, if only I could be too. I'm no use to you or Nerissa or Lucy or your father. I have failed in everything. I wish I could disappear or die."

Percy drew her close again, as if to shield her from further harm. "Shhhh, shhhh, shhhh. Soft now. Come, rest in this bosom, my own stricken dear. You've had a terrible accident. It's all my fault entirely. God took our child, not you. There was nothing you could do. No mother ever loved a child more than you." He paused, then lifted her chin with his right hand to look at her eyes, saying "I'll tell you what. When this year's crop is baled, we'll go back to New Orleans. Everyone you met there loved you. I'll get back to my law practice and in a year or two I'll seek a judgeship. Judah Benjamin can see to it that President Buchanan appoints me federal judge in New Orleans."

He refrained from saying they could try to have another child. In her state of mind, it would only have increased her sense of loss and of failure. And if she didn't conceive? What might it do to their marriage if they could not have another child? Percy did not want the Moorhead line to end with him. But he suppressed such thought. Even to consider them would be a betrayal of his wife when she needed him most.

"But what about Bolingbroke and your mother and your poor father? They depend on you. And Pompey and Julius and Odessa and Leddie and Little Jay and all the rest. You couldn't leave them under Calvin." Always, she reminded him of duty and piety, of his responsibilities to others and the need for firmness of purpose.

Again, Percy tried to comfort his wife. "Shhhh, shhhh. There's nothing more important to me than you and our life together. We can find a man to manage the plantation. I don't think my father will last much longer. Dr. Shay says he thinks he is weaker now than ever before."

"No," Phil said with determination. "We will stay here. This is now our home. You can't just give it all up."

Three days later, Percy sold Niobe without telling Phil. He didn't need to. She would have protested that she would try again to ride. But when she saw the empty stable, she was relieved.

Late spring and summer passed unmarred by crisis or traumatic incident. To any observer, there was pastoral peace on the twin plantations, Bolingbroke and Jericho. Calvin Bunch came and went without causing trouble. If he were gambling, he was not losing very much or his creditors were complacent. Sheriff Lurty had paid no calls to impose liens from any losses Calvin may have sustained.

Members from the St. Francisville church congregation called upon Miss Lucy and Miss Eliza and Miss Philomena once or twice a week to express their condolences and assure the Moorhead women that the dead child was resting in the arms of the Lord. The church ladies mostly engaged in pleasantries and persiflage with Lucy while Phil sat in silence. Two of them thought they were being helpful when they volunteered what a person should do to treat a yellow jacket's sting. One even asked what little Rand had done to the insects to make them attack him so. They were not observant enough to notice the deepening depression of Mr. Percy's wife. Because Phil said so little, they could not notice that her speech was becoming more slurred. They did not see the flush of her cheeks from the alcohol she was consuming each day. She never displayed self-pity. She drew within, a once-bright flower fading, wilting, losing all color.

Percy, however, could see the deterioration of his wife's state. He knew she was becoming increasingly dependent on drink to get her through each agonizing day. It deepened his grief. Yet what was he to do? He knew his wife and loved her too much to confront her, to accuse her of self-pity and demand that she sober herself. To hide the wine and alcohol would subject her to the indignity of sneaking around to acquire more. The friends she had in St. Francisville she had isolated herself from with the death of Rand. They had children with whom their child had played; now they had children and she had none. A common bond had been severed. She had been close to Westie's wife, Polly, but she was in New Orleans.

Percy called upon Dr. Shay in town in late August to see if there were a medical approach that might help Phil.

The doctor replied sympathetically. "From what you tell me, your wife has a sickness of the heart, not the body. Depression and despair are not an uncommon response to a loss of a child. They are not unreasonable. We can inoculate ourselves against some diseases, but only time can heal a wound of the soul. Men occupy themselves in work and escape the deep pains. A mother cannot."

Percy appeared distraught to the doctor. He said, "I can't watch her become destroyed by this. I just cannot."

Dr. Shay knew little about Percy Moorhead, even though he had visited the Moorhead home weekly for a year to check on Howard's condition. Percy was too reserved for Dr. Shay to penetrate. The physician watched the deterioration of Philomena after the death of Rand. Percy, he could tell, was determined to find some solution, despite his own despondency.

"And you can't let it destroy you," the doctor gently continued. "Let me suggest this. When we have a trauma so great that life cannot be continued on the same course, a complete break may be the answer. It can be in either direction: forward or backward. A forward break entails uprooting from everything and starting over in a new place. Some people even take on a new name and identity. The old self is gone and a new one unburdened by the trauma and the past begins a new life. Texas. California. China."

"And backward?" asked Percy, looking up from his gaze at the floor.

"A disturbed person returns to a time and a place before the trauma, when life was good and untroubled. In your wife's case, I don't think that would be New Orleans. That's where her child was born and had his first home. Perhaps Virginia. Didn't you tell me her mother still lives there?"

"Yes. Richmond. Or perhaps we could go to Williamsburg. We have happy memories there."

"I'm afraid I can't offer you anything better than a radical disruption of your lives. I think that's your best chance for her recovery. A complete break. Backward or forward."

Percy shook his head slowly. "We've already had disruption."

Percy walked from the doctor's office to the bank and brought his accounts up to date. Wilson, the middle-aged, balding clerk who handled his transactions, said a man had been making inquiries about the plantations and about Mr. Moorhead. He thought the man was asking about the older Moorhead, not about Percy himself.

"Did he have a name?"

"Didn't get it. Had an accent. Irish or English or Scots, they all sound alike to me." Wilson was a little hard of hearing even when he was paying close attention.

"What did you tell him?"

"Said I knowed Mr. Howard Moorhead maybe 20 years. A good man. Only now he can't speak or walk owing to his condition. No point in trying to see Mr. Howard, I told him."

Percy was puzzled. "Any chance this was about my brother-in-law's debts? Did he ask about Calvin?"

Wilson rubbed his hand on his cheek for a minute as he tried to recall the men and the conversation. "Come to think of it, he did say something about other members of the family and who they might be. Never did say why he was asking."

"Thank you, Wilson. If you see him again, send a boy to get me." The family had enough problems. Percy was afraid that Calvin was introducing more.

His concern aroused by the inquisitive stranger, Percy walked a couple of blocks, past the construction site of the new Episcopal Church, to the West Feliciana courthouse. He asked the records clerk, Enoch Singletary, if there were any inquiries in the past few weeks about the Moorhead family or the two plantations they owned. Singletary, a lanky, taciturn man in his early forties, was making entries in the mortgages register that was open on the counter.

"Reckon so." His eyes squinted when he looked beyond his work lamp. His vision was nearly as bad as Wilson's hearing.

"Who was he?"

"Them. Two men." Singletary seldom volunteered information, and, when pressed, parted with it reluctantly.

Percy pressed him. "Well, who were they?"

"I reckon one was a lawyer. He knew his way about property records. Other was a well-dressed man. Foreign accent. I heard the lawyer one call him Mr. Boil I think."

"Was the lawyer from around here?"

"Never seen him."

"And this Boile. What was he like?"

"Maybe Englishman. Maybe Irish. Bout your father's height. Older than you, maybe ten, twelve years older."

"So about forty?"

"Give or take."

"What were they interested in?" Percy was at a loss to understand why strangers were poking around in his or his father's life.

"Took notes out of the purchase and sales books. And the slave records. Taxes. Liens."

"Anything else you recall?"

"Well sir, they seemed to know something about you and your father. They said it was awful about your father's condition. And terrible what happened to your little boy. Didn't want to disturb you none, they said."

"What about my sister's husband, Calvin Bunch?" Calvin had already caused too much mischief for the family.

"He come up. They seemed to know he doesn't own much. Said he wouldn't give them no trouble."

"They said or you said no trouble?"

"They said it."

Asked Percy, "Meaning what kind of trouble?"

"Meaning I don't know."

Eating alone at the Meyer Hotel, Percy reflected on the inquiries at the bank and the courthouse and found them disturbing. Someone was gathering information on him or his family. He had no enemies, and as far as he knew neither did his father. Calvin was, of course, another matter. It would be best not to mention this to anyone at home. If he seemed to be probing about Calvin, both Eliza and his mother would resent it. If he asked Calvin, he could not expect an honest response.

He might, however, gently broach to Philomena the possibility of a trip or even a move to Virginia. He must be cautious. In her unpredictable state, it might deepen her depression if she thought it would disrupt his life and future as master of Bolingbroke or his prospects of a judgeship in New Orleans. Or she might be so eager that there would little time to prepare properly for a move and to take steps to establish a law practice in Richmond. The decision would have to be his and his alone.

The doctor had clarified matters, but there was no one else for

Percy to talk to. He was at the mercy of forces beyond his control and the whim of fate. What was happening to him now arose from events in the distant past, before his birth, across an ocean, on another continent. It was not anything he had done, and nothing in his own past, that would bring him loss. Nothing he could do could prevent grief.

Philomena's condition had reached the point where Percy thought he could wait no longer. She was losing her grip on reality, wandering and muttering to herself. He could no longer trust her to care for his father. He instructed Odessa and Leddie to take over entirely the old man's needs and gently to remove Phil if she tried to intervene. Lucy would sit with her husband for a few hours at a time but never volunteered to feed him or change his clothing. Percy knew it was likely he would have to take Philomena to Richmond permanently. It would take him three or four days in New Orleans to close out his law practice and make trip arrangements for the two of them to Virginia. Then he would return to Bolingbroke to take Phil away from this place of loss and sorrow for both of them, a move more for her sake than his.

And what to do about the plantation and his father's desire to free Bolingbroke's slaves? He could sell the plantation, but Louisiana law did not allow emancipation of slaves, nor even permit a master to take slaves to a free state. Perhaps, thought Percy, he could move to another slave state but one that allowed emancipation by an owner. He knew that his former roommate from Princeton, Alfred Cuthbert in Georgia, was finding ways to free slaves he inherited from his father though encountering difficulties. No matter the problems, Percy would find a way. Or so he planned, before he learned of the new threat from the mysterious visitors inquiring about the Moorheads.

Chapter 48

# Farewell, Father

When he got to New Orleans, Percy called on Westie Haydel and appointed him his business agent. He sent a telegram to Phil's mother in Richmond telling her they would soon visit her. A letter to him and Phil a month earlier from Mrs. Emily Randolph had told them she had been deeply saddened by the loss of the grandson she had never met. She was distressed that she could not comfort her grieving daughter. The trip she had planned to New Orleans had been called off when yellow fever had overwhelmed the city. Within hours, she sent a return wire to Percy telling him to hasten if they could. She was eager to see them again.

The clients whom he still had Percy referred to the law firm of Benjamin, Bradford & Finney. The lease on his office had only three months remaining on its term, so he took no steps to clear it out. He had to keep his files intact until he found a place for storage. He gave Louis, his assistant, notice that he would no longer need his services but asked him to remain until the end of the lease. Some of his clients might need access to files or assistance in the transition to other representation.

Next, Percy visited Linton Scruggs, the manager of Toulouse Gardens, to tell him of his plans and have him notify other investors in the syndicate. He would retain his interest but would no longer serve as attorney for the gaming casino. Scruggs wore his shallow smile and expressed regret but said he was not surprised.

"Why is that?" asked Percy.

"A man gave me the impression you might be leaving the business."

"What man?"

Scruggs shrugged. "An Irishman. Sharp dresser. He was asking about you and your father – whether your father was a part owner like he'd heard. He wanted to know how much of an interest you had in the business. He was here a week ago or thereabouts."

Percy's alarm was immediate. He had thought it likely the stranger was making inquiries because of Calvin Bunch. Now Percy felt he was threatened. He told Scruggs, "If he comes back, tell him I have no intention of relinquishing my ownership. Let me know if you hear from him."

"Well, you can probably catch him. He walked by the window not five minutes ago. Going toward the river. Don't know how you missed him if you came from that way. Wearing a low brim felt hat with a feather. Small cigar in his mouth."

Percy turned and walked hurriedly out the door. He caught up to the man near the end of Canal. The man was not surprised as Percy stopped him. He seemed to know Percy.

Percy demanded angrily, "Have you been making inquiries about me?" He did not like the look in the man's eye.

"More about your father than you." The stranger drew on his cigar and exhaled smoke in a way that suggested studied indifference in the face of the Percy's anger. His manner and speech were patronizing.

"You've been snooping around in St. Francisville and Bayou Sara. And now here. Why? Who are you?"

The stranger was as calm as Percy was angry. Coolly, he replied, "Fair enough. The name is Grady Boyle. I have come from

Dublin on a matter of family business. Your father would understand. Unfortunately, it appears he is incapable of communication. I am in no hurry. My business will wait."

"If it concerns my father, it concerns me. I demand you state your interest." Percy was visibly upset but also intimidated by the man's cold self-assurance. Few people had ever caused Percy to lose his composure. Boyle remained mysterious, relishing an assumed superiority over Percy. He had peeled away a layer of Percy's self-mastery in conditions of stress.

"In good time, Percy Moorhead. What does a man really know about his father? The father creates a myth, telling his child only what he wants him to believe. He omits important details, changes facts to fit the story he wants others to believe. Perhaps he even deceives himself. But a man's past has a way of finding a man and intruding itself. As you will learn in good time. In good time. Adieu, for now." He tipped his hat in manner that was insolent, even menacing.

Boyle's confident assertions, though cryptic, unnerved Percy. He wanted to confront the man and strike him down if he refused to provide answers. But he restrained himself, perhaps in fear that Boyle would provide answers that could not be tolerated. He hurried to board the northbound packet boat that would carry him home.

ॐॐ — ॐॐ

Three days after Percy returned to Bolingbroke, his father died, peacefully, in his Bath chair, under a blanket. Percy had rolled him out into the autumnal sun for breakfast. Howard Moorhead raised his head slightly, and his eyes seemed to come to life, suddenly aware of his surroundings one last time. They had met Percy's for an instance. An ineffable exchange occurred, a last moment of shared existence, of shared consciousness. It was as though Howard Moorhead was giving his son one final reassurance of paternal love and devotion, that even this would be all right. His father would be there for him even when he was no longer there.

Percy held a spoon of oatmeal and milk, poised to feed it to his father. But then the last breath passed from his lips. His chin slowly descended to his chest.

"Father?" There could be no answer. The old scout was gone.

Percy stood upright, looking down on the husk that had been his father, now empty, inanimated. Tears came to his eyes, gently. Tears and memories. There would be no sobs, no anguish. He called out to no one. He slowly set the oatmeal to one side and sat beside his father for fifteen, twenty minutes. Whoever it was who said that a man's life does not begin until his father is dead misspoke. A son is never free of his father. A father's life cannot be judged without an account of the son's life. The son carries his father's name and his reputation. The two are joined for all time, for they are inseparable and reciprocal. Each created what the other became, the one a continuation of the other.

Finally, Percy stepped inside. In a low voice he called out, "Mother? Mother, he's gone."

Lucy put the book she was reading into her lap and slowly closed it. She looked over in Percy's direction. Through the door she could see the lifeless body of her late husband of more than thirty years. As though speaking to him and not to her son, she said softly, "What will become of me? What of Eliza?" Sadly, her reaction did not surprise Percy.

Lucy, as well as Percy, knew that with Howard Moorhead's death, life with Calvin would be different. The presence of Howard, even silent and incapable of action, had been a constraint on the behavior of Calvin. The boundaries that fenced his impulses were now removed. Who could say what he might do?

Two days later, the Moorhead cemetery received its second coffin only four months after its first. Again, Pompey fashioned the funeral furniture — cypress and pecan, lined with fabric made from cotton grown on the decedent's own land, cushions filled with Spanish moss gathered from his own trees, beech and oak.

Among the mourners, the most bereaved was Philomena Moorhead. Howard Moorhead had become the father she had lost at an early age. He had welcomed her into his family wholeheartedly. His death following so closely the death of her child made the loss that much greater. At the foot of the grave stood Lucy, Percy, and Philomena. Off to one side were Eliza and Nerissa. A dozen or more from the town were present. Outside the wrought iron fence were most of the slaves of the two plantations. Not only did they feel the loss of a man whose treatment was never cruel or malicious, they also feared what might come of them now that the familiar, kindly master was gone.

As the minister gave the final words of the valediction, Calvin Bunch came riding up on his bay gelding. He had absented himself two weeks ago and was unaware of the death of Howard Moorhead. He was disheveled and far from sober. He dismounted and said in a loud voice, meant to be jocular, "Did somebody die? You all look like a funeral." Several in the back of the group shushed him, and he realized that it really was a funeral that he had come upon. Muttering to himself, he turned and led his horse towards the house of Jericho Hill.

Percy felt violated by Calvin's rude intrusion but said nothing as he walked with his mother and his wife from the cemetery to the house. They walked around to the front of the house and Percy saw something more disturbing than Calvin. A man was sitting in a single horse buggy, stopped on the road where it topped the ridgeline. He recognized the jaunty, feathered hat of the man he had encountered in New Orleans, Grady Boyle. The man fixed his eyes on Percy for a minute, then he turned the coach and drove away.

After Percy saw his mother and wife into the house and settled with others who would comfort them, he had a boy saddle his horse. Quickly, he galloped off after Boyle. He arrived at Bayou Sara just as the paddle-wheeler departed from the landing, headed down river. If he could have leaped onto the boat, he would have. He could demand in a loud voice to the man who gazed at him from the upper deck, "Why are you here? Why are you disturbing me and my family?"

With a mischievous expression, neither a smile nor a sneer, Boyle called down, "A man should attend his father's funeral, shouldn't he?"

For a moment Percy was uncomprehending. Suddenly, however, it became all too clear. His expression changed from confusion to consternation. A sudden chill seemed to close around him, squeezing the breath from his chest. He was seized by an ominous fear, a premonition of more terrible things to come.

"Yes," Boyle shouted as he receded. "In good time, I told you. You understand now. And we will see more of each other. Brother."

రావా — ఆసౌ

Percy said nothing to Phil about Boyle. She was far too distressed. That evening she was close to a breakdown. She could not eat. She paced back and forth in the house. With a lantern she walked out into the dark night, to the cemetery and sobbed over both graves, Rand's and Howard's. When it began to rain, she returned, dripping, mourning clothing completely soaked. She told Percy, "I loved your father. With him gone and Rand I don't think I can remain any longer. Please, please can we go back to Virginia? All I have now are you and my mother. I haven't seen her in six years."

"Of course, love. Calvin and my mother and sister will just have to manage. We'll go to New Orleans as soon as we have gathered your things. We will be with your mother before you know it. I will wire to New Orleans for tickets." He soothed her but could not get Boyle out of his head. What was the man up to?

Brother? Or had Percy misheard him?

The next morning Phil began packing her belongings. Seeing the activity, Lucy asked what was happening. It looked as though this was more than a short trip back to New Orleans. Percy asked his mother to have Calvin and Eliza and Nerissa to please come into the living room in a half hour. While they gathered, Phil continued packing in the bedroom upstairs.

Percy stood in front of his family and spoke to them while pacing. "Let me be direct. Phil and I are moving. To Virginia. Probably Richmond. This will be permanent. Before he became ill, father had written no will. Under Louisiana law I will inherit most of his property, including Bolingbroke. That was the arrangement he and Mother made - Bolingbroke plantation was his separate property. She kept title to Jericho Hill. The New Orleans townhouse he deeded to me when Phil and I were married."

"No will?" interjected Lucy. "Where does that leave me?"

Percy replied, kindly, "I will explain all, Mother. "The two plantations have been operated together for thirty years. It would be irresponsible of me to sell Bolingbroke even though I have no intention of making this my home ever again. I doubt Jericho Hill could be self-sustaining standing alone. The accounts are mingled together, and the slaves work on both properties as though they are one. But, we'll need to disentangle them. Slowly would be best for everyone. Mother, I imagine you'll want to stay in this house where you've lived since I was born. As long as it's mine, it will also be yours."

His mother frowned but said nothing. He continued, "So, here's what I plan to do. I assume, Calvin, you will want to take over managing Jericho and help mother. It's hers but will eventually go to you and Eliza. For the time being I will make Julius the overseer of Bolingbroke Hall. He has the background and ability to do it for now. I've written out everything that needs to be done for the next eight weeks. Pompey can help him, or Pompey could assist on Jericho."

Percy waited to see if his mother or Calvin would object. The effective control of both plantations was being handed over to the two sons of big Tom. Calvin had no familiarity with the laborers on either plantation. Percy expected that Calvin would wonder who would manage the accounts of both plantations; he had prevented until now Calvin from incurring any debt. He pretermitted any questions about expenses.

Percy told them, "I'm giving my power of attorney to the president of the bank in St. Francisville. He'll be able to endorse any debts incurred by Julius for Bolingbroke. After I get Phil settled in Richmond and I set up a law office, I'll come back here and will hire a permanent overseer to manage Bolingbroke. That should be in just a couple of months."

Lucy spoke after Percy paused. "Are you sure this is the right thing to do? I know you've had losses. This seems so sudden." She didn't want Percy to leave her alone to deal with Calvin or with the plantation.

Percy nodded slowly, but before he could speak, Calvin intervened.

"You do what you need to do, Percy. We can manage this." He spoke reassuringly, sympathetically. He could afford a generosity of spirit finally. After waiting for years, he would now be free of both Moorhead men. Until Percy could hire a white man to oversee Bolingbroke, Calvin expected to take control of both plantations no matter what instructions Percy handed down. Julius and Pompey could do nothing to oppose Calvin. No slave could rebuff a master.

"Thanks, Calvin." Percy was desperate for any justification for leaving the responsibilities behind. In a conflict of duties – to his father's memory and his aspirations for Percy, to his mother, to his sister, to all the residents of the plantations, to his remaining clients – those to his wife rose above all others. In his state of mind, it did not occur to Percy that perhaps Grady Boyle had already been in communication with Calvin. His lawyer's skills had failed him; he had not anticipated what Grady Boyle had planned and hinted at.

The morning of their departure was steel grey, a drizzle in the air. Despite the mildness of the weather, Philomena wore a long, dark coat. She paid no attention to the mud on her shoes as she walked to the Moorhead family plot and laid final flowers on the grave of her only child. Percy stood next to her with his arm around her. He was sad himself and still sadder that he was unable to shelter her from her grief. He helped her into the buggy. She did not look back as they rode towards town and the riverboat landing. Two hours later, the *Natchez Belle* blew its whistle and headed down river.

Phil remained in the cabin all the way down river to New Orleans. Percy brought her food to the room. She hardly touched it,

"You need to eat," he said kindly.

"Yes, I should," she replied wanly. But she did not eat. Sorrow neglects hunger. Percy hoped her gloom would lift as they proceeded toward Virginia.

Percy stored their two trunks at a transfer office next to the levee. They walked to the townhouse. He made his wife as comfortable as he could, removing her coat, placing food before her that he had picked up at the corner grocery.

"I haven't been here for two years," Phil said, looking around, remembering happier times. "I had forgotten what it was like. I was a good hostess, wasn't I? A good mother?"

"You are the best," Percy said. "A wonderful wife and mother. We will have a happier life in Richmond."

"We were happy, weren't we?" She was pale, worn, but briefly less despondent.

"Yes. No one could have made me happier than you, Philomena. And God gave us five happy years with Rand. I don't think we can ever escape fate. Death had an appointment with us. He would have found us wherever we went."

After Phil ate a few bites, she seemed to improve. Percy had several final things to do before they left. He asked her, "Will you be okay while I go to my office for a while?"

"Yes. Would you see if my music box will play a song for me?"

Percy wound it and walked to the door.

"Don't be too long," Phil said, anxiety in her voice and haunting her face. "I worry I'll lose you next."

At his office near the Custom House, Percy's clerk Louis Cutrer told him a man name Boyle had been by to see him, leaving a note that said he could be reached at the St. Louis Hotel. Percy spent two hours with Louis going over business that must be attended. When Percy got to the St. Louis, he could not bring himself to go to Boyle's room. Uncharacteristically, he went to the hotel bar and ordered a whiskey. Soon, he heard a voice behind him, "You have come to see me, I suppose."

Turning, Percy saw Boyle. The Irishman was several inches shorter than Percy, about the same height as Howard had been. His hat was in his hand. His hair was thinning, receding from a high forehead.

"Yes. What do you want with me?" Percy was curt. He had wanted to avoid the confrontation.

Boyle said coolly, "We can discuss this here. Or at my lawyer's office. As you prefer."

"Here is fine. A seat by the window." The two men moved from the bar.

Grady Boyle picked up a bottle of bourbon and two glasses and took them to the table Percy had gestured to. He poured bourbon into both glasses. Percy did not pick his up.

"Suit yourself," Boyle shrugged, taking a drink. "I know it's not easy learning you have a brother. It came as a surprise to me, too."

"I gathered that was your meaning at the boat landing." Percy would not accept the possibility the man was his brother.

"It's not as bad as being abandoned by a father."

Scoffing, Percy said harshly, "Are you saying you're my father's illegitimate son? That he had a bastard?"

Boyle shook his head in mock sympathy and leaned forward, a grim half-smile on his lips.

"Poor Percy. You simply do not understand. *You* are the bastard child. *I* am the legitimate son, the only one."

Percy recoiled as if struck. "That's absurd."

"Not at all. About forty years ago, your father – our father - was a ship's purser. He was well-trusted by the merchants he worked for. A very able, shrewd young man. Like yourself, my brother. Highly regarded. Until he betrayed them. After the next to last port on a voyage, in Marseille, he betrayed the ship and helped to steal the ship's cargo, including a chest of precious metal. A bargain with pirates. When he got back to England, he gave himself a fancy new name – Moorhead. Granville Howard Moorhead, businessman. Abandoned me and me mum in Dublin. Me, just an infant. His crooked course took him here, to New Orleans. Only, everything he made was based on the fortune he stole from that ship and shared with the pirates."

Percy returned the Irishman's gaze and said with more conviction than he felt, "That's a fanciful story. Can you show a word of it is true?"

"Oh, it's true all right. I have papers. And I will take them to court. My lawyer has them."

"To what end? Do you simply wish to destroy my father's name and mine?"

Boyle jeered, leaning back in his chair, "Your father's name? His name was Boyle. Redmond Boyle. Me mum is Maureen Boyle.

He abandoned the poor woman."

Percy spat out, "I don't believe a word this."

"Believe this, then. Since Redmond Boyle was my father and was married to my mum lawfully in Dublin, I am his only legitimate heir. The lawyer representing me tells me I inherit everything owned by my father whether he was called Boyle or Moorhead when he owned it and when he died. What the law counts is legitimate blood and not a name. I am his heir, his only heir. There's no will, is there?"

Percy was shaken. It showed in his voice as he said, "I can't believe this. It cannot be true. Not my father. He was an honest, honorable man."

"We shall see. If you wish to consider a settlement of this that does not require litigation, I suggest you contact my lawyer, Sumner Clausen. He already knows everything we need to know about your father's property and circumstances."

Defiant, Percy said, "You expect me to give up without a fight?"

"Suit yourself. If you are reasonable, it need not go too bad for you. Otherwise, you lose everything. This is not your doing or mine but our father's. No man can fault a man demanding what the law says is his."

Boyle stood, took a final drink to empty his glass and left. Percy was stunned. It seemed so improbable, so unlike his father. Yet, this Boyle was confident. He finally picked up his own glass and drank the whiskey. And then had another shot.

As he fumbled in his right pocket for a couple of coins to leave on the table, an awful thought struck Percy. In his left pocket, under his folding pocketknife, was his lucky coin. His father had given it to him when he left for Princeton. He withdrew it now, opening the thin leather piece he had wrapped it in for protection, the 40-franc 1807 Napoléon that he had carried in his pocket for a dozen years.

Could it have come from the chest that Grady Boyle claimed was pirated off the coast of France? His father had attached some significance to the coin. Was it a souvenir, a trophy of his father's piracy? Was this coin a residue of ill-gotten funds that launched his father's business ventures in New Orleans? Another question for his father that his father would never answer.

Chapter 49

# Now Philomena

Philomena was asleep when Percy returned to the townhouse in early evening. He had spent several hours walking around New Orleans in troubled uncertainty. He could not tell her of this outlandish claim by a man from a foreign country. She had as much trust in Howard Moorhead as did Percy. Sitting alone downstairs, he decided the only thing to do was to continue as he planned. Pick up the steamship tickets in the morning and depart in early afternoon. Make his wife as comfortable as possible. When he got into bed, he found Phil was under a blanket and in a wool nightgown. Her skin was now moist, almost clammy. He replaced the blanket with a lighter cover and fell to sleep.

When Phil awoke, it was after seven. Percy had gone out briefly and returned from a bakery with bread and butter and a tray of fruit. She ate a small amount, indifferently.

Percy asked, "Do you feel well enough to travel?"

"I do not feel well enough to stay," she said hoarsely. Was that a shiver Percy observed? "This place will crush me if we don't leave today. Before anything else terrible happens to us."

"I never knew you disliked it so."

"No, I loved this city. And our life here. And our child. The weight of those memories is more than I can endure now. Now, it is time to go home." Percy had never heard his wife so insistent. "No more. No more," she repeated wearily.

"We should see a doctor. You have a runny nose, and you are coughing. You were very warm last night."

Phil recoiled. "No! Just hay fever. A little cold. No doctor! Please, no doctor. Please." She was frightened at the thought of another minute more in New Orleans than necessary. A doctor might demand that she remain.

Percy helped Phil dress. He was reluctant to proceed on the journey. She, however, was determined. Delay, he decided, would be worse for her than staying.

"Will they have hot tea on the boat?" she asked.

"Yes. As much as you could want."

Phil walked slowly from the townhouse. Though it was only a short distance to the levee, Percy hailed a coach to carry them. He assisted her on board into a cabin. The trip to Mobile would take less than twenty-four hours, but he had reserved a cabin so they might rest without company. Even before the vessel steamed out into the river, Phil was slumbering in the chair in their cabin.

Percy removed his wife's shoes and rested her legs on a cushion. He walked to the salon and had himself a cup of coffee and brought his wife fresh hot tea. When he entered the cabin, Phil was still in the chair. Now she was shivering.

"I'm cold," she said. It was a rather warm afternoon for November, near 5:00, the sun shining.

"Let's get you in bed, under the covers," he said. She felt weak and shaky as he guided her into the bed. Her fever had returned. He found an extra blanket under the bed and spread it over her. Her breathing was shallow, and her heartbeat was fast. Percy worried that maybe they should have stayed in New Orleans.

"Water, please," she said. He poured a glass from a pitcher on a table under the cabin window. She sank back into the bed. Percy felt her forehead again; her temperature was now hot.

"Let me go find a doctor," he said with urgency.

"Stay," she whispered. But she drifted asleep, her hand still on his arm. He gently removed it. Walking swiftly again to the salon, Percy went around the room, asking if anyone knew a doctor aboard. Soon, a doctor Cassibry identified himself as a Mobile physician, returning home. Percy led him to the cabin. He needed only a few minutes to reach his diagnosis.

"Pneumonia," he said. "The symptoms come on quickly."

Philomena stirred as the doctor felt her forehead and pulse. Her teeth chattered, and she was shaking every few minutes.

"What can we do?" asked Percy.

The doctor replied in a tone that seemed to Percy indifferent. "As with other pulmonary rheumatic inflammation, we usually prescribe bleeding and mild purgatives, perhaps calomel. Saltpeter and small amounts of antimony. We must take her off the boat when we reach Mobile. In the meantime, keep her warm and give her black tea and chicken-broth."

Percy refrained from saying what he thought, "Damn it man, this is my wife, not just another patient."

The doctor returned to his poker game in the salon. She was just another patient.

Percy did not leave his wife's side for the rest of the voyage, seated in a chair next to her, holding her hand. The steam engine beat rhythmically, almost soothing in its regularity. He felt its vibrations through the floor throughout the night. He prayed, wondering why the gods had sent him another misfortune. Would they be so cruel as to take this dear and loving wife from him? She had given him love his mother begrudged him, and warmth, of which his father seemed incapable.

The captain was informed of his passenger's condition. As the boat docked, he sent two crew members with a canvas litter to carry her from the cabin. Dr. Cassibry reappeared and instructed a coach driver to take Philomena and Percy to Mobile Hospital and put her in the care of the Sisters of Charity. He would be along shortly.

Phil drifted in and out of consciousness for the next thirty-six hours. She mumbled and murmured indistinctly, never coherent. The nuns made her as comfortable as they could. Dr. Cassibry visited and administered powders in solution. A little past nine in the evening, Philomena breathed her last troubled breath.

Percy bent over her and kissed her forehead tenderly. A nun pulled the sheet over her face. As he exited the hospital, Percy asked the receiving clerk where the nearest funeral home was. Waking the undertaker, he instructed the man to take Philomena's remains from the hospital and prepare her a coffin for transport to Richmond. He walked into the moonlit night, dabbing tears from his cheeks.

ᖬᖬ — ᖨᖨ

The journey by steamboat up to Montgomery and then by train to Richmond took another three days. At each stage, Percy oversaw the transfer, never trusting others to follow the shipment directions affixed to the wooden box holding Phil's coffin. At the Richmond station he supervised the loading of the box onto a wagon and rode with the driver to the funeral home. Exhausted, he checked into the Exchange Hotel, where he had proposed to Phil in October 1851. His grief drove out all other earthly concerns and allowed only fitful sleep.

In the morning Percy called on Emily Randolph. When she saw Percy alone and grim-faced, she knew that her daughter was dead. She sank into her living room sofa and briefly wept. She and Percy visited for two hours.

Putting her hand tenderly over purses, Emily said, "I never regretted her moving to Louisiana with you, Percy. Her letters were all happy, very happy. She said Judge Tucker would have been so proud of your success in law. And there was joy in her son. She was glad that Rand could have at least one grandfather. As you know, her own father died before she even knew him well. She loved your father as though he were her own."

Percy patted Emily Randolph's hand with his free hand, "She took such good care of my father in his final days."

"Did he pass? Except for your telegram, I've heard nothing from Philomena since little Rand died."

"Yes. Only a couple of weeks ago. That precipitated our decision to relocate to Richmond. With both our son and my father gone, she wanted to come home to you."

Emily Randolph was touched. "And you were willing to give up your life in Louisiana?"

"Anything for Phil's well-being. I feel I failed her, not bringing her sooner."

"Don't blame yourself, son. What now, for you?"

Shaking his head, Percy responded, "I can't say. Other than my wife and child, my life has been centered on maintaining our plantations and my law practice. I've detached myself from both of those with no expectation of going back to Louisiana. Something came up just before we left, a crazy Irishman. I may have to go back and deal with him." Only now did Percy's thoughts have to reorient themselves. Without Phil, there was no reason to remain in Virginia.

"Can you stay a few days? We should have a service for Philomena at her church here. Her cousin Beverley is here on a visit. And a few of her friends should be invited."

"Bev? What's he doing now? Last I heard was he was printer to the Senate."

Emily Randolph was surprised. "I guess Philomena didn't tell you that he's the American commercial consul in Liverpool."

"Really! We had lost touch. That's an important role for anyone interested in the cotton trade. I met with a predecessor of his when I was there a few years ago. Very helpful on trade matters. That was Tom Crittenden. Good man. I heard he was followed by a man with no background in business or law – that writer from Massachusetts, Hawthorne. President Pierce's friend. Why a man who wrote a book favorable to an adulteress would qualify as an American trade representative escapes me. I'm glad he was replaced by Bev."

"Yes," said Emily. "It's a good post for a wealthy man or a dishonest one but not so rewarding for an honest man. Bev lent money to some of President Buchanan's friends who had forwarded his appointment. They have been reluctant to repay, thinking his appointment was repayment enough. He's home on a visit to address his financial indebtedness. He'd like to obtain the post of Marshal of the District of Columbia so he can leave England. Perhaps you could put in a word with Senator Benjamin and Senator Slidell. I know Philomena and Mr. Benjamin were good friends."

ৡৡ — ৯৯

The service for Philomena Randolph Moorhead was held three days later at St. John's Episcopal Church. Percy's luggage had been lost in transit, and he bought a new suit at a Richmond haberdasher. A black mourning bow was pinned to his sleeve. Looking down at it, he felt there should be three. An hour's wake with a closed coffin preceded the service. Percy, Emily Randolph and cousin Beverley received visitors to the wake. Most of those attending were friends of Emily or Phil and were unknown to Percy. The only one he recognized was the woman who was hostess at their wedding reception. She was dressed in mourning clothes herself. Later, Emily reminded him that she was Mrs. Robert Stanard, Martha, whose husband had recently also passed away. Percy told Beverley he was grateful that circumstances permitted his presence; it would have pleased Phil. If both he and Beverley should return to Virginia, he hoped their acquaintance could be renewed.

Beverley Tucker gave the eulogy, recalling his little cousin as a girl growing up in Richmond and seeing her at their uncle's home in Williamsburg on frequent visits. There she had met her future and beloved husband. The loss of her only child had broken her heart and her health. He spoke of her grieving mother and her late father and the loss that all who knew and loved Philomena felt.

When Percy stood to speak all that he knew to say were a few words directed to her and not to the other mourners, a few lines of poetry they had shared one evening at Bolingbroke before a warm fire:

> Let us melt, and make no noise,
> No tear-floods, nor sigh-tempests move;
> 'Twere profanation of our joys
> To tell the laity our love.

Interment was next to her father's and mother's sites in Hollywood Cemetery. Emily Randolph's headstone was in place with the date of death left to be inscribed. When he returned to Bolingbroke, Percy would have to get his father an appropriate headstone. Should he get his own as well? Should he ask his mother about her burial – next to Jim Willis at Jericho or to Howard Moorhead at Bolingbroke? He knew what the answer should be but whether that accorded with her heart was far less certain. Why could she not have reciprocated her husband's devotion? But had Percy himself failed his loving wife? No, that brief period with Diana Watkins was never love. Yet . . . . Yes, he had failed. If he could only undo what cannot be undone. If only the past were not immutable. Now, it was too late to make it up to Phil. Now, he felt anguish and remorse as well as grief.

Chapter 50

# Moorhead Boyled

Percy sat quietly at counsel's table as proceedings convened in late January 1859 in the court for the Seventh Judicial District, Parish of West Feliciana, Albritton, J. presiding. The judge announced that the hearing was the opening of a succession for the intestate decedent, Redmond Boyle, also known as Granville Howard Moorhead. Petitioner, Grady Boyle, was represented by his counsel, Sumner Clausen. The petition prayed that Boyle be named as executor of the deceased. Looking over the fourteen men and women seated in the cold court room before him, Judge Albritton inquired if anyone appeared in opposition to the petition. Percy Moorhead, a black crepe band on his left arm, asked to be recognized as appearing on his own behalf. He informed the judge he was the son of the decedent, Howard Moorhead, and the rightful heir of his estate, along with his mother Lucinda Willis Moorhead, who owned a half-interest in the community existing between the decedent and herself.

"Is Mrs. Moorhead present?" The judge did not know Lucy Moorhead by appearance. Before becoming judge his practice had been primarily in Jackson and Clinton. He was a red-faced man whose bald pate made his ears seem oversize. In his early fifties, he owed his judgeship to the Barrow family, to whom he had kinship through his wife.

Lucy stood slowly, her black bodice and dress and equally dark shawl showed her to be a widow in mourning. Next to her were her daughter and Calvin Bunch, neither wearing emblems of mourning. She looked at Percy, hesitated, then responded in a low voice from behind her silk veil, "We do not wish to be heard at this time, your honor."

Percy was caught off-guard. He looked at his mother, but she averted her eyes. He had not conferred with her, but he had no reason to think she wouldn't try to protect her own interests and Eliza's.

"Very well. You may proceed, Mr. Clausen."

Attorney Clausen introduced himself as a New Orleans lawyer representing Mr. Grady Boyle, late of Dublin, Ireland and a resident of New Orleans for two years, more or less.

Clausen was about thirty-five, tall, thin, a full head of dark hair, penetrating blue eyes. He appeared efficient, ready and relentless. A gray wool day-coat sheltered him from the chill air that persisted despite the bailiff's poking at the oak logs in the fireplace to one side of the room.

He began, "Let me get right to the point, your honor. The man known in this community and to his New Orleans business associates as Howard Moorhead was in fact Redmond Boyle, formerly of Dublin, Ireland and Bristol, England. Prior to his taking up residence in New Orleans some time prior to the year 1820, he was employed aboard English merchant ships. Until he disappeared nearly forty years ago, his principal residence was Dublin where he had a wife and infant, Grady Boyle, whom you see seated with me."

Grady Boyle nodded to the judge. The judge acknowledged him with a courteous nod.

Lawyer Clausen resumed his recital of facts. "After an incident in the Mediterranean Sea, Mr. Boyle absconded with his employers' monies, leaving behind his wife and son in needy circumstances. Despite hardships, Mrs. Boyle raised her son in a Christian home and provided the best she could for him. Three years ago Mrs. Boyle learned from a visitor to New Orleans, who had returned to Dublin, that her husband was living there under an assumed name. That he was calling himself Moorhead. After hesitation and consulting with her priest, she informed her son Grady of his father's apparent existence in a foreign land."

The judge appeared interested. "Please continue," he said.

"Naturally, this was startling news to Grady Boyle. What man does not wish to know his father? Mr. Boyle settled his affairs in Ireland and came to America looking for the man he understood to be his father." The attorney paused for effect. "To find in the fulness of time the circumstances and meaning of his paternity. He felt he owed it to his mother, who though not infirm was in no condition to travel abroad to confirm a truth she knew was written on her heart, that somehow, somewhere her husband was still alive. Once in New Orleans, Grady learned that the rumor his mother had passed on to him was true. By the time Grady Boyle found his father, Redmond Boyle had suffered a stroke and was living on his plantation, Bolingbroke Hall, only a few miles from this courtroom. To his further surprise, Grady discovered that he had a younger brother, Mr. Percy Moorhead."

Clausen turned in the direction of Percy so that the judge would look to Percy, as he had with Grady Boyle, the one obviously frustrated and angry, the other calm and collected.

"And Grady had hoped that Percy would welcome learning the truth about his father, as disappointing as it might prove to be, and greet a brother with an embrace. Alas, Percy Moorhead would not hear of it and spurned every overture that Grady Boyle has made towards his heretofore unknown sibling."

Shaking his head, Percy muttered, "Not true. Not true."

The judge admonished him, "Mr. Moorhead, you will address

the court if you have anything to say. Do you understand?"

"Yes, your honor." Casting his eyes downward, Percy was suddenly conscious of a food stain on his shirt just above the top button of his suit jacket. Never in his practice in New Orleans had he appeared in so unkempt a condition as now.

Clausen was succeeding at portraying Percy as an embittered, wrathful and unreasonable litigant, aided by the persistent scowl on Percy's face throughout the proceedings. Would the judge have been more tolerant if he had been aware of Percy's loss of son and wife? Percy was not helping himself. He was too distressed to act sensibly in his own interest.

Clausen continued, "So, now that his father has died, it is with great reluctance that Grady Boyle appears here as your humble petitioner to claim his birthright as the only legitimate child of Redmond Boyle and to vindicate the rights of the wife Redmond abandoned. Under the laws of Louisiana as well as natural justice, Grady Boyle is the rightful heir of Redmond Boyle. Although Redmond was living under another name – to wit, Moorhead – all the property he acquired in that name under Louisiana law was also the property of his wife even though she remained in Ireland. It is that property that makes up his estate, as his only lawful wife was Maureen Boyle of Dublin. In a word, though it is an ugly and unpleasant word, Redmond Boyle was a bigamist."

Percy stood and demanded: "Your honor. This is a nice fable. But there is no proof that Mr. Clausen can put forth that would establish that Redmond Boyle and my father Howard Moorhead are the same man."

The judge frowned at the interruption. He tapped his gavel firmly at the annoyance.

"Mr. Moorhead, I know you are an attorney yourself. You know very well that you cannot be heard until the petitioner has finished his case. You are correct in saying he has the burden of establishing his claims by a preponderance of the evidence. And unless I am mistaken, he plans to place before this court evidence of those very facts. I will suffer no more interruptions in these proceedings. Do I make myself clear?"

"But, sir, these are unfounded insults to the reputation of an honorable man who cannot speak in his own behalf," Percy insisted with agitation. "I cannot listen in silence to lies. He was my father." Percy was not endearing himself with the judge. So cool and collected representing others, Percy could not control his feelings in a case he knew to be a great injustice. Sleepless nights had clouded his judgment.

In a tone bordering on patronizing, the judge told Percy, "No one doubts your parentage, Mr. Moorhead. Mr. Boyle makes the same assertion, that the decedent was father to both of you. You must hear the facts even if they prove most disturbing to you. Proceed Mr. Clausen."

In spite of the warning Percy continued to object to his treatment, saying, "Your honor, if I fail to make timely objections, I may be deemed to have waived them. Mr. Clausen is making assertions of fact and law that he knows to be wrong. In the petition he makes claims against Jericho Hill and argues that Bolingbroke Hall must be treated as community property. My father kept the two plantations separated from ownership as community property. It's in the public records." Despite his courtroom experience representing others, Percy had difficulty restraining himself when his own identity was under fierce assault.

The judge was about to tell Percy to sit down and be quiet again, but Clausen spoke.

"You honor, Mr. Moorhead mistakes our purpose here today. Our principal purpose is to obtain the appointment of Grady Boyle as the executor of the estate of Redmond Boyle. Exactly what property belongs in a complete inventory of that estate will require further deliberations. Mr. Percy Moorhead is correct that the parish records show an attempt to maintain a separate property status for the two plantations. The two were governed as though they were one by Redmond Boyle. Grady Boyle, we will establish shortly, represents his mother as well as himself in this proceeding. Maureen Boyle has rights to one-half of all property acquired by her husband in Louisiana as part of the community existing between them during their marriage, which only ended on his recent death. That he tried to keep Bolingbroke Hall separate property from his invalid marriage to Lucy Willis can have no effect on the community property of Mrs. Boyle. Every bale of cotton ever sold from Bolingbroke was owned one-half by Mrs. Boyle. Every slave acquired to work Bolingbroke is owned one-half by Mrs. Boyle. We believe the facts will ultimately show that the assets of Bolingbroke were used to benefit Lucy Willis's separate property of Jericho over much of the putative marriage. As we disentangle the affairs of the two properties we will show that Lucy Willis owes a substantial debt to Mrs. Boyle to compensate her for the misuse of her community property. Because of the intermingling of the operations of the two plantations, many of the assets Lucy and her daughter might assert as separate property on Jericho are in reality owned one-half by the estate of Redmond Boyle *alias* Moorhead. When income from Bolingbroke – one-half of which belonged to Mrs. Boyle – conferred benefits on Lucy Willis's Jericho, Mrs. Boyle has a right to be reimbursed."

The judge interposed a question. "It appears there are two wronged women here. Doesn't Lucy Willis have her own claim of wrongdoing by her supposed husband?"

Clausen was ready with an answer. "As I have advised Grady Boyle, if Lucy Willis was ignorant of Redmond Boyle's status as a married man, she may claim rights as a putative wife under our civil law though not under the common law. Likewise, if she was in good faith, then Percy Moorhead under the precedent of *Patton v. Cities of Philadelphia and New Orleans* may eventually have a claim to some portion of Bolingbroke and the New Orleans townhouse –

at most a quarter interest and then only upon the termination of the usufruct of Mrs. Boyle. That, of course, assumes that there is property remaining after all the debts of Bolingbroke have been satisfied."

The judge was clearly discomforted by the complexity of the issues raised by counsel for Grady Boyle. He said to lawyer Clausen, "So you don't expect to resolve all these particulars today?"

"Yes, your honor. That's correct. We are confident, however, that if you will appoint Grady Boyle as executor and authorize him to sell all immovable property that is in the name of the decedent, the remaining issues will sort themselves out."

"You may continue," said the judge. With a gesture of his right hand the judge directed the bailiff to put more wood on the fire. As he complied, the burning logs crackled and cast sparks and smoke upward.

Clausen stepped from the lectern to the counsel table and picked up a sheaf of papers. He began introducing a series of documents into evidence, asking the court to accept them as exhibits which he had marked by appropriate number. He held up each exhibit for all to see, with the confidence of Mark Antony showing the Roman crowd the wounds in Caesar's toga. With each document introduced, attorney Clausen passed the exhibit to Percy Moorhead for his examination. They included:

1. Death certificate of Dr. Alfred Shay that Granville Howard Moorhead died on September 25, 1858.

2. Affidavit that Redmond Boyle and Maureen O'Neal were married in Dublin on May 5, 1815.

3. Baptism certificate of Grady Boyle, son of Redmond Boyle and Maureen Boyle, who was born on April 11, 1816.

4. Affidavit dated January 12, 1857 of Mrs. Redmond

Boyle, sixty-one years of age, wife of Redmond Boyle, whereabouts unknown, that she is a resident of Dublin, Ireland and appoints her only son Grady Boyle as her agent with full power of attorney to act on her behalf.

5. Preliminary inventory of the assets of Redmond Boyle, *alias* Moorhead. The list included Bolingbroke Hall and its 1253 acres, more or less, of improved land, all of the slaves appertaining to the said plantation, all of the horses, mules, cattle and other farm animals belonging to the plantation, a carriage or buggy and three wagons, and a town home in New Orleans.

The inventory listed a series of investments of indeterminate status, including an interest in Toulouse Gardens. In his distressed state, Percy noted this last item as odd but assumed it was an error, not something worth raising when so much more was at stake, especially the townhouse.

Percy stood and spoke, "Objection, your honor. The townhouse is mine. My father gave it to me on my marriage in 1851. I have his deed conveying it to me. Even if the townhouse had been community property with Grady Boyle's mother, as head and master of the community he had full power to alienate it."

Clausen did not hesitate. "Perhaps Mr. Moorhead thinks it so. And his father may have intended it. However, it is firmly established in the law of this state that an unrecorded deed has no effect on third persons, even if they have knowledge of its existence. Mr. Moorhead failed to record the deed as an examination of the records of the Parish will establish."

Lawyer Clausen looked at Percy as he savored a triumph on a precise point of Louisiana property law, the so-called race to the courthouse: the first person to record a deed wins, irrespective of knowledge or good faith. Every attorney admitted to the Louisiana bar had to demonstrate knowledge of the rule. He saw Percy's face flush in frustration as he realized that Clausen was correct, that

Percy had not had the foresight to protect against this contingency.

Looking again at the judge, Clausen drove home the knife. "He cannot do so now as the rights of the petitioner have superseded any claim he may have. Mr. Boyle has already filed in the parish records of Orleans a claim of his mother and himself to the property, subject of course to the rulings of this court."

"Even so," Percy trying to recover after a serious setback, shot back, "nothing in any of these exhibits, even if true, establish that Howard Moorhead and Redmond Boyle are one and the same man." Percy attempted a rhetorical flourish, an effort at mild self-deprecation, saying, "Until then, I am not the putative bastard Mr. Clausen makes me out to be." It fell flat.

Clausen was as patient as Percy was agitated. Without looking at Percy, he said calmly to the judge, "Mr. Moorhead would be correct, your honor, if my presentation were finished, which it is not. We seek not to sully Mr. Moorhead's character, recognizing as we do the lenity of the civil law, which does not burden the secondary offspring with the transgressions of the father. We are here to vindicate the rights of those to whom Redmond Boyle had primary obligations, his legitimate wife and son, those whom he abandoned. With your honor's permission, I would like to continue."

The judge said sternly, "Counsel is correct. Mr. Moorhead, if you interrupt again, I will hold you in contempt. Please proceed, Mr. Clausen."

"Thank you, your honor. Petitioner calls Mr. Jack Bayfield." The attorney turned his attention to the rear.

From the back of the court came an old man, gray and white hair and beard, who had been waiting in the antechamber. His face was deeply creased. Several teeth could be seen missing as he gave his oath to tell the truth. Percy had never seen nor heard of the man.

Lawyer Clausen established that Jack Bayfield was born in

Dorset, England, that he was sixty-two years of age, and was a resident of New Orleans. He asked Bayfield to tell the court of his acquaintance with the decedent, Mr. Boyle.

In a rasping voice, Bayfield said, "Yessir. I knew Mr. Boyle when I was on the crew of the *Hybla*. Years later I made my home in New Orleans. Ran into Mr. Boyle on Canal Street. I come up to him and says, 'Mr. Boyle. You remember me?' He said he didn't. I told him it must have been a mistake. I followed him and learned he was calling his self Moorhead."

"Now Mr. Bayfield, can you think of any reason why Mr. Boyle would want to pretend not to know you?"

Percy stood and said, "Objection. Calls for speculation from the witness. He can only testify to his own personal knowledge."

The judge did not wait for Clausen to respond. Visibly irritated, he said, "Mr. Moorhead, for the last time, this is a succession proceeding. It is not a criminal trial. The rules of evidence allow a certain latitude when a man's liberty is not at stake."

Clausen said, "Thank you, your honor. Mr. Bayfield is not experienced in the rules of court as is Mr. Moorhead. He has led the life of a simple and honest seaman and laborer. Now, sir, please tell the court about your personal knowledge of Mr. Boyle and why it stuck in your memory after many years."

With a toothless grin, Bayfield proceeded as prompted by the proficient lawyer representing Boyle. "Yes sir. I was just a young buck. On my first voyage. As I say, it was on the *Hybla*, out of Bristol. We was doing coastal trading in the Mediterranean. Dangerous it was, too. What with the wars and all. No steamboats in those days, just sail. *Hybla* wasn't near as big as some of them traders. But she was fast enough and could go in and out of ports that some of the big ships couldn't. Nimble, she was. Me, I was a general hand on deck. New, you know. Just learning the ropes. Been on lots of other ships since then. But this was my first. You don't forget your first ship. No sir, not your first ship."

Smoothly, Clausen interjected, "Forgive me for interrupting you, Mr. Bayfield. But we need to connect your experience on the *Hybla* with Mr. Boyle, the man later calling himself Moorhead."

"Right sir, right. Old Jack was getting there. Well sir. You're gonna remember your first ship if it gets caught by pirates. That's what happened to the *Hybla*. We was trading in Marseille for a few days and back into the voyage when we was on a heading to our next port which was Barcelona. We'd already been to Genoa and was on our last coupla stops. Out of nowhere comes up a corsair. Cap'n Rogers was gonna make a run for it, but they fired a shot across our bow and then one up high into a sail just to show us they means business. So Cap'n Rogers hove to and they boarded us. I thought we was all dead. Some of them maybe was Turks and some musta been French. We couldn't say which. We was all lined up on the quarterdeck so's they could keep an eye on us. Three of 'em went inside the cabins like they knew where they was going and came out with a box so heavy two of 'em just barely could handle it. Maybe it was two. I figured it musta been gold or silver that we didn't even know was on board. They may'uv took one or two of our crew over to their ship, hostages we thought they was. Then they put the rest of us in two lifeboats. I was in one and Cap'n Rogers and Mr. Boyle was in the other. After we watched the pirate ship sail away, I heard the Cap'n and Mr. Boyle arguing with each other. They was getting on it pretty fierce. I couldn't hear what they was saying."

Looking at the judge, Clausen asked the old sailor, "Now, this Boyle, what did he do on the *Hybla*?"

"Yessir. Mr. Boyle, he was the ship's purser. He handled all the commercial transactions at the ports where we stopped. Paid us our wages, too."

"And what happened next? What happened when you finally made it to Cette."

"Like you say, we made it to Cette, some French fishermen helping us. Cap'n Rogers found us shelter with an Englishman he knew. That's when he had Mr. Boyle arrested."

"Arrested?" As though he was surprised by this revelation, Clausen looked around the courtroom to observe the reactions of the Moorhead family and asked, "For what?"

"He told us that he suspected Mr. Boyle helped the pirates. It was like they knew we was carrying gold and they knew right where it was. They must'uv had a key, he said. Said too that someone had fouled the lock to where the muskets was kept. So's we couldn't defend ourselves from boarding. It was an inside job, he said."

"Was Mr. Boyle ever charged with piracy?"

"Don't see how he could be. He escaped the French a few days later. Or they was bribed. Cap'n Rogers was mighty upset. He was waiting for us to get on a merchant ship going to England and have Boyle charged and tried there. But Mr. Boyle, he slipped away. Next time I saw him was on Canal Street in New Orleans. Reckon he musta got his share of gold and set himself up mighty pretty. If he had helped them pirates and got tried, I reckon he woulda been hung. Musta got clean away."

Percy said, "Objection. Pure conjecture by the witness and no evidence at all in his knowledge."

Boyle's lawyer said, "We'll accept that objection. Truth is, Mr. Bayfield, you don't know how Mr. Boyle became Granville Howard Moorhead and how he became rich. And no one else seems to know either."

Bayfield eagerly agreed. "Yessir, that's a fair statement."

"So," continued Clausen, "it really doesn't matter whether he aided a piracy. Your testimony to us is only of interest as to the identity of Howard Moorhead as the Mr. Boyle you knew on the *Hybla*. And you are absolutely certain that the two men are one and the same."

"Yessir. It is God's own truth that the Mr. Boyle I knowed on the *Hybla* in 1815 was the Mr. Moorhead I saw in New Orleans."

"I have no more questions of this witness."

Percy looked at a few notes he had written as Bayfield spoke. He stood and stepped over to the witness chair to confront the witness.

"I have just a few. Mr. Bayfield, did you accompany Captain Rogers back to England?"

"No sir."

"Did you go back to England?"

"No sir. Not right away."

"When did you get to England?"

"Well, I didn't."

"So, you've never been back to England?"

"As far as I know, Mr. Boyle never did neither."

"You don't know one way of the other, do you? As far as you know, he may have gotten back to England and cleared his name."

Bayfield was belligerent. "If he cleared his name, I don't know why a man would take another name. I can tell you for sure Mr. Boyle was calling himself Moorhead and wouldn't answer to Boyle when I saw him. Same man. I'm positive of that. I swear to that."

Percy turned to the judge, "Your honor, the witness is being argumentative. Please instruct him to simply answer the questions put to him."

The judge frowned, annoyed at Percy's persistence, and said, "Mr. Bayfield is making a good point. He's testifying from his own knowledge that the man who called himself Boyle at one time changed his name to Moorhead. I'd wonder then the same thing myself."

Frustrated, Percy continued, "All right then. You said the

pirates took one or two crew members hostage. What happened to them?"

"Never saw them again. If they was hostages. We took a count of crew at Cette and figured we was missing one or two."

"Did you know them? Couldn't they have been in league with the pirates?"

"Couldn't say. We had musket and sabers pointed at us and scrambling into lifeboats and I can't say I was paying as much attention to them as I was to getting out of there alive."

"So, the two could have been the ones who betrayed the *Hybla*."

Clausen said, "Objection. Counsel is speculating and testifying. The witness has said he wasn't sure if one or two or indeed if any crew members were missing."

The judge said, "I'll let the witness respond if he cares to."

Jack Bayfield seized the chance to assert himself. "It wasn't them others that Cap'n Rogers was blamin'. It was Mr. Boyle."

Clausen nodded in satisfaction with the witness's statement.

Percy resumed his questioning, "Mr. Bayfield, where did you go after the piracy of the *Hybla*?"

"I was a seaman on another trading ship."

"What sort of trading ship?"

"Bringing goods to the Americas."

"You mean slaves, don't you?"

"Not always. That trading got more difficult over time."

"When did you first come to New Orleans?"

"Bout fifteen years ago. Couple years afore the Mexican War I reckon."

"What sort of work do you do now?"

"Mostly carpenter. Not much now. Too much pain in my hand

joints. I'm getting to be an old man."

"How did you come to be in this court room?"

"Bout a year ago I heard a man was asking around about Mr. Moorhead. So I found him out and told him what I remembered."

"Is Mr. Boyle or his lawyer paying you to testify?"

"They both told me you'd ask me that and that it would not be lawful for me to accept any money for my testimony."

"So is your answer 'No?'"

"Yessir."

What Bayfield didn't testify to was that he was promised a steady position on Mr. Boyle's plantation when and if the litigation proved successful.

Clausen said, "Petitioner rests, your honor."

"Mr. Moorhead, do you have any witnesses?"

"Yes, your honor. I call the decedent's widow, Mrs. Howard Moorhead."

"Any objections, Mr. Clausen?" asked Judge Albritton.

"No objections, your honor. If he weren't going to call her, we would have." Clausen was not displeased.

Lucy – Lucinda, now preferred – stood slowly at the second row of seats of the courtroom. As the years had accumulated, her bearing had become more erect, her manner more stiff. Her deep black hair, not fully covered by her bonnet, had lost its sheen and texture and was increasingly flecked with gray. Her eyes were proud and animated, but they were set in flesh that was no longer taut and rose-tinged. She carried herself with reserve and dignity as she walked to the witness stand.

Passing her son, Lucinda Moorhead whispered, "Don't do this to me, son. This will not go well."

After being sworn as Lucinda Pugh Willis Moorhead, she was seated. Carefully, she removed her black felt bonnet and held it in her lap. Percy asked his mother if she had ever heard anyone call her husband by a name other than Moorhead.

"No, no one ever did. I never knew him by any other name."

"Did your husband ever speak of his life before he settled in New Orleans?"

"Must I answer such questions? I've lost both my husbands. I've been through enough."

"I'm sorry, Mother. I want to save you what is yours in Bolingbroke. Please answer the question."

"If I must. Yes. He said he learned business on a ship. He was the ship's purser."

"Was it the *Hybla*?"

"What does it matter, Percy? I can't say it wasn't. Anyway, it doesn't matter. I've settled with Mr. Boyle. I'm not contesting the point."

Judge Albritton was surprised, though not as much as Percy. He leaned forward and said, "You're accepting the fact that Howard Moorhead was once named Boyle and married to another woman?"

Turning to the judge, she said, "I'm not contesting it." She was relieved to speak to the judge rather than Percy. "I'm settling it. I don't know what else I can do. Mr. Boyle says there may be many debts owed by my husband, and I can't lose Jericho Hill. If he can sell Bolingbroke Hall, he'll let me keep Jericho free and clear."

The judge said, "You know the effect of this is to undercut your son's case as the legitimate heir to his father's estate?"

Lucy looked to the judge for understanding, for compassion for the suffering she had endured. "Judge, sometimes I think I never knew Mr. Moorhead. He was a good husband. He always took care of us – me, my daughter, and our son, Percy. All our servants. But there was so much about him I didn't know. If my son fights this and loses, I could lose everything, too. He's just going to have to take care of himself. He always has. He's always been self-sufficient."

There was silence in the courtroom. Percy Moorhead was stunned and speechless. He had to put his hand on counsel's table to support himself, to keep himself from falling over, dizzy. All eyes were now on him. He regained his composure but could think of nothing to ask his mother. She stood and left the witness chair.

Finally, Judge Albritton spoke, not without sympathy. "I suppose there's nothing else to be heard in this case. Mr. Clausen, if you will prepare the papers putting Mr. Boyle in possession of all movable and immovable property of the estate as executor of the decedent's estate I will sign them. This will include the townhouse in New Orleans. However, I will assume that some of the movable property in the townhouse belongs to Mr. Percy Moorhead. Is your client agreeable to allowing him a reasonable time to remove such items?"

"Of course, your honor. We harbor no ill-will for Percy Moorhead. He's as much a victim of Redmond Boyle as his first son, Grady. Had he been agreeable, Mr. Boyle would have entered into a settlement with him for an equitable distribution of all of the property between them. However, he refused to believe the truth about his father. Even now, Mr. Boyle recognizes the ties a man feels to his childhood home and will allow Percy Moorhead to remove any personal property from the house that he wishes to take within the next few days. By that house, we mean Bolingbroke Hall."

"Very generous, Mr. Clausen," said Judge Albritton. His glance at Percy as much as said he wished Percy were as cooperative as Grady Boyle's attorney.

Clausen continued, "And with respect to the New Orleans townhouse, shall we set the date as two weeks from today's date, by which time the respondent must have vacated the premises?"

"Very well. What further today?"

Clausen said, "With all due respect to Mr. Percy Moorhead, as we said earlier, he is the son of a putative marriage. He does have some rights of heirship, subject to the usufruct of Mrs. Boyle during the remainder of her life. He will ultimately benefit from Grady Boyle's compromise with Lucinda Willis for that settlement reflects the estate relinquishing claims to her, and this will flow to him as one of her two heirs. The sale of Bolingbroke Hall and the townhouse, if and when they occur, and of other assets will be treated as an equitable partition among the parties. When the transactions are complete, an appropriate accounting will be made to Mr. Percy Moorhead, taking into consideration that he will gain benefits by his mother's settlement."

"How long do you anticipate?" asked the judge.

Clausen glanced at Percy, then told the judge, "I've seen these take two to three years."

"Mr. Moorhead, do you have objections to the proposed equitable partition?"

Percy saw no alternative. His mind was reeling. "No, your honor, subject to my right to appeal."

"Duly noted. You know of course that an appeal will only delay a sale and winding up the estate. Hearing no further objection, the court so rules. And with that, the court is adjourned."

Chapter 51

# Recrimination

Outside the courthouse, Percy and his mother immediately fell into a fraught argument, despite the cold wind and ash-gray clouds. "Mother," he demanded, "you gave up without a fight! How could you?" He felt betrayed by his own mother. He continued, "The documentary evidence was thin. The only evidence linking Father to Grady Boyle was the testimony of a man about events of forty years ago. I'm sure he perjured himself. He was bought and paid for by Grady Boyle. Could you not see that? When you said you settled I could see from the judge's demeanor the case was over. Surely, he would have had sympathy for a widow showing her grief and facing the loss of her principal home – even if he had no goodwill for me. And we could always have appealed."

With a disparaging look and colder than Percy could remember from any earlier exchange with his mother, Lucy said, "Percy Moorhead, don't be so quick to judge your gray-haired mother. I did the only thing I could do."

His frustration growing, Percy demanded, "Do you have so little faith in your son and my ability to pursue a claim in law?"

"My problem is not with you, Percy. It's with your father. You are not in possession of all of the facts."

Percy was taken back. "No? What am I missing?"

"This," she said, pulling a small notebook from her handbag. She handed it to Percy.

Looking skeptically at the object, he said, "What's this?"

"I found it in your father's desk, in a false compartment in the back of a drawer. See for yourself."

Opening it, Percy found it was identified as "Purser's log, *Hybla*." Turning the pages, he saw it was the accounts for four voyages of the *Hybla*, merchant schooner of Bristol, trading on behalf of Forster & Co.. The writing was in the precise small hand he recognized as his father's. One group of pages showed disbursements for supplies, another for goods sold or exchanged together with price or value and from and to whom payments were made. The pages in the back identified banks and merchants and financial transactions made with each. Next to each entry on this page were the initials, RB, in his father's hand.

Percy stared at the book in disbelief. How could it be so? How could he be so wrong about his father? His mother's stern expression did nothing to lessen the blow. His wretched acceptance that Bayfield's testimony may have been true vindicated her decision to settle, to salvage what she could out of a marriage of thirty plus years based on a lie, married seemingly to a stranger whose past she could not recognize. Was Howard Moorhead no more than a thief in league with pirates?

ᘒᘒ — ᘓᘓ

Leaving what remained of his family, Percy rode his horse directly to Bolingbroke from the courtroom. He summoned Pompey, Jessie Mae, Julius, Leddie, and Odessa into the living room. He seated them on the sofa; they were reluctant to sit where only whites usually sat. Standing opposite them, he said, "I'm afraid I have terrible news. A man claiming to be an older brother of mine, an Irishman named Grady Boyle, has been declared the heir of my father. He is now effectively the owner of Bolingbroke and all the property that was owned by Howard Moorhead. He will be taking over the entire plantation and selling it. I have only a few days to vacate anything that is mine."

"What's gonna happen to you, Mister Percy?" asked Leddie.

"I suppose I can go back to the practice of law in New Orleans. But I'll have to find a new place to live. He's even taken the townhouse my father gave to me and Philomena."

"God rest her soul. She was a beautiful person," said Leddie softly.

"What about all us that belongs here?" Julius asked, apprehensive.

"I wish I could tell you, Julius. My mother and sister will continue to own Jericho Hill. And Calvin Bunch will be running it, as bad as that might be. These two plantations have been run together for so long it will take a little time to sort out what belongs to what."

Odessa spoke, unable to hold back irritation in her voice, "You mean who belong to who. We not talking just mules and wagons, we are talking about the slaves that belongs to Miss Lucy and them who belong now to this Boyle." Odessa's Creole lilt and enunciation had been replaced by the voice and language she used in talking with the other slaves on the plantation. Without Howard Moorhead, without Percy Moorhead, she was just another slave, not the free daughter of a wealthy French planter.

Feeling helpless, Percy could only say, "Truly, Odessa, truly, I am sorry. It will take time. What happens to a division of property between Bolingbroke and Jericho will be entirely between my mother and this Boyle. If I could, I'd buy freedom for you five and Little Jay, too, of course. The law won't even allow us to free slaves anymore. The state of Louisiana is trying to force all free people with African blood to leave the state. Right now, I don't know what is even mine. I have some investments in New Orleans, but they may not be worth much. Since my son and wife died, I've neglected everything trying to keep up these two plantations."

Apprehensive, even fearful, Pompey asked, "What we do now, Mister Percy?"

"I'll do whatever I can for you. I can't make any promises. I wasn't able to protect myself. All my life, I've had good fortune. You'd have thought I the heavens favored me. Now, it looks like everything is against me. I've had taken from me the last thing I thought was solid and incontestable – my good name: Moorhead. My father, in death, seems to have abandoned me and all I believed I held dear. In court today, I became little more than a bastard in the eyes of the law and in the eyes of men. Am I Percy Boyle? Or is my name Willis because my mother was Mrs. Willis?"

Percy had been looking at the vacant fireplace in the cold room. He became aware again to whom he was speaking. An abrupt shift came in his voice, the self-pity suddenly dissipated.

Embarrassed, he said, "Listen to me! Here I am moaning about my fallen state to you. And you've spent your lives in my state, only worse. In the eyes of the law and of white people, you are just as illegitimate as I am now. You have no family name because the law denies you family and name except the name your owner allows you. If I am bankrupt, I am allowed to own at least the clothes on my back. You don't even have that."

Percy asked Pompey and Julius to inform all the slaves, one by one, not *en masse*, of the developments of the day and how they would probably affect Bolingbroke and Jericho. If they were to inquire whether they would stay at Bolingbroke or would be sold elsewhere, tell them it is too soon to know.

࿇࿇ — ࿇࿇

Percy went upstairs to the room of his boyhood, the room he had shared for a few years with his beloved wife and collected a few items of clothing and mementoes. Outside, the sunlight fading, he took a long look at Bolingbroke. Fixing his eyes on the hand carved sign bearing the plantation's name, he considered taking the sign from above the porch. But he rejected the thought as he wondered whether his father had chosen the name in a dark moment of infinite jest or mischief. Did not Bolingbroke contain and conceal his father's own name, Boyle?

*Chapter 52*

# A Gold Watch

When Percy arrived at his law office in New Orleans two days after the dismal day in the West Feliciana court, he found his clerk, Louis Cutrer, organizing the few files that remained in the office. He asked, "Have you found another employer yet, Louis?"

"No sir." Cutrer, twenty-five, was from Donaldsonville, a town upriver, where his father had a store next to the landing. The senior Cutrer supplied boiler wood and provisions for steamboats that regularly stopped there.

"I may have to resume my practice here in New Orleans. Would you be willing to stay on?"

"Certainly, Mr. Moorhead. I hope I can be admitted to the bar some day with your help."

The clerk saw the weariness in Percy's eyes, in the way he held his shoulders. His posture made him now appear two inches shorter and much older. Louis wanted to give him some encouragement. If it meant passing up other opportunities, he would.

Percy said, "Good. I was moving to Virginia for Philomena's sake, but now . . . You've probably heard that I've lost the plantation too."

"Yes sir. I heard something. It's unfair. Terrible on top your other losses."

"Over the next few days, I'm going to be clearing out of my townhouse. And looking for a new place to rent. When you have the time, I want you to go to the city and parish records to locate any and all transactions that have anything to do with Howard Moorhead or Redmond Boyle. Anything. Anything at all, no matter how trivial. No man can have achieved the business success in this city that my father did without leaving traces in records." Percy hoped to find some clue that would lead to proof that his father was never named Boyle.

"Yessir. I can do that." The clerk, like Percy, was diligent and competent. If there were records, he would ferret them out.

"Thanks. Anything else we need to discuss?"

Recalling a recent visitor, Louis told Percy, "A few days ago a woman left something for you."

"A woman?"

"Yessir. A small package. I left it on your desk in case I wasn't here when you came back."

"Did she say who she was?" Percy was startled by the sudden thought it might be Di Watkins, back to haunt him with shame and guilt.

"No, sir. She didn't say. She was a light-colored woman. Quadroon. Or octoroon. Older woman, very soft-spoken. Grey hair. Nicely dressed. A free woman, I would guess from her manner. A rich woman's servant maybe."

The description gave Percy a sense of relief but left him curious.

❧❧ — ❦❦

At his desk Percy opened the small box Louis had left for him. Inside was a gold pocket watch. Engraved on the back were the initials _G.M.H._ A small note was in the bottom of the box. He unfolded it. In an elegant hand it said "From your pere. M." He wound the watch with its key and found it to be in good working condition. Perhaps the colored woman who delivered it was the servant of one of his father's business associates. On the interior of the case, in small letters, the watch's makers were identified as Grimalde & Johnson, Strand, London, 1815.

Obviously, it had been his father's. Less obviously, the date and initials suggested his father was going by the name of Howard Moorhead at a time that Grady Boyle said their father was known as Redmond Boyle. Could the date have been before the alleged piracy of the *Hybla* that same year? It was undoubtedly a valuable watch. Why was it not in his father's possessions? New Orleans was too large a city for Percy to try to track down the woman of color without a clue as to whom she might work for. Could it be the link to his father's past that he sought?

ʀʀ — ʀʀ

It took Percy a couple of days to remove his clothing and personal property from the townhouse and put the things he wanted to keep in two chests in storage. He searched the place diligently to see if his father had left any clues to his past, another logbook perhaps. But there was nothing.

Next, Percy had to take stock of what might be left of his finances. On hand, for himself and what remained of his law practice he had only a few hundred dollars in ready cash and receivables. He decided it was time to visit his old friend and banker Westbrook Haydel, whom he had not seen in over a year. Perhaps he would need a loan. He called upon him at the Canal Bank building, at the corner of Magazine and Natchez, trying not to display the discouragement and despondency he felt. Westie walked from around his desk and put his arm around Percy.

"God, old friend, you've suffered the misfortunes of a character from the Old Testament. Polly and I said it couldn't get any worse for you after losing Phil. Now this Boyle thing. Just awful."

"Bad news travels quickly."

"It has always been so. Especially if money is involved."

Percy opened up to his friend. "Well, I've lost my townhouse as well as my plantation. A month ago, I was worth half a million dollars. Now I just have a few hundred dollars and my stake in Toulouse Gardens. I need to borrow a couple of thousand to find a place to live and carry me until I can resume my law practice. Aside from wanting to see a friendly face, that's why I'm here. Relatively speaking, that's not much and my signature ought to be the only security you need."

Westie's expression of concern changed little, but his tone did. He took his hand from Percy's shoulder and sat behind his desk. "I wish it were that simple, Percy. If it were me, we'd have no problem. But there are others to whom I must answer – my associates, my father-in-law."

"Of course. I'd be glad to put up my interest in the supper club."

Westie pursed his lips and looked Percy in the eye, now a bearer of more bad news. "That's where the difficulty arises, Percy. Two of the other investors in Toulouse Gardens have been by to see me. That's how I knew about Boyle. You'll recall your father co-signed the note you used to purchase your share. They are uncertain whether he merely signed as surety for your obligation to our firm or whether he – and now Boyle – acquired an ownership interest in the gambling hall. I tried to explain that it was you who owed us the money still outstanding and your father only guaranteed payment as the debt came due. Yet, I had to admit, that in the event of your insolvency we would need to proceed against your interest in the investment as well as seeking money from your father's estate. Should Boyle pay the outstanding money owed, then the interest in Toulouse Gardens would devolve to him as

Howard Moorhead's heir. So yes, they are exposed to Grady Boyle taking over your interest in the establishment."

Percy reflected on the legal implications for a moment and said, "I suppose the only way to avoid that is for me to pay the note in full. How much do I owe?"

"A little over $12,000 remains. It is already overdue. We have simply been renewing the term by a year for the past two years."

Percy could only be candid. He always was. "I don't have it. As I resume my practice, I'm sure it won't take me long."

Leaning forward with his elbows on his desk, his fingers closed together in front of him, Westie said, "Look, Percy, I can lend you money from my own account. As a friend I can do no less. But for the firm – we can't renew the note in light of the loss of the security in the form of Bolingbroke Hall."

Percy saw that the friend Westie had been replaced by Westbrook Haydel, Banker.

"As my friend, any suggestions? Surely you face people with problems like mine often enough."

"I'm reluctant to advise you. I have to look not only to you but to the credit of this investment house and the people who have entrusted us with their money."

"Please, Westie." It was a new experience for Percy to plead, but now he had no choice.

Shifting in his chair, the banker said impassively, "I know this will wound you. Unpleasant as it may be, it would be the prudent thing to do. Your associates asked me what would happen if they paid off the note. I explained the only way that would work would be for them to buy you out. Purchase your interest."

This was unpleasant, yes, but Percy saw it could be a way to get money quickly. If he were to start his practice again, he would need a substantial sum. "That's not unreasonable. It must be worth $30,000 at least."

Now Westie had to provide more discouraging news. "Who am I to say what it's worth? You have to remember that when you started, it was the only establishment of its kind. Its success brought in imitators and competitors. McGrath & Company's gambling house on Carondolet has taken many of your regular customers. Others have gone to Laurine & Cassidy. We couldn't turn them away when they looked to us for financing. The revenue for your establishment isn't what it was. Fewer gamblers now and smaller wagers. The banking panic last year hit New Orleans like everywhere else. The elegance of Toulouse Gardens is not valued as it was when you first opened."

Percy looked at the floor, glumly. "Are we becoming coarser?"

Westbrook continued after clearing his throat, reluctant to state what he knew. "I heard them say the most they would offer you was to pay off the note and throw in a couple of thousand. You might get $15,000 if you hold out. Or maybe less. You wouldn't clear more than a couple of thousand."

Discouraged, Percy replied, "Not what I hoped to hear, Westie."

"I'm afraid there's more you won't want to hear. The two men said Boyle already owns ten percent in Toulouse Gardens."

"How?" Percy had thought there could be no more surprises.

"It's listed in the inventory of Howard Moorhead's estate. The judge put him in possession and his attorney has already filed it of record in this parish."

Suddenly, Percy recalled the inventory he had looked at in the courtroom. "That's not possible. I thought Boyle was just listing a claim to my ten percent."

Westie declared flatly, "No, it was your father's. I'm certain. I checked."

"When did my father get an interest in the casino? He can't have. I'd know. He'd have told me."

"Maybe so. But he was concealing it from someone. He purchased it with a counter letter through a New Orleans attorney. From a Mrs. Diana Watkins."

"Diana? When?" Percy's confusion was complete. Again, Di haunted him. "She was a manager at the casino."

"Maybe two years ago. He paid her cash. The full value and then some. The attorney who represented her in the transaction was candid with me. Your father purchased on the condition that she leave New Orleans immediately and never return."

"Oh my God, that's why she left. Where did she go? Did she leave a forwarding address?"

"Apparently not. But the attorney thought she could be reached through her husband."

Quickly, Percy sought to correct Westie. "There's some mistake. She's a widow."

Shaking his head, Westie told Percy, "Hardly. Not even divorced. She abandoned a husband in Steubenville, Ohio before landing here. He's some sort of agent for manufacturers of farming equipment. A slick salesman. You know the type – smooth-talker, ladies' man. Schemer. I'm told he came looking for her not long ago, thinking he had a share of the inheritance of her father as belonging to him. Showed up at Toulouse Gardens claiming to be a part owner. That's how he came to know about the counter-letter and the attorney. No one else knew your father had been a purchaser. Boyle heard about it when he was inquiring into your interest. Perhaps your father bought her interest to increase your holdings in the casino. With your interest and his together, you'd have had more control. He must have thought it was a good investment."

Percy stood and walked over to the window. He looked out. New Orleans suddenly looked very different to him. How little he knew his father. Or Diana Watkins. How could he not have seen that even her claimed assault in the streets had been a ruse to gain

Percy's sympathy? He had been an easy mark. She had used him, but to what end? What had Rev. Mr. Hope said in class at Princeton? – *We live life forward but understand backward*. Somehow, probably from something Percy had told him, his father understood, intuitively surely, that Percy had become intimate with Diana. She was a threat to Percy's marriage and to Howard Moorhead's family. Immediately and decisively, Howard had taken steps to remove the threat. How could he have known that Diana was a liar and a cheat? Did his father have so much greater an insight into the hearts and minds of others than Percy had? After a few minutes, he turned and said with resignation.

"All right. I'll give you my power of attorney. Do what you can for me, Westie."

## Chapter 53

# Meeting Maisie

W
hen he returned to his law office, Louis Cutrer told him he had found a tax notice for a property on Old Levee Street, with a receipt for it being paid by his father six years earlier. Percy did not recognize the property description. It was not listed in the inventory of property compiled in the succession proceeding. Perhaps it was something his father had sold or managed for a client. Desperate for any link to his father's past, Percy felt compelled to track it down.

A trip to the city tax and property records revealed that the property was in the name of M. Dastugues. Formerly, it had been in the name of G. Moorhead. So, his father had owned it and must have sold it to Mr. Dastugues. Maybe it was to cover Calvin's losses when the cotton bales had gone up in flames with the wharf fires.

The brisk cold breeze of the late afternoon brought tears to his cheeks as Percy walked down Canal Street toward the Levee Street address. The winter sun would soon descend. He pulled his hat lower. Soon, he arrived at a small shop, identified as Lalande & Co.. Its wood and glass door was held ajar by an iron casting in the form of a somnolent cat, painted yellow. Another precursor of death? Or was it a reminder of Di's cat, Cheddar? A modest sign in the window declared that a customer could purchase combs, brushes, jewelry, stationery, fine perfumery, and flowers.

Pulling open the door, Percy found, to his right, a long, low cabinet with glass tops through which he could see the wares offered by the shop. And behind were open shelves with more items and bric-a-brac, tastefully laid out. Behind a counter at the rear of the shop was a woman of light complexion. He guessed she must be one of New Orleans's *gens de couleur*, a free woman-of-color employed as the salesclerk. She was in her early to mid-fifties, with a trim figure and salt-and-pepper gray hair. She matched the description of the woman who had brought his father's watch to his office.

"Pardon me. My name is Percy Moorhead. I'm looking for Mr. Dastugues."

"Yes, Percy. Please do come in. But you'll find no Mr. Dastugues here." She knew who he was and apparently expected to see him. Her speech was articulate and carried no trace of a common background.

"Forgive me if I seem impertinent, but I have reason to believe that my father sold this property to Mr. Dastugues. The property records show him in the chain of title. I'm looking for him."

Seeing his lack of comprehension, she said, "I thought you might be coming. It's a risk I took. I don't mind. If you will give me a few minutes to close the shop, we can go upstairs and I will offer you some tea." She put away several pieces of jewelry that were on the counter and walked past Percy to the door.

"I've never met you, have I?" Percy was puzzled. The woman was completely at ease with his visit. "It's a simple question I would like answered concerning Mr. Dastugues."

Maisie was enigmatic. "The question is simple, but the answer is not. I will answer it. But it needs to be in an appropriate setting. Not where we may be interrupted. You are Howard Moorhead's son."

Percy could not help but feel a momentary jar at a colored person referring to him and to his father by their Christian names. He had never referred to his father as anything other than Father or Dad or Mr. Moorhead. Even his mother referred to him during life as "Mr. Moorhead" when speaking to others. This woman saw Percy's expression and immediately understood.

With a wry glance back at Percy, she said, "Your surprise is no surprise. You have no idea who I am. Your father was a complex man, with many parts. No one knew them all."

She locked the front door of the shop and led Percy to a door behind the back counter. They mounted stairs to an apartment just above the shop. Passing through a bedroom, they went to a living room/pantry that overlooked the street below. She had Percy remove his jacket and sat him at a table while she prepared tea in a brass spirit kettle. It was an elegant utensil which Percy would not expect to see in modest surroundings.

"Sugar?" she asked, offering him a bowl after pouring a cup of tea.

"Yes, please." He took two spoons.

She took the chair opposite him and sipped her tea. "Where shall we begin? My name is Maisie Dastugues. There is no Mr. Dastugues, except my father who is dead for many years. I did not buy this shop from your father. It was his gift to me. When his grandson was born. Your Randolph. Before that, the title was in his name."

"Why would he give you his shop?"

Pausing to sip her tea again, she said, "It was always my shop. The title he held in his name until the end, when he deeded it to me. He said he owed me that much. He would no longer see me. At least not in intimacy. We would still be friends. And he came to have tea every few months. Just as you and I are enjoying a cup together. He would tell me of you and Philomena and Randolph.

He was so proud of you. And the family you began. It was only with his passing that I learned that he had fallen ill nearly two years ago. I knew only that he had stopped calling on me altogether."

As she spoke, Percy came to understand what he was reluctant to accept – that Maisie Dastugues was his father's octoroon mistress. Delicately, he interrupted her,

"How long?" It was little more than a whisper.

Sounding reflective now, Maisie said slowly, "How long were Howard Moorhead and I together? Yes, naturally, a son would want to know. Sometime before he married your mother. A year? Two years? I couldn't say. When he married, he stopped seeing me. I was expecting it. Of course. White and colored cannot marry. But later, he came back. Sometime in the year after you were born. Whatever Howard felt for your mother, a man must have a certain intimacy. Now, I'll say no more about that. She is your mother. In his own way, he was always faithful to her. His love, his affection for her, were genuine. No other woman could enter his heart. She had given him what he most wanted in all the world – a son. I never met her. Once I saw them in the street together, walking with you. You were six, I think. She was a handsome woman, tall and strong. I could see why Howard chose her to be your mother."

Percy flushed, suddenly overcome with a sense of loss for his father. Her simple statement unlocked a hidden compartment of his father's soul, a father's love that he could never share in words with his son. Yet. And yet. Here this same woman was another secret of his father. Could he think his father dishonest for having a separate life in New Orleans for all the years that he, Percy, was growing up at Bolingbroke? It was just as incomprehensible to him as his father really being an Irishman named Redmond Boyle. Wasn't his father cheating on Percy as much as on his mother if he had a secret life with this woman of color? But how could he condemn Howard Moorhead for the same infidelity of which he himself was guilty? How was his relationship with Diana less blameworthy?

"How did you meet?" He was asking, how did this come about, this meretricious relationship that antedated his marriage to Lucy Willis, for better or worse, in sickness and in health.

Maisie was precise, even if becoming wistful at her memories. "Like many such meetings in New Orleans. An octoroon ball. The quadrille of the quadroons, I think someone called these social events. I was a pretty girl from a good family, my mother a free woman-of-color who was mistress of a white married man. My father was once a government official, a kind man, generous like your father. He sent me to Paris for two years when I was 13. He died shortly after I returned. What was my mother to do? Girls like me were groomed to be what I became. If we were lucky. Many weren't lucky. Prostitutes, until youth and beauty were no more. No longer exotic. I was fortunate. I had Howard Moorhead. He could be distant, unreachable. Or calculating. But he was also sentimental. And loyal. There was something in his past. I don't know what. More than anything as he grew older, he wanted peace."

"And the watch? It was you who left the watch for me?"

Maisie offered Percy a cookie. He declined. She continued, "I should have returned it to him. But I was selfish. He had forgotten it here some time ago. He thought he had lost it. I wanted to keep something of his. To remember him. It was the only time I was ever dishonest with him. He had taken himself from me when your son was born. I resented him even though he still came to visit. When I heard he had died, I decided it was something I had no right to keep. It should be yours."

Percy nodded in a gesture of thanks.

Maisie continued, "I hear this Irishman has taken everything from you. You must have something of your father's, no matter what you may think now. You were the most important thing in his life."

Reluctantly, Percy asked, "Does my mother know about you and my father?"

Shaking her head, Maisie said, "No. I wouldn't think so. I wouldn't want her to know. One part of me didn't want you to know. But you are my only connection to him. I can't entirely lose someone who was so much of my life. Do you understand?"

"Did he ever tell you that he was Redmond Boyle?"

"No. I never knew anything of his past. He spoke sometimes of his years at sea. But nothing more. Nothing of a father and mother. Nothing about any other child or wife. I don't believe he was capable of such deceit. It is out of character for him not to live up to commitments. He mentioned an uncle who had done him a great kindness. He said he had found a way to repay the debt he owed him."

It occurred to Percy that this woman was attempting to get support from him, playing upon his sympathy. Did she want something in return for the watch? He asked, "Did he continue to support you? Are you unable to take care of yourself now that Grady Boyle has taken everything?"

Percy's distrust was obvious, with his questioning of her motives. Defensive, she insisted, "Oh no, don't suspect me of seeking anything from you. I have no needs. I have this shop and these rooms where I live. Your father and I set this up years ago and he deeded it to me five years or so ago. I make enough to live on and put some aside for when I will need it. I need nothing from you."

Percy was disappointed in himself for his skepticism. His father would not have associated with a woman of low character.

"What does the name mean, Lalande & Co.?"

"Nothing at all. Not a person, not a good or item. Your father chose the name. It is my little shop and none of my customers have any reason to think I am the owner. It suits us that they assume I am a store clerk for an absent proprietor."

"Did the sign say you sell flowers?" A memory was called up by the sign at the door. He hesitated. "Do you sell pink roses?"

"I do when they are available." Maisie did not immediately recognize why this would interest Percy.

"Did you ever sell pink roses to a man called Ja-Boo?"

"Ja-Boo. Your father's man."

"Yes. A few years ago, Ja-boo helped me in dealing with Alderman Duplessis and his factotum, a man named Plauché. Somehow, he used two pink roses. I've never understood what he did."

"Oh, Duplessis and Plauché." She smiled as she recollected, then laughed lightly. "That was Howard. Oh, he was sly. He had such an understanding of people and their weaknesses and deceptions. And he enjoyed himself so much with that one. I remember now that he said he was going to use flowers to help you. He must have taken pink roses from the shop. He said he needed four identical flowers. I told him to help himself. It must have been four pink roses."

"Four? I had one and Plauché had one. That's all I knew about."

"He had Ja-Boo see that they were delivered to all four of you. The third would have been the alderman. The fourth was to Josie Barton."

"Josie Barton? Who's Josie Barton?"

Maisie stood and carried the empty teacups to a wash basin, saying, "Some called her Jo-Jo. She's moved to Texas now. She's back with the judge, they say. After he left town, she had a house on Philippa Street."

Percy interrupted. "By house, you mean brothel?"

Unapologetic, she responded, "Call it a brothel if you will.

House seems nicer. Not all the young women who find themselves in the house of a Josie Barton think of themselves as prostitutes. For some, a period of residence is a means of passing into polite society, where young women become ladies and acquire a few social graces."

"Social graces?" Percy had had no experience with brothels.

"But yes," Maisie responded. "Josie would school them. A wealthy planter, maybe a widower, from Concordia or Calcasieu may take a lady friend home after a week in New Orleans. She will be a freshly minted coin, all shiny in a small town who know only that she is a descendant of the first convent girls who settled New Orleans."

Softening, Percy said, "And the judge? That would be the judge who fled the state after he was caught forging notes of indebtedness?"

She nodded. "The same. The judge's passions were aroused by Josie. She claimed to be from an old family in New England. Her maternal grandfather signed the Declaration of Independence. The first anyone knew of her in this town was as the wife of a policeman. Cuddy Conway. Then she caught the eye of the judge. How he loved an audacious woman! Soon she was sharing his bed and he didn't much care who knew."

"How did this involve Gerald Plauché?"

"Plauché, he was working for the judge. When Cuddy discovered what his wife was up to, he beat her up pretty good. The judge and Josie had Plauché frame Cuddy for robbing the home of the same businessman whose name the judge had forged. Cuddy went to jail, and Josie and the judge flaunted their relationship. The businessman and the judge were so thick together, the judge was certain the man wouldn't say his signature had been forged or that his house had never been robbed. And the judge was right. What the judge hadn't taken into account was that Josie had told Cuddy enough about the judge that Cuddy was able to get the judge's enemies to expose his misdealings. That's when the judge took himself off to Texas. Secrets. Everybody's got secrets."

"How did I miss all that?"

"You were off in Mexico and Virginia. Before you set up with Mr. Benjamin."

"I'm a little lost," said Percy. "How do we get back to the roses?"

Sitting again across the table from Percy, Maisie said, "I was coming to that. So, you see, the judge moved to Texas. Cuddy got out of jail when it came out that he was framed. He was glad to put three states between him and Josie. Alderman Duplessis needed someone like Plauché. An operator behind the scenes who knows New Orleans secrets. Everyone has secrets, didn't I tell you?"

With just the hint of a smile, Maisie went on to explain how Duplessis and Plauché set Josie up with a house and a few young women they already knew. The alderman protected Josie Barton's new house from interference by the city and the police, while he and Plauché got a share of the house receipts. Josie's "girls" were expected to learn as much secret information from their clients as they could. More than a few New Orleans officials and businessmen had regular girls at Josie's. A man will tell a prostitute many things to show how important he is and what all he knows, thinking she won't tell anyone else. A man pays for an illusion and then he is fooled by it. Those secrets were money in the bank for the alderman when he used them to defeat an opponent or get support. No one ever got robbed at Josie Barton's. Except their secrets.

"The roses?" Percy asked.

"Don't you see? The only way the system could work is if the patrons to Josie Barton's did not know that everything that went on there went right straight to the leading alderman of the district. If it became known that Josie worked for Plauché and the alderman, their scheme would come to an end. When someone delivered the same type of flower to each of the three at the same time on one day, they knew someone was on to their collusion. They wouldn't know who. But they would have conferred with one another in some sort of panic. You can guess the rest."

"So, when I showed up at a meeting with Plauché the next day with the same kind of flower, it appeared it was a message to them that I knew about their arrangement. If they tried to hold me up on the casino project, I could bring down their whole operation and the alderman's career. But how did Ja-Boo know all this?"

"He didn't. As I said, it was all Howard. He had Ja-Boo carry out his plan."

"Including me in the plan." Percy marveled at his father's cleverness.

"The plan was for you. If you had known all that was going on, you wouldn't have been able to carry it off. Your father always said you were intelligent and crafty, but you were incapable of guile."

Percy was surprised. He was gaining a new perspective on what his father thought of him, thoughts Howard had never shared with him. "I don't know if that is compliment or criticism. But how did my father know all about the operation? Surely, he didn't deal with the likes of them regularly."

"I told Howard about Josie and her two business partners."

"You? How?"

Maisie spoke firmly, if softly. "No, I was never a prostitute, whatever else I may have been expected to be. One of the girls who was for a time at Josie Barton's house was like a daughter to me. Her mother and I were belles at the octoroon balls at the same time. The daughter of my friend was fair enough to pass for white. She never knew who the father was. That girl could never pass into white society in New Orleans without people asking about her background. If a man liked her enough to take her away from Josie Barton's and set her up as wife or mistress, well, that was a different story. No one would ever know her mother wasn't white. That girl, she looked to me for guidance. When Josie got drunk sometimes, she'd say things that let her know what the arrangement was and that was passed on to me. She'd see Josie meet with Plauché."

"What happened to her?"

Maisie laughed, "She's married now to a sixty-two-year-old white man and has 2000 acres in Napoleonville. She's got a little boy now, white enough to be governor of this state someday."

"Why couldn't my father tell me about the alderman himself? I feel like he's the *deus ex machina* in my life."

"I don't know about that. What I can tell you is something that should be obvious to you. You would have asked him the same questions you've been asking me. Always the how? The why? He said you never stopped asking questions once you started speaking. He also told me he had never lied to you, Not a single time. If he told you nothing, he didn't have to lie to you about me."

"Or about who he was, I suppose. Look where he has left me. Should my name be Percy Boyle?"

Maisie spoke to Percy as if she were lecturing to him. "No. You are Percy Moorhead, the son of Howard Moorhead. You should be proud of that. Whether he was called by another name doesn't matter. He was who he was. You are who you are. No matter if this Grady Boyle takes your land and your money, he can't take from you who you are. Your father would have told you the same thing. A man is not what he has but who he is."

"Then I guess I better go out and be who I am," he said with a rueful smile. "I won't pretend you aren't a shock to me, Maisie. I never would have thought my father . . . . Well, I'm glad you've been candid with me. If I might return, I may have more questions."

"Please do," she said, standing again. Percy noted her quiet dignity, evident in the way she held herself. She showed him the way downstairs and out of the shop, Lalande & Co.

෨෨ — ෧෧

Darkness was descending as Percy departed Maisie's. Her revelations about his father somehow comforted Percy. It added depth to what he knew of him. If Howard Moorhead showed such care and tenderness to Maisie, he was not the sort of man who would abandon a wife and child in Dublin.

Nearby, Percy could hear sounds from the steamboats tied along the levee. Laughter. Music. Couples strolling along the river. He walked up the levee and gazed up and down the river. What should he do with his life? He turned and walked over to the statue of Andrew Jackson, triumphal on a rearing horse. As though the Battle of New Orleans had been fought by cavalry. As though he were Napoleon at Austerlitz. A misrepresentative, grandiose monument, raised to a hero of a useless battle, fought when the war was already ended, forty years after a meaningless event. The city fathers who erected it cynically celebrated the ascendancy of a political party that embraced Southern extremism. Seeing the direction of the political tides, even Judah Benjamin had become a Democrat. Howard Moorhead was never a political man. But his disapproval of President Jackson had been evident to Percy as a boy. "A crude man, a coarse man, lacking in basic decency and manners," his father had said. New Orleans was now reflecting the same bumptious qualities, a disdain of civility, an intolerance of broader culture.

Despite his determination of only days earlier, he now couldn't imagine returning to the practice of law in New Orleans; it felt as if he had landed in a foreign, hostile port. Boyle had dispossessed him of all that he thought was his – in New Orleans and in Bayou Sara and St. Francisville. Should he start fresh elsewhere? Texas, like the disgraced judge? Or Missouri, like Judge Tucker had done? Or even California? Or return to a place familiar, to an earlier self before the blows of fortune he had suffered? Now he was determined – he would spend a last night in the townhouse and the next day return to Bolingbroke to tell his remaining family goodbye. Then he would start over again in Virginia.

*Chapter 54*

# Massa Calvin Kills

The crisis at the two plantations had started ten days before Percy met with Maisie, just after Percy departed for New Orleans on the daily packet steamer. Lucy had quickly moved all of her belongings from Bolingbroke to Jericho Hill. She appointed Calvin Bunch to be in charge of the settlement of all relations between the two plantations. He readily acceded to all of the demands of Grady Boyle and his lawyer, eager to seize his new role, free of the confines imposed by Howard and Percy Moorhead.

Grady Boyle announced his intent to sell all of the slaves of Bolingbroke as quickly as possible. He would receive ready cash and be free of the burden of the expenses and responsibilities of maintaining them. More than sixty had been acquired by Howard Moorhead in his name. These and their offspring passed unquestionably to Boyle's control as executor. More than thirty others had been owned by Lucy when title to Jericho passed to her on Jim Willis's death and others who were subsequently added to Jericho. Pompey was among these, along with other offspring of the thirty. Births and deaths among the slaves were nearly balanced over the thirty-two years of marriage of Howard and Lucy. Julius had been born at Jericho and entered on the books there, and Lucy held title to Leddie as a gift from Howard, so the couple and their child were to remain at Jericho. Odessa, however, was to be sold at auction. Her papers showed her as purchased by Howard Moorhead. She was to be separated from her son and her grandson.

More than twenty of the younger slaves were offspring in which one parent belonged to Bolingbroke and the other was owned by the owners of Jericho, Lucy and Eliza. There had never been a reason to distinguish between them and to decide whether title to the child went to the owner of the mother or the father. Calvin was impatient with legalisms, so he quickly agreed to Boyle's proposal that they sell all the young slaves in dispute and divide the money in proportion to the number of slaves owned by each plantation, five-eighths to Boyle and three-eighths to Lucy, Eliza and Calvin. Under the arrangement, nineteen children were to be separated from their parents. Pompey learned that his ten-year-old son, Joshua, and the boy's mother, Jessie Mae, with whom Pompey lived, were among those to be sold at auction in the coming weeks.

An agent for slave dealers in Louisiana and Mississippi lived in Bayou Sara. His name was Jacobs, and he was employed by Boyle to identify and list the names of all the slaves to be sold. Jacobs advised that notice of the sale should be given in newspapers in Jackson, Mississippi, and that the slaves in the coming weeks be fed well and groomed to fetch a better price. He would arrange armed guards to transport them to Jackson within a month or so. The agent also recommended to Boyle that he separate all those to be sold from the rest and keep a vigilant eye on them. Slaves who feared a change of masters often ran away. Boyle agreed that it would be prudent; he hired three men from St. Francisville to confine and keep watch over his property.

Shortly after breakfast, a week after Percy had left, Calvin called together all of the slaves who were to remain at Jericho. The morning was cold, in the mid-thirties, not unusual for the first week of February. Frost was on the grass, and mist appeared on the breath of the men, women and children waiting for Calvin to speak, some shivering. He stood on the steps of the porch to the house, leather riding crop in hand, wearing a wool jacket and a warm beaver hat. Looking down from the second story window was Lucy Moorhead. Her presence made it clear to all the slaves assembled below that Calvin Bunch spoke for her.

Calvin, in a falsetto voice, called out, "Listen up. You already heard what's happening. I'm gonna be sure you understand what this means to you. Now y'all are used to taking directions from Pompey. He's gonna be the head nigra. But there's a change. He's been too much like his pappy, Big Tom. Too easy-going. Too soft. Howard Moorhead was soft and left it all to Big Tom. But he's dead, and his son might as well be as far as any of y'all are concerned."

Calvin walked back and forth on the porch, tapping his crop in his left palm. "I'm in charge now. You nigras been loose-reined too long. Some of you think you can leave off the plantation and visit and go to town whenever y'all take a mind to. Not gonna happen anymore. Ain't gonna be any visiting from y'all's friends from nearby. Ain't no nigra coming on or off this plantation who doesn't come to me first. Y'all understand?"

His words produced only shock and dismay, as he expected. They needed to know their place under their new master.

He shouted, rapping his leather crop on the porch rail twice with force. "I didn't hear y'all. If y'all understand, I want to hear it."

"Yessuh," came a few voices.

"Again, damn it,"

"Yessuh, Massa Calvin," more loudly.

"Now y'all go on about your business. Y'all know what y'all supposed to do. It ain't all that cold."

All the slaves left except Pompey and Julius.

"Whatch ya'll want?" the white master demanded.

Pompey spoke first, walking alongside as Calvin sauntered

towards the barn.

"Mr. Calvin, I'm gonna try to run this place like you wants me, but I sure would be obliged if you could find a way to keep my Jessie Mae and my boy with me. It'd be a big help to me."

With disdain, Calvin said, "Well now, we can't all have everything we want, can we?"

"She's my woman and Josh's my boy, the onliest chile I got."

Calvin turned and spoke to him, scornfully. "Don't you see, Pompey? Jessie Mae and you been together at least 10 years. And you ain't got but the one little pickaninny? Somethin' wrong there. I'm guessing it's her and not you. You're a big fine buck. Oughta have more like you instead of like Julius here. Hell, he ain't much bigger than his mama. He can read and write and figure, but hell I can do that myself. What we need is more like you. I'm planning on breeding you with Julius's woman and see what we get." He laughed and then sneered when Julius's angry look caught his attention.

"You can't do that," Julius said with ill-concealed fury.

Calvin spit out, "You don't tell me what I can do and can't do, boy. I'm in charge here and you ain't got Howard Moorhead or Percy Moorhead to run to. They treated you and your momma like you was family. It's time you learned your place."

Julius seethed, "You may be the boss but everybody knows you ain't half the man Mister Percy is. And you ain't gonna take it out on me."

Calvin exploded with anger, "No nigra's gonna talk like that to me."

He began beating Julius with his riding crop, first across the shoulders then the top of his head and face as the black man crouched to protect himself. A cut opened on Julius's left cheek and blood spurted.

"Mr. Calvin, don't do that," pleaded Pompey trying to restrain the white man's right arm.

"You too, you black bastard?" Calvin withdrew his arm and stepped over to the barn. He picked up an axe handle. Pompey turned aside to ward off the blow as Calvin struck. The axe handle came down hard on Pompey's shoulder. He fell to his knees. Calvin swung again, this time grasping the handle with both hands. The blow struck the back of the slave's head with a loud crack. Pompey lay lifeless, blood oozing from his skull, a thick red running through his kinky black hair, into the dirt.

Calvin stood over the body, breathing hard. He looked over at Julius with rage still in his eyes and on his bloated red face. Julius took two steps backwards. While looking at Julius, Calvin bent over and felt at Pompey's waist. He found the Damascus steel hunting knife that Pompey had inherited from Big Tom. Still looking straight at Julius, he inserted the blade between Pompey's ribs, near his once-beating heart. He looked pleased with himself.

The screen door at the side of the house swung open as Lucy Moorhead ran out, frantic. She had seen it all from the window. Dismayed, she cried out, "Calvin, what have you done?"

Calvin responded. "Damn nigra had it coming. He shouldn't have tried to stop me. He as good as attacked me."

"Is he dead?"

"Yeah." He looked over at Julius and spoke again to Lucy. "And I say it was Julius here who did it. Fighting with his own brother. Like Cain and Abel. He'll hang for it."

Julius stammered, "You saw it, Miss Lucy! It was Calvin. He did it. Not me."

Lucy Moorhead looked at Julius. She looked at Calvin. She said nothing.

Calvin looked at his wife's mother, saying "Get me a pistol, Lucy."

Julius knew what the pistol was for. Calvin was going to shoot

Julius and blame Pompey's death on him. That was why Calvin stuck the knife in Pompey, so he could claim Julius stabbed Pompey with their father's knife.

When Lucy began walking slowly back to the house, Julius did not wait to see if she would get the pistol. He set out running.

## Chapter 55

# Flight to Kwa-zembe

When he got to the Middlebrook farm, Julius sent word by a slave named Selina for Odessa to come meet with him at a corn shed. Calvin wasn't smart enough to take Julius's wife and son into custody before getting the law after him, to hold them hostage to get Julius to turn himself in. Someone was sure to think of it before long.

Odessa arrived at the Middlebrook corn shed a little after noon. She found her son crouched behind a stack of bushel baskets. The bleeding had stopped from the cut on his cheek, but she saw it was a severe wound. She dabbed it tenderly with the edge of her skirt.

"Momma, Calvin killed Pompey," said Julius, distraught. "He meaning to kill me next."

"Everybody knows you knows that," she said. "We gotta get you away, far away. And Leddie and Little Jay."

"How we gonna do that, Momma?"

"I've been thinking on it. Percy Moorhead won't let this happen but he's not hereabouts. We gotta get y'all somewhere safe til we find him. You know Kwa-zembe?"

"I heard of it. Hideout for maroons, runaways. Is it for real?"

"Yes. I been there twice to tend the wounds of runaway slaves.

They owe me somethin' for all that. Not gonna let them tell me no."

Odessa explained to Julius how to find his was to a meeting place for a guide to the runaway camp. She said she would see to it that when darkness fell, Leddie and Little Jay would meet Julius at a hollow oak on Frenchman's Bayou. After hugging him, she slipped out of the shed, careful that no one had seen her come or go.

Julius spent three more hours in the shed, gnawing on ears of corn and resting. Then he, too, left the shed, and walked stealthily through the woods. He came to a pond where he took a shallow pole boat and dragged it across a damp field until he came to the bayou. He poled his way up the bayou until he came to the meeting place, the hollow oak. After an hour's wait, he saw Leddie and their son making their way cautiously in the dark. She carried a bundle with clothing and some food. He was cold and hungry and glad to see his wife and child.

"What you hear happened?" Julius asked his wife while he eagerly ate bread and dried beef jerky.

Urgently, her words flowed out. "Calvin's told everybody you killed yo' brother. Said you did it with Big Tom's knife he give you."

"You believe 'em?"

Leddie reassured Julius. "Wouldn't be here if I didn't believe it happen the way you tole Odessa. Where we goin'? She wouldn't say."

Pointing over his shoulder, he said, "Swamp. For now. Place called Kwa-zembe." Julius settled his wife and child in the boat and pushed it away from the bank with his pole.

Leddie held her son close to herself in the boat. She was frightened. She had heard stories about Kwa-zembe. It was so deep in the swamp it took two days just to get there. Some of the slaves said it was a prison where the white man sent the worst of their slaves and kept all of them in cages guarded by the same malevolent mastiffs they used to hunt runaways. Others said it was a peaceful settlement, a refuge of round huts just like an African village, where there was plenty of food and everyone shared what they had. The village elder was an ex-slave named Razmus who had lost his papers that showed his master had freed him just before he died. The whites said Kwa-zembe was the worst place on earth, a place where runaway slaves went when they had nowhere else to go, that half of them were cannibals. That it was these ex-slaves and fugitives who kept packs of dogs they trained to attack all white men. That it was a leper colony, its inhabitants marked by corruption of their flesh. Some said it didn't even exist, that it was a fiction made up by black folks to encourage the rebels among them to think they had somewhere to go if they would only escape their bondage.

Leddie was scared to her bones, but she trusted Julius. She soothed Little Jay as he whimpered, telling herself she had to be strong for her child, strong for her husband. Julius would get them through this nightmare.

Kwa-zembe was more than white myth and black fantasy. It was a clearing in a deep swamp, a small patch of land between the hell of slavery and the hope of freedom, a place of transition in which slaves could be purged of their bondage. Its population was fluid. Many were maroons or runaways who were listed in sheriffs' offices and in newspaper ads as wanted and whose capture would bring reward. Others were free blacks who had committed crimes and were wanted by the law for that reason. More than a few were free but couldn't prove their status and were subject to seizure and sale. Their only transgression was their dark skin, their African features.

From time-to-time bounty hunters, alone or in small bands, penetrated the swamp to find the camp, defying the copperheads and moccasins and alligators. Most never came out. Three or four who did emerge after days of being lost were covered in bug bites and had contracted dysentery or malaria. They vowed never to try it again. Their stories deterred other attempts by bounty hunters and slave-catchers.

Julius poled the boat for more than an hour through the bayou until it merged with a broader, shallower expanse that was swamp, dense with cypress trees and knees that jutted up everywhere. Spanish moss brushed their faces. From trees came shrieks of owls and gruntings of frogs, from water the sound of the bateau brushing against bulrushes. In unison above, male cicadas in branches rattled their tymbals, filling moonlight with a hum that grew loud then soft in cycles of five or seven minutes. Mosquitoes were an unceasing annoyance. Leddie swatted them from Little Jay's cheeks and ears as best she could. The boy's bony arms and slender legs were covered by a thin blanket where he nestled next to his mother.

After two more hours, they suddenly perceived a dim light as a man uncovered a lantern. He told Julius his name was Mingo. He was a maroon who had made Kwa-zembe his home for three years since escaping a cruel master in Opelousas. Deep scars on his back from repeated lashings had made it impossible for him to travel any distance northward without being identified as a runaway. Even if he made it as far as Illinois or Ohio, who could say but that he would be returned for more beatings under the fugitive slave law? Some states, called free, banned former slaves from entry entirely. How was a black man who couldn't even read know the different laws from state to state?

Life was rude and primitive in the make-shift shanties crudely constructed in the depths of the swamp. But it was a life less fettered, less demeaning. Even if it meant death, a desperate man like Mingo would rather live as a fugitive than go back to fourteen-hour days in blistering heat, chopping the stalks of cane whose distilled sugar made the white man wealthy. Mingo's hands still bore scars and callouses from wielding the cane knife.

Julius and Mingo helped Leddie and Little Jay from the boat then sank it to hide where they were traveling from by foot. Wordlessly, Mingo led the three fugitives over an unseen trail through the swamp, a snake-like ridge of land just below the surface of the swamp waters that the dwellers of Kwa-zembe could traverse in safety. Little Jay was tired and grumpy. He did not understand what was happening. Julius carried the seven-year-old across his hip, the boy's frail arms around his neck. Only a person familiar with the natural markings of fallen trees and hollow trunks could follow the sinuous route that, after two hours of wading and walking, would end at the secret hideaway of nearly eighty souls living beyond the reach of the white man.  Most were men but a dozen women were among them and a handful of children.

Mingo brought his travelers to a small fire and retired to his lean-to shelter with a roof of palmetto fronds over bamboo shoots. They were cold, tired, wet and hungry. A woman gave them blankets and dry clothes. Someone else handed them each a plate of beans and squash and lard biscuits. They were pointed to a make-shift tent where they could sleep that night. Julius and Leddie lay together under thin blankets, Little Jay between them, huddling for warmth against a chilly night.

Julius swore to himself he would do all in his power to see no harm came to his wife and son. He wished he had the strength of Big Tom or Pompey. Poor Pompey, thought Julius, killed for trying to help his younger brother! Poor Pompey, lacking Julius's intelligence but a gentle, generous soul who never complained about losing birth's lottery. Neither had chosen their parents nor their servitude to the white man. Perhaps the shrewdness of his mother would get Julius through this. He fell asleep wondering how the inhabitants of this small village of outcasts could maintain themselves in the middle of an impenetrable morass.

ॐॐ — ৯৯

The next morning Julius learned more about Kwa-zembe by observation and questions. It appeared they were on a small island of two or three acres in the swamp, though it could hardly be distinguished from any other part of the swamp. No trees had been felled to open it up, no field created for growing a crop. Men appeared busy, some caulking a rowboat, others nearby setting a trotline whose snoods would yield a catch of catfish and bass. Two others were stretching a seine net between trees to dry and repair it. Beaver and muskrat hides nailed to boards were drying in a sunlit opening. A stout woman with a bandanna around her head brought a breakfast of grits and ham and coffee to their tent.

Mingo came by a little later and asked about their sleep. Then he took Julius to a two room cabin off to one side of the dry land. He pulled aside a canvas flap that served as a door and bade him enter. Seated in a large wooden chair furnished with cushions of different colors was a one-eyed black man. He was about fifty, had a short beard that was going to gray and wore an old leather hat. His remaining eye was red, fierce and wary. As far as the white man's law was concerned, he was still a slave. The laws of Louisiana did not, however, hold sway in the sovereign jurisdiction of Kwa-zembe. A large dog with a ravaged face was at his side. Looking up at Julius, the man did not rise. Mingo said simply, "This is Razmus."

The chief of Kwa-zembe said "Sit," pointing to a crude bench next to a window. Mingo turned and left.

"They say your name be Julius. You tried to kill Calvin what married the Willis daughter." His voice was guttural, his speech more a series of grunts than sentences.

Julius replied, "I wish I had. Truth is, he killed my brother Pompey."

"You be the boys of Big Tom. That right?"

"Yep. Calvin is trying to make me guilty of killing Pompey. But I did'n. Truth is, Pompey tried to stop Calvin from beatin' me. Calvin cracked his head open with an axe handle. Then he took the knife and stuck it in his chest and said I stabbed him."

"How you know to get with us?" Razmus didn't sound welcoming.

"My mother's Odessa. She knows this place. She sent a message to y'all then told me where to meet someone if y'all was gonna help. Truth is, I did'n know y'all would `til Mingo showed up where he was supposed to. We be mighty grateful."

Razmus complained, "Can't say I's too happy to take you in. Only reason we been here long as we has is most'f us not wuth lookin for. If your mama wasn't Odessa, you wouldn't be here. We owes her at least that much."

"How do y'all do it? Must be eighty-ninety folks here."

Razmus said desperate men can learn what it takes to stay alive in mighty awful conditions. His deep voice explained, "Plenty of meat in the swamp. Coon. Rabbit. Squirrel. Gator. Wild hogs. All of 'em be taken with traps or spears. No gunshots give away their location. Every other food we needs come from plantations near the swamp. We looks like any other field nigger when we go pick corn or beans in the morning. Steal clothes off clothesline while they be drying. Take tools out of barns at night. Some of the men here has family still living where they run away from. We stay live cuz we keeps outta sight. We don't make no trouble. Now what you plan on doin' next? Y'all can't stay here."

"Just don't know," Julius replied reluctantly. "This is the furtherest I've ever been. I never been more than fifteen miles from Bayou Sara. I read and write English and French. I read books on France and England and America. I know there are states where there are no slaves, but I can't say how to get there. They's all thousand miles away."

Razmus leaned forward, "Lissen now, they ain't gonna come afta you cuz you killed a nigger. They gonna come afta you cuz white man says you tried to knife him. Sooner y'all leave here, better it is fer everone."

"Is that what he's saying?"

"At's what we hearin now. Calvin be stirring in the town to get up a posse. Come after you. You here be bringin' the white man down on us."

## Chapter 56

# The Bunch Posse

T he report Razmus received was mostly accurate. Calvin had gone into St. Francisville with a wagon bearing the body of Pompey, the distinctive Damascus blade knife still sticking up from the dead man's chest. The wound of the skull was at the back of the head and not visible where it was cradled in rolled-up burlap. No one would examine the corpse once the knife wound was seen, once the white master had described the murder by a jealous brother. Calvin had demanded that the sheriff form a posse to go after Julius and the two other runaway slaves, Leddie and Little Jay.

Seymour Lurty, the sheriff, was well aware of Calvin Bunch's small acquaintance with the truth, and with the burdens he had imposed on Howard Moorhead and then on Percy.

"Calvin, this was just one nigger killing another. We have that all the time," said Sheriff Lurty, the chief law enforcement official of the parish.

Indignant at the sheriff's reluctance to act, Calvin complained, "Seymour, he was going to knife me, too."

Sheriff Lurty was skeptical. If he went chasing after every slave that ran away, he'd have no time for any of his other duties. Runaways were an owner's problem, even if it involved killing another slave. Squinting and pointing a finger at the corpse, he observed with a drawl, "But Calvin, I'm looking at that knife right now, still stuck in that black carcass. How's a nigger going to stab you if he didn't have that knife?"

Flustered, Calvin said angrily, "Well, he coulda got it. If you won't do your job, I'll do it myself." He stalked away. Sheriff Lurty was popular in the parish. Calvin Bunch was not.

Calvin found the slave agent Jacobs in a saloon two blocks from the sheriff's office. Jacobs told him where he might find men who could be hired as bounty hunters at Bayou Sara – at the China Grove Hotel or working as hands at Henshaw and Haile's stables. After some haggling over whether they would be paid by the day or on a reward basis, Calvin had his men. A day later, Calvin and three hired hunters were outfitted and set out on horseback to track down the three runaways, Julius and Leddie and Little Jay. Most owners used slaves to hunt runaways. But not Calvin. He didn't trust a slave to hunt a slave. He might run Calvin in circles or turn on Calvin himself. One of his three hired hands, Monte Williams, said he guessed a runaway with a woman and child would try to get to Kwa-zembe. A woman with a child would have to go slow. Nobody else would take them in. Awful hard to hide three people together, he opined. Monte was a gambler. He had experience fighting in Nicaragua with William Walker, the filibuster.

"Can you find it?" Calvin demanded.

"I can get us purty close, I reckon."

"How much danger for us?"

Monte's confidence often became bluster, especially with a man of such little experience as Calvin.

He said, "You can't believe them stories people tell. There's four of us, four long-guns, six revolvers between us. No matter how many they is, they ain't gonna get killed over three runaways. They'll give them up before taking fire from us. Like it was in

Nicaragua."

"You ready?" Calvin asked the other two men – Vernal Bostwick and Chance Landry. They nodded in the affirmative. Neither was as bright as Monte Williams. They were attracted from their work at the stable by Calvin's promise of a generous bounty for capturing or killing Julius. Both counted on the more experienced Monte Williams to tell them what to do.

"Let's do it," said Calvin with bravado. He was leading a charge by his own little cavalry.

Tracking skills did not take Calvin's search party to the vicinity of Kwa-zembe. When they got to the swamp they had to leave their horses. After thrashing about in the mud and muck of the swamp for four more hours, after chigger bites and thorns and a thirty-minute downpour, they decided to rest and warm themselves by a fire. A fugitive woman returning to the maroon camp saw them and left hurriedly to warn Razmus. She was seen by one of Calvin's men, and they followed her. In her haste to warn, she failed to follow camp procedures for concealing entry.

Realizing they had stumbled on the camp, the four white men spread out, forty feet between them. A sentry in a tall beech tree whistled a warning to the camp. Monte was closest to him and shot the man with his rifle. The sentry fell, wounded but not dead. When Monte waded into the swamp towards the wounded sentry, another fugitive slave shot Monte with an arrow that pierced his chest just above his heart. The white man fell with a curse. He struggled in the shallow water for a few minutes, grasping the arrow but only increasing its pain. Bleeding profusely, he quickly died from the fatal wound.

Calvin was wading through the muddy swamp off to the right, headed to the dry side of the camp area. He spotted Little Jay, who had wandered from the main part of the camp. Emerging from the muck, Calvin ran to the confused boy, lifting him with his left arm and pointing his pistol at the boy's head.

Leddie screamed as she saw her son in jeopardy. She ran to snatch him away from his captor. Still holding the boy, Calvin shot Leddie in the chest with his revolver and then the head. She was only ten feet from him, and he was firing without aiming; even as bad a shot as Calvin couldn't miss at that short a range.

Julius was behind them as events unfolded, chopping wood from fallen limbs. His only thought was to kill the man who held his son and shot his wife. With his hatchet he struck Calvin in the back of the neck, instantly severing the white man's spinal cord. Calvin's body went limp, dropping Little Jay and his pistol.

Julius picked up Calvin's pistol and fired it twice at another of the bounty hunters, Chance Landry, who was closing in on him, twenty feet away. The man fell face down, groaning. Julius stood over him and put another bullet in the man. The remaining searcher, Bostwick, knew he was outnumbered. He dropped his rifle and ran back in the direction from which they had come. He had taken a bullet in the left shoulder, fired by someone in the camp. It was near dark.

At the sound of shots, Razmus came running. He found Julius carrying Little Jay into the camp. Razmus said, "Now you gone and done it, nigger. See why I dinna wanna take you in. Now they gonna bring war on us."

Razmus was right.

Bostwick, the wounded slave stalker, cowered in the swamp for three hours, not daring to move lest he be discovered. Recovering from the initial shock of the bullet, he began a painful journey back to the trail they had followed to locate Kwa-zembe. In another two hours, just past midnight, he arrived at New Troy, owned by Lester McEachern, known to his friends as "Jolly," and his family of seven. Bostwick's banging on the door awakened Jolly.

"Good God, man, what's happened to you?" said McEachern as he looked at the blood-covered man now slumped on his porch.

"Shot," was all the exhausted man could answer. His face was clawed by thorns and brush. Algae-inflected mud ran up and down his trouser legs after wading hip-deep through the swamp.

Jolly called to his wife as he helped Bostwick into the kitchen and sat him in a chair. As Laurel McEachern began dressing Bostwick's bullet wound, Jolly handed the man a tumbler of whiskey and soon a second.

By two in the morning, Bostwick's story to the McEacherns had grown to his being the sole survivor after he and his intrepid fellows were assaulted by a force of fifty armed renegades. They had killed ten fugitive slaves before being overwhelmed. Growing more alarmed as the story was told, Jolly began sounding his plantation bell. Within an hour a fevered chorus numbering a dozen bells had chimed in, sounding fear throughout the parish.

Not long after sun-up, a crowd of men gathered at the town hall of St. Francisville, holding guns and talking excitedly. Soon the events were transformed into a slave rebellion led by Julius and by a fearsome runaway black giant named Razmus. Bostwick, the surviving member of the slave-catcher posse, reported that he had heard them say more were coming from all the plantations from twenty miles around. They were stealing their masters' guns. Two barns had already been burned, though no one could identify where they were.

The town constable called out the sheriff and the sheriff sent a rider to Baton Rouge to notify the governor in person – no telegram, for fear of spreading the story. It would be sure to draw a response from Governor Wickliffe, for the governor's home, Wyoming Plantation, was not far from where the killings occurred. His own interests were directly threatened. Immediately, he called to action the head of the Louisiana Militia, General DeRussy. In less than twenty-four hours a company of a hundred men were assembled and were on a steamboat sent north from Baton Rouge, with full gear and supplies.

Shortly after the militia departed the state capital, Percy's steamboat from New Orleans put in at Baton Rouge to offload passengers before continuing up-river to Bayou Sara. Noticing the excitement that seemed to grip a crowd of people greeting debarking passengers, he stepped off the boat to inquire of the news.

An excited barber whose shop was nearby, called out loudly, "It's a slave revolt. Up near St. Francisville. Governor's called out the militia. DeRussy's been sent to put it down."

"Where?"

"Place called Jericho," exclaimed the barber. "Nigger killed his brother and then killed their owner."

"Lucy Moorhead?" demanded Percy.

"Naw. Man named Bunk or Bunch. Something like that."

Percy grabbed his bag from the boat and paid for a horse and saddle at the livery stable. Riding fast up the post road would get him there quicker than the steamboat which was scheduled to stop at Port Hudson, after its layover in Baton Rouge.

## Chapter 57

# Enlisting Odessa

Percy leaped off his exhausted horse at the entrance to Jericho and rushed inside. Eliza was sitting in a chair, sobbing. Lucy was near her, pacing impatiently, distressed that she could do nothing to help her daughter. Nerissa was closed off in her room upstairs.

Looking back and forth to both women, Percy sought answers. "What's happened? Someone in Baton Rouge said Calvin is dead. I got here quick as I could."

Eliza looked up accusingly. "Oh, Percy, did you have to leave when you did?"

"Yes. I did," suddenly irritated with his sister, despite his sympathy for her loss. "Boyle had me on a short fuse to clear out of my house in New Orleans. Now tell me."

Eliza continued, sorrow and anger together in her voice. "It was Julius. He stabbed Pompey and was going to kill Calvin, but then he ran off. Calvin went after him into the swamp with some men from town, and then he killed Calvin. You and Howard never accepted Calvin, and now he's dead."

Percy turned to his mother. He was surprised that she had let Eliza pour out the story. There must be a reason. Did his mother also blame him for Calvin's actions and death?

"Is that right, Mother?"

Lucy was evasive. "That's what Calvin told us and Sheriff Lurty." She would avoid lying if she could. But she knew Percy would see through her. He did, immediately. Eliza's account was too improbable to be accepted. Eliza wasn't lying. She was merely gullible.

"It's not something Julius would do," Percy said flatly. He surmised that Calvin had killed Pompey.

Lucy turned her anger to her own son. "Calvin was right. Your father was too lax with the workers. If he had been stricter, this would never have happened." She put her hands on the shoulders of Eliza to reassure her.

Eliza looked reproachfully at Percy, as though she too blamed him. "I've lost my husband, Percy. And it was the nigras that did it. Don't you go and try to say Calvin brought this on by trying to impose discipline. There's no other way when we're surrounded by all of them. Calvin's murder shows that."

"Your sister's right, son," Lucy interjected harshly. "What's done is done. Whether Julius was at fault in killing Pompey is beside the point now. You've got to stand with family. Calvin may have been in the wrong, but he was still family. You've got to step up and look after your family. We're your responsibility, not Julius. No one else is going to look after us. It's your duty."

Without responding, Percy turned and began striding to the door.

"Where are you going?" Lucy was shocked that he was leaving.

Without looking back, he said impatiently, "I think I've heard enough to understand what happened. Maybe I can keep it from getting much worse."

"Don't you walk away from me, Percy Moorhead." She had lost a husband and a son-in-law. Now she was losing a son. Yet she had learned nothing.

Percy continued on without a backward glance. Outside, he saw more clearly what he failed to notice in his rush to get to Jericho. On the porch at Bolingbroke were two armed men, shotguns at the ready. A third was seated on his father's favorite bench in the yard, the one nearest the two fig trees.

Percy surmised that they were Boyle's guards, looking after his human property. One informed him that Boyle himself had gone to Woodville to meet with a potential purchaser of Bolingbroke. No one was to be allowed onto or off his plantation.

No slaves of either plantation could be seen. They were sheltered inside cabins or in one of the barns, afraid to come out. Or, thought Percy, some may have gone to join Julius, others had become fugitives. He had no way of knowing. Both plantations were now in turmoil. With Calvin dead and Percy dispossessed, all of the slaves on both expected to be sold, their families broken up. The lives they had known for thirty plus years were dissolved by a court order recognizing the claims of an Irishman they never heard of and by the ascendance of Calvin Bunch as the ultimate beneficiary of the misfire of Jim Willis's pistol, thirty-five years ago.

⁂ — ⁂

Percy found Odessa in the cabin she had shared with Big Tom for thirty odd years, where she had given birth to Julius and had raised him and Pompey. She was sitting silent in the cane and cypress chair Big Tom had made for her when she had nursed their child. He squatted next to her, compassion in his voice; his expression was tender. "I know Julius didn't kill Pompey," he told her. "It wasn't in him."

"Don't matter now," she said wearily. "The only one who could say different is dead. That be Calvin. Your mama saw it. But she won't say different. Not Miz Lucy."

"Did you talk with Julius?"

"He sent for me a few hours after it happened. Told me all

about it. Told me where to send Leddie and Little Jay to meet up with him."

"What'd he say?"

"He said Pompey tried to help him when Calvin was beating on him with that horse whip he carried. Calvin whopped Pompey upside the head with an axe handle and kilt him. Tried to make it look like Julius done it. Your mama was going after a pistol to shoot Julius when he run away."

"So Leddie and Little Jay are with Julius?"

"Guess so. I've heard nothin' from them." Percy sensed resentment and reproach in her flat answer. He had let her and her family down by being away at a time of crisis; when everything was falling apart, he had taken off and left them to fend for themselves. Here were the consequences.

"I'm here now," he urged. "I want to see if I can help them. Will you come with me?"

"They saying Calvin is dead. And that Julius did that too."

Percy tried to coax Odessa from her chair. "Let's go see what we can find out for sure."

Odessa was reluctant. She declared tearfully, "They gonna kill him. No matter what, they gonna kill him. You lost your son. Now I'm gonna lose mine. And my grandbaby."

Percy reassured her. "Not if we can stop it. Do they have any idea where to look for him?"

Odessa heard his determination. She trusted him again, saying, "He is headed for the maroon hideout. What they call Kwa-zembe. I sent 'em there. They owed me that much. Two times I risked myself to help wounded runaways who took shelter with Razmus."

"Can you get us in the right direction?"

"Yes," she said, finally acceding to Percy's imploring.

Percy hitched up a buckboard wagon to the horse he had hired in Baton Rouge. The two set off to find the militia.

## Chapter 58

# The Insurrection

Leaving Bolingbroke behind them, Percy and Odessa rode thirty minutes southward until they came to a wagon trail which they followed to an open field about four miles southwest of Governor Wickliffe's plantation. The field ended in a line of thick brush and trees, behind which could be seen a glimpse of the bayou that fed into the swamp. The hastily assembled company of militia had arrived an hour before Percy and Odessa. Setting up a base camp, with a dozen tents, they numbered at least ninety men. Seven tracking dogs were on leashes tied to one of the wagons. They stirred anxiously, eager to begin the work for which they were trained.

Dark clouds obscured the late afternoon sun, making it difficult to distinguish shape and figure from shadow. Percy pulled the handle of the wagon's brake and left the wagon and Odessa on the path a short distance from the camp. As he approached the tents, he saw an older officer who was directing the men and walking from squad to squad to supervise, obviously the man in charge. To Percy's surprise the officer was someone he knew. It had been ten years since Percy had last seen him, but he immediately recognized the soldier who had sworn him into the Louisiana volunteers for the Mexican campaign, Lewis DeRussy, now general of the Louisiana militia. He was heavier now, and getting up in years, but he still projected authority.

"General, I'm Percy Moorhead. I served with you in Mexico."

"And so you did, Moorhead. I remember. You more than served me. You saved me, at no little risk to yourself. I would've drowned. Last I saw you was Tampico."

"Yes. You sent me on to Vera Cruz and General Scott."

With night ineluctably approaching, DeRussy was impatient to get the camp ready, but he took time to ask Percy, "I don't suppose this is a social call. You must have heard we have a situation here. What's your connection?"

"Unfortunately, it concerns my family, General. One of the dead men is my brother-in-law."

"Sorry to hear that. Talk to me while we set up the camp. Are you here to claim the body?"

The question surprised Percy. He asked, "It's here? I didn't know the body had been brought out of the swamp. I heard that one of the four men who went in escaped. That he saw my brother-in-law killed."

"There's three bodies down by the bayou. One of the farm owners nearby said someone left them there this morning, before daybreak. Didn't see who."

"Let me go see," Percy said.

The general saw that his officers were carrying out his instructions. He said, "I'll come with you."

Percy explained to DeRussy that he was in New Orleans closing out his law practice when the events unfolded on the plantation but told him little else. DeRussy said it was his understanding that a slave belonging to Mr. Bunch had murdered his own brother over who was to be the head slave on the plantation. The killer was going after Mr. Bunch to stab him too when he was interrupted by the lady of the house who had a pistol. The sheriff was reluctant to pursue escaped slaves into the depths of the swamp without a large posse, so Mr. Bunch went after the killer with three associates from town. The wounded man who came back said he saw a slave fitting the description of the killer attack Mr. Bunch. Slender, light-colored mulatto, medium height, about thirty.

Percy asked, "Did he say anything about a woman and child with the man?"

"No," said the general, shaking his head.

The two men arrived at the three corpses. All three were on their backs, arms folded across their chests. Their faces and hands had been cleaned of mud, muck and blood.

"You know them?"

Looking down, Percy said without emotion, "Just the one in the middle. Calvin Bunch. My sister's husband."

Percy felt no sorrow at Calvin's death, only disgust, and not just with Calvin. No, he blamed Grady Boyle as much as Calvin. Were it not for Boyle, Percy could have prevented a clash of Calvin with Pompey and Julius. And their confrontation came from the brutal fact of slavery itself. Did slavery come about because of men like Calvin Bunch or were men like Calvin Bunch a product of slavery?

"May he rest in peace," said DeRussy respectfully.

"Thanks. It might be a first time for Calvin."

Percy didn't share with DeRussy his rueful reflections as he stood over the body of his in-law who had caused him trouble from their first meeting. The institution of slavery was evil not just for the bondage it imposed on the African but for corrupting the souls of men like Calvin Bunch. That good men like Howard Moorhead participated in slavery and that good men like Judge Tucker defended the institution itself did not diminish its corrosive effects on white society – of which Percy himself was a part. Even Christianity was debased by slavery: No Africans were taken as slaves to make them Christians; they were baptized Christians as balm for the white conscience, not for the black soul.

"Trouble?" DeRussy sensed Percy lost no love on the dead man.

Sounding as grim as his thoughts, Percy said, "My sister's father had a violent ending. Might have expected the same for her husband." Percy remembered a story of DeRussy's son-in-law killing a lawyer over DeRussy's daughter and fleeing to Mexico. He was sure DeRussy would understand family difficulties. This was another reason he was glad DeRussy was in charge. And he was a clear thinker in a crisis, calm and decisive.

"Who are the other two?" Percy asked.

"Don't know their names. Part of some sort of posse that Bunch got up." Gesturing in the direction of the camp, he added, "See that man back at the wagons with his arm in a sling, near the hounds? Calls himself Vernal Bostwick. He's the one who got out wounded. He thinks he might help in the search even if the scent they left behind was too faded for the dogs to follow back into the swamp."

"If he was a man who would go with Calvin, he could be trouble."

Now walking rapidly back to the encampment, DeRussy shrugged and said, "Let's get on with what we got to do here."

"What have you been told to do, General?"

"My orders are to wait until I hear from the governor. We have a man at the telegraph office in town. Governor doesn't want a lot of people killed in his back yard, white or black. There's a half-blind old darkie said his daughter came to him last night from Cazembe or whatever they call this place. She said they sent all the women and children away. Since they were all going to die if we go in, they might as well put up a fight and try to break out."

DeRussy kept talking to Percy as they walked by the line of tents. The militia men milled around uncertainly. DeRussy and

Percy were the only ones among them who had fought in combat. Drilling once a month on a parade ground did not prepare a man to face a desperate foe in a thicket or swamp. DeRussy was unsure whether he could count on these inexperienced volunteers.

Implicitly trusting someone who had once rescued him, DeRussy shared his concerns with Percy, in case he could offer guidance. "Lot of folks around here are mighty nervous. Abolitionists up north are encouraging the slaves to rise up where they are. Don't know what it means that they brought out the bodies. Maybe they figure we won't come in if they send them out for a Christian burial. The sheriff has some men out trying to find anyone that might have come out of there. They might can tell how many men are there and what arms they have."

Before Percy could respond, a messenger on horseback galloped up to them. With his mount snorting and stamping its hooves in the damp earth, the man struggled to report to DeRussy that the sheriff's party had found a woman hiding in a barn who had come out of the settlement. She claimed there were more than a hundred men in there. They were well armed with guns they had stolen from farms and plantations. And they had gunpowder.

"Has the governor been informed?" asked the general.

"Yessir. The sheriff sent him a telegraph message right away."

DeRussy turned to Percy again, "You must live around here, don't you?"

"Yes. Most of my life."

"I thought so. Now tell me what we might be facing. Slave unrest? Rebellion?"

Knowing DeRussy would trust him, Percy was frank. "I can't sugar-coat it, General. The slaves of this parish outnumber the whites four to one. Owners in Virginia and Tennessee sell their difficult slaves down the river to end up here. Runners. Troublemakers. Draw a circle ten, twelve miles out from where we stand, it would enclose maybe ten thousand slaves. Even if they have no guns, all of the adults can get their hands on axes, hatchets, machetes, hoes, and iron bars. A thousand adult male slaves are within an hour's walk of this field. It would take fewer than a hundred to kill everyone on thirty plantations around St. Francisville before you could march this company back to town."

"That's a grim reality." DeRussy looked at the gray February sky. "We've less than an hour of sunlight left. Maybe we should act quickly while they're unorganized. If someone is going around stirring the pot, we couldn't respond. Nat Turner gathered his mob and went farm to farm in the night, killing men, women, and children in their beds."

He added ominously, "Same sort of thing happened down at LaPlace, when five plantations were burnt to the ground. We need to shut this down before it spreads."

Turning from Percy, DeRussy gave orders for all the men to have their guns ready and to be prepared to go into the swamp as soon as the command was given. Then he and Percy sat on camp stools with cups of hot coffee. The temperature had now dropped into the low forties. An overnight freeze was expected.

Warmed by the coffee, DeRussy opened up to Percy. "Newspapers will be all over this. One in New Orleans has been saying this insurrection was coming. Blaming it on the legislature. They made it impossible for a slave to get free even if his master will give or sell freedom to him. No hope for freedom, no reason not to rebel."

Percy made no comment. It was his own assessment.

Just then another rider galloped up. He reported the governor had instructed DeRussy to wait for reinforcements. Two hundred-fifty more militia and volunteers were being mustered. Wickliffe was sending them upriver by steamboat in the morning. Frowning but complying with the limits imposed on him, DeRussy sent word down the line for the men to eat and post a watch at each tent through the night.

Now, at dusk, Sheriff Lurty rode into the camp. He was a lean, grave man, about forty-five, with a short black beard. He took DeRussy aside, within Percy's hearing.

Concern lining his face, the sheriff warned, "General, you need to know the folks in town are close to panic. Hotheads getting liquored up, threatening to start shooting all the men slaves. I closed all the bars in town and at Bayou Sara. Imposed a curfew starting now. No one, white or black, outside after six til six tomorrow. Every landowner in the parish is sitting up with a gun and locked behind their doors."

The news was not reassuring to DeRussy. He asked, "How many deputies do you have to keep order?"

The sheriff shook his head slowly. "Six. Good men. But they're worried about their families. They want to be at home to protect them."

"We've got reinforcements coming. I can give you ten of my men if that'll help."

Lurty welcomed the offer. "I may need them tomorrow. Starting first thing in the morning, we're gonna move all the women and children into the churches in town where they'll be safe and guarded. Some of the planters are setting up a vigilance committee. They plan to go from farm to farm and arrest any slaves who are suspected of favoring rebellion."

DeRussy frowned. He couldn't go chasing around the countryside rescuing planters in new spots of fighting. But he wouldn't tell the sheriff how to do his job.

The sheriff looked around at the camp's tents then left. He had not been gone an hour when a group of seven rough-looking men showed up at the camp, three on horseback and four on a two-horse wagon. When Sheriff Lurty had closed their saloon on Bayou Sara, they saw an opportunity to shift from drinking to fighting. If there were black men to be hunted down, they were ready to be crew for a neck-tie party.

General DeRussy demanded that they leave, but they were drunk and defiant. The general had them arrested for violating the sheriff's curfew, confiscated their guns, and had all seven tied to their wagon. Vernal Bostwick came over to sit with them. They were friends of his and of Monte Williams, with whom they had often played Bourré in Bayou Sara. Bostwick pointed in the direction where Monte Williams and Chance Landry lay, next to Calvin. This set them to muttering and cursing at being held prisoner.

A half-moon was shining across the field by nine that evening, the clouds clearing as the weather turned colder. At the edge of the swamp, among the trees, just across the bayou, torches began to appear. Within a half hour, seventy or eighty torches were burning about one hundred fifty yards from the militia camp. Many were stationary. Some were moving from side to side.

Apprehensive, Percy stood near DeRussy as the general ordered all the men to the alert. It looked like the slaves from Kwazembe were massing. DeRussy called for the six wagons to be put in a line and overturned in front of the tents. Seeing Percy was unarmed, DeRussy gave him his own pistol and told an orderly to get him another. Reluctantly, Percy accepted it and tucked it under his belt.

Percy peered into the darkness, looking for some sign that there was a way to de-escalate before either side opened fire. Instead, whistles and hoots began sounding in the distance, from where the resinous torches were hissing and spitting. Owl hoots and crane calls and goose honks, or so they seemed. Percy knew that no owls or cranes or geese massed at night. Nor did they burn torches. Now followed more mimicry and torches on their left flank. A vagrant cloud passed in front of the moon, adding to the gloom.

DeRussy called his four officers together in his tent. He included Percy in their council, to their surprise. Scowling in the lamplight, DeRussy laid out his concerns. "I don't like this. Are we in the middle of a slave insurrection? There could be hundreds out there. Maybe they're planning to attack us tonight. We can't shoot what we can't see. We can't go into that swamp in the dark. If they have even half as many men as they do torches, we'll be wiped out. We've turned over a hornet's nest."

The officers were just as uncertain. Only Percy spoke.

"General, I have a suggestion, if I may." He made himself sound far more self-assured than he felt. He needed the confidence of these officers if he was to have any chance of averting a catastrophe.

"Sure, Moorhead."

Looking first to the general and then to each of the other officers, Percy explained, "I grew up with the slave who's at the center of this engagement. Maybe Julius will talk to me. Let me go and see if I can find out what might come next. His mother is still nearby. She's waiting for me in a wagon a little ways back. I'll go get her. Then we'll see if the men out there will meet. They won't kill me if she's with me."

The officers under DeRussy were immediately attentive to a proposal that could avoid an armed battle with slaves and fugitives who had nothing to lose. Percy's deliberate manner gave them assurance that he might be able to carry it off; his misgivings were not apparent to them.

The general was skeptical. "Moorhead, you might just set them off. If they kill you walking towards them, I'll have to go after them no matter. You may be putting all these men in danger."

Percy appealed to the general's military instincts to act on the best information about an opponent. "Look, at least I might see how many men are really out there. And whether they have guns. They might, might not. It's better than waiting here for them to make the first move."

DeRussy appraised Percy carefully: "Moorhead, you know

more about this than you've let on."

"Yes," Percy acknowledged. "Only now is it relevant. I know he didn't kill his brother. My brother-in-law did that, then tried to pin it on Julius. And I know he's got a wife and child with him who he would want to protect."

Accepting the new intelligence, DeRussy responded, "All right. Give it a try." The other officers nodded their approval. DeRussy added, "Keep that sidearm I gave you ready. You may need it. One thing, Moorhead. You stay out in the open. Make them come out to talk to you. If you get out of my sight, I'm coming in after you." The general trusted Moorhead. He owed him at least a chance to prevent a bloody conflict with an uncertain outcome.

Percy insisted, "No sharpshooters. No surprises."

"No, not at night. And it would put you in too much danger. You have my word."

The six men exited the tent. Tracing his way in the dark back to his buckboard, Percy found Odessa waiting, warm under a horse blanket.

Ten minutes later Percy and Odessa each held a torch and began walking side by side across the field. Frosty vapor could be seen from their breath. Percy held the torch in his left hand and a white flag on a pole in his right. On the far side of the field there now appeared the figures of three black men, Razmus, Mingo and Julius.

Percy approached them slowly, Odessa a few steps behind, hesitant to make a misstep in a tense confrontation.

From fifteen feet away Razmus spoke first. "You here to take your slave away?"

Percy ignored Razmus. He spoke to Julius, who stood to Razmus's right. "I know you didn't kill Pompey, Julius."

Julius stepped closer. To Percy, he appeared older, fatigued and despondent. "That don't matter much now, does it?" he said listlessly. "There's three white men dead. I killed Calvin, only cause he killed Leddie. Calvin was going kill Little Jay, too. Holding a gun to his head."

Surprised, Percy shook his head sorrowfully. "My God. Leddie's dead? I didn't know." Calvin Bunch was a worse man than Percy had thought.

Odessa gasped and stepped closer. "Oh, no!" She put her hands on Julius's arm. Fearfully, she asked, "Where's Little Jay?"

"He's safe, Momma."

Percy now turned to Razmus and asked, "Why'd you bring the bodies out?"

"Keep the white man from having to come get 'em," the large black man explained, defiance in his voice and righteous anger on his face. "We didn't ask for no trouble. They come looking for it."

Percy demanded, "Why are you looking for.it now? Looks like you are setting up an insurrection."

Percy studied the black man and saw he was not hostile to Percy. Why, he wondered. Had he been privy to the exchanges between Razmus and Julius, Percy would have understood: When Julius had seen Percy and Odessa across the field, he had told Razmus that Percy must have come to prevent a massacre. One of the dead white men was Percy's brother-in-law, but the two were as good as enemies. Percy, said Julius, was not seeking to retaliate for Calvin's death. Razmus believed him. Instinctively, Razmus saw Percy as a white man with whom he might negotiate.

Razmus was as direct as he was formidable: "We done heard state militia coming for us. Coming to Kwa-zembe, wipe us off this here earth. If y'all be send'n army in, we got no chance. Better if we stir a commotion and come out all at once and scatter. Mo' of us get away than waiting til y'all come to kill us all in one place."

Percy looked now to Julius whose silent nod assured Percy that he should believe what Razmus was saying. Percy understood that

Razmus was taking him into his confidence, conveying that the torches and noisemaking were an elaborate bluff. "You'd rather not fight, I take it."

The wary eyes of Razmus rolled across the line of tents, the overturned wagons, the armed men standing or crouched, to see if any were about to open fire. Alert as he was to danger, he did not see just behind the tents the small group of louts who were noiselessly working to free themselves with the help of Vernal Bostwick. To Percy, he answered, "What we gonna do? We be living at peace back in the swamp til this nigger brought the trouble in. Couldn't just turn him away when he come. Now it's done too late."

Trying to sound hopeful, Percy said, "Maybe not too late. If I take Julius out now, he'll be given a trial. Maybe we can establish that he didn't kill Pompey and that it was my sister's husband who did. Jury might just send him to prison."

Julius was cold and fatigued, conflicted by having to deal with Percy and his mother at the same time, answering also to Razmus, and anxious to save his son. He snapped crossly, "Didn't kill Pompey. But I did kill Calvin. Can't change that. Bounty hunter that got away saw me do it. With a hatchet."

Percy urged Julius, "But you acted in self-defense. We can show that."

Irritated, Julius shook his head. "Percy Moorhead, your daddy once told Big Tom you had more smarts than sense. You may have a lot of learning in the law. But you know it as a white man. You don't know what the law says to the black man. You don't understand."

"All right, I'm listening, Julius."

Frustrated that he had to spell it out, Julius told Percy what every slave, male or female, young or old, learned from their earliest years. "What I know is this. Calvin Bunch was in his rights in white man's law to seize a runaway nigger like me, whether I was right in running away or not. He could use any force he wanted. Under white law I had no choice except submit. There ain't no right of self-defense against violence to the slave. Black child learns that before white child is ten year. The law will kill me one way or another."

Percy knew that Julius was right. They had grown up together, both nursed by the woman who stood next to them in this desperate hour, both guided by Big Tom, the closest of friends until the color line came between, demanding that society's racial strictures be adhered to with no exceptions. Those same racial codes mandated that no slave who killed a master could escape execution.

But Percy had to stave off a confrontation by whatever arguments he could use. "Look, if you come in with me, I may persuade the commanding officer there's no reason for all of them to go chasing after everyone into the swamp. Too cold a night to go wading and shooting up and down the bayou. No reason we can't all go somewhere warm."

Razmus now stiffened. Was Percy setting up a trap, playing a white man's trick? He said, "Them three dead white men is three reasons enuf."

Suddenly, Julius offered himself as a solution to the impasse.

"If I'm gonna die, I'd just as soon die here. How about if you hang me in front of those soldiers? You tell them I killed all three of the white men and maybe they'll go away. If a white man's gonna kill me, might as well be you, Percy."

Percy recoiled, "I can't do that, Julius."

Julius meant it. If he would die soon, he might demand one last concession from Percy. He played upon the sense of guilt he knew Percy carried in his heart. "Sure you can. You told me about that boy you killed in Mexico. You had to do it to save your own people. You gotta do it now, too. But you gotta do something for me."

"What?" Julius had struck a nerve.

"You gotta raise Little Jay," he implored. "You gotta see he gets free and gets an education." He turned to his mother as witness to a pact. "Ain't that right, Momma?"

Shaking her head, Odessa said, "You thinkin' something good come out of this. But not this way." Turning to Percy, she stammered out, "No, no, no. Not this. Not this, Percy Moorhead. You can't."

"You'll know where to look for Little Jay, Momma. He ain't in the swamp now. We got him out early this mornin'. You know where I'd send him."

Odessa nodded. She knew.

Percy said, "I give you my word I'll do that, like he was my own son. But that doesn't mean I can kill you. Just come with me now."

Julius had Percy's word on Little Jay. Now he pleaded for his mother. Shivering now at the cold, he added shakily, "You gonna take care of Odessa, too? Don't let her be sold to strangers. Calvin was gonna sell her. Boyle's gonna sell her."

By the light of the torch, Percy could see tears in Julius's eyes. Like Percy, Julius had lost his wife and had suffered at the injustices brought on by the Irish stranger. Fighting back his own tears, he could not help but say, "I promise." Percy didn't know how he would do this, but do it he would.

"Where's that leave the rest of us niggers?" demanded Razmus. Nothing in the negotiation protected him and those who depended on his leadership.

Percy turned to Razmus and responded, "You tell me what you want. I know the general doesn't want a fight. I can't speak for him or for the others who are coming tomorrow. But I think he'll trust me."

Percy had a grudging respect for this scarred and hardened man. In spite of his years of suffering at the white man's hands, he wanted only peace; survival, not vengeance. He sought to protect his band of followers who had looked to him for refuge.

Razmus bargained with Percy. "I just need a little time is all. You draw this thing out. We goin' slip way while y'all all bunched up."

Percy wanted to seize on an end to the confrontation. But how could he know he wasn't being played the fool by a cunning opponent, one who had every reason to hate the white man? "I'm not setting you up just so you can attack while they're distracted."

"Naw," Razmus scoffed. "Ain't but fo'teen men here. And some of them already gone off. Take their chances goin' north."

Skeptical, Percy said, "Looked like ten times that."

"To'ches stuck in trees can look like an army in the dark. Men see in the dark what theys fear in the dark."

Percy believed Razmus. If he was telling the truth, there could be no attack. Without an attack, Percy knew DeRussy wouldn't make any move until more militia arrived the next afternoon. He said to Razmus, "All right. I can buy you some time. That's something I can promise." Percy, the lawyer, always looked for a negotiated settlement. The crisis was coming to an end, he had every reason to believe.

Razmus and Percy each examined the face of the other for signs of deceit. They found none. Percy took Julius by the arm, turned and began to walk slowly back to the camp, Odessa following a step behind. The dampness around them began to turn into a light snow that hung in the air. Razmus and Mingo looked on.

Percy had gotten fifty feet when he heard a rifle shot ring out. A bullet whizzed past him. Then a second shot. Next to him, Julius suddenly slumped to the ground, bleeding from a bullet to his chest. And then followed a ragged volley of a dozen shots.

DeRussy shouted out furiously, "Cease fire! Cease fire! Who fired those shots?"

Percy saw that two men had come out in front of an overturned wagon, two of the town rowdies who had been tied up. They must have fired the initial shots. Vernal Bostwick had loosened their ropes. He wanted a bloodletting after what he had suffered in going to search for Julius. His buddies saw their chance to start the fight at little risk to themselves, with the Louisiana militiamen to do the fighting that they started. They were not so drunk that they couldn't shoot straight. Some of the nervous, undisciplined militiamen had joined in. Whether from fear or excitement or thinking that General DeRussy had ordered it could not be said.

Odessa was crouched over, beside Julius, crying. Percy looked behind him and saw one of the black men was down. It seemed to be Mingo. He was victim of the first bullet that had passed by Percy. Had it been intended for Percy? Razmus must have escaped.

One of the shooters now pulled a pistol. He was walking toward Percy and Odessa, intending to shoot both of them at close range. DeRussy was the closest man to him. Seeing what was ready to occur, the general grabbed a rifle and hit the man in the back of the head with the butt. He called over two militiamen to drag the unconscious man away and told them to put him in irons. Others arrested the remaining shooter who had set off the round of firing. He struggled but was subdued. At the general's command, two more of the militia grabbed Bostwick by the shoulders. He cried out in pain when they fastened cuffs to his arms behind his back.

Percy heard DeRussy shout out at his men, "Damn it, no one gave an order to shoot."

An officer ran to him and asked, "Shouldn't we give chase, General?"

Upset that his men would even question him, DeRussy again shouted angrily, "Goddammit. Our orders were to wait. We've not been fired on. You will restrain your men. Immediately."

Looking around warily, DeRussy determined that there was no movement in the areas where the torches were still burning. He walked cautiously to where Percy, Odessa and Julius were. Odessa was seated on the ground, cradling her dead son in her arms, softly moaning and rocking back and forth. DeRussy could hear a few words in French from her. To Percy it sounded like a soft creole lullaby that she had sung to him as a child.

DeRussy came to Percy, who stared vacantly at the dead black man. He said gravely, "I didn't break my word, Moorhead. You have to know that."

"I know," he said numbly.

DeRussy continued, "Everyone was watching what was in front of them, not the men behind them. Those peckerwoods were spoiling for a killing. They will be punished."

"I know," Percy repeated, still without emotion.

The general needed to assess if a threat remained. "Help me out here. Tell me what took place when you were talking. Were those the leaders? I've got decisions to make immediately. I have to report back to the governor."

Percy looked at the commanding officer. "It's over, General. You can tell the governor there's nothing more."

Uncomprehending, DeRussy insisted, "But all these men. The reports."

"All show. Like the sticks we used for guns after we lost ours in the shipwreck of the *Ondiaka*. Like the watchfires you left for General Cos while we escaped. Tactical tricks used since time immemorial. There were never more than a dozen or so men putting those torches in the trees and on bushes. Whooping it up to make us think they were an army. All the while they were slipping away while we focused on the shining things."

Grudgingly accepting Percy's intelligence, he asked, "Who is this you were bringing out?"

"This was Julius," Percy said sadly, gesturing to the body. "My closest friend growing up. Saved me from drowning when I was a boy." He gestured at Odessa, saying, "Her son. He admitted to killing my brother-in-law. Said he saw Calvin murder his brother at my family home. He saw Calvin shoot his wife when they were in the hidden camp. Calvin was going to kill his son, too. Julius had to kill him, whether the law would agree of not."

"You believe what he said?"

"Yes. He was ready to walk out of here to certain execution to prevent further killing. He said he killed one of the other men in the posse. The other dead man over there was called Mingo. You can report they can be blamed for the three white men killed in the swamp, and they wounded the scoundrel you've got over there, Bostwick. The maroon settlement wasn't ready to sacrifice themselves for one slave in trouble."

"But the insurrection? What shall I tell the governor?" DeRussy had too much information to assimilate it all at once. He had been dispatched to put down an insurrection.

Percy shook his head. "General, there was no rebellion in the making. They were prepared to give Julius up if it would help them get away after breaking up their camp. Julius knew he couldn't get far. He asked me to hang him right here. I told him I couldn't do it. He was willing to let me turn him over to you if it could be done without violence. I told him I knew you to be a good man who I served under a long time ago. And you had given me your word."

DeRussy heard no rebuke in Percy's voice. His statement was without affect, merely a report of what had been said. Nevertheless, DeRussy was unsettled by the events. There had been a breakdown of discipline. Every soldier knows such moments. Every conscientious leader feels a responsibility when it occurs under him. DeRussy felt it now.

"It sounds like you've suffered a double loss, Moorhead. Friend and brother-in-law. But you got us through this. What can I do?"

"Give me one of your men to help load those two on my

wagon."

Motioning to his orderly, DeRussy said, "He's here now." He shook Percy's hand: "God be with you."

After retrieving his buckboard, the orderly and Percy put Julius's lifeless form in the bed of the wagon. Then they drove to the place in the field where the bodies of the three white men lay. They lifted the corpse of Calvin Bunch and set it next to Julius's body. It was a poignant moment for Percy. Two men whose lives had been lived next to Percy, now lying in death together, each responsible for the death of the other.

Was Percy himself at fault? From the start Calvin Bunch meant to displace him, wanting to control both plantations. Lacking intelligence, Calvin's only means of achieving his goal, after taking a wife to serve the purpose, were violence and dumb luck. Should he have been much more forceful in tamping Calvin down? He had been reluctant to confront his mother or his sister, as had been his father. Was he indifferent to the plantations, enjoying himself as a lawyer in New Orleans, too ambitious in rising to the top of his profession? Perhaps, he reproached himself. He had too often ignored Calvin and the damage he inflicted. But, as much as he despised Calvin, Percy would bring his body back to Eliza. She was family. Family sentiments had to be respected or there would be no family.

Again on the wagon seat with Odessa beside him, Percy shook the reins to urge the horse into the night, leaving the militia camp behind them. The snow's increase had begun to settle on the dark and uncertain path in front of them. Time, some say, heals all. But how could the passage of time undo all that had been done? The lives of the two men now dead in the wagon-bed behind them, one slave, one free, had been bound together on the plantation now taken from Percy. Their deaths were final. The past is fixed and unchanging.

Percy's past had been an illusion, exposed by Grady Boyle. Is not the future as inexorable as the past? Percy grimaced at the thought. It was too bleak for him to accept.

Snapping the reins again, he told the tired horse to keep trudging. "We must trudge on," he repeated. Rest was not possible.

Her hair flecked with snow, Odessa's expression was inscrutable as she turned to Percy. In a voice barely audible over the wagon's creaking and rolling on the rough road, she said, "He never lied to you, Percy."

"How can you know that? The name. The family. The mistress. The piracy. His money's sources."

"I saw him at your birth. I saw him look at you. He would never lie to you. He never lied to you."

Yes, thought Percy. He never lied. He had only concealed the truth. But what was the truth that he concealed? Was Grady Boyle's version the truth? Percy was too weary to reason it through and too far from evidence to sift the matter thoroughly. He would have to be patient.

The past would have to wait.

He would find it in a foreign country.

Made in the USA
Columbia, SC
08 November 2024

28930258-50df-4cec-a632-feeddf6f065dR04